SOCIOLOGY
AND
HISTORY:
METHODS

The Sociology of American History
RICHARD HOFSTADTER *and* SEYMOUR MARTIN LIPSET,
editors

Sociology and History: Methods
Turner and the Sociology of the Frontier

SOCIOLOGY
AND
HISTORY:
METHODS

Edited by *Seymour Martin Lipset*
and
Richard Hofstadter

✤ ✤ ✤

Basic Books, Inc., *Publishers*

New York   London

Contents

SOCIOLOGY
AND
HISTORY:
METHODS

✿ 1 ✿

Richard Hofstadter

HISTORY AND SOCIOLOGY
IN THE UNITED STATES

History has a mixed inheritance and has come to have a mixed identity. It is partly amateur, partly professional; partly literary, partly "scientific." But its basic inheritance, the quality that sets it off most clearly in its character and aspirations from the social sciences, is its literary and humanistic background. For generations, for centuries, history was first of all a story to be told and understood, and its success depended upon the sweep of the narrative line. It was primarily a literary metier, and to achieve greatness in historical writing meant more than anything else to achieve literary excellence.

To a degree this remains true, but the role of history has been complicated by other than literary aspirations and literary models. Our sense of where it stands today may be made more acute by a look at the ground over which it has come. If first we consider narrative history in its pristine form, we may be struck by its relative simplicity of purpose. It was usually written in response to the drama of some great cause—the rising national state or the nationality, Protestantism or Catholicism, the liberal or conservative view of politics, a party or a class, a group or institution. Of course, individual historians have not always had the simple partisan identifications that this suggests, but my point is that to a large degree the public function of history was of this kind, and the task of narrative history was shaped by such commitments. There was a premium on the drama of the story, on the role of great characters with high purpose, good or evil. It was simpler, in constructing a narrative that did not wander too far from a central story, to feature a main line of events involving the politics of church or state, the drama of diplomacy and war. Those historians—and there have always been some—who hoped within the framework of the narrative to deal with the unfamiliar and the less dramatic, with social history and the lives of the multitude, have always felt themselves to be embattled, to be pressing against the weight of a great and imposing tradition.

Narrative history was also distinguished from much modern academic historical writing by the character of its authors and its audiences. It was intended to reach not a small professional public but a wide educated audience. In American experience the eminent narrative historians of the nineteenth century were gifted and dedicated amateurs, usually men of wealth and leisure who could command the help of copyists and amanuenses and afford the luxury of travel. They could also afford, if worst came to worst, to spend years on a masterwork that turned out to be commercially unsuccessful, as in the case of Henry Adams, whose great nine-volume history sold only three thousand sets. Adams called history "the most aristocratic of all literary pursuits, because it obliges the historian to be rich as well as educated," and suggested that if history became consistently popular and profitable, "the luxury of its social distinction would vanish."

While the basic inspiration of the great narrative historians came from literature and philosophy—there were no social sciences as models—they had scholarly standards and methods defined by the canons of accuracy and verification. Their intellectual morality, their conception of accuracy and rigor, called for an examination of as many of the original sources as their energies could encompass. They were storytellers whose stories were supposed to be scrupulously true.

In the last decades of the nineteenth century, the situation was decisively changed by the emergence of academic history-writing, which developed in this country under the tutelage of the German seminar and under the inspiration of the scientific ideal made dominant chiefly by the prestige of Darwinian science. A new corps of historical workers came into being, middle class rather than patrician in their personal backgrounds, and dependent upon the prerogatives and the training of the university. They soon found themselves writing for a different, more specialized audience than that aimed at by the older narrative historians. The goal of the narrative historians had been to reach as wide an audience as possible, given their intellectual concerns and the level of their work. The new professional historians were writing mainly for a professional audience—that is to say, for each other—a luxury made possible by the emergence of scholarly journals and the university presses. Their purpose, too, as they conceived it, was different. They were to engage in a detached, objective, more "scientific" search for causes and relationships. Where the narrative historians had not been much inhibited about retelling a story familiar in its essentials, the academic monographers felt more deeply the imperative of research—the imperative of finding new subjects, untapped sources, new interpretations or reinterpretations. Prestige came from using new materials, hitherto seen by the eye of no other historian, or from a revisionist argument imposingly documented. The concern with objectivity, the professional audience, and with discovery or novelty all accorded better than the canons of the narrative historians with the dominant ideal of scientific inquiry. It became possible at last for some historians—though by no means all—to think of history as a "science" that would, with enough patience and enough cumulative evidence, establish grand generalizations or historical laws.

But, in the main, it is important to remember how superficially the ideal of science established itself, even among most of those historians who, under the spell of Darwin and Spencer or Comte and Quetelet or other masters, aspired to give history a sound academic standing by emulating scientific methods. For most of them science meant not much more than the effort to achieve objectivity and to adopt a skeptical and critical attitude toward their sources, an attitude hardly unknown to their predecessors among the narrative writers. On the whole, this simple canon led more often than not to eschewing generalizations and speculation, and it led historians to avoid considering the role of hypotheses and guiding principles, rather than subjecting such hypotheses and principles to a sophisticated scrutiny. John W. Burgess' account of the method of history teaching at Columbia, prepared in 1885, was representative:[1]

We seek to teach the student, first, how to get hold of a historic fact, how to distinguish fact from fiction, how to divest it as far as possible of coloring or exaggeration. . . . We undertake . . . to teach the student to set the facts which he has thus attained in their chronological order, to the further end of setting them in their order as cause and effect. . . . After the facts have been determined and the causal *nexus* established we endeavor to teach the student to look for the *institutions and ideas* which have been developed through the sequence of events in the civilization of an age or people.

Nothing could have seemed cleaner or simpler than this dedication to the fact. Searching in 1909 for "methods of investigation which are strictly scientific," George Burton Adams thought that all technically trained historians were in basic agreement "that the first duty of the historion is to ascertain as nearly as possible and to record exactly what happened." [2]

When American historians ventured beyond this naive version of science to reach for generalizations, the generalizations were likely to be conceived along the lines of nineteenth-century evolutionism, which itself proved to be a fragile plant. When, for example, they spoke of "the comparative method" as applied to political institutions, what they had in mind was the application of the "germ theory" of modern Anglo-American liberties, which traced free and democratic institutions back to the German forests. This feeble biological analogy gave birth to some of the dullest institutional history ever written, but it did not last long. It is quite likely that some of the subsequent skepticism of American historians about history as a "science" stems from this abortive and ill-considered flirtation with inadequate and truncated scientific models.

In drawing a line between the old tradition of narrative history and the new academic history that had taken shape by the end of the nineteenth century, I have been dealing with archetypes, somewhat abstracted from reality. There was continuity as well as discontinuity in the historical profession, and it is important to remember that despite the modish regard for "scientific" history, there was never a time when the old literary ideal died out, not even among the most dedicated fact-hunting writers of monographs nor the most ardent spokesmen of historical "science." There are, I believe, no seminars in which the instructors do not try to prevail upon their students to see that their monographs are well written and in coherent narrative order; none in which some considerable labors are not expended upon matters of art and style. This is important because it bears upon the profound difference in models that still separates history and sociology. A further consideration is that the new professional history writing in the United States did not supplant or destroy the old narrative history of the nonacademic practitioners; rather it grew up alongside it. The tradition of the dedicated amateur persisted along with the historical form that amateurs had made distinguished, though in the twentieth century the dedicated amateur is much less likely to be a gentleman of inherited wealth or a retired businessman and more likely to be a journalist or politician in the tradition of Albert J. Beveridge and Claude Bowers or George Fort Milton and Douglas S. Freeman. Moreover, an especial prestige still adhered, even among the professionals—and perhaps especially among them—to those historians who, like Allan Nevins or Samuel Eliot Morison in our time, could move at ease in both the world of demanding professional scholarship and the world of popular history. Finally, it must also be said that the function of narrative itself did not by any means disappear from monographic work. If, as C. Wright Mills has said, "history is the shank of the social sciences," the narrative is also the shank of history. The new monographic writing somewhat subordinated the narrative and focused on smaller and more constricted narrative sequences, but it could no more do without its narrative framework than it could without its sense of time.

While academic history was developing its own professional ethos, the life around it was becoming more complicated and more challenging. Other social disciplines, new and old, were getting a more secure foothold and developing their own methods of work. Professional economics and political science, long established in the academic curricula, were proliferating; sociology and anthropology also won a place on academic faculties between the 1890's and World War I. By the 1920's historians could not help but be aware that they were surrounded by other disciplines having many points of common concern with them, but having different and more expansive conceptual frameworks, more ample theoretical interests, and, in some respects, more precise methods. At points the other disciplines seemed to be living up more adequately to the scientific ideal. In some way, history seemed to be missing something.

Quite aside from its partial and ill-fulfilled fealty to "science," history, in the wake of World War I, felt under a stronger imperative to be relevant and useful to the present. It was these considerations that underlay the growing post-war urgency about "the New History," which James Harvey Robinson had begun to preach at Columbia even before the war began. Robinson appealed to his colleagues to make history increasingly relevant to the present and its problems, to look at political events in their social and economic environment, to write history which took account of the experiences of the common man, and to cooperate with the social sciences. The most ambitious response of historians writing United States history was the multivolume *History of American Life* series, edited by two Columbia graduates who were much influenced by Robinson and Beard, Dixon Ryan Fox and Arthur M. Schlesinger.

What this series showed, however, was that historians were trying to write a kind of sociological history without having any sociological ideas. They had discovered—or rather rediscovered —the common interests they had with sociologists in a wide variety of aspects of human behavior—marriage and the family, religious and social institutions, education, urbanization, and many others—but they had not yet discovered unifying ideas with which to put these concerns into intelligible relations. Although the editors found their authors among the more gifted professional historians of their generation and invested incalculable efforts of their own to put some of the volumes into shape, the product, at least considered as a historical genre, was nothing better than a still-birth, and the conception of social history with which the works began was obsolete long before the last of the twenty volumes came off the presses. An important lesson had doubtless been learned, though it was largely a negative one: interesting and important social history could not be produced in a series of volumes moving rapidly in sequence from one "sociological" subject to the next—from sewage disposal to popular entertainment, to sports, to changing fashions—without a firm conceptual framework upon which to order the whole. If history was to be more sociological, it must also have more ideas and a better sense of method.

The search for a more satisfactory connection with the social sciences was not ended by this failure, but even those historians who were most in favor of the marriage realized that it would be no simple matter to make the arrangements. During the 1940's and 1950's there occurred a notable resurgence of intellectual and entrepreneurial history, whose exponents felt more keenly than the less innovative political historians the need for a sociological orientation; and it is hardly coincidental that among the historians of their generation Merle Curti in intellectual history and Thomas C. Cochran in economic and entrepreneurial history were especially prominent in trying to persuade their colleagues and students to take a sociologist's view of the historical process. In the main, however, most of the articles on the relation of history to the social sciences written during the last fifteen years have expressed disappointment over the little that has been accomplished. "The inclusion of history," Cochran wrote in 1955, "as a full-fledged cooperating member of the social science group has not appealed to most historians in the United States," and he was even uncertain that the younger generation was any more receptive than their elders. Eight years later, A. S. Eisenstadt, though conceding that there were a few conspicuous instances of "a new departure in recent American historical writing" and citing eight books all of which had been written in the 1950's, was still able to endorse Cochran's judgment and felt obliged to conclude that "the orientation underlying present American historiography is conventional and conservative." [3]

But this judgment may be unduly sweeping. There is no longer, if there was before, a single orientation underlying American historiography and holding the overwhelming majority of its practitioners completely in its sway.

Those historians who wrote favorably about sociology in the 1950's, even though they may have felt themselves to be embattled with their colleagues, were increasing in numbers. In 1954, a group of historians gathered by the Social Science Research Council undertook to persuade their colleagues of the validity of what they called "the social science approach," and produced a bulletin (No. 64) whose very title, *The Social Sciences in Histori-*

cal Study, bore evidence of their commitment. But this commitment was no sooner made than another S.S.R.C. conference issued another, much more circumspect statement about the relationship between history and social science.[4]

The truth is that the profession has been, and still is, engaged in an active and healthy debate between conservatives and innovators in which the "orientation" toward related disciplines is one of several questions at issue. The character of this division is well illustrated by two recent presidential addresses of the American Historical Association delivered only a few years apart. In 1957, William L. Langer, a historian whose distinguished reputation rests largely upon diplomatic history of a conventional kind, found it regrettable that many historians "have a tendency to become buried in their own conservatism" and argued that "if progress is to be made we must certainly have new ideas, new points of view, and new techniques. We must be ready, from time to time, to take flyers into the unknown, even though some of them may prove wide of the mark." The particular flyer that he urged in this address went well beyond the now-conventional reminder that the other social sciences should be regularly consulted to the assertion that the historians should make themselves much more receptive to the findings of modern depth psychology than they have been hitherto, and in particular to "psychoanalysis and its later developments and variations as included in the terms 'dynamic' or 'depth psychology.'"[5] To argue this case represented an innovative daring greater than that shown by the usual advocates of interdisciplinary work; even many of these have drawn the line at having any truck with Freud or depth psychology. And yet, in trying to exemplify how the new history, receptive to depth psychology, might for instance take a new view of the later Middle Ages and the era of the Reformation, Langer threw out some historical suggestions that might well have seemed congenial to more-old-fashioned historians who admired Huizinga's *Waning of the Middle Ages*.

Five years later, Carl Bridenbaugh undertook in his presidential address to warn his colleagues against "the dehumanizing methods of the social sciences." Not only did he have little faith in the ability of the other social disciplines to carry on in the spirit of humanism, but he attacked modern urban-reared historians for their inability to understand rural America, and hence by implication, though not directly, challenged the possibility itself of valid historical knowledge concerning periods of history which have not been directly experienced by the historian.[6] Clearly if an American reared in cities cannot really understand the history of the earlier rural America, it is unlikely that an American, whether reared in city or country, can really understand, for example, classical antiquity or the later Middle Ages or the era of the Reformation, and it becomes especially unlikely if his angle of vision is further distorted by such new-fangled preconceptions as those of psychology. That the issue may not be so unnegotiable as it appeared from these words is suggested when one examines Bridenbaugh's own writings on early America, which are by no means devoid of insights which, while amply humanistic, are at the same time informed by a certain sociological awareness.

It has been clear all along, then, that the many historians who have argued for closer ties to the social sciences have done so in the teeth of a good deal of resistance. It may be well to say a little about this resistance, and in particular the specific resistance to sociology. The objections of conservative historians to being "sociologized" have varying degrees of importance and deserve varying degrees of respect and credence. But I think that at the heart of the matter lies a general fear of being deprived of one's intellectual identity. At a very primitive level, some historians, when it is suggested to them that their work might acquire a whole new dimension, think that they are simply being reproached for shoddy work or intellectual superficiality. More reasonably, many a historian—and this includes some who are more receptive to sociological conceptions than they are to sociological methods —feels that he is being asked to work with tools that he has not been trained to use. This objection rests upon a solid bedrock of fact; even today, when a consistent interest has developed among many graduate students in "interdisciplinary" work, the institutional arrangements for cross-field training are of the most casual and rudimentary nature. Then there is always the knotty question of style: historians are repelled by the texture of sociological writing, and they complain that sociologists use a vast mass of superfluous jargon. Some of these objections are both superficial and unfair; there is no more point in rebuking the sociologist for employing technical terms necessary to his trade—say, "reference groups" or the "F-scale"—than there would be in rebuking the historian for talking about paleography or palimpsests or the physician for his aorta and gluteus maximus. There is in both fields, and will undoubtedly continue to be, a great deal of bad writing. The difference perhaps lies chiefly in the fact that in the historical profession an inferior style is taken as an obstacle to publication; and it is probably true that in history a smaller proportion of the bad writing sees the light of day.

There is, I believe, also an element of professional deformation in bad sociological writing. As a lately arrived discipline, which has a strong drive toward generalization, sociology felt obliged to justify itself by taking on an air of profundity, and its practitioners fell into the trap of imagining that an idea gains in force and dignity the more abstractly it is expressed. Many historians unfortunately have felt all too free of any need to gather the general implications of their findings. One trait that almost all historians have in common is a certain love of facts for their own sake, and even those who feel obliged to generalize are happily quite capable of understanding and using the fact-bound monographs of their fellows who recognize no such obligation. No doubt there is something here that is related not only to differences in aims and methods but also to the way the personnel of the two disciplines is recruited. It is not true that history is an "ideographic" discipline, which deals only in unique facts, but it is certainly true that historians are men for whom a mass of apparently unique facts still offers certain undeniable delights. To them it is incomprehensible that anyone should fail to understand or share this pleasure.

I have thus far left out, however, the deepest distinction between the two disciplines that has kept them apart: it is that good history is almost invariably written in a personal voice, and all the examples of great history we have illustrate this fact. This is something that even historians who are quite committed to the mutual need of history and sociology will not sacrifice. The misunderstandings that have hitherto separated the disciplines can be overcome not by flouting this profoundly ingrained feeling of historians but rather by showing them that there is a possible historical genre in which the personal voice still remains and for which the sociological imagination is of the highest value. Such examples are not lacking, either in contemporary or in traditional historiography.

A point of still further resistance, which may be shared by historians who are relatively well informed about social science and which still troubles many sociologists, is the argument that sociology in fact, whatever it may ideally be, has become ahistorical if not actually antihistorical, and that this state of mind militates against cooperation. This view of the case is founded upon the preponderant energies that have gone into highly focused, narrow, though sometimes very finely wrought empirical studies since the end of World War II. Just as historians are often vulnerable to the lure of a new mass of documentary materials, without giving sufficient advance consideration to what they might get out of it, so sociologists have been fascinated by that which could be precisely measured without troubling themselves about what results of intellectual significance the measurement might yield. For them, highly developed methods of microanalysis have had the same fascination as piles of unused documents for the historian, and both situations have had their own consequences in the way of professional deformation.

But few sociologists, however absorbed in them, care to defend the proposition that such microanalytic efforts should have a monopoly of professional energies. In recent years, as the companion essay by Seymour M. Lipset (which follows) indicates, there has been a heartening resurgence of interest in historically informed sociological work. Many sociology departments have begun to look for historical sociologists who have some promise of restoring to the discipline some of the quality that was imparted to it by the great historical sociologists of the era of Weber and Simmel. No doubt we are only in the early stages of this resurgence, and historical sociologists are still hard to come by. For a long time, sociology departments were not taking the trouble to find or train such talents; the whole process of graduate training was absorbed in empirical work, often of a kind for which rich grants were easy to get.

It is significant, too, that even those sociologists who have deplored this tendency, and who have argued for a return to the older tradition of macroscopic analysis and political relevance, have been unable to live up to their own demands. For example,

David Riesman and the late C. Wright Mills come readily to mind as sociologists with a strong interest in macroscopic historical change. Such works as *The Lonely Crowd, White Collar,* and *The Power Elite* make significant comparisons of contemporary phenomena with those of the remoter historical past. Yet their actual historical dimension is quite thin, having much more the character of Veblen's "conjectural history" than of full-fledged historical sociology. The proffered pictures of the inner-directed man of the nineteenth century or of the relatively rational and orderly political discussion that supposedly preceded mass culture and the domination of the power elite are purely abstract archetypes, usable because they pose a point of contrast to imputed contemporary realities, but not themselves developed in historical depth. The questions whether the realities were as they are imagined, and whether they do in fact offer sound points of contrast, are left to the historians. No one, for example, who has read Mills' contrasting pictures of the derationalized public political discussion of the 1960's and the imaginary rational political "publics" of an earlier era is likely to be persuaded that here the sociologist had given as serious thought to the politics, say, of 1828 or 1840, or 1884 as he had to the politics of the Eisenhower era. And, indeed, for a sociologist committed on principle to the importance of history, *The Power Elite* constituted an ironic, though largely implicit and unarticulated, attack upon the relevance of history to the study of power, since it assumed that the actual historical setting in which political decisions arose could be ignored in favor of a career analysis of those who made the decisions.

In spite of all these difficulties, the barriers between the two disciplines have visibly melted during the past decade, as these pages testify, and the complaints of sociologically-minded historians in the mid-1950's about the indifference or hostility of their colleagues now seem less justified. The sense of smug self-sufficiency among historians which, for a generation or more, seemed a formidable obstacle is encountered with much less frequency. The old idea that the historian has done his job if he gathers together a lot of related facts and puts them on a chronological framework in creditable prose is now largely dead among the younger generation of historians. No doubt a certain amount of historical work of this kind will continue to be done, but this is not what the able younger historians aspire to do. They now have before them enough models of another kind of achievement; they consider it their business to attack significant problems of historical change, and in their attack to use all the intellectual weapons that can be brought to bear from all the relevant disciplines. Increasingly they are asking during the years of their graduate training how they can acquire the necessary instruction.

Many young historians today apparently find that sociology, while it has enough points of convergence with history to be emiently usable, also has just enough differences to offer a special kind of stimulation. The sociological imagination is related to the historical imagination but represents an amplification of it rather than an alternative to it. Both its concepts and its methods have much to offer, and the coming generation of historians finds itself more intrigued than alienated. They begin to see historical problems in a fresh light and to find new ways of getting at them. An acquaintance with sociological literature has sharpened their feeling for occupational structure, social stratification, and social mobility; for the family and the whole kinship order, especially as it is related to economic and political power and to the pattern of social mobility; for religious institutions and religious styles, as they bear on economic and political conflicts; for the problems of church and sect; for the social role of ideologies; and for the history of immigration as the history of acculturation and contrasting styles of life and thought. Familiar historical concerns, like class and status, have been pursued with new and interesting consequences. Moreover, they have been pursued with new methods: quantification has been used in some areas where historians were previously content to make impressionistic generalizations, and some of the old impressionistic generalizations have not been able to stand the test of a quantitative analysis. Systematic career-line studies, comparative history, content analysis, and the sociology of knowledge have all had their repercussions in historical study.

Probably the chief impact on historians of their increasing exposure to sociology has been a growing awareness of the complexity of their task and of the variety of methods available to them which hitherto have been little used.

For a long time historians were slow to show an interest in

quantification, even in areas in which it is readily possible. Two generations have now come of age since Charles A. Beard, in his famous book on the Constitution, showed the way to a systematic analysis of a group of men connected with a single event, anticipating by many years the emergence of Namier's variety of structural history. And yet, despite the general acceptance among historians of his argument, only recently challenged in formidable works, little interest was shown in his methods. Today, however, there is a renewed interest in systematic career-line analysis and in quantitative studies of historical personnel, stimulated to a considerable degree by an interest in the study of social mobility.

Another type of inquiry, long neglected and now beginning to find its place, is the use of comparative history to illuminate events. As employed by such writers as David Potter, Stanley Elkins, and Eric McKitrick, this method promises to help break down the parochialism that has all too long beset American writers on American history. Again, the sociology of knowledge and a rather impressionistic, but not less significant, kind of content analysis have made their way into historical writing in the work of such historians as Albert Weinberg, Henry Nash Smith, John William Ward, and Marvin Meyers. This methodological breakthrough has many sides, for the historians have undoubtedly learned as much from philosophers like Lovejoy and from the textual preoccupations of the new criticism as they have from sociology.

A further area in which historians have been impelled to reconsider their previous ways of work has to do with what they have learned about behavior—on the one side, from public opinion polls, and on the other, from depth psychology. As Lee Benson pointed out some years ago, historians had not yet begun to give serious consideration to the loose interpretations they were in the habit of making about voting patterns in elections, even though the process of voting decision was now considerably better understood, old assumptions about the whys and wherefores of voter choice no longer seemed plausible, and new quantitative techniques were available to test such interpretations.[7] Historians had been all too ready to believe that masses of people, to whose minds they had a far less direct access than the modern pollster in contemporary affairs, were in fact decisively influenced by the manifest content of campaigns and the more or less rational discussions of issues which it was possible for the historian to study in his usual documentary way. A generation of public opinion polling and the analysis of voter choice and voting patterns has cut the ground from under their assumptions, handed down from textbook to textbook, and those assumptions will have to be systematically reconsidered. Many of them, perhaps most of them, will not survive. One of the first of the techniques that will have to be employed is that of analyzing each election through comparisons across time, which requires at least some rudimentary quantitative techniques.

Earlier judgments about political behavior were also based upon certain psychological assumptions that are beginning to be questioned. The generation of Beard, Turner, and Parrington worked with postulates that seemed greatly to oversimplify their task but that now seem to many historians greatly to oversimplify our history. Their conception of political man was at bottom—even though they may not always have been prepared to defend it—highly rationalistic. Political man, as they saw him, was a direct descendant of economic man. In politics he sought to realize his interests, of which he had a fairly clear and basically accurate conception, and which he saw and defined almost exclusively in economic terms. American history could therefore be viewed largely in terms of the struggle of economic classes or subclasses over certain basic questions. The economic picture might be modified to a degree, as in Turner's case, by sectional or regional determinants, but the fundamental fact of social class and economic self-consciousness, the fundamental priority of social and political conflict among the concerns of the historians, were not profoundly affected by this. Parrington even attempted to apply to American literature and thought a schematism which was far too constricted in its sense of the human psyche even to bear the burden of interpreting our political history, not to speak of our literary achievements. Today, under the impact of a more informed sense of the considerations that enter into human action, the simple synthesis offered by the progressive historians is breaking down. Historians are replacing their economic man with a creature who is prey to a variety of motives and concerns. The single-minded concentration on class and region is being varied by a concern for status and role and their effect on social action. The almost obsessive concern with conflict as the central theme of historical writing has given way to an understanding that multivariate analysis is needed to put the forces of history upon an intelligible framework.

What is emerging in our time, as one may hope this volume will illustrate, is a new historical genre—a genre, to be sure, that comes to us not without distinguished predecessors from a long historiographical past, but which only in our generation, and only in ample scope during the past fifteen years, has begun to be cultivated intensively. The new genre is part narrative, part personal essay, part systematic empirical inquiry, part speculative philosophy. Just as the monograph did not displace the old-fashioned narrative history, the new genre of analytical history will not displace the traditional professional monograph. There is room in a complex intellectual culture for all three, and perhaps more besides, to live side by side. But the new analytical history, with its complex conceptual task and its enlarged frame of reference, offers a kind of inquiry that is as much differentiated from the traditional academic monograph as the monograph itself was from the older historical narrative. What is basically true today—and the influence of sociology is much to be thanked for this—is that the historian now has at his disposal a larger conceptual apparatus and a wider range of methods of work. It is hard to believe that the old narrative historian's regard for style will not have an important place in the new genre, or that the sound monographer's feeling for fact and ingenuity with sources will not also be incorporated. Perhaps history written with sociological awareness will also have something to offer to sociology, notably in breaking down its parochialism about time, and in restoring to it some of the magisterial command of the great early masters of historical sociology.

Notes

1. John Herman Randall, Jr., and George Haines, IV, "Controlling Assumptions in the Practice of American Historians," *Theory and Practice in Historical Study*, Social Science Research Council Bulletin No. 54 (New York: 1946), p. 32.

2. *Ibid.*, p. 33.
3. Thomas C. Cochran, "History and the Social Sciences," *Relazioni del X Congresso Internazionale di Scienze Storiche* (Rome, September 4–11, 1955), p. 481; cf. pp. 482–484, 489; A. S. Eisenstadt, "American History and Social Science," *The Centennial Review*, VII (Summer 1963), 259, 261.
4. R. D. Challener and M. Lee, Jr., "History and the Social Sciences: The Problem of Communications," *American Historical Review*, LX (1956), 331–338.
5. William L. Langer, "The Next Assignment," *American Historical Review*, LXIII (January 1958), 284–285.
6. Carl Bridenbaugh, "The Great Mutation," *American Historical Review*, LXVIII (January 1963), 326.
7. See his essay in Mirra Komarovsky, ed., *Common Frontiers of the Social Sciences* (Glencoe, Ill.: The Free Press, 1957).

✤ 2 ✤

Seymour Martin Lipset

HISTORY AND SOCIOLOGY:
SOME METHODOLOGICAL CONSIDERATIONS

American sociology has been criticized for having departed from the historical concerns of its nineteenth century European founders. This departure was characterized by a shift from a macroscopic to a more microscopic focus on society, from studies of social change and aspects of total societies, viewed in a historical and comparative perspective, to the study of interpersonal relations, the structure of small groups, and the analysis of the decision-making process, accompanied by an emphasis on improving the quantitative methodology appropriate to these topics. This change suggested to its critics that modern sociology had lost contact with its original intellectual traditions. The writings of men such as Alexis de Tocqueville, Max Weber, Robert Michels, and Vilfredo Pareto were apparently of contemporary interest only insofar as they had attempted to specify functional relationships and social psychological processes of the type that interested latter-day sociologists.

There are many examples which indicate ways in which sociological research has made major errors by ignoring historical evidence. Oscar Handlin and Stephan Thernstrom have given us an illustration of the weakness of an ahistorical sociology when they demonstrate how W. Lloyd Warner misinterpreted a number of patterns in his Yankee City series of studies of a New England community by relying on contemporary reports concerning past patterns and ignoring the actual history of the community as available in documentary sources.[1] Thernstrom has also pointed out the weakness of many assumptions made about rates of social mobility. He indicates that both sociologists and historians have erred in their interpretations concerning the extent of social mobility in mid-nineteenth-century America by relying either on impressionistic accounts by contemporaries concerning the presumed high rates of upward movement, or on logical deductions concerning an inherent need for a high mobility rate in a rapidly expanding economic system. His detailed quantitative analysis of the actual movement of unskilled workers in Newburyport, Massachusetts, a century ago, suggests a rate of mobility that is lower than has been found in studies of contemporary communities.

The Revival of Historical and Comparative Sociology

In the last decade, the situation with respect to sociological concern with historical topics has begun to change. There has been a significant revival of historical and comparative sociology. This revival has taken many forms, including interest in the sociology of science, concern with the determinants of change in intellectual life, interest in the evolution of national values, study of past patterns of electoral behavior, analysis of changes in religious life, and the like. The growth of interest in such problems is so recent that many with an interest in sociology, including some in the profession itself, are unaware of the extent to which leading sociologists have become involved in these fields of inquiry.

A significant source of the renewed interest in historical and comparative sociology has been the emergence of the body of inquiry which has been called the sociology of development. This term refers to interest in the processes which affect propensities to "modernize" total societies. As a field of research, it parallels the work of economists on problems of economic development. And just as economists concerned with economic development have recognized that much of what is conventionally termed "economic history" is actually the study of economic development, and that generalizations concerning economic development which are relevant to contemporary "developing economies" can be tested by reference to the past history of developed economies, so sociologists interested in problems of societal modernization and

nation building in Africa and Asia have come to understand that
the "old states" of the world have much to tell us about these
problems. In sociology, as in economics, interest in comparative
development has involved a renewed concern with historical analysis.[2]

The re-emergence of historical and comparative sociology does
not reflect any general feeling on the part of sociologists that the
emphases on quantitative techniques, rigorous methodology, and
systematic theory, which have characterized the work of the discipline in recent decades, were misguided. If there is any criticism
of these efforts, it is only that they had the temporary effect of
narrowing the focus of concern from the macroscopic (total society) to microscopic (small unit) problems, and from concern
with patterns of social change to the analysis of the processes determining group behavior, regardless of time or place. In a sense
the swing back to the macroscopic and the historical involves an
effort to relate the new methodological and theoretical developments to the analysis of total social systems and social change.
Much of the logic of inquiry developed and tested with respect to
experimental and microscopic sociology and to analysis of current
contemporary processes has proven applicable to macroscopic research, including comparative and historical.

Sociological Approaches

If the sociologist has erred in the past by ignoring historical data,
the historian has erred in the eyes of the sociologists by ignoring
concepts and methods which are as available and useful to the
historian as to the sociologist. This does not mean that sociologists
seek to turn historians into historical sociologists. From an ideal-
typical point of view, the task of the sociologist is to formulate
general hypotheses, hopefully set within a larger theoretical
framework, and to test them. His interest in the way in which a
nation such as the United States formulated a national identity is
to specify propositions about the general processes involved in the
creation of national identities in new nations. Similarly, his
concern with changes in the patterns of American religious participation is to formulate and test hypotheses about the function

of religion for other institutions and the social system as a whole. The sociologist of religion seeks to locate the conditions under which chiliastic religion occurs, what kinds of people are attracted to it, what happens to the sects and their adherents under various conditions, and so on. These are clearly not the problems of the historian. History must be concerned with the analysis of the particular set of events or processes. Where the sociologist looks for concepts which subsume a variety of particular descriptive categories, the historian must remain close to the actual happenings and avoid statements which, though linking behavior at one time or place to that elsewhere, lead to a distortion in the description of what occurred in the set of circumstances being analyzed. As Lewis Namier has put it:

The subject matter of history is human affairs, men in action, things which have happened and how they happened; concrete events fixed in time and space, and their grounding in the thoughts and feelings of men—not things universal and generalized; events as complex and diversified as the men who wrought them, those rational beings whose knowledge is seldom sufficient, whose ideas are but distantly related to reality, and who are never moved by reason alone.[3]

To use concepts and methods developed in sociology or in the other social sciences, however, does not turn the historian into a systematizing social scientist. Rather, these offer him sets of categories with which to order historical materials and possibly enhance the power of his interpretive or causal explanations. Thus, looking at the findings of social science may give a particular historian certain ideas as to types of data to collect which may be pertinent to his problem. For example, in recent years students of stratification have formulated the concept of status discrepancy as an explanatory variable. Status discrepancy refers to situations in which individuals or groups are ranked at different levels of prestige or reward on various dimensions of stratification. A college graduate who is a manual worker is high on one dimension—education—but low on the other—occupation. A political boss may be much higher on the power dimension than he is on prestige. College professors may be higher in prestige than they are in income, and so on.

The students of status discrepancy have postulated that those who are in discrepant positions will behave differently in specific ways from those whose statuses are congruent, i.e., all relatively on the same level. It has been suggested, for example, that individuals subject to status discrepancies are likely to be more liberal politically than others who are in the same income, occupational, or other stratification category as themselves. They are also more likely to react in extreme fashion with respect to political and religious behavior. Clearly, a concept such as this may be of use to the historian. It indicates the need to consider the possibility that the varying status positions might explain the deviation from expected behavior of some individuals or groups in the past. I do not suggest that the sociologist can furnish the historian with certain definite facts to incorporate into his analysis; just the opposite is true—the sociologist is complicating the work of the historian by indicating that he ought to examine even more factors because evidence drawn from sociological studies suggests that these may be relevant.

To take another example, work in sociology and social psychology on attitudes has indicated that the conventional contemporary American definition of liberalism (which assumes that to be liberal means to support socioeconomic policies which favor redistribution of community resources in favor of the underprivileged, the welfare state, trade unions, civil rights for Negroes and other minority groups, civil liberties for unpopular minorities, internationalism, liberal immigration policies and so forth) turns out to create major analytical problems when the actual attitudes of samples of the general population are examined. Opinion studies suggest that there are at least two dimensions of liberalism, economic and noneconomic. The first refers to support for welfare-state reforms, trade unions, planning, redistributive tax policies; the second includes backing for civil rights, civil liberties, internationalism, and similar issues.[4] Moreover the evidence indicates that the less income people have, the more likely they are to be liberal on economic issues, while higher education is closely correlated with noneconomic liberalism. Since the better educated are generally more well-to-do than those with less education, one finds that poor and less-educated people are liberal on economic issues and illiberal on noneconomic ones, while well-educated and well-to-do people tend to be liberal on noneconomic measures and illiberal on economic ones.[5] There are, of course, many who are liberal on both; such a position characterizes the intellectual community and is the policy fostered by the liberal wing of the Democratic party and organizations such as trade unions and civil rights groups which support the liberal coalition. There are those who are illiberal on both dimensions; these include Southern conservatives, lower class Republicans, and many right-wing organizations and political leaders.

The significance of this distinction for the historian is fairly obvious. It should be possible to discover to what extent similar variations existed in the past. Thus, as one illustration, this distinction may be reflected in the fact that in debates over the suffrage in New York State, Federalists and Whigs favored equal suffrage rights for Negroes and whites (noneconomic liberalism), but the Federalists sought to preserve a property franchise (economic class illiberalism). The Democrats, on the other hand, opposed a property requirement, but showed little interest in Negro suffrage.[6] The hypothesis would suggest that xenophobia, nativism, and anti-Catholicism had a strong appeal to less-educated lower-class persons all during the nineteenth century. Thus, the Whig and Republican alliances with nativist and "Know-Nothing" elements may have been their primary means of securing lower-class support away from the Democrats.[7] Such hypotheses might be tested by analyses of the various referenda conducted before, as well as after, the Civil War, which dealt with issues of Negro rights, as well as with suffrage rights for the foreign-born, prohibition, and other noneconomic issues.

In urging that historians apply generalizations developed in contemporary analysis to the past, I am not suggesting that they should assume that such propositions have always been valid, or even that the same relationships among different factors will probably help account for given past events. It is quite possible that under the different conditions of pre-Civil War America, anti-Catholic or antiforeign prejudices were not located preponderantly among the lower strata. However, the hypothesis does suggest the need to investigate the relationship between class and prejudice during that period.

Another group of concepts which may be useful for historians is that subsumed in the terms "frame of reference" and "reference

group." These concepts involve the assumption that, to understand the behavior of individuals or groups, it is necessary to locate the framework within which they evaluate or compare stimuli. Implicit here is the assumption that two events or measures
which are objectively similar when judged against an absolute
standard may have quite varying consequences when viewed
from different frames of reference. Thus, an income or occupation which places a man close to the top of the stratification system in a small community may locate him in the lower-middle
class in a large city or in the nation as a whole. To specify social
location in relative rather than absolute terms may enhance explanatory analysis. To cite an example from my own work, a
study of voting patterns in the elections of 1860 indicated that the
extent of slavery in Southern counties correlated with the way in
which they voted in the presidential race and the subsequent secession referenda. However, if counties are classified in terms of
whether they ranked high or low in proportion of slaves in the
South as a whole, the correlation is quite low. If the classification
of high or low is made within state lines, then the correlation is
much higher. High slave counties within state boundaries behaved
similarly politically, even though the statistical meaning of high
proportion of slaves varied greatly from states with many slaves
to those with few.[8] Thus, it would appear that the relative position of areas within the frame of reference of state politics
strongly affected their reaction to the secession question.

The concept of reference group has, of course, emerged largely
within social psychology as a way of conceptualizing the group
authorities from which individuals derive their standards of judgment. To understand the behavior of historically relevant actors,
it may often be necessary to locate or impute their reference
group, e.g., to determine whether a given political leader judges
his actions by comparison with his estimate of those of his note-
worthy predecessors, whether a man relates his present behavior
to those standards held by his peers when he was young, and the
like. Such guides to action may not be located by examining the
immediate external pressures on a decision maker, but require detailed biographical knowledge which permits imputations concerning an individual's reference group. As Thomas Cochran,
however, points out: "In many cases empirical evidence short of

that from interviews by skilled psychologists will not suffice to establish a reference group. Occasionally such information is plausibly given in autobiographies." [9]

There are, of course, many examples of the fruitful use of sociological concepts and hypotheses by historians. Stanley Elkins and Eric McKitrick applied concepts developed in the context of a sociological study of political participation in a contemporary New Jersey housing project to an analysis of the nineteenth-century frontier. Robert Merton has demonstrated the way in which new communities with a homogeneous population faced with a period of problem solving involve a very large proportion of citizens in politically relevant community activities. And Elkins and McKitrick were able to locate comparable processes and factors in new prairie frontier settlements, thus using Merton's propositions to locate the processes underlying many of Turner's assumptions about frontier democracy.[10]

In his study of the formation of political parties in early American history, William Chambers used Max Weber's analysis of the role of charismatic leaders in postrevolutionary situations to interpret George Washington's role in encouraging the trend toward a rational legal basis of authority.[11] He also examined some of the sociological propositions that have been advanced in a comparative context concerning the social requisites for democracy, and related these to the social structure of the early United States. Thus, the explanation for the success of early American democracy is linked to generalizations about factors associated with democratic institutions on a world-wide scale.[12]

Robert Lamb's interest in explaining some of the factors involved in American economic development (particularly in the cotton textile industry) between 1787 and 1816 was explicitly premised on the application of systematic social science approaches to a particular set of events. As Lamb described his method:

[W]e need models descriptive of the structures and functions of national and international communities at moments of time, and of their changes through time. These models should be made by students of entrepreneurship, working with political, social and economic historians. To build such models we need, for example, to trace the pattern of a given social structure such as an extended-kinship system at a moment of time, study its connections with the surrounding community, and follow its changes over time.[13]

In addition, Lamb argued, the weakness of efforts to analyze early American economic development lay in large part in the lack of experience by entrepreneurial historians in dealing with such models. One needed a model with its subsumed hypotheses to indicate the kinds of data to collect, the relationships which needed tracing, and so on. He developed his own research within the context of a model of community decision making. His concern with the decision-making process led him to look for the effective basis of the influence by the successful entrepreneurs on their communities and regions, which he traced to the extended kinship system and family connections.

The efforts of sociologists to differentiate a number of stratification dimensions and to suggest that incongruent positions, high in one dimension, low in another, would affect behavior in determined ways have been applied in various analyses of different events in American history. Thus, the emergence of the temperance movement and the various stages it has taken since the early nineteenth century have been explained in terms of reactions of groups to the tensions inherent in conflicting stratification positions.[14] A number of writers have discussed status tensions as a source of support and leadership for the abolitionist movement.[15] Stanley Elkins applied the analysis of the French sociologist, Emile Durkheim, of the social conditions which result in *anomie*, a social state in which individuals feel disoriented, unrelated to strong norms—and hence more available for recruitment to new movements—to an understanding of the emergence of the abolitionist movement. He suggests the intense expansion of the 1830's resulted in a situation "in which limits were being broken everywhere, in which traditional expectations were disrupted profoundly." [16]

The study of ethnic prejudice and nativist social movements is clearly one in which the substantive interests of historians and sociologists overlap. And here again, propositions concerning status tensions have informed the analysis of historians. John Higham has pointed to status rivalries occasioned by upward mobility as the basic set processes which underlie the conflicts of different ethnic and religious groups. He has applied on the level of broad historical events the same sort of analysis of these tensions that one may find in the detailed community studies by sociologists of the frictions fostered by ethnic and religious status conflicts.[17]

A comprehensive discussion of the application of the concepts of social science to the work of the historian may be found in the report of the Committee on Historical Analysis of the Social Science Research Council. It is interesting to note that the one sociological concept discussed in any detail there is that of social role. The interest in this concept seems to reflect a concern with the need to specify clearly the expectations held by a group or society concerning behavior associated with a given status or position. As Thomas Cochran put it:

Much of the value of history, whether viewed aesthetically or scientifically, depends on assumptions or generalizations regarding anticipated uniformities in role-playing. . . . Knowledge of the intricacy of role analysis can also guard the historian against over-simplified views of the pattern of social interaction.[18]

Perhaps as significant as the interchange of concepts between sociology and history is the transference of methods. Lee Benson has pointed to the failings in much of American political history occasioned by the fact that many historians have attempted to explain political shifts without doing the necessary research on easily available voting statistics.[19] Much as the sociologist prefers to deal with quantitative data drawn from interviews, the historian seems to prefer qualitative materials drawn from printed matter, diaries and letters. The "reasons" often given by historians for the defeat of a particular party may be tested through a simple statistical analysis of voting returns. We can find out, for example, how many of the gains made by the Republicans between 1856 and 1860 occurred in areas which were sharply affected by the depression of the late 1850's, or were shifts to the Republicans of Know-Nothing votes, as contrasted with increases from districts which had shown concern with the slavery issue. Research on the election of 1860 in the South indicates that the division between Breckenridge and Bell, the two candidates who secured most of the vote in that region, correlated greatly with the lines of electoral division which formed around the Jacksonian

Democrats three decades earlier. Specifically, Breckenridge, the secessionist Democrat, secured the bulk of his votes from the traditionally Democratic poor-white areas where there were relatively few slaves; while Bell, the antisecessionist Constitutional Union candidate, received most of his votes from areas characterized by plantation agriculture, a high ratio of slaves, and a past tradition of voting Whig. In subsequent referenda and convention delegate elections in late 1860 and early 1861—held not on party lines but on the issue of union or secession—the majority of the plantation areas, which voted for the Constitutional Unionists, opted for secession, while the majority of the low slavery counties, which had backed the secessionist Democrats in the presidential election, voted for the Union. Analysis of shifts of sentiments and behavior of this kind provides firm evidence regarding the trends and processes at work in the American population during the crucial years before the Civil War and raises questions concerning assumptions of a consistent relationship between party policies and opinions of party supporters.[20]

In his effort to spell out ways in which historians may verify generalizations about national character differences, Walter Metzger detailed the way in which sociologists handle multivariate analysis in survey research. As he points out, one of the major problems in drawing conclusions about national character is to distinguish among attributes of societies which are properly characteristic of the culture and those which result from the fact that societies vary in their internal composition, containing more of certain groups or strata than another. Thus, the question may arise as to whether society A differs from B because it is predominantly rural, or Catholic, or has a much higher level of education, rather than because basic values or "character" vary. To test out these possibilities he suggests a simple trick of the sociological trade (one familiar in this discipline but surprisingly little appreciated by historians), namely, to hold factors constant as is done in intranational opinion research. One may compare Catholic Canadians with Catholic Americans, or college-educated Canadians with Americans of comparable education.[21]

In yet another area of political history, the sociologist Sidney Aronson has tested the various assumptions made by historians concerning the supposed introduction of the spoils system by Andrew Jackson. Aronson carefully coded the social background characteristics of the higher civil servants in the administrations of John Adams and Thomas Jefferson, and of John Quincy Adams and Andrew Jackson, much as one does with interview data. He is able to show that the overwhelming majority in all four administrations came from the socioeconomic elite.[22] This study offers another example of the way in which contemporary observers may be deceived about what is happening around them, particularly when they are making statistical guesses about facts which actually are unavailable to them. The ideology of a group may lead it to claim to be doing things which in fact it is not doing. Thus, Jackson sought to appeal to a mass electorate, and the claim that he was throwing old Federalists from office and replacing them by good plebeian Democrats may have been good politics. Both friend and foe alike may have agreed in print concerning his actions, and thus misled not only contemporaries but also future historians.

Paul Lazarsfeld has pointed out the utility for historical research of the opinion survey, a method long used by sociologists.[23] He has called the attention of historians to the enormous quantities of information on a multitude of issues which have been gathered by commercial and academic polling organizations over the past three decades. Unlike historians dealing with pre-New Deal events, contemporary historians of the New Deal period have available to them, as will historians in later decades or centuries who will study the twentieth century, fairly reliable data about the state of public opinion, voting behavior, and various other activities such as church attendance, membership in voluntary organizations, drinking and gambling habits, and much more. In evaluating Roosevelt's or Eisenhower's role in a foreign policy crisis, the historian will be able to know what the American people thought of the issues. He will be able to differentiate as to the characteristics of those who attended church regularly, as to shifts in sentiments toward McCarthy or racial integration, and so on.

To do this, however, the historian will have to take courses in survey analysis—he may want to learn certain statistical techniques so as to know how to make up various attitude scales, or to evaluate the validity and reliability of his results. And to maximize the use of survey data for future historians, those of the present may want to dictate some of the questions which are asked by contemporary pollsters. For the sake of future generations of historians, it may be useful to repeat the identical questions about certain attitudes and behaviors every few years so that a reliable estimate of changes may be made.

At the moment, however, few historians, including those dealing with the modern period of American history, seem to have been aware of the uses of survey data for their problems. One may point to books on the 1930's which make inferences concerning the social base of the Coughlin movement, isolationism, and popular attitudes toward the third term or toward Roosevelt's proposal to enlarge the Supreme Court, which were written in apparent ignorance of the body of opinion data dealing with these matters. And in a number of cases, historians relying on their interpretation of election results, or assuming that congressional or press reaction reflected predominant trends among the public, have been quite wrong in their conclusions. Such mistakes are not likely to recur since many younger historians have now begun to apply quantitative techniques to the study of political history.

While the sociologist believes that he might help the historian methodologically, he would like assistance from the historian to test some of his generalizations about changes in social structure. Many social scientists have presented hypotheses concerning the relationship of changes in the occupational and class structures to other institutions. It has been suggested, for example, that the development of a predominantly bureaucratic and tertiary economy, oriented around leisure and consumption, has led to a change in many fundamental patterns such as child-rearing practices, the content of American religion, or the modal personality structure. In *The First New Nation* I have questioned the validity of many of these propositions concerning fundamental changes in American values and behavior, but for the most part, I, too, relied heavily on extant reports of subjective observations.[24] The techniques of content analysis, which involve the coding of qualitative documents so as to permit quantification, have obvious applicability to efforts to verify assumptions concerning the direction and extent of such changes. Analyses of diaries and other autobiographical materials, coding of the themes of ministers' sermons, and examination of newspaper discussions of how to raise children could undoubtedly tell us a great deal about social changes.[25]

Some indication of the utility of content analysis applied to a historical issue may be found in a study dealing with the extent to which consciousness of being Americans rather than British colonials, overseas Englishmen, or residents of a particular colony, existed among the inhabitants of the colonies prior to the American Revolution. Richard Merritt analyzed the symbols in newspapers from Massachusetts, New York, Pennsylvania, and Virginia from 1735 to 1775. He found a sharp increase in reference to American rather than English events, and in the use of the term Americans.[26]

It is important to recognize that values expressed in the mass media at any given time may not be a good indicator of popular attitudes. Thus a recent analysis by Fred Greenstein, which compares a "forgotten body of survey data" from the late nineteenth and early twentieth centuries (questionnaire studies of school children's ideals and occupational aspirations) with comparable ones from recent years, reports little change over a 60-year period. His results contradict the assumption of writers such as David Riesman, William Whyte, Eric Fromm, and others, that the achievement goal or "Protestant ethic" has been declining in American life. The one major change which seems to have occurred is a decline in references to national heroes, particularly to George Washington. Since some studies of the themes of children's textbooks or popular fiction do indicate changes in "achievement orientation" and in the occupations of fictional idols, these findings argue for the thesis that changes in social ideology, as expressed by popular or textbook writers, need have little relationship to variations in the underlying popular values. And latter-day intellectuals who conclude that intellectual consensus equals popular agreement may be confounding "rationalization with reality." [27]

Comparative History

Basically, all social science is comparative. Social scientists, sociologists included, seek to formulate generalizations which apply to all human behavior; to do this, of course, involves specifying the conditions under which a given relationship among two or more variables holds true. And it may be that these conditions make a given proposition unique, it may occur only under conditions which rarely happen. The fact, however, that a combination of circumstances occurs uniquely or rarely does not mean that its conditions cannot be presented in terms of general concepts or categories. The test, of course, of any proposition is the analysis of varying conditions in which it should predict behavior.

In attempting to account for a specific pattern of behavior which has occurred in a given part of the world, for example, the casual relationship (if any) between the emergence of Protestantism and the rise of capitalism, it is clearly necessary to engage in comparative research. Without examining social relations in different nations, it is impossible to know to what extent a given factor actually has its suggested effect. For example, if it is true that the German *Ständesstaat* (rigid status system) has played an important role in determining the authoritarian pattern of German politics, how does it happen that a similar structure in Sweden is associated with a very different political culture? Again, the fact that the American rates of mobility are not uniquely greater than those in countries with class-conscious politics obviously raises a number of questions: [28] Why has there been consensus concerning the relative "openness" of American society? Perhaps the emphasis placed in the value system on equality of opportunity or on social equality in interaction is more important than the "invisible" rate of mobility. Or is the image of a uniquely open society fostered by the American standard of living, which has been higher than that of any other country for many generations, which has permitted the great majority of the population to greatly improve their living standards from one generation to the next, and which has narrowed the gap in consumption standards among the classes more than in other countries?

Questions such as these are as important to historians as to sociologists. Many historians have long recognized that the study of national behavior is enhanced by comparisons of similar developments in different countries. Such comparisons can provide the historian with some controls for evaluating the significance of the factors which he uses for interpretive purposes. Few historians or sociologists have taken advantage of the magnificent laboratory for comparative analysis afforded by the twenty-three independent states of the Americas. These nations vary considerably with respect to the stability and nature of political institutions and rates of economic development. To account for such differences among any two or more of them some have pointed to variations in their religious ethos, differences in their pattern of frontier settlement, varying constitutional arrangements, differences in their system of class and ethnic relationships, and so on. A brief look at some of the problems which have been raised by this type of analysis may illustrate the utility of such research in depth for both disciplines.

Perhaps the most systematic efforts to account for structural differences between countries by comparative historical analysis have been done by Canadian scholars. Canadians are forced to learn almost as much about the United States as Americans do, and they know their own country as well. Thus, many of them continually raise questions as to why various differences between the two countries have occurred or exist. S. D. Clark, a former historian turned sociologist, and various other Canadian historians, such as Frank Underhill, Harold Innis, and A. R. M. Lower, have suggested that Canada is a more conservative or traditional country culturally because it is a nation which has emerged out of a successful "counter-revolution," while the United States represents the outcome of a successful revolution.[29] They have urged that if one looks at developments north *and* south of the American border after 1783, it is clear that the success or failure of the Revolution had major consequences on the core national values which have informed behavior, on the nature of class relations, on the extent of education, on the type of religious organization, and so on. In each case, Canada developed a more conservative pattern showing greater respect for authority and law and order, greater emphasis on hierarchy, more conservative religious behavior, and lesser economic development. Canadians writing on these topics have tried to show how emphases endemic to a Tory image of society have been successfully fostered in the settled portions of the Maritimes which were before 1783 essentially part of New England. At the same time in the United States there has been an extension of many of the egalitarian and universalistic emphases inherent in the dogmas proclaimed in the Declaration of Independence.

The strength of the left tradition in the United States and of the conservative one in Canada has had continuing influences. Thus Clark points to the fact that the failure of the effort to annex Canada to the United States in the War of 1812 represented a second defeat for the democratic or revolutionary forces in Canada. The frontier farmers there were pro-American. And this defeat unleashed a second series of internal events which reinforced the conservative values and institutions in Canada. Again, during the Jacksonian period in the United States, Canada had its Mackenzie-Papeneau rebellions which were defeated.[30] Canadian independence occurred in 1867, not as a result of a triumphant democratic movement, but rather under the leadership of the Canadian Empire oriented Conservatives. It reflected Britain's desire to reduce her overseas commitments.

Subsequent American reform movements such as the Populists and Progressives had their parallels in Canada, but the latter had much less ideological effect on the nation as a whole. And the period which witnessed the American reformist left hailing the triumph of the New Deal found their Canadian compeers resorting to the creation of a third party (now called the New Democratic party), which has remained weak. The weakness of the democratic or left political tradition in Canada is related to the fact that it has been identified with the United States. To preserve a national raison d'être, Canadians have been obligated to denigrate the populist egalitarian American democracy and to hold up as a positive model various aspects of the more elitist British society. Thus S. D. Clark and Frank Underhill have argued that while the predominant political tradition in the United States has been a leftist and populist one, Canadians live in a country which must defend its refusal to join the revolution and praise the values of political moderation, cultural conservatism and respect for elites. And various Canadian scholars have interpreted comparative trends in Canadian literature, education (many fewer Canadians attend university than Americans), the family (lower divorce rate), attitudes toward law and order (lower crime rate), elites (greater respect), and religion (less sectarian innovation) as derivative in large part from the differences in the political events forming the two nations.[31] Few, if any, American historians have sought to explicate their interpretations of the conservative or leftist character of the American Revolution, the American political tradition, or American institutions by looking at the way in which Canada developed within a highly similar ecological environment. I would argue strongly that no one should work in United States history without also dealing with Canada.

The effort to relate variations in the value system and institutions of nations to the differences in their key formative experiences provides a good illustration of Max Weber's methodological dictum that current differences among social structures may often be linked to specific historical events which set one process in motion in one nation or unit, and a different one in a second. Weber, in fact, used the analogy of a dice game in which each time the dice came up with a certain number they were loaded in the direction of coming up with that number again. That is, a decision in a certain direction tends to reinforce those elements which are congruent with it. In other words, historical events establish values and predispositions, and these in turn affect later events.[32]

The general thesis laid down by Frederick Jackson Turner concerning the impact of the frontier on various characteristics of American society has led to a number of efforts to test it in the context of other frontier societies such as Canada, parts of Latin America, and Australia.[33] Presumably it might be argued if various elements in the experience of colonizing a frontier land resulted in individualism, egalitarianism, and high political participation in the United States, similar consequences should have occurred in other pioneer settlement countries. Students of the Australian frontier, however, have pointed to the fact that their frontier experience was quite different from that of both North American countries. In America, each individual attempted to find his own plot of land. The Australian agricultural frontier, on the other hand, was much less hospitable in terms of climate, and family agriculture was less practical. Many of the frontier enterprises involved large-scale cattle and sheep grazing, both of which required considerable capital if the enterprise was to be worthwhile. "The typical Australian frontiersman in the last century was a wage-worker who did not usually expect to become anything else." [34]

There are, of course, other differences which have been suggested to account for the varying nature and influences of the Australian and American frontiers. Thus the absence of strong aboriginal resistance in Australia as compared with the Indian wars in the United States may have weakened the need for strong local community life in Australia.[35] And the frontier, regardless of the institutions and values which it fostered, necessarily had much less impact on Australia than on the United States, since the relative size of the frontier population as compared to the urban one was much less in the former because of geographic factors.[36]

Although frontier geographic conditions in the two North American states were quite comparable, these frontiers also differed greatly in large part for reasons derivative from their varying political histories discussed above. Inasmuch as Canada had to be on constant guard against the expansionist tendencies of the United States, it could not leave its frontier communities unprotected or autonomous. "It was the established tradition of British North America that the power of the civil authority should operate well in advance of the spread of settlement." [37] Law and order in the form of the centrally controlled North West Mounted Police moved into the frontier before and along with the settlers. This contributed to the establishment of a much greater tradition of respect for the institutions of law and order on the Canadian frontier as compared with the American, meant the absence of vigilante activity in Canada, and enabled Canada to avoid the Indian Wars which were occurring south of the border, since the Canadian government kept its word to the Indians and the Mounties prevented "renegade whites" from upsetting the Indians.

The pervasiveness of the government legal controls on the Canadian frontier seriously weakened the development of an excessive emphasis on individualism which characterizes the United States.[38] There has been no particular glorification of the frontiersman in Canadian writing as there has been in the United States.[39] The development of the Canadian frontier, in fact, did not simply follow on population movements impelled by natural social pressures, as occurred in the United States. Rather, the Canadian government felt the need deliberately to plan for the settlement of the West. As the Canadian sociologist S. D. Clark has put it:

Canada maintained her separate political existence but only by resisting any movement on the part of her population which had the effect of weakening the controls of central political authority. The claims to the interior of the continent were staked not by advancing frontiersmen, acting on their own, but by advancing armies and police forces, large corporate enterprises and ecclesiastical organizations, supported by the state. The Canadian political temper, as a result, has run sharply counter to the American. Those creeds of American political life—individual rights, local autonomy, and limitation of executive power —which have contributed so much to the political strength of the American community have found less strong support within the Canadian political system.[40]

A recent effort to explain why Brazil—the largest, most populous, and most richly endowed of the Latin American states—has done so much more poorly than the United States also emphasizes the varying nature of frontier settlement in the Americas. Vienna Moog points to the differences between "bandeirantes" and "pioneers" as a key source of the varying patterns of development in his native Brazil and the United States. As Adolf Berle summarizes his thesis:

Bandeirantes ("flag-bearers") were the explorers and settlers of the interior of Brazil, as "pioneers" were the conquerors and colonizers of the great unoccupied heartland of the United States. The difference lies in their motives and ideals. The Brazilian bandeirantes were perhaps the last wave of colonial conquistadores. The American pioneers, though of all kinds, were predominantly Reformation settlers. The resulting civilizations set up by the two groups of wilderness-conquerors were therefore quite different, despite many elements common to both.[41]

Moog relates the varying nature of the Brazilian and United States frontiers to the facts that for three centuries in Brazil the main motive for going to the frontier was to get rich quickly, to find gold or other precious minerals, and that labor whether in urban or rural occupations was denigrated as fit only for slaves while the English and later American settlers looked for new homes based on their own work.[42] These differences are linked to varying cultural traits and motives for seeking new opportunities on the frontier. In Brazil the bandeirante is credited with the geographic enlargement of the country, much as the pioneer is in the United States. "In the United States a thing, to be capable of arousing enthusiasm, must bear the label of pioneer; in Brazil . . . it must merit the epithet of *bandeirante*." [43]

The history of Argentina offers yet another example of the way in which the social structure of an American frontier was determined by the predominant structure and values established in colonial times. Values and structures endemic in the settlement of an open frontier neither served to influence the social organization of the rural community nor helped shape a national democratic outlook. Argentine agriculture developed much like that of Australia, with large cattle and sheep ranches which used many workers, either as hired help or as tenants, and preserved a hierarchical status system. Various efforts to encourage small landholding failed after Independence because of the power of the large landowners. And subsequently, in the latter part of the nineteenth century, it proved to be impossible to apply meaningful homestead legislation to Argentina, although there was a general belief among Argentine experts that United States prosperity and development was attributable to its policy of encouraging land settlement in the form of family homesteads. The Argentine pampas, which closely resembled the prairies of the United States and Canada, remained in the hands of a small class of large landowners. "Churches, schools, and clubs did not develop in rural Argentina for the simple reason that settlement was dispersed and often temporary." [44] And as in Australia, the urban centers of Argentina, particularly Buenos Aires, became the focus for immigrant settlement. "Rather than a frontier, Argentina had a city." [45]

The argument that the varying characters of the Brazilian, Argentine, Canadian, and American frontiers flow from differences in their early values assumes the perspective taken by Max Weber which stresses the role of core values in influencing the institutional structure of a nation. As applied here, it suggests the need to modify the assumptions of many historians who accept variants of the Turner thesis, that the frontier experience was a major, if not the major, determinant of American egalitarian values.

Rather, the comparisons with Brazil, Argentina, and Canada would suggest that the egalitarian character of the American frontier was in some part determined by the values derived from the revolutionary political origins and the Calvinist work ethos. The thesis that basic social values shaped the frontier society has, of course, been advanced by a number of historians. Thus Henry Nash Smith has sought to show how the rural frontier settlements established in the West on the Great Plains reflected not only the physical environment but also "the assumptions and aspirations of a whole society." [46] He has argued that revisions in the Homestead Act, which would have permitted large farms and a more economical use of arid lands, as in Australia, were opposed by the new settlers because *they believed in the ideal of the family farm.*

It should be clear that a concern with the influence of economic, ecologic, and value elements in determining given national developments or traits is not a matter of dealing with alternative mutually exclusive hypotheses. Rather as in the case of Weber's discussion of the relative contribution of economic and value factors in the rise of capitalism, one may conclude that different variables are each necessary but not sufficient to produce the results sometimes credited to one of them alone. Thus, the comparative data indicate that an open unsettled rural frontier need not result in egalitarian, individualistic, and democratic institutions and values. On the other hand, political movements which stress such values have found great difficulty in institutionalizing them in the countries whose ancient structures have been able to resist political efforts to change values. The American and French revolutions espoused similar ideologies and societal outlooks. The American, developing in a new society with an open frontier, could impose its values on the culture. The French failed to do so; the rightist culture supporting throne and altar has remained a powerful force in France to the present.[47] Thus it may be argued with Weber that the appropriate structural environment for a given development requires the emergence of facilitating values, or that necessary values will not result in the anticipated changes unless the structural conditions are propitious.

The emphasis on the role of values in national development links studies of historical change with basic assumptions in contemporary sociological theory. Seen in the light of Weber's methodology, the sociological emphasis on key values in a social system is an effort to relate the operation of the system to elements rooted in its history. This general line of argument which stresses values as the key source of differences in the rate of development of economic and political institutions has been countered by some students of Latin America who point to the Southern states of the American union as an example of a subculture which has been relatively underdeveloped economically, which has lacked a stable democratic political system, and which has placed a greater emphasis on violence and law violation to attain political ends than the rest of the country. And as these scholars point out, the white South is the most purely Anglo-Saxon and Protestant part of the United States.

The American South is held to resemble much of Latin America, including Brazil, in having an institutional structure and value system erected around a plantation (or latifundia) economy which employed large numbers of slaves, and which after the abolition of slavery continued a two-caste system, with a stratification hierarchy correlated with variations in racial background. From this point of view, the clue to understanding the economic backwardness and political instability of Brazil and much of Spanish America lies in their structural similarities with the American South, rather than in those values which stem from Iberian or Catholic origins.[48]

Such an argument concerning the relative influence of these different factors on development may lead us to return to a look at Canadian differentiation. French Canada, historically, has been less developed than English Canada. Much of its economic development has been dominated by entrepreneurs from English speaking backgrounds.[49] Though not as politically unstable as the Southern United States or most of Latin America, Quebec has long exhibited symptoms of political instability (i.e., an opposition-party system is perhaps less institutionalized there than in any other populous province); charges of political corruption, illegal tactics in campaigns, violations of civil liberties, and the like, seem much more common in Quebec than in the English-speaking provinces.[50] Quebec is certainly Latin and Catholic (if these terms have any general analytic or descriptive meaning), but it certainly has not had a plantation culture, nor a significant racial minority, though it could be argued that the English-French relationships resemble those of white-Negro, or white-Indian in the other countries of the Americas.

Various analyses of the weakness of democracy in Quebec do argue that religious-linked factors are among the relevant ones. As Pierre Trudeau has put it:

French Canadians are Catholics; and Catholic nations have not always been ardent supporters of democracy. They are authoritarian in spiritual matters; and since the dividing line between the spiritual and the temporal may be very fine or even confused, they are often disinclined to seek solutions in temporal affairs through the mere counting of heads.[51]

And many have pointed to the differential in the economic development of the two Canadas as evidence that Catholic values and social organization are much less favorable to economic development than Protestant ones. As S. D. Clark has reasoned:

In nineteenth century Quebec religion was organized in terms of a hierarchy of social classes which had little relation to the much more fluid class system of capitalism, and sharp separation from the outside capitalist world was maintained through an emphasis upon ethnic and religious differences and through geographic isolation.[52]

Sociologists interested in the factors which have differentiated French-Canadian economic development from other parts of North America have divided over the extent to which the social structure of Quebec has been determined by values inherent in the culture of a rural Catholic traditional "folk" society, as many sociologists and anthropologists have suggested. The University of Montreal sociologist, Phillippe Garigue, has argued that the culture of New France was mainly a commercial and urban one, that its frontier was commercial (fur trade) rather than rural, that a large part of the population lived in towns, and that many were Protestants or otherwise anticlerical. He argues that in nineteenth-century Quebec one found a farmer rather than a peasant culture, that rural French Canadians basically bore more resemblance to the farmers of New England in their orientation toward making money from the land than they did to Norman peasants. Consequently he denies that the lack of French-Canadian economic leadership stems from specifically French, Catholic, or traditional peasant society traits. Rather he would blame it on the consequences of being subjected to foreign, i.e., English, rule.[53] Garigue does not deny the existence of a distinct French-Canadian value system, but he argues that the emphasis on it was a consequence of a minority group seeking weapons to resist those with power, much as English speaking Canada has constantly sought to emphasize whatever differentiates it from the United States. French-Canadian priests, politicians, and intellectual leaders have sought to foster the elements of a unique culture, "even if sometimes this was done on an imaginary base." [54] And recently, sociologists from the University of Montreal have reported on studies which show that mid-nineteenth-century Quebec was much less religious than the twentieth century province, that anticlericalism was stronger and church attendance lower.

These are not the only issues involving comparative sociological hypotheses which seek to account for variations in social, economic and political development in the different American countries.[55] One of the key topics for discussion in American political history is the explanation of the absence of significant "third" and/or ideological or class-conscious parties in American politics. Many of the explanations have focused on seemingly unique elements in American society, as contrasted to those of European nations, with their class parties and multiparty systems. Thus the absence of a feudal past and the consequent lack of concern with estate (fixed status-group lines) values have been suggested as reducing the pressures for class parties; the supposed existence of greater opportunity has been alleged to reduce backing for class consciousness; the greater wealth of the country is said to have reduced the tensions among strata; the presence of many diverse ethnic groups has been held to inhibit class politics since parties appealed to diverse multiclass ethnic groups. Others have stressed the role of the American constitutional arrangements, the requirement to choose one man to hold the executive power, as pressing for a two-party system, while forms of parliamentary government facilitate multiparty systems. To some extent such hypotheses may be scrutinized in the context of analyzing the various American nations, which vary on a number of these factors and in their political systems.[56]

Efforts at formulating and testing comparative historical generalizations may not only seek to examine the relationship between given structural and value elements and specified consequences such as do most of those discussed above, but may also look at types of events in the lives of nations and ask what are the factors which affect differential reactions to similar problems. Thus in his analysis of the failure of the Reconstruction period to settle the conflicts between the North and the South which had reached a determinate outcome on the battlefield, Eric McKitrick has looked at the way in which the vanquished were dealt with by the victors in other wars. He has pointed out that normally the vanquished have accepted and peacefully adjusted to their defeat, much as has occurred in Germany and Japan after World War II. He has sought to specify some of the conditions which inhibited efforts at further resistance by the defeated to major social changes introduced by the victors. And his explanation of the failures of the Johnson Reconstruction lies in the unwillingness of Andrew Johnson to behave as a victor should have done if he were to have received respect and obedience from the vanquished. In a sense, his book is a case study in one subarea of the sociology of conflict which deals with the resolution of violent struggle in which there is a definite winner or loser.[57]

If much of comparative history and sociology seeks to point up and account for variations among nations, this emphasis also may lead to highlighting the effects of common experiences or factors. Thus, in recent years, a number of studies have sought to specify the conditions facing new nations or other postrevolutionary societies which seek to establish legitimacy, to find a basis for national linguistic and value consensus so as to have a stable national society which does not rest on force, or which will not come apart during the strains of major crises. Most of this literature deals with the contemporary new nations or with Latin America. Some, however, have included the United States in this category and have sought to re-examine early postrevolutionary American history with a view to learning how the United States dealt with these problems. Methodologically these studies have taken various forms. Karl Deutsch and a group of historians have spent some considerable time working over the histories of a number of nations, including the United States, which were successfully created out of independent subunits, so as to formulate propositions which held true in most of these occurrences.[58] On the other hand, Chambers and I have sought to specify propositions about the requirements for stable new nationhood from the literature of latter-day new nations, and to re-examine American history to see to what extent such propositions could inform historical inquiry, and conversely, to develop propositions from a detailed historical case study which might be useful in analyzing contemporary events occurring under comparable conditions.[59]

Concern with the social requisites of new nationhood also has inspired the work of Robert Lamb and Richard Merritt, dealing with prerevolutionary America. Both recognized that the creation of a new nation, or even united colonies in rebellion, required, as Lamb put it, a new *national* elite which had to be in communication within itself, and which had a consciousness of kind. He traced through the interconnections which emerged in terms of personal, family and business ties among members of the elite in Virginia, Pennsylvania, New York and Massachusetts.[60]

Merritt, discussed earlier in a slightly different context, sought to demonstrate that a national consciousness had emerged before the Revolution through an analysis of the symbols in the colonial press which showed a steady increase in use of the term "Americans" and a decline of words which in any way pictured the colonists as transplanted Englishmen.[61] Both studies, it should be noted, were consciously concerned with general processes of national development and refer their work to those interested in these larger issues. Thus Lamb has addressed himself, in part, to "those interested in the role of elites in the formation of new nation-states"; and Merritt has suggested that "the evidence provided by the American experience is useful in testing current ideas about nation-building. . . ." [62]

Most recently, Louis Hartz and a group of historians have introduced the concept of the "fragment" society or culture to characterize those *new societies* which were formed out of the overseas nations settled by Europeans—the nations of the Americas, Australasia, and South Africa. The concept of the fragment refers to groups which emigrated from European countries to settle abroad as coming from parts or fragments of the mother culture. Despite all their variations they represent for Hartz a common body of experiences in being "fragments" of Europe which developed very differently from the mother cultures since they did not embody the European "whole." Many important European strata, values and institutions, usually those associated with the privileged classes, never reached the "new societies." All of these societies "in the midst of the variations they contain, are governed by the ultimate experience of the American liberal tradition." Each left behind in Europe an ancient source of conservative ideology in the form of the traditional class structure. Hence in British Canada, the United States, and Dutch South Africa, particularly, enlightenment doctrines could dominate. In Australia, created by a fragment of nineteenth-century Britain, radical principles carried by working-class immigrants could form the national tradition unhampered by the need to compromise with powerful Tory values and supporters. But over time, the very absence of a traditional right transmutes the liberal or radical doctrines into conservative dogmas of the "fragment." It is impossible to build an ideological left in the fragment cultures because there is no hereditary aristocracy against whom to rebel, and because the philosophical bases on which an ideological left might be founded are already institutionalized as part of the received liberal and radical tradition of the society.

In stressing similarities among these nations, Hartz is, of course, sensitive to the many differences among them. Thus, he relates the varying attitudes towards race relations in these societies to the strength or weakness of feudal remnants. Feudalism as a system of defined statuses may more easily accommodate hierarchical race differences, as may be exemplified by the situation in Brazil. Enlightenment or radical values which have predominated in the United States, South Africa and Australia find it more difficult to encompass such differences and foster policies of complete separation such as "white Australia," South African apartheid, the "separate but equal" doctrine of the American South, or a massive moral struggle for real equality and integration as in the United States as a whole.

There can be little doubt that the concept of the fragment, like other concepts employed in the comparisons among new nations, points out interesting hypotheses about sources of similarities among the societies they subsume. At the moment, however, comparative analysis is faced with the difficulty that many of its most illuminating ideas are used by their proponents as literary devices, as ways of organizing a mass of information, not as means of testing specific alternative hypotheses. One may point to contradictory propositions advanced by different exponents of the comparative method which are not explored. Thus, Louis Hartz contends that the major factors forming the American liberal ethos derive from the fact that it is a fragment culture, a new society. The assumption requires that he find that the American Revolution was a relatively moderate revolt, that it was not a basic source of the American institutional system. In line with this thesis, Hartz and Kenneth McRae treat English Canada as a liberal Enlightenment society, not very different from the United States. Hartz and McRae argue that the two English speaking American nations never had an aristocracy, a fount of conservative elitist anti-enlightenment values. But Robert Palmer, in his treatment of the late-eighteenth-century revolutions in America and Britain, assumes that the American Revolution was a major dynamic event which not only greatly changed the course of American society, but also strongly affected the character of the subsequent revolutions in Europe. He traces strong similarities among the American, French, and other revolutions. To do this, he postulates:

"Aristocracy" [is] characteristic about 1760 of the society established in all countries, including the Anglo-American colonies. . . . Family self-perpetuation, inter-marriage, inheritance of position, and privileged or special access to government and to its emoluments or profits are found to have been common phenomena over a wide range of institutions—the governors' councils in the British American colonies, the two houses of parliaments of Great Britain and Ireland, the parliaments and provincial estates of France, the town councils and estates of Belgium, Holland, Switzerland, Italy and Germany, the diets of Hungary, Bohemia, Poland and Sweden.[63]

In Palmer's language these were "constituted bodies." He attempts to show that in many of these countries movements based on Enlightenment ideas emerged directed against the power of the "constituted bodies." These advocated equality as a reaction to the fact that an "aristocratic resurgence" was occurring in which "exclusiveness, aristocratic class-consciousness, and emphasis on inheritance were increasing. . . ." [64] And he contends that the revolution succeeded in the two countries in which the agricultural population collaborated with urban middle-class leaders—France and the United States—but failed in other countries of Europe because of political apathy or weakness of their agrarian populations.

It would not be appropriate to evaluate the head-on controversy between Palmer and Hartz here. In my own writings on American history in a comparative context, I have assumed that the American Revolution was a major revolution, which had enormous consequences in forming American values, political system, and general institutional structure. One must face up to the issue, however, as to whether it is possible to evaluate the utility or validity of different organizing comparative concepts such as "fragment," "new society," "new nation," "aristocracy," and "revolution."

To a considerable degree, the issue in comparative analysis often involves evaluating the same fact as meaning "as much as" or "as little as." Thus, one way to judge how "revolutionary" the American Revolution was is to see how many were removed by the upheaval. Palmer attempts to deal with this problem by comparing the number of emigrés who left the United States and France after the two revolutions. If we accept the French Revolution as a standard for a "real revolution," then the fact that there "were 24 emigrés per thousand of population in the American Revolution, and only 5 emigrés per thousand of population in the French Revolution" argues that "there was a real revolution in America." [65]

Hartz also compares the American and French revolutions to evidence his opposite thesis that the American Revolution had *relatively* little effect. He points out that contemporary American conservatives hail the revolutionary heroes, while in France "the royalist still curses the Jacobin." [66] Palmer would reply (in fact, the two ignore each other) that the French emigrés returned to France after the Restoration while the American did not come back to America, and that this fact made for great differences between the two countries, that the American Loyalists are forgotten.

The sense in which there was no conflict in the American Revolution is the sense in which the loyalists are forgotten. The "American consensus" rests in some degree on the elimination from the national consciousness, as well as from the country, of a once important and relatively numerous element of dissent.[67]

Clearly the issues posed here concerning different macroscopic judgments can rarely be resolved by empirical tests. The way in which one looks at data depends in large measure on the questions asked, the theory employed, and the classifications used. It is obvious that in dealing with complex alternative interpretations, no matter how rigorous the methodology employed, most historians and sociologists basically present an argument which they then "validate" by showing that there are more positive than negative data available. Most of the concepts used, however, such as revolution, class, aristocracy, are necessarily very imprecise. They leave a great deal of room for the analyst, wittingly or not, to find reasons for selecting those indicators of a concept which best fit the over-all conceptual framework he is using. And when existing data are confirmatory, most of us are not motivated to look further. It is only when data are in conflict with our theory, hunches, or prejudices, that most social scientists decide there must be something wrong with the data or with the concepts underlying the selection of the data, and look further. In reading the work of others, we are normally inclined to accept their findings as both valid and reliable, as long as they agree with our predispositions. Disagreement, however, results in efforts to re-analyze the evidence and to demonstrate that previous work has drastically oversimplified, or simply ignored, many data.

It is important to recognize that by looking at the same problem from different theoretical perspectives, we increase knowledge even if the conclusions seem contradictory. Different conceptual frameworks lead one man to highlight certain aspects which another ignores. Often, findings which are not congruent with one another merely reflect the fact that different scholars have used different concepts. Thus Hartz, in stressing the differences between pre-Revolutionary America and Europe, emphasizes in his conception of the European class structure the notion of a feudal rigid status system. Palmer, on the other hand, has a very different conception of aristocracy on both sides of the ocean, which basically sees the late-eighteenth-century societies as governed by small oligarchies whose members are closely related to one another.

Historians and social scientists should not feel inhibited to admit that one of their main analytical procedures is what I call the "method of the dialogue." In large measure the very meaning of scholarly verification in history has been the re-examination of the same problem by different scholars operating with alternative approaches. As long as men agree concerning the meaning of hypotheses and the nature of evidence, the dialogue can result in replication and the growth of knowledge. The sociologist can and has contributed to the dialogues in historical analysis by introducing concepts and methods which expand the possibilities available to the historian.

Many scholars, both historians and sociologists, despair of the value of introducing the methodological approaches of sociology or the other social sciences into historical work. They point to the fact that given historical situations are determined by a multitude of factors and that it is impossible to perform the methodological operation of holding other factors constant, or randomizing them, as can often be done when studying large numbers of individuals. The social psychologist or sociologist dealing with a sample of 2,000 people may compare the consequence of a factor being present or not among people who are comparable on a variety of other variables. The historian or the historical sociologist cannot do so. This does not rule out the utility of applying sociological generalizations to historical events. The sociologist engaged in a historical case study uses it to draw out generalizations that can apply to all similar cases, say of postrevolutionary office-holders, of reactions to authority in systems in which public offices are directly responsible to the people, and so forth. One may compare reactions to events within the same larger national system, regional differences, for example, in which many over-all factors are obviously being held constant. There is no necessary clash between developing general sociological hypotheses and taking historical specificity into account. T. H. Marshall argues that sociologists must accept historians as experts and rely on their accounts of events.

[S]ociologists must inevitably rely extensively on secondary authorities, without going back to the original sources. They do this partly because life is too short to do anything else when using the comparative method, and they need data assembled from a wide historical field, and partly because original sources are very tricky things to use. . . . It is the business of the historian to sift this miscellaneous collection of dubious authorities and to give to others the results of their careful professional assessment. And surely they will not rebuke the sociologist for putting faith in what historians write.[68]

Clearly we may apply the logic of science to the study of social systems with as much justification as we apply it to the analysis of individuals and institutions. Despite the fact that no two individuals have the same growth pattern or history, experts from varied fields continue to make generalizations about individual behavior by comparing instances in which the circumstances of development have been similar. It is true that there are fewer societies than there are individuals to compare and that hypotheses about the operation of a specific variable in the evolution of the former are less subject, therefore, to explicit verification than are generalizations about the operation of variables in individual development. Although the logic and approach of science can and should be used in historical sociology, it is obvious that work in this field cannot validate hypotheses with the rigor normally associated with the concept of a science. That this is so should only highlight the challenge. No discipline can select its research problems solely from those which are easy to study with extant methods. Those sociological problems which lend themselves to experimentation, to rigorous quantification, to explicit testing of mathematical models, are now relatively easy to study. Those in which it is difficult to isolate variables, in which one must deal with numerous factors and few cases, require a high level of theoretical and methodological ingenuity. As Karl Deutsch and the group of historians working with him on problems of history and comparative method point out:

Since historical cases can best be compared in only some of their aspects, and practically never in all of them, any comparison means the sacrifice of a great deal of detail, much of it important information. Yet to draw limited comparisons from only partly comparable data is of the essence of human thought. Throughout our lives we all apply selected memories from the past to our decisions in the present and to our expectations for the future. If we elaborate this time-honored practice and call it the "case method," we can hope to be more explicit in the techniques we use, in the assumptions we make, and in the data we leave out.[69]

One may hope that the new generation of historical sociologists are as creative methodologically as their more quantitative and experimental brethren have been in the past two decades.

Notes

1. See Handlin's reviews of two books of W. L. Warner and associates, "The Social Life of a Modern Community," *New England Quarterly*, XV (1942), 556, and "The Social System of the Modern Factory," *Journal of Economic History*, VII (1947), 277; and Stephan Thernstrom, *Poverty and Progress: Social Mobility in a Nineteenth Century City* (Cambridge: Harvard University Press, 1964), and his chapter in this book.
2. See T. H. Marshall, *Class, Citizenship, and Social Development* (New York: Doubleday, 1964).
3. Lewis Namier, "History and Political Culture," in Fritz Stern, ed., *The Varieties of History* (New York: Meridian Books, 1956), p. 372.
4. See G. H. Smith, "Liberalism and Level of Information," *Journal of Educational Psychology*, XXXIX (1948), 65–81; and "The Relationship of 'Enlightenment' to Liberal-Conservative Opinions," *Journal of Social Psychology*, XXVIII (1948), 3–17. See also Herbert H. Hyman and Paul Sheatsley, "Trends in Public Opinion on Civil Liberties," *Journal of Social Issues*, IX (1953), No. 3, 6–17.
5. See S. M. Lipset, *Political Man* (Garden City, N.Y.: Doubleday, 1960), pp. 96–130.
6. Marvin Meyers, *The Jacksonian Persuasion; Politics and Belief* (Stanford, Calif.: Stanford University Press, 1957), pp. 189–190.
7. S. M. Lipset, "Class, Politics, and Religion in Modern Society: The Dilemma of the Conservative," *Revolution and Counterrevolution: Change and Persistence in Social Structures* (New York: Basic Books, Inc., 1968), pp. 246–303.
8. Lipset, *Political Man*, pp. 344–354. I did not report the methodological analysis in this discussion.
9. Thomas C. Cochran, "The Historian's Use of Social Role," in Louis Gottschalk, ed., *Generalization in the Writing of History* (Chicago: University of Chicago Press, 1963), pp. 107–108.
10. Stanley Elkins and Eric McKitrick, "A Meaning for Turner's Frontier," in Richard Hofstadter and S. M. Lipset, eds., *Turner and the Sociology of the Frontier* (New York: Basic Books, Inc., 1968), pp. 120–151.
11. William Nisbet Chambers, *Political Parties in a New Nation* (New York: Oxford University Press, 1963), pp. 36, 42, 95.

12. *Ibid.*, pp. 99–101.
13. Robert K. Lamb, "The Entrepreneur and the Community," in William Miller, ed., *Men in Business* (Cambridge: Harvard University Press, 1952), p. 93.
14. Joseph Gusfield, *Symbolic Crusade: Status Politics and the American Temperance Movement* (Urbana, Ill.: University of Illinois Press, 1963).
15. David Donald, *Lincoln Reconsidered* (New York: Vintage Books, 1961), pp. 19–36; Stanley Elkins, *Slavery* (Chicago: University of Chicago Press, 1959), pp. 165–167.
16. *Ibid.*, pp. 165–166.
17. John Higham, "Another Look at Nativism," *Catholic Historical Review*, XLIV (1958), 148–158.
18. See Cochran, *op. cit.*; see also Walter Metzger, "Generalizations about National Character: An Analytical Essay," in Gottschalk, *Generalization in the Writing of History*, pp. 90–94.
19. Lee Benson, "Research Problems in American Political Historiography," in Mirra Komarovsky, ed., *Common Frontiers of the Social Sciences* (Glencoe, Ill.: The Free Press, 1957), esp. pp. 114–115.
20. Lipset, *Political Man*, pp. 344–354.
21. Metzger, *op. cit.*, pp. 99–100.
22. Sidney Aronson, *Status and Kinship in the Higher Civil Service* (Cambridge, Mass.: Harvard University Press, 1964).
23. See Paul Lazarfeld's article in this volume.
24. S. M. Lipset, *The First New Nation* (New York: Basic Books, Inc., 1963).
25. An example of such research may be found in Clark E. Vincent, "Trends in Infant Care Ideas," *Child Development*, XXII (September 1951), 199–209. In this study Vincent analyzed the literature of infant care from 1890 to 1949 dealing with "breast versus artificial feeding," and tight versus loose feeding schedules.
26. See the chapter by Richard Merritt in this volume.
27. See Fred I. Greenstein, "New Light on Changing American Values: A Forgotten Body of Survey Data," *Social Forces*, XLII (1964), 441–450. Greenstein cites a number of studies of changes in values as measured by content analyses, and also many studies of children's beliefs and values made since the 1890's.
28. See S. M. Lipset and Reinhard Bendix, *Social Mobility in Industrial Society* (Berkeley: University of California Press, 1959).
29. This thesis is elaborated in Frank Underhill, *In Search of Canadian Liberalism* (Toronto: The Macmillan Co. of Canada, 1960); A. R. M. Lower, *From Colony to Nation* (Toronto: Longman's, Green and Company, 1946); J. M. S. Careless, *Canada. A Story of Challenge* (Cambridge: Cambridge University Press, 1963).
30. See S. D. Clark, *Movements of Political Protest in Canada* (Toronto: University of Toronto Press, 1959).
31. For evidence concerning these differences see Dennis Wrong, *American and Canadian Viewpoints* (Washington: American Council on Education, 1955); Kaspar Naegele, "Canadian Society: Some Reflections," in Bernard Blishen, Frank Jones, Kaspar Naegele, and John Porter, eds., *Canadian Society* (Toronto: Macmillan Co. of Canada, 1961), pp. 1–53; Lipset, *Revolution and Counterrevolution, op. cit.*, pp. 31–63.

32. Max Weber, *The Methodology of the Social Sciences* (Glencoe, Ill.: The Free Press, 1949), pp. 182–185.
33. See F. J. Turner, *The Frontier in American History* (New York: Holt, Rinehart and Winston, 1962). For a collection of some of the American literature discussing and evaluating Turner's theses, see Hofstadter and Lipset, eds., *op. cit.*; my essay there includes the discussion of the frontier here, I have repeated the analysis in both volumes since it seems relevant to the different contexts.
34. Russel Ward, *The Australian Legend* (New York: Oxford University Press, 1959), p. 226. See also Carter Goodrich, "The Australian and American Labour Movements," *The Economic Record*, IV (1928), 206–207; Jeanne Mackenzie, *Australian Paradox* (London: Macgibbon and Kee, 1962), p. 106; Brian Fitzpatrick, *The British Empire in Australia, An Economic History* (Melbourne: Melbourne University Press, 1941); and Fred Alexander, *Moving Frontiers. An American Theme and Its Application to Australian History* (Melbourne: Melbourne University Press, 1947).
35. Ward, *op. cit.*, p. 36; G. V. Portus, "Americans and Australians," *The Australian Quarterly*, XIV (June 1942), 30–41.
36. Ward, *op. cit.*, p. 30.
37. Edgar W. McInnis, *The Unguarded Frontier* (Garden City, N.Y.: Doubleday, 1942), pp. 306–307.
38. A. R. M. Lower, "Education in a Growing Canada," in Joseph Katz, ed., *Elementary Education in Canada* (New York: McGraw-Hill, 1963), p. 8.
39. Claude T. Bissell, "A Common Ancestry: Literature in Australia and Canada," *University of Toronto Quarterly*, XXV (1956), 133–134.
40. S. D. Clark, *The Canadian Community* (Toronto: University of Toronto Press, 1962), p. 214.
41. Adolf A. Berle, "Introduction," Vianna Moog, *Bandeirantes and Pioneers* (New York: Braziller, 1964), p. 9. See also Charles Wagley, *An Introduction to Brazil* (New York: Columbia University Press, 1963), pp. 74–75.
42. Moog, *op. cit.*, pp. 119–121.
43. *Ibid.*, p. 171.
44. James R. Scobie, *Argentina* (New York: Oxford University Press, 1964), p. 124. For a discussion of the way in which efforts to encourage farming on the North American pattern were defeated, see pp. 78–81 and 121–130.
45. *Ibid.*, p. 130. The impetus for the "growth of cities, which would eventually make the Argentines Latin America's most urbanized people . . . came from (the extensive) agricultural exploitation of the pampas. The immigrants who were drawn to Argentina in the late nineteenth century found the land already controlled by *estancieros* (large landlords) and speculators. With the ownership of land largely beyond their reach, the newcomers accumulated in Argentina's port cities, especially in Buenos Aires."
46. Henry Nash Smith, *Virgin Land: The American West as Symbol and Myth* (Cambridge: Harvard University Press, 1950), p. 124. For similar points of view see George W. Pierson, "The Frontier and American Institutions," *New England Quarterly*, XV (1942), 253; and W. W.

Rostow, "The National Style," in E. E. Morison, ed., *The American Style: Essays in Value and Performance* (New York: Harper & Brothers, 1958), pp. 247, 259.

47. See John Sawyer, "The Entrepreneur and the Social Order. France and the United States," in William Miller, ed., *Men in Business* (Cambridge: Harvard University Press, 1952), pp. 7–22. "The French case offers striking testimony to the tenacity of inherited patterns. Here the old institutional structure was most violently assaulted; here more than anywhere else in Europe new ideas and institutions emerged triumphant in the Revolution and the Republic. . . . Yet France . . . carried forward elements of the European past that have remained widely diffused to this day. Over the centuries when commercial capitalism was enlarging its place in the national life, a series of historical turnings kept peculiarly alive aristocratic values and patterns . . ." (p. 13).

48. See Gilberto Freyre, *New World in the Tropics. The Culture of Modern Brazil* (New York: Vintage Books, 1963), pp. 71–72, 82–87, 193–195.

49. See Bernard Blishen, "The Construction and Use of an Occupational Class Scale," *Canadian Journal of Economics and Political Science,* XXIV (1958), 519–531. Yves de Jocas and Guy Rocher, "Inter-Generational Occupational Mobility in the Province of Quebec," *Canadian Journal of Economics and Political Science,* XXIII (1957), 377–394; John Porter, "Higher Public Servants and the Bureaucratic Elite in Canada," *Canadian Journal of Economics and Political Science,* XXIV (1958), 483–501.

50. One French-Canadian analyst has argued recently that "historically French-Canadians have not really believed in democracy for themselves." He suggests "that they have never achieved any sense of obligation towards the general welfare, including the welfare of the French-Canadians on non-racial issues." Pierre Elliot Trudeau, "Some Obstacles to Democracy in Quebec," in Mason Wade, ed., *Canadian Dualism* (Toronto: University of Toronto Press, 1960), pp. 241–259. On the general problems of, and weakness of democracy in Quebec see Herbert Quinn, *The Union Nationale* (Toronto: University of Toronto Press, 1963), esp. pp. 3–19, 23, 65–67, 126–129, 131–151; Gerard Dion and Louis O'Neill, *Political Immorality in the Province of Quebec* (Montreal: Civic Action League, 1956); Arthur Maheux, "French Canadians and Democracy," in Douglas Grant, ed., *Quebec Today* (Toronto: University of Toronto Press, 1960), pp. 341–351; Frank R. Scott, "Canada et Canada Français," *Esprit,* XX (1952), 178–189; and Michael Oliver, "Quebec and Canadian Democracy," *Canadian Journal of Economics and Political Science,* XXIII (1957), 504–515.

51. Trudeau, *op. cit.,* p. 245; see also Quinn, *op. cit.,* pp. 17–18.

52. Clark, *The Developing Canadian Community,* p. 161.

53. Phillippe Garigue, "St. Justin: A Case Study in Rural French Social Organization," *Canadian Journal of Economics and Political Science,* XXII (1956), 317–318; see also Philippe Garigue, *L'Option politique du Canada français* (Montreal: Les Editions du Levrièr, 1963), pp. 52–65.

54. Phillippe Garigue, "Organisation sociale et valeurs culturelles Canadiennes-françaises," *Canadian Journal of Economics and Political Science,* XXVIII (1962), 203; see also Garigue, *L'Option politique du Canada français,* pp. 29–49; and *Études sur le Canada français* (Montreal: Faculté

des sciences sociales, University of Montreal, 1958). The traditional position which Garigue rejects has been presented by Leon Gerin, "L'Habitant de St. Justin," *Proceedings of the Royal Society of Canada*, IV (1898), 139–216; Gerin, *Le Type économique et social des Canadiens* (Montreal: Editions de l'Action Canadienne-français, 1937); Everett Hughes, *French Canada in Transition* (Chicago: University of Chicago Press, 1943); Horace Miner, *St. Denis* (Chicago: University of Chicago Press, 1939); and Jean-C. Falerdeau, "The Changing Social Structure," in Falerdeau, ed., *Essais sur le Quebec contemporain* (Quebec: Les Presses Universitaires Laval, 1953), pp. 101–122. For a recent reply to Garigue which defends the position of unique elements in the culture see Herbert Guidon, "The Social Evolution of Quebec Reconsidered," *Canadian Journal of Economics and Political Science*, XXVI (1960), 533–551.

55. For a discussion of different approaches to the problem of American uniqueness which draws on the same evidence that is presented below, see S. M. Lipset, "The 'Newness' of the New Nation," in C. Vann Woodward, ed., *The Comparative Approach to American History* (New York: Basic Books, 1968), pp. 62–74.

56. See E. E. Schattschneider, *Party Government* (New York: Rinehart & Company, 1942), pp. 65–98; Lipset, *The First New Nation*, pp. 286–316.

57. Eric McKittrick, *Andrew Johnson and Reconstruction* (Chicago: University of Chicago Press, 1960).

58. See Karl W. Deutsch, S. A. Burrell, R. A. Kann, M. Lee, Jr., M. Lichterman, R. E. Lindgren, F. L. Loewenheim, R. W. Van Wagenen, *Political Community and the North Atlantic Area* (Princeton: Princeton University Press, 1957).

59. Chambers, *op. cit.*; Lipset, *The First New Nation*. R. R. Palmer also points to the "typical problems of a new nation" which faced the United States in very similar terms. See *The Age of the Democratic Revolution. The Struggle* (Princeton: Princeton University Press, 1964), pp. 518–522.

60. See memorandum by Robert K. Lamb presented in Karl W. Deutsch, *Nationalism and Social Communication* (New York: John Wiley, 1953), pp. 18–20. See also Lamb, "The Entrepreneur and the Community," for another report on the same research presented in the context of analyzing the conditions for economic development.

61. See the article by Richard Merritt in this volume.

62. Lamb's memorandum in Deutsch, *op. cit.*, p. 19, and the article by Richard Merritt in this volume.

63. R. R. Palmer, "Generalizations about Revolution: A Case Study," in Gottschalk, ed., *op. cit.*, pp. 69–70. Here Palmer summarizes the second and third chapters of his book, *The Age of the Democratic Revolution: The Challenge* (Princeton: Princeton University Press, 1959).

64. *Loc. cit.*

65. Palmer, *The Age of the Democratic Revolution: The Challenge*, p. 188. He also compares the compensation paid for confiscation of the property of counter-revolutionaries by the British government and the French Bourbon restoration. The sums were similar, holding population size constant.

66. Louis, Hartz, *The Founding of New Societies* (New York: Harcourt, Brace, and World, 1964) p. 82.

67. Palmer, *The Age of the Democratic Revolution: The Challenge,* pp. 189–190. On the meaning of the elimination of the Tories and their outlook from American life see William H. Nelson, *The American Tory* (Oxford: The Clarendon Press, 1961).

68. Marshall, *op. cit.,* p. 38.

69. Deutsch et al., *op. cit.,* p. 15; for detailed analyses of different aspects of the comparative approach applied to American histories, see the various essays in Woodward, ed., *op. cit.*

❦ 3 ❦

Stephan Thernstrom

QUANTITATIVE METHODS IN HISTORY:
SOME NOTES

Doubtless it is true, as historians are fond of telling their freshman classes, that the study of the past enriches the mind and liberalizes the spirit, undermining the instinctive parochial prejudices of those who have been exposed to only one culture, one world view, one way of life. But it does not follow, I fear, that historians as a breed are conspicuously liberal and open-minded in their reception of new methodologies and new research technologies. With respect to the subject of this essay—quantitative studies in history, particularly the potential uses of the modern electronic computer in historical research—it can only be said that historians have been conservative and unadventuresome. Some currently visible portents, however, suggest that this may not long continue to be the case. It seems appropriate, therefore, to raise some questions about both the possible uses and possible abuses of the computer and the habit of mind it engenders.

I.

First, a word about the character of the resistances which have made some of my fellow historians reluctant to employ the com-

Stephan Thernstrom is Associate Professor of History at Brandeis University. He is the author of *Poverty and Progress: Social Mobility in a Nineteenth Century City.*

The background of this chapter is explained in a note at the end of the chapter.

puter. These resistances, of course, have little to do with the computer itself—intimidating beast though it is. They stem rather from hostility toward the concepts and analytical techniques which the computer seems to impose upon the user—theoretical constructs, and quantitative techniques borrowed from the other social sciences. The suspicion certain professional historians feel toward such borrowing borders on the pathological, as witness the claim of one distinguished American historian that "almost all important questions are important precisely because they are not susceptible to quantitative answers." [1] I will avoid flogging this tempting horse at length, though I fear that it is far from dead. Let me say only that anyone who is not blindly and irrevocably committed to the view that all legitimate history is ideographic rather than nomothetic should concede two points.

One is that there are a great many historical problems of importance which *demand* the analysis of overtly quantitative data—voting statistics, information on wages and prices, population figures, etc. That among the vast mass of such unexploited materials are some kernels of genuine significance for historians can hardly be denied by any reflective person. Second, and this is more controversial, it should be clear that the fabric of even the most conventional historical account is studded with terms which are in some sense *implicitly* quantitative—"representative," "typical," "widespread," "intense," "growing." [2]

It is by no means always possible to translate these intuitive, implicit judgments of magnitude or typicality into explicit hypotheses for which verifying or diversifying evidence of a quantifiable kind can be produced—I will indicate later, e.g., some reservations about the quantitative indexes yielded by such procedures as content analysis—but there are some encouraging examples of imaginative index construction in the other social sciences, examples historians could profitably emulate in some instances. At the very least, the commitment to substitute an examined generalization for an unexamined one alerts the historian to the full implications of what he is saying, and, as W. O. Aydelotte reminds us, checks his natural instinct to remember best those cases which best fit his own prejudices and preconceived hypotheses. [3]

I hasten to concede regretfully that an investigator's sloppiness is sometimes merely displaced rather than eliminated by the procedure I describe (the return of the repressed, as it were), so that unexamined generalizations are converted into examined generalizations accompanied by numerical indexes which themselves rest on unexamined and questionable premises. Thus the recent quantitative analysis of Supreme Court decisions which assigned numerical weights to each of 26 factors which appeared in opinions in right-to-counsel cases without giving any account of just how it was decided which "factors" appeared in which cases.[4] But I would draw from this not the moral that as machines grow more intelligent the men who use them grow more stupid, but only the truism that people of all methodological persuasions make mistakes.

One common objection to quantitative historical research is that evidence amenable to quantification is often scarce or nonexistent. Two things should be said about this. One is that the raw evidence need not come in numerical form to allow some quantitative manipulation. A little imagination will often suggest ways of handling quantitatively even such radically qualitative materials as words—for instance, Richard Merritt's recent study of symbols of American national awareness in colonial newspapers between 1735 and 1775, based on the crude but useful procedure of tabulating changes in the frequency of different place-name symbols.[5] Second, data which are overtly quantitative are far more readily available than is commonly supposed; in my own field of specialization, for instance, American urban history, there are literally tons and tons of untapped material in manuscript census schedules, local tax returns, city directories, school attendance records and similar sources. The problem has been not a lack of sources, but either ignorance of the existence of these sources or a lack of knowledge of what to do with them. Admittedly, this evidence is often of low quality because of the primitive process by which it was gathered and recorded, but this is hardly an objection to quantitative analysis itself. Indeed, the researcher with a sophisticated knowledge of quantitative techniques is much better equipped to use these materials with proper caution than is the conventionally trained historian, who, if he examines them at all, is prone to rely upon his intuitive judgment of what they portend.

Another common objection to quantitative historical research is that the availability of data susceptible to quantification may exert an unduly coercive intellectual influence upon the scholar, who may forget the large issues and turn his attention to trivial matters about which statistical data happen to be available. The historian becomes an applied mathematician, preoccupied with perfecting his technique and less and less concerned with the substantive issues which initially engaged him. There is some force in this argument; C. Wright Mills' argument about the ascendancy of the trivializing "higher statisticians" in sociology and the abandonment of the intellectual concerns of the classic tradition is overdrawn, but sufficiently true, I think, to worry about.[6] But are scholars sympathetic to quantification really any more exposed to trivializing pressures than those working with other types of evidence—diplomatic notes, let us say? Historians very often let the availability of unanalyzed data rather than their prior perception of a significant problem determine their choice of subject; thus the cult of manuscript sources; thus the presumption of aspiring biographers that anyone who "hasn't been done" and who left personal papers behind is worthy of painstaking study by virtue of that fact alone. At least it can be said that the new barbarians who may flock into quantitative historical studies should be a little less parochial than the old barbarians and will be forced to know a little more about what is happening in other related disciplines. If some develop an unhealthy preoccupation with chi-squares and two-tailed t-tests, others will read Durkheim or Piaget or someone else and begin to see their problems in a new way.

II.

With the space at my disposal here I cannot pretend to offer any systematic survey of recent quantitative social research which the historian could profitably know about. A hasty, very unsystematic glance at a little of this work, however, may be of some value.

It should be recalled, of course, that our generation is hardly the first to see that measuring and counting have a role to play in historical study. Arthur F. Bentley's *The Condition of the Western Farmer as Illustrated by the Economic History of a Nebraska Township*, after all, was published in 1893. Bentley has now been appropriated by the political scientists as a Founding Father, but even if he be read out of the historical guild as a heretic, other instances could be cited of quantitative work by historians whose legitimacy can hardly be challenged; Crane Brinton wrote *The Jacobins: An Essay in the New History* thirty-five years ago. The French, of course, have done much of interest along these lines; the splendid recent work of the *Annales* group is the culmination of decades of development.

It should also be observed that the advent and growing accessibility of modern electronic computing devices has not drastically altered the research strategies followed by quantitative toilers in the historical vineyard. Such techniques as multivariate analysis and content analysis are relatively new, and they depend to some degree on the high-speed computer. But, on the whole, electronic data-processing devices have been used by historians to do in months much the same thing they used to do in years, or to put familiar questions to bodies of evidence which seemed so vast as to be utterly impregnable to historians of the precomputer age. One thinks of the Bailyns' study of an early eighteenth-century Massachusetts shipping register which included information about 1,696 vessels and some thousands of investors in these vessels.[7] If the tactics of the Bailyns seemed radical to some, the questions they asked and answered with their deck of IBM cards were straightforward; most of them had been asked before by historians who could answer them only by guesswork. I make this comment about the familiarity of the topics and procedures of many recent quantitative studies as an observation, not as a criticism, for I think that this is quite defensible. I do hope that more widespread use of quantitative methods will work some change in the intellectual perspectives of the historian—in the questions he asks as well as in the way in which he attempts to answer them; I hope, in particular, that greater interest in quantification and a parallel interest in social theory which should go hand in hand with it will turn attention to a series of basic problems in social history which have been sadly neglected. But I would emphasize that quantification in history is neither so new nor so necessarily radical in its implications as either the Maoists, as it were, of the quantitative revolution or the Goldwaterites would have us believe.

It is hard to know what to single out among the spate of recent historical studies which fall under the general rubric under consideration here: Aronson's statistical critique of the myth of the Jacksonian spoils system, Benson's reinterpretation of Jacksonian Democracy (or should I say his effort to demolish Jacksonian Democracy?) on the basis of election statistics for New York State, Lawrence Stone's fascinating tour through the corpse-strewn landscape of English social history in the century before the Puritan Revolution, Charles Tilly's investigation of the relationship between urbanization and counter-revolutionary political upheaval in the Vendeé all come to mind.[8] In addition, there is the whole field of economic history, where work of this kind is superabundant, so much so that some of its practitioners have adopted a new disciplinary label for themselves—cliometrics.[9] Their research has already proven so valuable that I think we can forgive them that grating neologism.

One important study which raises a problem I might comment upon is Merle Curti's analysis of population turnover, occupational mobility, patterns of property acquisition and related phenomena in a Wisconsin frontier community in the 1850–1880 period.[10] Certainly *The Making of a Frontier Community* deserves to be called a pioneering study of the Wisconsin pioneers it deals with. Curti was the first social scientist to use original manuscript census schedules as a means of tracing the changing social position of individuals; he was also the first historian to employ data-processing machines for grass-roots social history. The data in the book are an invaluable point of comparison for anyone studying these phenomena, and the how-to-do-it methodological appendix is very useful. But the central conclusion of the work—that it provides powerful objective support for Turner's frontier thesis—is utterly unconvincing. Curti had the imagination to dig out and the integrity to include in the book some materials on the property structure of a Vermont county in the same period, materials which actually subvert the author's case for the frontier theory. This perhaps is a useful reminder that neither the raw statistical data nor the computer will speak for themselves and that the task of interpreting statistical results is as difficult and fraught with error as other tasks of historical interpretation.

Indeed, it is perhaps more difficult in one way, for the precision of quantitative data tends to foreclose the common procedure of making sense out of a mass of materials by offering an intuitive generalization which best fits one's own interpretative predilections. Probably this is the reason that quantitative historical studies have more often been effective in dissolving and destroying older categories and hypotheses than in suggesting equally powerful and persuasive new ones. This is what Richard Hofstadter calls "the paradox of quantification," and it is an issue worth grappling with.[11] There is something familiar and inviting in the notion that the grey fact dooms even the most vibrant and imaginative generalization, that the intellectual universe is destined to remain forever divided between those bold souls who rear grand interpretative structures on sandy, intuitive foundations and those computer-equipped termites who undermine these structures without offering new ones to replace them, but I remain skeptical of this.

I would concede a certain atomizing, fragmenting bias in some quantitative techniques, to be sure. The use of currently fashionable methods of multivariate analysis to break down a concept into discrete elements and to weigh the effect of each separate element offers many illustrations; my favorite is the study of urbanization as a variable in the presidential election of 1928.[12] The authors found that when they "partialled out" such variables as Catholicism, immigration, anti-Prohibition sentiment, etc., and examined the effect of "pure" urbanization, i.e., the percentage of people in an area who live in cities, they found a slight *negative* correlation between urbanization and the vote for Al Smith. The authors, of course, had castrated the concept of a city by separating out from it a series of elements which were not accidentally but integrally related to it in the society they were studying. The chief conclusion we might draw from the study, though perhaps not one to the liking of the authors, is that a city is more than a mere agglomeration of bodies. Treating it analytically as if it were nothing more reveals that nicely. A similar argument could be made concerning Lee Benson's multivariate analysis of New York State voting patterns in the Jacksonian period. After partialling out a host of variables—the most important of which was ethnic background—Benson found no significant class differences between the Whigs and the Democrats. But a social class too is more than a mere agglomeration of occupations, and one may seriously doubt that Benson has really shown what he thinks he has shown in his very interesting book.

All this is only to say that certain statistical techniques artificially fragment social reality and that the investigator who employs them should have on hand all the king's horses and all the king's men to aid him in interpreting the findings yielded by such techniques. It is not to say that we may generalize this disclaimer into an excruciating paradox of quantification. The examples Hofstadter gives to illustrate this presumed paradox, and other examples one might think of, strike me as transitional phenomena. Admittedly, the most obvious implication of many recent quantitative historical studies is that the received interpretations in the field are either incorrect or too ambiguously formulated even to be judged correct or incorrect. But the sophomoric urge to destroy all previous interpretations and to wallow in the ineluctable, seemingly uninterpretable complexity disclosed by exhaustive quantitative study seems to me just that—sophomoric—and I think that soon upperclassmen will be using these techniques in a more constructive fashion and will go beyond naive historical nominalism.

Suppose we take Hofstadter's *Age of Reform* as a fine specimen of imaginative historical writing. Is there any inherent reason why the status revolution theory could not have been given a clearer operational specification, and why it could not have been more carefully checked against quantified evidence? I don't mean simply that some tables, some numbers, would have been useful. What concerns me more is that the author failed to take elementary precautions which a scholar trained in quantitative social research should have taken. One such precaution would have been to seek information about possible control groups against which to compare the groups whose supposed status anxieties were being explored. If it were to turn out that the social origins and current status of conservative Republicans were actually identical to those of Progressives, the author's inferences about the link between status anxieties and political behavior would have to be reconsidered. (Recent work by Samuel P. Hays and others suggests just this conclusion.)[13] Another elementary point concerns the tactic of generalizing about the social position of large occupational or

ethnic groups on the basis of slender impressionistic evidence, for
instance, Hofstadter's comments about the legal profession in the
latter half of the nineteenth century. There are actually two
problems here. Much more solid evidence is needed about the
situation of the legal profession as a first step. Second, and perhaps
more important, is the question of whether the generalization
about the profession as a whole applies with particular force to
those individual lawyers who participated in the Progressive
movement. It is possible that lawyers as a class might not be faring
too well at some point in time, but that the behavior Hofstadter
was attempting to explain was engaged in by just those elements
of the profession which had least reason to feel status grievances
(again a point suggested by recent studies). Sociologists have long
been familiar with this problem—they face it each time they attempt to translate ecological correlations into statements about individuals.[14] The only real solution to it, and one open to Hofstadter after all, is to investigate samples of individuals to be sure that
the correlation holds at that level.

I won't linger any longer over the supposed paradox of quantification, except to add that this pessimistic view of the function of
quantitative research concentrates too narrowly on the *testing*
function—which is to some degree inherently destructive, I suppose—and overlooks the fact that in superior scientific work theory, interpretation, and empirical study are creatively inter-
twined, that new quantitative findings suggest new interpretations
and force as well the reformulation of old ones. It ignores the fact
that *anomalies* disclosed by quantitative study are a powerful impetus to theory construction, a point ably developed by Thomas
S. Kuhn in his paper, "The Function of Measurement in Modern
Physical Science," and by Robert K. Merton in his famous discussion of "the serendipity pattern." [15] And one thinks of Schumpeter's comment that "we need statistics not only for explaining
things but in order to know precisely what there is to be explained," which again points to the constructive functions of
quantification.

The foregoing examples of quantitative historical research have
involved such materials as voting records, economic statistics, data
summarizing the social characteristics of groups of men. Some attention should be given as well to quantitative studies of materials

of quite a different kind—words, sentences, paragraphs. I am a little less enthusiastic about the possibilities here, but there can be no doubt, I think, that more and more work of this kind will be done in the future and that it merits discussion.

One ingenious use of the computer to attack a historical problem—Mosteller's count of the frequency distribution of such minor words as "by," "from," "to," and "upon" to infer the authorship of the disputed Federalist papers—seems quite persuasive to me, but authorship problems are a small and special class, and I don't see that the methodology of the study can be easily extended to other issues.[16] The technique known as content analysis has much wider application, however. By breaking down the contents of a document into units which are first labeled by a human coder or by the computer itself with the aid of a dictionary programmed into it, and then mechanically tabulating these units, content analysis purports to provide both a more objective and systematic and a more sensitive rendering of meaning.

There are genuine advantages to this procedure, especially when one is asking rather simple questions of otherwise unmanageably large bodies of material, but the results it yields can be no more sensitive than the coding rules or dictionary employed. Many historical issues involve ideas and relationships which cannot be reduced to rules which a machine can follow; one thinks, for instance, of Perry Miller responding to a sermon by Jonathan Edwards. Doubtless a computer—at least if its dictionary were prepared by someone who knew as much about Puritanism as Perry Miller—could pick out certain things in a text that a Perry Miller unassisted would miss, things of consequence in some instances. A computer can attend to a great many things at the same time and a man cannot. In one scanning of a text it can answer questions which would take one of us fifty painful readings to answer; it can disclose the recurrence of key words, themes, and constellations of images that would be extraordinarily difficult to detect in other ways. But it is hard to imagine how an IBM machine could be given a set of formal instructions which would equip it to ferret out certain of the most important and yet most subtle connections to be found in an Edwards sermon or something similar, connections which are often ones of delicate emotional shadings, connections which are poetic rather than prosaic,

This is an excruciatingly obvious point, but those who preach the gospel of content analysis have not heeded it sufficiently.

Another limitation of content analysis, and indeed of much of the quantitative work now going on in the social sciences, is suggested by research on communications and decision-making on the eve of World War I now being carried out by Ithiel de Sola Pool at M.I.T. and North, Holsti, and others at Stanford.[17] The authors are political scientists, but they hope to influence the thinking of historians as well. The problem is that their work has been aimed at testing largely psychological propositions of such simplicity and such universality as to be of little interest to the practising historian: "People pay more attention to news that deals with them"; "The higher the stress in a crisis situation, the greater the tendency to rely upon extraordinary or improvised channels of communication." The difficulty is not that these propositions are self-evident common-sense truths and thus unworthy of testing; this common complaint against social science research is usually unfounded, partly because it ignores the fundamental principle that for each and every cliché there tends to be an equal and opposite cliché, partly for reasons too complex to examine here. What bothers me is that generalizations of such cosmic sweep, presumably true (or at least interestingly false) of all times and all places, seem arid and empty, seem to have no relevance to the problems that bother me. While I urge that historians attempt to translate their intuitive generalizations into explicit generalizations, the generalizations I have in mind are less abstract, less sweeping, and more powerful; they are to some degree relative to the context to which they refer, applying to such entities as "American farmers in the twentieth century" or even "middle class residents of large American cities in the period since World War II," and might be considered the counterpart in history to what Merton calls "theories of the middle range." [18]

Perhaps it was unfair to single out isolated instances of these cosmic psychological propositions. Pool, North, Holsti and others are using such propositions as building blocks for models. At least the more sophisticated of the model-builders do not claim any necessary correspondence between their models and reality. Pool, for instance, concedes "it is perfectly clear that individual psychology accounts for only a small part of international politics. However, the best way to ascertain what part, if any, individual psychology plays in the determination of political behavior is to postulate the truth of the extreme propositions and then see what conclusions it leads to. We can then compare those conclusions with reality." Presumably the comparison would yield some such finding as that, let us say, 24 per cent of the behavior of the historical actors being put under the microscope may be explained by the laws of individual psychology, and the remaining 76 per cent would then be tested against an economic model, a sociological model, a balance of power model, and perhaps an astrological model. Another line of inquiry would be to see if this 24 per cent figure remained constant when normal rather than cataclysmic historical events were being examined—possibly the laws of psychology explain more of normal behavior than of crisis behavior, possibly the opposite relationship holds. I would certainly admit that there are fields of social science which deal with phenomena which have been described and conceptualized so as to allow the invention and manipulation of highly abstract and elegant mathematical models; certain problems in economic history and many problems in demography are clearly suited to this strategy. But I think the aim of looking for something in human society to correspond to the periodic table of elements in chemistry, as Barrington Moore describes it, is ill-suited to history, and to most of sociology and political science as well.[19]

One reason is that many important historical phenomena have not been well described, much less conceptualized. Lord Bryce's dictum, "It is Facts that are needed; Facts, Facts, Facts. When facts have been supplied, each of us can try to reason from them . . ." sounds incredibly naive today—we all know that facts are not born but made—but if you examine a historical problem like the one which most interests me, the nature of the American class structure in the past, you appreciate what Bryce had in mind. And where the facts have been gathered in abundance, they rarely are the right facts—the facts that seem strategic to someone interested in social science explanation, the facts that permit comparison with other historical situations and the development of intermediate generalizations. Beyond these tactical objections to universalist models in history, I would add that I frankly doubt that it will ever be possible to create a science of society, a science of politics, and a science of history along the lines envisaged by Pool. I needn't go into that here, since even if I am wrong about that my tactical arguments seem to me sufficient for now.

And so I would conclude this rambling and eclectic discussion of the knotty problem of models with the comment that even the most enthusiastic devotee of interdisciplinary cross-fertilization should allow for some division of labor. I see the role of the historian as that of developing and refining the materials which will permit intermediate or low-level generalizations about social phenomena. Other social scientists will naturally seek to extend the range of these intermediate generalizations and to test their ultimate limits, but long before the initial generalization is converted into a proposition of sufficient abstractness to apply universally, the historian will likely have lost interest in it and have gone back to his business of dealing with events and processes in a limited context. To the extent, therefore, that content analysis is carried out by scholars dedicated to testing universalist models of human behavior, it is unlikely to influence the mainstream of historical writing.

III.

A few remarks about my current research on the social history of modern Boston will illustrate some of the intellectual opportunities opened to the historian by the computer and some of the problems he must resolve to seize those opportunities. This research, still in progress, grew out of my belief that the existing literature in the field of social history dealt inadequately with social structure and basic social processes. Even the best work in the field, I felt, depended excessively on evidence which was at one remove from the daily lives of individuals. My Newburyport study offered several examples which supported the premise from which I began: that some important historical processes could not be understood without microscopic study of individual human actors.[20]

There are grave limitations, however, to the usual microscopic historical study. Biographers can overlook these limitations by persuading themselves (or deluding themselves) that their subjects are intrinsically important. But the social historian who seeks to treat the lives of common men rather than very uncommon men cannot evade the problem of giving general meaning to his findings. The easiest tactic is to describe one's microscopic examination of an obscure group or neighborhood or community as a "case study," a useful phrase which lends an attractive aura of generality to one's painstaking study of the social origins of Armenian grocers in Boston's North End. But of what is this hypothetical investigation a case study? May we generalize from the Armenians to the Greeks, and from them to the Italians and Jews? What does a study set in the North End tell us about the South End, the West End and other neighborhoods of that sprawling complex, Greater Boston? Historians and sociologists alike have been reluctant to consider such questions. Thus William F. Whyte's classic field report on youth in the North End, *Streetcorner Society*, leaves us in the dark as to how much of what the author describes reflects basic patterns of working class life in American cities, and how much is due to the particular ethnic group (Italians), the particular neighborhood (the North End), or the particular historical period (the late thirties) Whyte dealt with. Nor does Herbert Gans' interesting recent work, *The Urban Villagers*, which treats working-class Italo-Americans in the West End in the late fifties, go very far beyond *Streetcorner Society* in this respect. Ideally, historical studies of the city should employ microscopic techniques for the depth and richness of detail they alone can provide, but should employ them on a sufficiently spacious canvas—spacious temporally as well as physically—to confront the problems that the label "case study" customarily obscures.

It is here, of course, that the development of the electronic computer affords the social historian a great opportunity, for only through mechanical means can the historian master the vast body of materials that he must consult to do a study of this kind. The sources for a comprehensive grass-roots social history of the sort I describe are readily available—manuscript census schedules, city directories, local tax records, school records and so forth—and they have occasionally been utilized by historians. But for the student who must collect and analyze it without the aid of electronic devices, the limits imposed by the sheer bulk of this material (and by the tedium it inspires) are very narrow My own little study of the social mobility of unskilled laborers in Newburyport, which was done without mechanical methods, probably involved about as much complexity and as much drudgery as the ordinary historian can stand, and that study dealt with something less than 10 per cent of the labor force of a city of fewer than 15,000 inhabitants. To trace and analyze the career patterns of several occupational and ethnic groups in a much larger community without mechanical assistance would be an impossible task. With the aid of a computer it is possible to draw together, examine, and comprehend the life histories of thousands and thousands of ordinary men and women. The microscope can thus be applied to a large enough population over a broad enough time span to provide a dynamic view of the whole of a complex social organism, including such matters as variations in social mobility opportunities during the course of urban growth and industrial change, ethnic differences in mobility patterns and the flow of population between districts of the city and into and out of the city itself.

I am now attempting something of this sort, employing a computer to map the demographic and social structure of Boston from 1880 to the present. I have fed into the computer information about three samples of the population in the community— one drawn from 1880 manuscript schedules of the United States Census Bureau, one from 1910 marriage license records, one from 1930 birth certificates. This information deals with a host of social characteristics—occupation, place of residence, age, ethnic and religious affiliations, property holdings, etc. Once the samples were drawn, the subsequent occupations, addresses, and property holdings of these men were recovered from later city directories and tax records, so that for a substantial cross section of the Boston population—a total of 8,000 men—I have abbreviated family histories which span several decades, down to 1963 in some cases.

These data shed light on such questions as the following. Did the Boston social structure become significantly looser or tighter over this period of 83 years? Were there notable differences between the mobility patterns of different ethnic and religious groups within the community, along the lines suggested by popular folklore about the characteristics of the Irish, the Italians, the

Jews, the Negroes, etc? What was the relationship between different forms of social mobility—between occupational, residential, and property mobility, for instance, and between intergenerational and intragenerational changes in social position? To what degree did the class structure of modern Boston, according to legend a stagnant, caste-ridden place, fundamentally resemble that of other large American cities?

This is not the place to report on my findings concerning these and other related issues; a full discussion will be available in the near future. It may be more useful to describe two of the large problems which are likely to bother any investigator who attempts a study of this kind, and to suggest an approach to them.

One of these is that it is extraordinarily difficult to trace and keep track of the residents of an American city over any substantial time period. There are countries whose historians are blessed with national population registers which draw together in one place the relevant information about any citizen, but that is not the case in the United States. The records available to the social historian, whether prepared by local, state, or national officials, are arranged by locality. This would not be a handicap in a relatively settled society. In Sweden, for example, a student of social mobility was able to draw a sample of fourth-graders in the Stockholm schools in 1936 and trace these young men in the 1949 Stockholm Register, with only 6 per cent of them disappearing in the interim.[21] But in any American community, I have learned from frustrating experience, one would be lucky to locate as many as *half* of the sample members after a lapse of thirteen years. Americans do not stay put, a severe problem because it means that the people whose career lines can most easily be traced—those who do stay put—deviate from the national norm in an important way. And that, of course, means that it is doubtful that the social mobility patterns of this stable minority are representative of the population as a whole.

I know of no way of eliminating this problem, but it can be made to seem less crippling. For one thing, prior awareness of it allows us to draw a sufficiently large sample to leave a respectably large number of cases even after the attrition produced by high population turnover. Second, it must be understood that a turnover of something like half a population in a decade is not so much a distorting influence to be frowned upon as a crucial datum to be thought about and made use of. The extraordinary population volatility that has been revealed by my historical studies of both Newburyport and Boston shapes the character of social life in many respects. We are coming to understand that there are close and complicated connections between physical movement and social movement, between social mobility, immigration, and internal migration from country to city and between cities.[22] These connections are literally forced upon our attention when we attempt to trace individuals over time in a given city and discover how many of them disappear over even a short period. By looking more closely at this process, and analyzing what brings people into the city and what determines who moves on and who remains, we can greatly enrich our understanding of modern society. In interpreting the social mobility tables yielded by a study of this kind, we will have to recall that they apply to only a portion of the urban population—to those who stayed in the city long enough to be counted at two intervals. But this inescapable difficulty is to some degree compensated for by the insight we thus gain into the interrelationship between physical movement and social movement.

A second broad problem is that of reducing the chaotic mass of raw data to some analytical categories, of developing, for instance, an occupational classification scheme to reduce the hundreds of specific occupations listed on the census schedules to some general types. Each reduction of this kind, of course, involves a *loss*. To know that a man is a "semiskilled laborer" is less revealing than to know that he is a streetcar conductor or an operative in a shoe factory. It is a cruel fact that we give up something every time we use a general social category; obviously we should strive to reduce our raw data to order in a way which gives up as little as possible. The point to stress here is that, contrary to the belief of many historians, in dealing with problems of this kind at least, a computer can tolerate much more complexity than an individual human being and can thus preserve a degree of concreteness that a historian working without a machine would necessarily sacrifice.

This for two reasons. First, it is very difficult (as I know from painful experience) for a man to cross-tabulate raw data employing more than a very few categories. If you are computing, for example, differing rates of occupational mobility in seven ethnic groups, it is impossibly tedious for you to utilize more than a half-dozen occupational categories (giving 42 cells), and even more tedious and difficult to consider the influence of other variables at the same time. With the cunning spaciousness of an IBM card at your disposal, however, and a tireless device to sort and count these cards, it is possible to use many more occupational categories and hence to remain much closer to the complex reality that the historian of a handicraft age had to abstract from.

A second reason why the computer permits a more complex and more concrete analysis in investigations of this kind is simply that in any study utilizing sampling techniques, the possibilities for refined analysis are severely restricted by the size of the sample. Even a good-sized sample of the population of a modern city, for example, will contain only a few Italian carpenters, so that to examine differences between literate and illiterate Italian carpenters would be impossible; to test the significance of literacy as an influence on career patterns one would have to lump together all carpenters or all Italians to have enough cases for meaningful analysis. But a machine, of course, can handle many more cases than a man; thus a much larger sample can be gathered, and a more subtle and concrete analysis carried out.

I would end on a note of chastened optimism. I do not believe that the computer will revolutionize historical writing, leaving orthodox historians the victims of technological unemployment. Nor do I believe that the over-all quality of quantitative historical work in the near future will necessarily be very high. Historians will find it difficult to learn enough about computers to employ them in a sophisticated fashion, and it is not unlikely that some who do succeed in mastering the computer will forget (or never learn in the first place) that technical competence in manipulating statistics cannot make up for ignorance of the social context which produced the statistics. But I remain confident that the remarkable increment the computer provides to our ability to do certain kinds of things to certain kinds of historical material, and the contact it will promote between history and the other social sciences, will prove of net benefit.

Notes

NOTE: This chapter incorporates portions of papers delivered by the author at the Yale University and Boston University conferences on Computers for the Humanities. The conferences were funded by the International Business Machine Corporation. The Yale papers first appeared in *Computers for the Humanities? A Record of the Conference Sponsored by Yale University on a Grant by IBM, January 22–23, 1965* (New Haven: Yale University, 1965), © 1965 by Yale University, with a foreword by George W. Pierson of the Department of History. In a revised form the conference papers have appeared in Edmund Bowles, ed., *Computers in Humanistic Research* (Englewood Cliffs, N.J.: Prentice-Hall, 1967), © 1967 by Prentice-Hall, Inc. Permission to incorporate into this chapter material from the author's conference papers has been granted by Yale University, International Business Machines Corporation, and Prentice-Hall, Inc.

1. Arthur M. Schlesinger, Jr., "The Humanist Looks at Empirical Social Research," *American Sociological Review,* XXVII (1962), 770.
2. Lee Benson, "Research Problems in American Political Historiography," in Mirra Komarovsky, ed., *Common Frontiers of the Social Sciences* (Glencoe, Ill.: 1957), p. 117.
3. William O. Aydelotte, "Quantification in History," *American Historical Review,* LXXI (1966), 803–825.
4. Fred Kort, "Predicting Supreme Court Decisions Mathematically," *American Political Science Review,* LI (1957), 1–12.
5. Richard L. Merritt, *Symbols of American Community, 1735–1775* (New Haven: 1966).
6. C. Wright Mills, *The Sociological Imagination* (New York: 1959).
7. Bernard and Lotte Bailyn, *Massachusetts Shipping, 1697–1714: A Statistical Study* (Cambridge, Mass.: 1961).
8. Lee Benson, *The Concept of Jacksonian Democracy: New York as a Test Case* (Princeton, N.J.: 1961); Sidney Aronson, *Status and Kinship in the Higher Civil Service* (Cambridge, Mass., 1964); Lawrence Stone, *The Crisis of the Aristocracy, 1558–1641* (Oxford, 1965); Charles Tilly, *The Vendée* (Cambridge, Mass.: 1964).
9. For excellent brief surveys, see Robert W. Fogel, "The Reunification of Economic History with Economic Theory," *Papers and Proceedings of the 77th Annual Meeting of the American Economics Association* (1965), pp. 92–98; Peter Temin, "In Pursuit of the Exact," *The Times Literary Supplement,* July 28, 1966.
10. Merle Curti *et al., The Making of an American Community: A Case Study of Democracy in a Frontier County* (Stanford, Calif.: 1959).
11. Richard Hofstadter, "History and the Social Sciences," in Fritz Stern, ed., *The Varieties of History* (Cleveland: 1956), pp. 359–370.
12. W. F. Ogburn and N. S. Talbot, "A Measurement of Factors in the Presidential Election of 1928," *Social Focus,* VIII, 175–183.
13. See Samuel P. Hays, "The Politics of Reform in Municipal Government in the Progressive Era," *Pacific Northwest Quarterly,* LV (1964), 157–169, and the literature cited there.

14. The classic discussion of the problem is W. S. Robinson, "Ecological Correlations and the Behavior of Individuals," *American Sociological Review*, XV (1950), 351–357; cf. O. D. Duncan, R. P. Cuzzort, and B. Duncan, *Statistical Geography* (Glencoe, Ill.: 1961), pp. 9–10.

15. The Kuhn paper is available in Harry Woolf, ed., *Quantification* (Indianapolis: 1961); Merton's discussion appears in *Social Theory and Social Structure* (Glencoe, Ill.: 1949), pp. 98–101.

16. Frederick Mosteller and David L. Wallace, "Inference in an Authorship Problem," *Journal of the American Statistical Association*, LVIII (1963), 275–309.

17. Ithiel de Sola Pool and Allan Kessler, "The Kaiser, the Tsar, and the Computer: Information Processing in a Crisis," *American Behavioral Scientist*, VIII (1965), 31–38; Ole R. Holsti, "The 1914 Case," *American Political Science Review*, LIX (1965), 365–378.

18. Merton, in *Social Theory and Social Structure*, pp. 98–101; S. H. Beer, "Casual Explanation and Imaginative Reenactment," *History and Theory*, III (1963), 6–29.

19. Barrington Moore, Jr., *Political Power and Social Theory* (Cambridge: 1958), p. 126. Moore's critique of contemporary social science in chapters iii and iv of this book, and in his newest work, *Social Origins of Dictatorship and Democracy: Lord and Peasant in the Making of the Modern World* (Boston: 1966), merits careful consideration by anyone interested in the subject of this essay. See also Lawrence Stone's "Theories of Revolution," *World Politics*, XVIII (1966), 159–176.

20. Stephan Thernstrom, *Poverty and Progress: Social Mobility in a Nineteenth Century City* (Cambridge: 1964).

21. Gunnar Boalt, "Social Mobility in Stockholm: A Pilot Investigation," *Transactions of the Second World Congress of Sociology* II (1954), 67–73.

22. Seymour Martin Lipset and Reinhard Bendix, *Social Mobility in Industrial Society* (Berkeley, Calif.: 1959).

❦ 4 ❦

Barnes F. Lathrop

HISTORY FROM THE CENSUS RETURNS

The original manuscript returns of the decennial census enumerations of the United States, beginning in 1790, have long been prized by genealogists, and in the last twenty-odd years have received increasing appreciation among historians.[1] Yet employment of this material in historical work remains on the whole so sporadic or so slight that the unprinted census records must still be classed as a great neglected source. The present article undertakes to describe the manuscript schedules, and to canvass their potential uses, in the hope of attracting more attention to the census source in general, and to the returns for Texas, 1850–1880, in particular.

The first six federal censuses, 1790–1840, were little more than crude enumerations of population according to status, age, and sex.[2] The first census asked of each family, besides the name of the head, only the numbers of free white males aged sixteen years and above, of free white males under sixteen years, of free white females, of all other free persons, and of slaves.[3] In successive decades the analysis by age groups was much refined, and inquiries were added, but the approach was not basically altered.[4] The

Barnes F. Lathrop is Professor of History at the University of Texas. He is author of *Migration into East Texas: 1835–1860*, and of numerous articles.

Reprinted from *The Southwestern Historical Quarterly*, LI (1948), 293–312, by permission of the author and the publisher.

investigator may find the original returns without peer on certain topics—name frequencies,[5] or ancestors, or size of slave-holdings —but the range of information is narrow.

The census of 1850 embodies a radical advance in the scope and technique of census-taking. The inquiries are divided into six schedules, each schedule printed on a sheet measuring 13 by 17½ inches. All six schedules are herewith illustrated in miniature (see Table 4–1): Schedule 1, Free Inhabitants, with two families enumerated;[6] Schedule 4, Agriculture, with four sample entries;[7] the heads of columns for Schedule 2, Slave Inhabitants, for Schedule 3, Mortality, and for Schedule 5, Industry; and the inquiries making up Schedule 6, Social Statistics. Schedules 1 to 5 required separate individual enumeration of each person or producer by visitation of all dwellings, farms, and establishments. For Schedule 6 the enumerator assembled as he saw fit the "social statistics" of his unit, usually a county.

The schedules employed in 1860 and in 1870 closely resemble those designed in 1850. Schedule 1, Free Inhabitants, 1860, calls for occupation of females as well as of males, and for value of personal estate as well as of real estate. Schedule 2, Slave Inhabitants, has an added column for number of slave houses. On Schedule 4, Agriculture, beeswax is divorced from honey. Otherwise the 1860 schedules are identical with the 1850 schedules. Before 1870 the Civil War and the Thirteenth Amendment canceled Schedule 2, Slave Inhabitants; hence in 1870 all persons—with the perennial exception of "Indians not taxed"—are enumerated on Schedule 1, Inhabitants. The more important changes in the schedule concern illiteracy, nativity of parents, and "constitutional relations." Minimum age for classification as illiterate, formerly twenty years, becomes ten years, and the abilities to read and to write fall under separate heads. Two new columns ask in respect of each person whether either parent is of foreign birth. Two concluding columns aim to find out who are adult male citizens, and to which of them the "right to vote is denied or abridged on other grounds than rebellion or other crime." Schedule 3, Agriculture, divides unimproved land into woodland and other unimproved, and has added headings calling for amount of wages paid during the year, gallons of milk sold, value of forest products, and "estimated value of all farm production, including betterments and additions to stock." Otherwise the schedule copies the 1860 schedule. Small alterations in Schedules No. 2, Mortality, and No. 5, Social Statistics, are not worth particularizing. Schedule 4, Industry, differs from 1860 chiefly in distinguishing between child and adult labor, and in asking for number and description of machines.

As the census of 1850 marked an epoch, so the census of 1880 began a "third era" in Federal census-taking. The schedules which had served for three decades were displaced by more precise and elaborate general schedules supplemented by numerous and encyclopedic special schedules; moreover, many topics were withdrawn partly or wholly from general enumeration and entrusted to expert special agents. The immensity of the expansion is evident in the increase of schedules from five containing 156 inquiries in 1870 to 215 containing 13,010 inquiries in 1880. The printed census report jumped from 2,524 pages quarto in 1870 to 19,305 pages quarto in 1880.

Even to mention all the schedules of 1880 is not possible here;[8] neither is it necessary, for the original returns of most of the 204 special schedules are thought not to be extant. Most lamentable for Texas is the apparent loss of the special schedules on cotton culture (265 inquiries), and on stock raising (482 inquiries),[9] employed in the preparation of E. W. Hilgard's *Report on Cotton Production*, and Clarence Gordon's *Report on Cattle, Sheep, and Swine*.[10] The schedules that survive appear to be only the twenty-three that were entrusted to the regular enumerators. Fortunately, these include the schedules of most importance for the nation as a whole, namely, the general population schedule and the general agriculture schedule. Also included are the general schedules for manufactures and for mortality, and nineteen special and supplemental schedules presently to be named.

Schedule 1, Inhabitants, 1880, is a moderately enlarged version of earlier schedules on the same subject. The student interested in economic analysis is distressed to find that the old columns on value of real and of personal estate are gone. Likewise absent are the 1870 inquiries concerning "constitutional relations." A most useful addition is a column calling for statement of the relationship of each person in the family to the head of the family. Another column shows the birthplace of each of the parents of every

TABLE 4-1
Census of 1850

Schedule No. 1—FREE INHABITANTS in........, in the County of........, State of........, enumerated by me, on the .... day of........, 1850, Ass't. Marshal.

Dwelling-houses numbered in the order of visitation.	Families numbered in the order of visitation.	Name of every person whose usual place of abode on the 1st day of June, 1850, was in this family.	Description Age.	Sex.	Color—white, black, or mulatto.	Profession, occupation, or trade of each male person over 15 years of age.	Value of real estate owned [in dollars].	Place of birth, naming the State, Territory, or country.	Married within the year.	Attended school within the year.	Persons over 20 years of age who cannot read and write.	Whether deaf and dumb, blind, insane, idiotic, pauper, or convict.
756	756	Wilson M. Brown	35	M	W	Farmer	1,000	S. C.				/
		Rachel Brown	31	F	W			Georgia				
		David P. Brown	8	M	W			Ala.				
		Robt. P. Brown	5	M	W			Texas				
		Nancy Brown	4	F	W			Texas				
		Eleanor Brown	3	F	W			Texas				
		John H. Brown	9/12	M	W			Texas				
161	162	Victor Pannell	50	M	W	Blacksmith	2,520	S. C.				/
		Barsheba Pannell	39	F	W			N. C.			/	
		Elisabeth Pannell	18	F	W			Ill.		/		

TABLE 4-1
Census of 1850

Schedule No. 1 (*continued*)

Dwelling-houses numbered in the order of visitation.	Families numbered in the order of visitation.	Name of every person whose usual place of abode on the 1st day of June, 1850, was in this family.	Description.			Profession, occupation, or trade of each male person over 15 years of age.	Value of real estate owned [in dollars].	Place of birth, naming the State, Territory, or country.	Married within the year.	Attended school within the year.	Persons over 20 years of age who cannot read and write.	Whether deaf and dumb, blind, insane, idiotic, pauper, or convict.
			Age.	Sex.	Color—white, black, or mulatto.							
		Lucinda Pannell	16	F	W			Ill.		/		
		Samuel R. G. Pannell	14	M	W			Mo.		/		
		Malinda Pannell	11	F	W			Mo.		/		
		Thomas J. Pannell	8	M	W			Mo.		/		
		Malona B. Pannell	4	F	W			Texas				
		Victor M. Pannell	2	M	W			Texas				
		Henry Brikle	20	M	W	Farmer		Germany			/	
		David William[s]	33	M	W	Heardsmann		Tenn.		/		
		Bershaba Williams	1	F	W			Texas				
		Victor P. H. Case	4	M	W			Texas				
		Alexander Mayfield	30	M	W	Sportsman		N. C.				
		Lewis Lee	36	M	W	Blacksmith		Indiana				

TABLE 4–1 (*continued*)

Schedule No. 4—PRODUCTIONS OF AGRICULTURE

Name of owner, agent or manager of the farm.	Acres of land improved.	Acres of land unimproved.	Cash value of farm.	Value of farming implements and machinery.	Live Stock, June 1, 1850.							Value of live stock.
					Horses.	Mules and asses.	Milch cows.	Working oxen.	Other cattle.	Sheep.	Swine.	
Jessee Dannell	230	410	2,500	150	5	6	17	6	20		150	1,240
Jno. Jennings	65	255	1,280	300	4		8	7	4		15	486
Dan Donahoe	14	1,000	222	180	9	2	24	10	200		12	1,127
William M. McMurry	15	305	500	10	2		4	2	9		60	302

Produce During the Year Ending June 1, 1850

Name of owner, agent or manager of the farm.	Wheat, bushels of.	Rye, bushels of.	Indian corn, bushels of.	Oats, bushels of.	Rice, pounds of.	Tobacco, pounds of.	Ginned cotton, bales of 400 lbs. each.	Wool, pounds of.	Beans and peas, bushels of.	Irish potatoes, bushels of.	Sweet potatoes, bushels of.	Buckwheat, bushels of.
Jessee Dannell			800				17			20	300	
Jno. Jennings	25		1,000	8					6		30	
Dan Donahoe			120									
William M. McMurry			250						4		150	

Produce During the Year Ending June 1, 1850

Name of owner, agent or manager of the farm.	Barley, bushels of.	Value of orchard products in dollars.	Wine, gallons of.	Value of produce of market gardens.	Butter, pounds of.	Cheese, pounds of	Hay, tons of.	Clover seed, bushels of.	Other grass seeds, bushels of.	Hops, pounds of.	Dew-rotted hemp, tons of.	Water-rotted hemp, tons of.	Flax, pounds of.
Jessee Dannell					140								
Jno. Jennings					500	3						5	
Dan Donahoe													
William M. McMurry													

Produce During the Year Ending June 1, 1850

Name of owner, agent or manager of the farm.	Flaxseed, bushels of.	Silk cocoons, pounds of.	Maple sugar, pounds of.	Cane sugar, hhds. of 1,000 pounds.	Molasses, gallons of.	Honey and beeswax, pounds of.	Value of home-made manufactures.	Value of animals slaughtered during the year.
Jessee Dannell								140
Jno. Jennings						60	50	100
Dan Donahoe								100
William M. McMurry								

TABLE 4–1 (*continued*)

Schedule No. 2—SLAVE INHABITANTS

Name of slave owners.	Number of slaves.	Description.			Fugitives from the State.	Number manumitted.	Deaf and dumb, blind, insane, or idiotic.
		Age.	Sex.	Color.			

Schedule No. 3—PERSONS WHO DIED DURING THE YEAR ENDING JUNE 1, 1850

Name of every person who died during the year ending June 1, 1850, whose usual place of abode at the time of his death was in this family.	Description.	Married or widowed.	Place of birth, naming the State, Territory or country.	The month in which the person died.	Profession, occupation, or trade.	Disease, or cause of death.	Number of days ill.
	Age. Sex. Color—white, black, or mulatto. Free or slave.						

Schedule No. 5—PRODUCTS OF INDUSTRY

Name of corporation, company or individual producing articles to the annual value of $500.	Name of business, manufacture, or product.	Capital invested in real and personal estate in the business.	Raw material used, including fuel.	Kind of motive power, machinery, structure, or resource.	Average number of hands employed.	Wages.	Annual product.
			Quantities. Kinds. Values.		Male. Female	Average monthly cost of male labor. Average monthly cost of female labor.	Quantities. Kinds. Values.

Schedule No. 6—SOCIAL STATISTICS

Name of Division [town, county, or city].	Valuation of Estate: Real and Personal.	Annual Taxes.	Colleges, Academies, and Schools.
	Real estate $ Personal estate $ Total $ How valued? True valuation $	Name or kind of each. Amount of each. How paid.	Number received from other sources. Character. rank, or kind. Number of teachers, etc. Number of pupils. Amount annually realized from endowment. Raised by taxation. Received from public funds.

TABLE 4–1 (continued)

Schedule No. 6 (continued)

Name of Division [town, county, or city].

Seasons and Crops.	Libraries	Newspapers and Periodicals.	Religion.	Pauperism
What crops are short. To what extent. Usual average crop.	Number. Kind. Number of volumes.	Name. Character. How often published. Circulation.	Number of churches. Denomination. Number each will accommodate. Value of church property.	Whole number of paupers supported within the year.
				Native. Foreign.

Pauperism.		Crime.		Wages.
Whole number on 1st June.	Cost of support.	Whole number of criminals convicted within the year.	In prison on 1st June.	Average monthly wages to a farm-hand with board. Average to a day-labourer with board. Average to a day-labourer without board. Average day-wages to a carpenter without board. Weekly wages to a female domestic with board. Price of board to labouringmen per week.
Native. Foreign.		Native. Foreign.	Native. Foreign.	

person enumerated. The remaining new items deal with "civil condition" (single, married, widowed, divorced), unemployment (number of months during the census year), health (nature of sickness or temporary disability "on the day of the enumerator's visit"), and permanent disability ("maimed, crippled, bedridden, or otherwise disabled").

Schedule 2, Productions of Agriculture, 1880, containing 104 inquiries, includes everything (except value of home manufactures) in the earlier schedules, and much not asked before.[11] Operators are to be designated owners, money renters, or sharecroppers. Improved land divides into tilled ("including fallow and grass in rotation") and untilled (permanent meadows and pastures, orchards, vineyards). Entirely new are columns on cost of fences and of fertilizers in 1879. Cost of labor, continued from the 1870 schedule, is supplemented by an item on weeks of hired labor, distinguishing white and colored. Grasslands are for the first time recognized as such, with one column to show acreage "mown," another, acreage "not mown." Inquiries headed "Movement—1879" ask in respect of cattle and sheep the numbers born, purchased, sold, slaughtered, and lost. Lost cattle, whether dead, strayed, or stolen, are entered in one lump figure; sheep are permitted no dereliction save death, but in death they enjoy choice among three columns according to cause (dogs, disease, or stress of weather). The old item on pounds of wool is altered into a request for fleeces and weight of the "clip, spring of 1880, shorn and to be shorn." [12] New columns relate to poultry (barnyard, other) and to eggs produced in 1879. No doubt the most important advance in the whole schedule is the inclusion in the enumeration of crops of columns calling for the acreage as well as the production of each crop. The only field crop added to the Southern schedule is sorghum (acres, pounds of sugar, gallons of molasses). Apple and peach orchards are singled out for return under three heads each (acres, bearing trees, yield in 1879). Acres and value of product of nurseries appear for the first time. The former wine column is broadened into a vineyard section covering acres, grapes sold, and wine made. Finally, with the 1870 item on value of forest products is a question as to cords of wood cut in 1879.

General Schedule No. 3, Manufactures, 1880, contains a mere

twenty-nine items; the principal additions deal with hours and wages of labor, months in operation, and details of water power and steam power. Certain classes of establishments are enumerated on special schedules as follows: No. 1, Agricultural Implements; No. 2, Paper Mills; Nos. 3 and 4, Boots and Shoes—Leather; Nos. 5 and 6, Lumber Mills and Saw Mills—Brick Yards and Tile Works; Nos. 7 and 8, Flour and Grist Mills—Cheese, Butter, and Condensed-Milk Factories; Nos. 9, 10, and 10a, Slaughtering and Meat Packing—Salt Works; and Nos. 11 and 12, Small Coal Mines—Quarries. These schedules, general and special, probably cover the bulk of the establishments in Texas and other agrarian states.[13]

General Schedule 5, Mortality, 1880, differs only moderately from its predecessors. The most informative new feature is a request for the name of the physician attending the decedent, and for an attestation or emendation by the physician to the enumerator's entry giving cause of death.

The old method of seeking "Social Statistics" was abandoned in 1880 in favor of a wide variety of schedules handled by special agents.[14] The regular enumerators were left with a few schedules classed as supplemental to general Schedule 1, Inhabitants, and deriving from certain queries made in the past partly under "Inhabitants" and partly under "Social Statistics." These supplemental schedules, known collectively as "Defective, Dependent, and Delinquent Classes," deal with the following: No. 1, Insane; No. 2, Idiots; No. 3, Deaf-Mutes; No. 4, Blind; No. 5, Homeless Children; No. 6, Inhabitants in Prison; and No. 7, Pauper and Indigent Inhabitants.

So much for description of schedules. Where can the returns of the schedules be had? In one form or another all those for Texas are to be found in Austin. The United States Bureau of the Census in 1919 distributed to state and other depositaries its entire holding of the nonpopulation schedules of the Seventh, Eighth, Ninth, and Tenth Censuses, 1850–1880.[15] The Texas State Library in consequence has for 1850 and 1860 the Texas returns of Schedules 3–6, for 1870 the Texas returns of Schedules 2–5, and for 1880 the Texas returns of general Schedules 2, 3, and 5, Special Schedules 1–10 (accompanying general Schedule 3), and Supplemental Schedules 1–7.[16] Of the population schedules for 1850, 1860, and 1870, complete microfilm copies (positives) are in both the Texas State Library and the Archives Collection of the Library of the University of Texas. The Texas State Library alone has film copies of the 1880 population schedule.[17] A rather small part of the population returns, 1850–1870, is available also in the form of photostats or retained copies.[18]

Census material, either from printed reports or from manuscript returns, must be used with steady awareness of the imperfections of the data. In planning an investigation based upon manuscript returns, the careful student needs to fortify himself by (1) a moderate excursion into the critical literature,[19] (2) close attention to the schedules, instructions, and procedure of enumeration, (3) inspection and comparison of returns actually made by several enumerators, (4) rumination upon the probable foibles of enumerators and the enumerated. An example or two under each head will illustrate the purpose of these exercises. The critical literature reveals such points as the gross under-enumeration of Southern Negroes in 1870, and the near worthlessness of the mortality schedules, 1850–1880, as bases for vital statistics. Attentive reading of the schedules and instructions shows that enumeration of farms, 1850–1870, furnishes no proof of ownership.[20] Even in 1880, when tenure is defined, the owner of property worked by tenants does not appear; post-bellum plantations thus commonly remain invisible. Comparison of the returns made by several enumerators reveals variation, sometimes large, in interpretation of instructions. James H. Harrison, assistant marshal for Henderson and Kaufman counties, 1850, so defined unimproved land that he found only 680 acres of it in the two counties. Rumination along the classic lines of finding a cow ("I figgered what I'd do was I a cow," etc.) suggests various types of probable omissions or mistakes; the probabilities may later be confirmed by evidence. Thus, one would expect carelessness in reporting products not common in the enumerator's locality; and both the assistant marshal for Bowie County, 1850, and the Superintendent of the Census, 1880, confess that such was the case.[21]

Far outweighing the faults of the manuscript census returns are certain obvious virtues. The greatest is an unrivalled inclusiveness which offers the investigator a high degree of certainty in generalization, and a broadened view of society. The superiority of generalizations based upon enumeration over generalizations based upon crude sampling—the usual alternative—is too patent for argument. The broadened view of society is possible because the census comprehends (errors excepted) every person, high or low. Only through its manuscript pages can one see a past wherein ordinary individuals appear in proportion to their numbers. Given ingenious and persistent study, the census returns will in time largely improve our knowledge of the common man in the mid-nineteenth century.

Certain uses of the census are self-evident. As a universal directory of persons, the manuscript schedules may be consulted for information about almost any known individual. This biographical wealth merits much wider and more habitual employment than it has received. The enumerations, not to be ignored even for men of great fame, have as their peculiar province the furnishing of facts about the multitude of relatively obscure persons who serve the historian either as actors or as sources. The utility of the data on individuals becomes the more impressive the smaller the unit of study. Simply as a work of reference, without analysis, the returns can perform countless services for the local historian.

Numerous opportunities are to be found in the study of census data on groups of individuals already known by name, such as the members of a convention or a legislature, the county officials of a state, or a block of the field and regimental officers of the late Confederate States Army.[22] Equally profitable, and perhaps easier to execute, are examinations of groups distinguished by birth, occupation, or other characteristics, such as the Irish or the Yankees, the blacksmiths or the physicians, in Texas.[23]

Informative as the manuscript returns are in a biographical way, they promise still more as sources for statistical and semistatistical studies. The printed tables for 1850–1880 are almost all either simple compilations of the totals of the several columns of enumeration, or distributions and correlations of data—usually color, sex, age, nativity, and occupation—that could not be totaled without prior classification. The room for further work lies both in supplying supplements to existing tables, and in making analyses not attempted in the printed reports.

Projects for the extension and refinement of existing types of census tables lack the attraction of novelty, yet by employing punch-cards and tabulating machines valuable work of this kind might be done. For example, the printed tables of proven worth include those classifying for each county (1) the inhabitants in 1870 and 1880 according to birth in selected states and foreign countries, (2) slaveholdings according to size in 1790 and 1860, and (3) farms according to size in 1860 and 1870, and size and tenure in 1880.[24] A reworking of the manuscript returns could provide comparable nativity tables for 1850 and 1860, slaveholding tables for 1850 (and back to 1800 in the older states), and farm size tables for 1850. The new data would be esteemed by students in several fields.

The larger and the fresher realm of census studies consists in the making of analyses of kinds not attempted in the printed reports. Since the number of potential correlations within and between censuses is astronomical, no one commentator can pretend to list all the varieties of meritorious census projects. It is practicable, however, roughly to subdivide analytic census research in terms of procedure, and to suggest topics of investigation under each head. According to the mechanics involved, and in order of increasing complexity, the several procedures are: (1) analysis of a single column of enumeration, (2) analysis correlating two or more columns in the same schedule, (3) analysis correlating columns in two or more schedules, (4) analysis correlating columns in two or more censuses.

New single-column analysis offers certain interesting possibilities. For example, a study of name frequencies could measure accurately the population elements in "mixed" regions like south Louisiana and southwest Texas. Again, many historians would welcome tabulations dividing cotton growers and other agricultural producers according to the sizes of their crops. Perhaps the prize columns for isolated analysis are those on value of personal and real estate; despite imperfections, they may be readily converted into tables showing, with probable validity, the distribution of wealth.

Informative correlations between columns may be made within the separate population, agricultural, manufacturing, and mortality schedules. Thus numerous items respecting agriculture, such as acreage, livestock, and amounts and kinds of crops, can be explored in conjunction with one another. The enumeration of free inhabitants also is susceptible of many manipulations. Its very arrangement by families invites research on the subject of the family. Another feature is the age column, which has unique value because it in effect introduces a time element into an otherwise static description. Extensive tabulations of property-holding by age would afford strong evidence on general economic opportunity; more refined analysis might measure the differentials in expectancy of "getting ahead" between different groups or different regions.

Tabulations of birthplaces by ages in 1850 would illumine the population movements of the preceding half century. A study of migration would be based on a simple correlation of the columns enumerating names, ages, and birthplaces.

The investigator need not confine himself to the contents of one schedule at a time. Through the link of the individual or the family, he can bring together data from two or more schedules. In ante-bellum Southern studies the customary first step is from the free to the slave schedule. Is the free individual slaveholder or non-slaveholder? If a slaveholder, in what bracket? The next move is usually to the agricultural schedule, whence farm items are added to the information acquired in the population schedules. In the case of an artisan or an industrialist, the manufacturing schedule may substitute for the agricultural schedule. Occasionally the mortality schedule adds a dismal bit. Accumulation of information from several schedules extends into the hundreds or above the number of fruitful correlations that can be devised within the limits of one census. Specimens of work already done along this line will be cited presently. Here a single illustration, involving the neglected Censuses of 1870 and 1880, will serve to demonstrate the importance of results obtainable by a correlation of schedules. The two censuses cover the period probably most critical in the adjustment of the South to free labor; yet the printed reports are fatally defective as measures of that process, because the agricultural schedule in 1870 ignored both the color and the tenure of farm operators, and the schedule in 1880, while recording tenure (owner, money renter, sharecropper), remained oblivious to color. In other words, existing statistics of farm tenure start in 1880, and the highly material division of owners and of tenants by color is first found in 1890.[25] The missing information for 1870 and 1880 is not, however, wholly irrecoverable, for the manuscript returns contain enough data to repair the worst defects. The schedules of inhabitants in the two censuses give the color of every person; and the column in 1870 on value of real estate permits reasonably correct sorting of farm operators into owners and nonowners.[26] Once correlation with the population schedules has been made, parts or the whole of the agricultural schedules can be retabulated in terms of tenure and color.

All types of analysis within the limits of a single census have one grave limitation: except as they employ the age column, they are incapable of showing change. To study change requires correlation or comparison of two or more censuses covering the same area or the same individuals. Work of this type promises the maximum rewards to be had from the census. It is, for example, entirely practicable, though by no means easy, to make from the manuscript returns a microscopic examination of leading features in the development of any settled locality from 1850 to 1860, or 1870, or 1880. It is possible, also, to follow the fortunes of any number of free individuals, especially men, through the same four censuses. Admittedly, so to trace individuals in quantity is a difficult job; but such statistical biography, even though it be less than perfect, holds uncommon promise as a way of describing social change.

Complex census studies of the several kinds mentioned demand so much labor that they must ordinarily be kept down either to a few topics or to a small area. The demerit of extensive examination of selected topics is that it necessitates rather rigid definition of technique and aims in advance of execution, and therefore incurs a danger that the findings may be warped by preconceptions and oversimplification. The prime advantages of wide-area work are the opportunities for comparison of subareas, and the sweep of the generalizations obtained. Major examples of this approach will be found in the trail-breaking studies conducted or inspired by Professor Frank L. Owsley of Vanderbilt University. These studies aim to show the economic structure and the late antebellum trends in Southern society by analysis centering around the landholding of slaveowners and non-slaveowners in numerous sample counties.[27]

Small-area analysis, while weak in breadth of generalization and instructive comparisons, has compensating advantages. An individual away from a research center may hope to accumulate the material requisite for one or a few counties, and to handle that material without equipment more esoteric than ordinary note cards and a calculating machine. Because intimate acquaintance with a limited body of material leads to novel perceptions, the intensive study can achieve variety, flexibility, and subtlety in analysis quite impossible on a large scale. The small-area approach also lends itself to an effective mixing of the statistical and the nonstatistical employments of the census, and to a ready integration of census data with information from other sources. Fine examples of such work are J. C. Bonner's "Profile" of Hancock County, Georgia, and the pioneer studies of groups of Wisconsin counties by Joseph Schafer, whose volumes proved, as he said, that "the great indispensable and hitherto almost universally neglected census source" enabled him "to disclose social and economic trends of which the conventional historical treatise is quite innocent," and to raise local history to general significance.[28] Frequently, too frequently, writers of town and county histories work solely for a home audience whose personal knowledge invests with sentiment and meaning long recitals of factual minutiae that merely bore or bewilder the outlander. But the historian of the small region can, if he will, find in local development sets of patterns and processes informative to the outlander and illustrative of man's behavior in society. The ways to this important end may vary; but the most promising, as a rule, is an astute and thorough use of the census.

The reader will inevitably have concluded that, whatever the value of the census, to attack it is to let oneself in for a deal of close and plodding work. The conclusion, though just, is partial, for census study has charms to redeem its pedestrianism. Scrutiny of the schedules turns up many diverting or unexpected facts. One may encounter in Cherokee County, Texas, 1850, a genuine "bee hunter," or in Smith County a farm family, illiterate, with daughters called Luzyephia and Artemisea, and a neighboring farm family, literate but less imaginative, with two young children (numbers seven and eight) "not named." One is informed about Refugio County, 1860, by an enumerator's explanation that he had "numbered many Dwellings without Families which is owing to the callings and occupations many of whom have a Camp or Cabbin occupied by one or more men for the purpose of attending to stock others who are engaged in catching Fish, Turtles &c all of which I have Denominated Dwelling Houses." Again, one finds that William Hogan, assistant marshal for the Navarro District of Texas (Navarro, Ellis, and Tarrant counties), filed with his return of Schedule 6, Social Statistics, 1850, an addendum containing not only a methodological "Note on various Schedules" but also a laudatory "Description of Navarro District." More consequential, however, than the garnering of tidbits is the salutary effect upon the investigator of grinding through an interminable list in which men, women, and children of all ranks, provided they be free, are accorded almost equal attention; no other exercise in historical research can give so abiding an impression of the overwhelming weight of plain people in American society. Census study offers, besides, a challenge to think, in that the devising of analyses calls for ingenious contrivance, and the interpretation of findings demands clear and prudent reasoning. Finally, there is a genuine intellectual satisfaction in those moments, at the end of tedious tabulations, when results begin to take on coherent form, sustaining a presupposition, uncovering a new bit of truth, or propounding yet more questions.

Notes

1. The priority in census exploration of genealogists and other seekers after personal detail is manifest in the annual reports, 1904 and following, of the Director of the Census. On census data in relation to genealogy, see Gilbert Harry Doane, *Searching for Your Ancestors: The Why and How of Genealogy* (New York, London: c. 1937), 144–156, pp. 232–235, and index under "Census." Joseph A. Hill, in "The Historical Value of the Census Records," a paper read before the American Historical Association, and published in *Annual Report*, I, 1908 (Washington: 1909), 197–208, made perhaps the earliest effort to interest historians in census subjects. A recent invitation to the census appears at pages 48–51 in that excellent manual, *Local History, How to Gather It, Write It, and Publish It* (n.p., [1944]), by Donald Dean Parker, revised and edited by Bertha E. Josephson for the Social Science Research Council. Examples of Texas studies depending in some part upon the manuscript census returns include R. L. Biesele, *The History of the German Settlements in Texas, 1831–1861* (Austin: c. 1930); Abigail Curlee, "A Study of Texas Slave Plantations, 1822 to 1865" (unpublished

Ph.D. dissertation, The University of Texas, 1932); A. F. Muir, "The Free Negro in Harris County, Texas," *Southwestern Historical Quarterly,* XLVI (January 1943), 214–238; I. T. Taylor, *The Cavalcade of Jackson County* (San Antonio: c. 1938); G. W. Tyler, *The History of Bell County* (Charles W. Ramsdell, ed., San Antonio: 1936); and Clarence R. Wharton, *History of Fort Bend County* (San Antonio: 1939).

2. Descriptions in this article are based upon examination of most of the schedules, and upon prolonged conning of *The History and Growth of the United States Census* (Washington: 1900; also issued as *Senate Document No. 194,* 56 Cong., 1 Sess., Serial No. 3856), prepared by Carroll D. Wright, assisted by William C. Hunt, for the Senate Committee on the Census. The bulk of this volume (pp. 131–910) is an unabridged printing of nearly the whole of the schedules of inquiry, instructions, etc., for the first eleven censuses, 1790–1890. The other principal feature (pp. 12–76) is a meticulous "Historical Review of the Federal Census." Only those abused superlatives, "invaluable and indispensable," adequately state the relation of the Wright and Hunt compilation to serious census study. The graphic representation of the schedules through 1850 in J. D. B. DeBow, *The Seventh Census of the United States: 1850 . . .* (Washington: 1853), pp. x–xii, proved useful in the construction of Figures 1–4, but for ordinary purposes the work of Wright and Hunt supersedes the descriptive matter scattered in earlier publications.

3. The original returns have been published in full by the Bureau of the Census under title *Heads of Families at the First Census of the United States, taken in the year 1790* (12 vols., Washington: 1907–1908).

4. The population schedules of 1820 and 1830 called for the number of foreigners not naturalized; the schedules of 1820 and 1840 asked the numbers of persons engaged in several occupations; the schedules of 1830 and 1840 contained questions about the numbers of various "defectives," such as the deaf and dumb; and the schedule of 1840 sought the names and ages of "pensioners for Revolutionary or military services" (the roster thus obtained was published as a separate volume in 1841). The answers to all of these inquiries were recorded family by family. The census of 1840 also collected information about numbers of students and schools, the data being returned in the form of district totals. The population censuses were supplemented by imperfect attempts to collect statistics of manufacture in 1810 and 1820, of manufacture and agriculture in 1840. The 1810 returns of manufacture are not with the other early census records, and presumably perished long ago. The present writer has not had opportunity to compare the non-population schedules of 1820 and 1840 with the printed reports compiled from them. Wright and Hunt, eds., *op. cit.,* give the impression that the returns of 1840 came in as district totals, which could be exhausted in the printed reports, while the returns of 1820 dealt with each establishment separately, and therefore embrace detail not shown in the printed report.

5. See Howard F. Barker, "National Stocks in the Population of the United States as Indicated by Surnames in the Census of 1790," American Historical Association, *Annual Report,* 1931, I (Washington: 1932), 126–359.

6. The first family, from Cherokee County, is fairly typical of East Texas farm families. The second family, from Henderson County, is something of an oddity.

7. Dannell was a planter in Bowie County; Jennings, a general farmer in Grayson; Donahoe, a piney woods stock raiser in Polk; and McMurry, a newly-arrived small farmer in Smith.

8. All or nearly all are printed in Wright and Hunt, eds., *op. cit.;* they occupy about 240 pages.

9. *Ibid.*, pp. 245–249, 261–273.

10. Hilgard's massive work occupies vols. V–VI (Washington: 1884) of the *Reports of the Tenth Census,* 1880; Gordon's is in the same set, vol. III, *Report on the Productions of Agriculture* . . . (Washington: 1883), pp. 951–1116. Hilgard frequently quotes or abstracts the returns of the cotton schedules. It is hard to tell from his report what use Gordon made of the schedules on his subject.

11. The version of the schedule used in the South differs from the one used elsewhere in that it omits broom corn and hops (together four items), and includes rice, cotton, and cane, plus a subdivision of weeks of hired labor into white and colored (together eight items).

12. The agricultural schedule of 1880 was supposed to exclude animals "kept beyond the frontier of close and continuous settlement, under the ranch system" (Tenth Census, 1880 vol. III, *Agriculture,* xv); such animals fell in the province of Gordon's special report. The attempted distinction, however well or ill observed, was by no means clean cut, and the student should not assume the agricultural schedule to be irrelevant to ranching. Casual examination of the returns reveals men such as Winn Traylor, with pasture of 30,000 acres and 5,000 cattle (Victoria County, page 19, line 7), or J. N. Simpson, with 4,000 cows—entered by the enumerator as "Milch cows"—and 10,250 other cattle (Taylor County, page 11, line 7).

13. Special agents collected the statistics of manufacture in several major industries and in all or nearly all towns and cities of 8,000 or more population. Wright and Hunt, *History and Growth of the United States Census,* pp. 63, 173–174.

14. The abandoned schedule was No. 4—hence the gap in number between the schedule of manufactures and that of mortality.

15. Report of the Director of the Census, September 15, 1919, in *Reports of the Department of Commerce, 1919* (Washington: 1920), p. 609.

16. The volumes in the Texas State Library appear to contain no returns of Special Schedules Nos. 11 and 12. The two schedules may have been withdrawn entirely from the regular enumerators. See Wright and Hunt, *History and Growth of the United States Census,* p. 174.

17. The originals of the population schedules, 1790–1880, and of the non-population returns, 1820 and 1840, are in The National Archives, Washington, D. C.

18. These are mentioned because most users prefer them to film copies. The Archives Collection has photostats of Schedules 1 and 2 of 1850 for the counties of Gillespie, Limestone, Milam, and Smith, and of Schedules 1 and 2 of 1860 for Bell, Gillespie, Limestone, and Smith. The State Library has photostats of Schedule 1 of 1850 for Goliad and Refugio, and of Schedule 1 of 1860 for twelve frontier counties. Much more substantial is the State Library holding of retained copies, 1870, from the records of the Secretary of State (Texas). The copies cover fifty-one of the counties with names falling alphabetically between Goliad and Zapata.

inclusive, and comprise, in addition to the population schedules, most, if not all, of the nonpopulation schedules.

19. The introductory and analytical sections of the printed reports often state frankly the shortcomings either of the census to which they belong or of earlier censuses. Wright and Hunt, *History and Growth of the United States Census,* while primarily descriptive, contains good appraisals. The most elaborate critique is one by members of the American Economic Association entitled *The Federal Census: Critical Essays* [American Economic Association, *Publications,* New Series, No. 2 (March, 1899), New York and London: c. 1899].

20. Instructions (1850) direct the enumerator to insert "the name of the person residing upon or having charge of the farm, whether as owner, agent, or tenant." The official interpretation of the term "slave owners" in Schedule 2 reads: "The person in whose family, or on whose plantation, the slave is found to be employed, is to be considered the owner—the principal object being to get the number of slaves, and not that of masters or owners." Wright and Hunt, *History and Growth of the United States Census,* pp. 153, 235.

21. Endorsement by Benj. Booth, assistant marshal, on his returns of the agricultural schedule; remark by General Francis A. Walker, Tenth Census, 1880, vol. III, *Agriculture,* viii.

22. Notice the use of census data concerning the members of the Mississippi secession convention in P. L. Rainwater, *Mississippi, Storm Center of Secession, 1856–1861* (Baton Rouge: 1938).

23. As a specimen of this kind of work, see Herbert Weaver, "Foreigners in Ante-Bellum Towns of the Lower South," *Journal of Southern History,* XIII (February 1947), 62–73.

24. The sizes of slaveholdings in 1850, and the birthplaces of the free inhabitants in 1850 and 1860, have been tabulated for states, but not for counties. Tables referred to here and above are in Bureau of the Census, *A Century of Population Growth* . . . (Washington: 1909), section XIV, and Tables 113–115; J. D. B. DeBow, Superintendent of the Census, *Seventh Census,* pp. xxxvi–xxxvii, and *Statistical View of the United States . . . being a Compendium of the Seventh Census . . .* (Washington: 1854), pp. 95, 116–118; Eighth Census, 1860, vol. I, *Population . . .* (Washington: 1864), pp. 616–623, and vol. III, *Agriculture . . .* (Washington: 1864), 193–221, 223–247, 248; Ninth Census, 1870, vol. I, *The Statistics of the Population . . .* (Washington: 1872), pp. 343–377, and vol. III, *The Statistics of the Wealth and Industry . . .* (Washington: 1872), pp. 339–366; and Tenth Census, 1880, vol. 1, *Statistics of the Population . . .* (Washington: 1883), pp. 496–535, and vol. III, *Agriculture,* pp. 28–101.

The copiousness and complexity of the printed census reports render hazardous any statement of what they do *not* contain. For a consoling instance of oversight by the Bureau of Census itself, see the assertion in *A Century of Population Growth,* p. 135, that the only previous classification of slaveholdings by size was that of 1850.

25. The first report on agriculture that takes account of race is in Twelfth Census, 1900; but Eleventh Census, 1890, vol. V, *Report on Farms and Homes . . .* (Washington: 1896), offers classification of owners and tenants by color.

26. Since labor and tenure arrangements in agriculture take many forms, a mere division of farm operators into owners and nonowners in 1870 cannot be regarded as satisfactory; but it would be much more enlightening than no division at all.

27. Frank L. and Harriet C. Owsley, "The Economic Basis of Society in the Late Ante-Bellum South," *Journal of Southern History*, VI (February 1940), 24–45; Blanche Henry Clark, *The Tennessee Yeomen, 1840–1860* (Nashville: 1942); Chase C. Mooney, "Some Institutional and Statistical Aspects of Slavery in Tennessee," *Tennessee Historical Quarterly*, I (September 1942), 195–228; Frank L. and Harriet C. Owsley, "The Economic Structure of Rural Tennessee, 1850–1860," *Journal of Southern History*, VIII (May 1942), 161–182; H. L. Coles, Jr., "Some Notes on Slaveownership and Landownership in Louisiana, 1850–1860," *Journal of Southern History*, IX (August 1943), 381–394; Herbert Weaver, *Mississippi Farmers, 1850–1860* (Nashville: 1945). Fabian Linden, "Economic Democracy in the Slave South: An Appraisal of Some Recent Views," *Journal of Negro History*, XXXI (April 1946), 140–189, is an elaborate criticism of the Vanderbilt studies, ending with a list of suggestions for further census work. See also Linden's review of Weaver's book, and Owsley's reply thereto, in *American Historical Review*, LII (January and July 1947), 338–340, 845–849.

28. Bonner's "Profile of a Late Ante-Bellum Community" is in *American Historical Review*, XLIX (July 1944), 663–680. Three books by Schafer constitute volumes II–IV of the *Wisconsin Domesday Book, General Studies*, published by the State Historical Society of Wisconsin. The titles are: *Four Wisconsin Counties, Prairie and Forest* (Madison: 1927); *The Wisconsin Lead Region* (Madison: 1932); and *The Winnebago-Horicon Basin, A Type Study in Western History* (Madison: 1937). The quotation is from the last volume, p. ix. See also Schafer, "A Rural Life Survey of a Western State," in J. F. Willard, ed., *The Trans-Mississippi West . . .* (Boulder, Colo.: 1930), pp. 291–308.

✿ 5 ✿

Bernard and Lotte Bailyn

INVESTORS AND INVESTMENTS

Tables 5–1 and 5–2 (see end of chapter) give basic information relating to ownership of vessels registered in 1698 or between January 1699 and October 1714. The data in Table 5–2 on home port of vessel and residence of investor for the period 1699–1714 differs from that presented in Table 5–1 for the year 1698 in that tonnage-per-owner figures, based on an equal division of shares, cannot be used for the 1699–1714 period. Frequently in this period the number of owners changed after a vessel was first registered, and in such cases it is obviously impossible to set tonnage figures for those who remained owners throughout.

The totals for these tables contain what is perhaps the most remarkable piece of information to be derived from the Register. No fewer than 903 residents of Massachusetts owned some part

Bernard Bailyn is Professor of History at Harvard University and editor-in-chief of the John Harvard Library. He is author of *Education in the Forming of American Society, The New England Merchants in the Seventeenth Century, Politics and Social Structure in Virginia*, and other books. He is editor of *Robert Keayne 1595–1656*, and of *Pamphlets of the American Revolution 1750–76*. Lotte Bailyn is Research Associate in the Laboratory of Social Relations at Harvard. She is author of *Mass Media and Children* and *Notes on the Role of Choice in the Psychology of Professional Women*.

Reprinted from Bernard and Lotte Bailyn, *Massachusetts Shipping 1697–1714: A Statistical Study* (Cambridge: The Belknap Press of Harvard University Press, 1959), pp. 56–73, by permission of the authors and the publisher. © 1959 by the President and Fellows of Harvard College.

of the shipping registered after 1698. Of these, the astonishing total of 544 were residents of Boston.

The relative magnitude of this figure may be gained by considering that the total population of Boston in 1710 was 9,000. Since the average family in this period had six members, and since the overwhelming majority though not all of the adult males in Boston were heads of households, a reasonable estimate of the number of adult males in Boston is one-fifth of the total population, or 1,800. Close to one out of every three adult males in the town of Boston during the first decade of the eighteenth century, therefore, was part-owner at least of a seagoing vessel.[1]

Such popular involvement in the ownership of vessels was not equally characteristic of all of Massachusetts, but there were high proportions in at least a few of the other towns. Population figures for all Massachusetts towns in 1710 are not available, but if the ratio between Boston's 1710 adult male population and its 1690 militia figures is applied to the other militia figures of that year, it may be said that in Charlestown one out of every four adult males held shares in shipping; in Salem, two out of every nine; in Gloucester and Newbury, one out of every six.[2]

Who were these hundreds of Massachusetts shipowners? What was the character of this shipowning population? What are the implications of such numbers for the economy of the province? One approach to answers to these questions lies through inspection of the occupations and titles of prestige listed by the owners.

The occupations officially stated by owners in the Register make clear the breadth of popular participation in the ownership of vessels, the degree to which the possession of shipping capital in this period had been parcelized. The list of owners includes not only merchants but people claiming a variety of humbler occupations. No fewer than 154 of the Boston investors who stated their occupations called themselves mariners; nine claimed to be shipwrights; five, blacksmiths; five, coopers; four, shopkeepers; two, traders; two, carpenters; two, sailmakers; one, baker; and one, ropemaker. Nor was the participation restricted to the male part of the population: nine of the owners from Boston were women; four of these listed themselves as widows.

More significant than the variety of modest occupations stated by the owners was the size of the group claiming to be merchants.

At first glance it would seem that the town of Boston was simply one great guild of merchant-shipowners, since no fewer than 207 owners—11.5 per cent of the adult male population—gave their occupations as merchant. But these 207 Bostonians were by no means all merchants in the traditional sense of that term. The use of this title in colonial America was lacking in precision just as the occupation itself had lost its once-traditional distinctiveness. In early eighteenth-century Boston people called themselves merchants who in Europe, including England, with its firmer institutional constriction of economic life and its clearer social stratification, would never have pretended to such occupational dignity.[3]

A dramatic illustration of the confusion and imprecision in occupational designations, reflecting deep-seated tendencies toward occupational mobility and a confusing flexibility in occupational roles, lies in the fact that sixteen of the Bostonians who called themselves merchants, elsewhere in the Register listed other occupations. Most often the alternative was mariner, but not always. One person used ropemaker alternatively with merchant; another, shipwright; another, shopkeeper. Moreover, no fewer than fifteen of the Boston shipowners who called themselves merchants stated also that they themselves were the masters of the vessels in whose ownership they shared. In four of these cases the individual concerned did not even list mariner as an alternative occupation.

In Boston, then, claims to the title of merchant were extraordinarily widespread. It was an occupational designation that could be assumed easily by anyone involved in trade or maritime activity, and it was not used exclusively when adopted. This expression of occupational mobility was to a much lesser extent evident in the other Massachusetts towns. Thus, although besides merchants and mariners there were among the Newbury shipowners a trader and a weaver; in Salem, two traders, two shipwrights, and a blockmaker; in Charlestown, a shipwright; and elsewhere in Massachusetts, a trader, three shipwrights, a carpenter, and a cooper— none of Newbury's nine shipowners who stated their occupations, only two of Charlestown's thirty-five, and three of Salem's thirty-seven gave more than one occupational title. Elsewhere in Massachusetts not one of the seventy-four shipowners who listed their occupations gave alternatives.

However different these lesser Massachusetts towns may have

been from Boston, the fact remains that participation in shipowning was remarkably widespread. Throughout the province the shipowning population extended far beyond the boundaries of a merchant-shipowning "class" defined in any traditional sense. It constituted a wide social spectrum. This social span was largely composed of a broad band of small entrepreneurs for whom artisan occupations touching maritime affairs furnished access to investment in shipping and to mercantile activities that made the designation of merchant seem reasonable, at least as an occasional usage. But it also included the complex reality behind what has loosely been called a "merchant aristocracy."

The Register contains information of a particular kind on this upper group, for titles of prestige as well as occupational designations were included in the entries. The honorific title Esquire, applied by the end of the seventeenth century to all magistrates and to a very few others as a mark of social distinctiveness, appears frequently in the Register.[4] But it appears only in particular circumstances. Fifteen Bostonians used the appellation Esquire; all but three of them used merchant as well, either together in the same entry or separately in other entries. Only one resident of Boston who used the term Esquire used any other occupational title than merchant.[5] Similarly, among the three Bostonian shipowners who called themselves Gentlemen the only alternative designation used was merchant. Elsewhere in Massachusetts such titles of distinction appear quite infrequently, but when they do they are found either unassociated with other occupational descriptions or only with merchant. Only three residents of Salem used the title Esquire; all three also identified themselves in other entries as merchants. The three Charlestown Esquires and the one in Newbury gave no other titles or occupations. Of the four individuals who called themselves Esquires in other Massachusetts towns none claimed a specific occupation; one of the two Gentlemen gave merchant as an alternative.

This peculiar use of prestige titles suggests that within the wide spectrum of the merchant-shipowning group there was an inner area of distinction. It lacked precise boundaries, and was defined not by institutional or legal demarcations but by an effective degree of common agreement.[6] Its implications run deep. In the environment of colonial America where traditional landmarks on

the social terrain were indistinct, there was already by the early
eighteenth century evidence of what would become the characteristic American practice; not of giving up efforts to mark out an
elite sphere but, out of necessity, of substituting voluntary, informal, vague, and highly impermanent demarcations for the more
precise boundaries defined by more stable social and economic
institutions.

The great spread of participation in Massachusetts shipping was
horizontal as well as vertical: its range extended not merely down
into the middle and lower regions of colonial society, but abroad,
into England and its commercial enclaves throughout the Atlantic
world.

Examination of the column in Table 5–2 labeled "Total
Massachusetts" shows the extent of this non-American participation. Seventy-nine residents of the British Isles owned shares of
Massachusetts' shipping registered between 1699 and 1714, though
it would be more accurate to say Boston's shipping since there
was only a single investment by a resident of the home islands in a
vessel based in any other Massachusetts town than Boston. The
fourteen entries under "Other British Isles" represent not a heavy
concentration in a single outport but considerable spread. The
town second to London in investments in Boston's shipping was
Exeter, with only four investments by four individuals. Taunton
followed with two investments; and the rest was held by residents
of five towns in the west of England and in Dublin and Glasgow.

Almost as many residents of England's Atlantic possessions
shared in ownership of Boston's shipping as did residents of the
British Isles proper. Most of the fifty-nine investors listed in the
"West Indies, etc." category gave addresses in the Caribbean Islands: nineteen were residents of Barbados, ten of Nevis, eight of
Jamaica, six of Antigua, five of Montserrat, four of St. Kitts, and
one of Providence Isle. But participation by Englishmen living
overseas was not restricted to West Indians. English inhabitants of
Oporto (eight) and Lisbon, Portugal (one), of Madeira (four),
Newfoundland (one), and Annapolis Royal, Nova Scotia (one)
also invested in Boston's shipping.

Thus, though none of the investors in Boston's or Massachusetts' fleet came from so far afield as the two "English Merch"

resident at Archangle in Rousha" who in 1713 shared ownership in the 150-ton *George Augustus* of London newly built in Boston, support was widely recruited throughout the Atlantic ports—throughout the length and breadth of England's Old Empire.

The question arises whether this geographical spread of investment represents a significant shift in the location of preponderant ownership. Analysis of the proportions of Massachusetts shipping held by the various regional groupings listed in Table 5–2 and a comparison with the equivalent data for the early period found in Table 5–1 furnish the answer.

There was no important shift in the geographical location of ownership; with one possible exception the proportional holdings by residential areas of the shipping of all the localities represented in the table remained essentially unchanged. To begin with the most important point, external control of Massachusetts shipping remained negligible. In 1698 residents of Massachusetts claimed 91.0 per cent of the investments in their fleet; they held 88.5 per cent of the investments of the vessels registered after that year. Residents of the British Isles owned only an insignificant part of the fleet in 1698; they could claim only 4.0 per cent of the investments thereafter.

Even upon closer calibration the proportions remain surprisingly constant. Bostonians held 69.5 per cent of the new Massachusetts investments; they had owned 67.0 per cent of the shares in the earlier fleet. They also retained almost to the percentage point their high claim to shares in their own vessels (80.2 as opposed to 80.8 per cent), a fact of particular importance in view of the growing concentration of Massachusetts shipping in the port of Boston. The percentage of investments made by residents of other Massachusetts towns in Boston's vessels declined from 9.4 to only 7.3.

There appears to be a similar constancy in the proportion of Boston's holdings in the shares of vessels based abroad. The most important of these, investments by Bostonians in vessels of the British Isles registered in Massachusetts, remained essentially unchanged in percentage terms: 15.4 per cent of all investments in this shipping after 1698 as opposed to 16.7 per cent in the early period.

The one possibly significant change in the geographical loca-

tion of investments concerns the shipping of the lesser Massachusetts towns. The residents of these communities held a greater
share of the shipping they registered after 1698 than they had of
the vessels they listed as of 1698. To put it another way, and perhaps more realistically, Boston's interest in the shipping of the
minor Massachusetts ports declined with the lessening in relative
importance of these towns as mercantile centers. In 1698 Bostonians held 13.3 per cent of the investments in the shipping of all
Massachusetts ports but Boston; of shares in the new acquisitions
they claimed only 9.0 per cent. At the same time the holdings of
the residents of these towns in their own vessels taken as a unit
rose from 80.8 per cent of the whole to 85.2.

The entries under the home port category "West Indies, etc."
have a peculiar interest. Almost all of these vessels were based in
the larger Caribbean sugar islands whose economy, by the early
eighteenth century, was closely tied in with powerful English
commission houses.[7] But the islands' shipping—at least that part
of it reflected in the Massachusetts Register—was not directly
dominated by absentee English entrepreneurs. English investments in the West Indian shipping registered in Massachusetts
were almost nonexistent. Thirty-three of the total 142 investors,
however, were Bostonians.

It should also be noted in this connection that residents of Boston alone of Massachusetts residents ventured widely abroad.
Fifty-eight Bostonians held shares in British shipping, but only six
residents of other Massachusetts towns did so. And only one of
these six was from Salem: the only person in the town to invest in
shipping based outside Massachusetts.

Perhaps the most revealing aspect of the problem of ownership
distribution in the Massachusetts fleet concerns the distribution
among individuals: the degree to which ownership was concentrated in the hands of a few among the large number of shareholders. The problem is to decide whether in the process of rapid
replacement a significant change in this balance took place.

In seeking to answer this question we are hampered to some extent by the lack of tonnage-per-owner figures. Nevertheless,
Table 5–3, which shows the distribution of ownership in all Massachusetts vessels registered between 1699 and 1714 in terms of

numbers of investments, provides at least a first approximation to an answer, and it may indicate whether the problem is worth pursuing further.

Table 5–4 showed that in the 1698 fleet the small owners—those who invested three or fewer times—held 69.7 per cent of the total number of investments. Table 5–3 shows that the equivalent lower portion of the investor group in the later period taken as a whole—91.9 per cent, or 1,027 people—held 1,541 investments: 52.1 per cent of the total number—a drop of 17.6 per cent. Conversely, the five leading investors in the early period—1.5 per cent of the whole group—controlled 11.9 per cent of the 587 investments. Of the 2,957 shares in the vessels added to the Massachusetts fleet after 1698, the same top percentage (seventeen people) controlled more than twice as large a percentage of the investments: 24.1 per cent.[8]

These figures certainly suggest that a decisive and significant change in the balance of ownership had taken place. Confirmation of this trend may be found in the one category of vessels in which tonnage-per-owner figures are available and entirely reliable: the solely owned vessels. Table 5–5 shows the distribution of ownership of vessels possessed entirely by single individuals, in terms of both numbers of investments and tonnages. Analysis of the comparable figures for the 1698 fleet (Table 5–6) made clear that the two leading owners of solely owned vessels—5.9 per cent of the group—had held 20.8 per cent of the investments in these vessels and 29.1 per cent of the tonnage. Comparison of these figures with their equivalents from Table 5–5 shows a radical change: the same top percentage of owners of the 386 solely owned vessels registered in the sixteen years after 1698 held 49.5 per cent of the investments in this category, and a minimum of 54.6 per cent of the tonnage.

Examination of solely owned vessels, then, amply supports the impression of an important shift in concentration of ownership. It therefore seems reasonable to seek means beyond those used in analysis of the shipping of the early period to probe the character and to assess the dimensions of this development. The data must be reanalyzed in such a way as to avoid the limitations of both previous tables and locate precisely the center of the change.

Table 5–3 was limited by its exclusive concentration on mere numbers of investments: it is at least possible that the increased percentage of investments claimed by the upper 1.5 per cent of the investors reflects not a material increase in control of shipping but simply a multiplication of holdings in small vessels. Table 5–5, on the other hand, though it included accurate tonnage figures, was limited to solely owned vessels: since this group formed only about a third of the total registrations (34.7 per cent), it might misrepresent the general development.

In Table 5–7 all elements of the situation are brought together in a different arrangement that not only avoids the weaknesses of both previous compilations but locates the heart of the change in ownership concentration.

The rows in this table divide all Massachusetts vessels into three tonnage categories: those 100 tons and over, those between 31 and 99 tons, and those 30 tons and under. The columns cross these divisions by three others which separate the vessels according to the number of people who held shares in them. The nine major cells that result represent nine categories of what might be called risk-units. The unit of greatest risk is that of the upper-left cell vessels of 100 tons or more owned by single investors; the bottom right cell represents the exact opposite: vessels of 30 tons or less owned by five or more people. Two sets of numbers are entered in the cells: the percentage of the total investments in each category owned by the biggest investors (defined as those who invested in ten or more Massachusetts vessels throughout the Register), and the percentage of the group involved in each category that such investors constituted. Subdivisions contrast the percentages of their holdings in Massachusetts' 1698 fleet with those in Massachusetts vessels registered in the subsequent sixteen years.

Looking first at the top row of the table, one can see that the frequent investors increased their holdings in some, but not all, of the largest vessels (100 tons or more), and the difference is important. They did not increase their proportion of investments in large vessels where the risk was small—where the total number of shareholders was five or more—but only where the co-owners were few. Thus, if two to four investors were involved not only did the percentage of their claims rise, but they themselves consti-

tuted an increasing portion of the investing group; but where five
or more investors were concerned and hence where the risk was
most widely spread, the percentage of their holdings in the largest
vessels declined.[9]

The interest of the most frequent investors in the medium-sized
vessels (31–99 tons) followed a similar pattern. Their investments
increased when they themselves owned the ships outright or
when they entered into combination with no more than three
others; but when the number of shareholders rose to five or more
the percentages of investments they held decreased. For the smallest ships the pattern is slightly altered: investments held by the
frequent investors increased in the case of the solely owned vessels and remained essentially the same for ships of medium risk;
they did, however, increase again for the lowest risk vessels.[10]

A further demonstration of the point involved will be found by
examining not the rows of the table but the columns, and particularly the second column, in which the risk element is kept at a
constant value of between two and four owners. In this medium-
risk category the concentration of holdings by the frequent investors increased markedly only in the case of the larger vessels. In
ships over 100 tons the high investors held a much greater proportion of the investments after 1698 than they did in those of that
year, and they also constituted a larger proportion of the group
investing; in ships between 31 and 99 tons they still held a larger
percentage of the investments, but the group had become more
open: frequent investors comprised a smaller percentage of the
people participating; in the smallest vessels of all they also formed
less of the group and here their investment percentages barely
rose at all.

Table 5–7 has demonstrated that the increasing holdings
claimed by the frequent investors, far from being a mere multiplication of low-risk investments, were in fact increases in investments in the larger vessels where ownership and hence risk was
shared by the smallest number of people. But general conclusions
drawn from this fact would be questionable unless it can also be
demonstrated that this area of increasing interest by the frequent
investors was not a decreasing portion of the newly registered
fleet: if the kinds of vessels in which the larger shareholders were

increasing their holdings were declining in number relative to the whole, the rise in investments still would not indicate a net increase in control of shipping.

To cover this possibility Table 5–8 has been prepared. In organization it follows precisely the plan of Table 5–7, re-creating the nine major risk categories subdivided by the two contrasting time periods. But the percentages entered in the cells are no longer the percentages of each category held by the big investors but rather the portions of the total number of vessels that each category and subcategory includes. Now, by comparing the entries in the same cells of the two tables, we are in a position to establish the absolute, not merely the relative, importance of the increasing holdings of the leading investors.

The relation between the two tables concludes the argument. The vessel categories in which the major shipowners were increasing their investments were those whose proportional contribution to the fleet was growing. The increases in proportions of the total number of vessels that took place will be found in much the same cells in which the increases in investments of the most frequent investors had earlier been seen: in the high-risk cells, where large tonnages were combined with small numbers of investors. Thus, to retrace the path followed in discussing Table 5–7, the percentage of vessels 100 tons or over in the fleet as a whole increased only when such vessels were solely owned or when they were owned by groups of from two to four. But, when the risk in these largest vessels was less, their proportional contribution to the fleet as a whole declined. The same pattern is seen for ships between 31 and 99 tons. The smallest vessels (30 tons and below) show a decrease for all levels of risk. Finally, the two-to-four column shows that when numbers of owners are held constant, increases in the relative size of the vessel group stand in direct proportion to tonnages. The relative number of vessels owned by two to four people rose when the vessels were 100 tons or over; they rose also when the tonnages ranged from 31 to 99; but they fell when the tonnage figures were 30 or less.

There can now be little doubt as to the meaning of the original ownership concentration figures for this period. In the successive replacements of the Massachusetts fleet as it had existed at the end of the seventeenth century, the leading shipowners—the sixty individuals who owned part of ten or more of Massachusetts' vessels recorded in the Register—owned an increasing portion of the province's shipping: they held increasing control of the growing part of the fleet, which was composed of the largest vessels involving the greatest risk. Concentration of ownership was indeed rising; the balance of holdings between the large and the small investors was shifting significantly.

Who were these major investors? Was there a change from the earlier period in the entrepreneurial groupings they formed as shipowners?

Table 5–9 contains the names, residences, and summaries of the holdings of all those who invested in ten or more of all the vessels listed in the Register. The figures for each of these sixty-nine individuals are divided first into categories of home ports of the vessels they invested in; they are then subdivided within these groups into time periods: 1697–1698 and 1699–1714. In each of these time periods there are separate listings of numbers of investments and of tonnages, the latter being the sums of the known tonnage-per-owner figures. A separate column lists the vessels and tonnages each person owned alone. The last two columns total all the subtotals and thus present the accumulated investments of the leading shipowners.

Several of the names, especially those at the top of the list, are familiar from the early period. The two leaders of the 1698 fleet Samuel Lillie and Andrew Belcher, still head the list of grand totals, though in terms of numbers of investments their positions have been reversed. Benjamin Gallop, third in 1698, is now seventh; Marston and Dyer, previously fourth and fifth, are now twenty-ninth and thirty-first. To such familiar names are added a large group of Bostonians who had held shares in the 1698 fleet but whose involvement had been minor; their holdings had risen rapidly in the decade and a half thereafter.

There is thus a good deal of continuity in personnel through the entire eighteen years of the Register. To be sure, there were a few important new arrivals from outside, such as John Lloyd of London and Timothy Harris of Oporto, but most of the newcomers were connected in one way or another to well-established Boston merchants. Thus, Jonathan Belcher, the future governor,

who returned from his first European trip in 1705 and immediately became deeply involved in shipping, was the son of Andrew
Belcher. It was with the prominent Boston merchant Louis
Boucher that the Londoner Paul Boucher appeared as a shipowner
in Massachusetts; and the two Wentworths, whose family roots in
Massachusetts went back to the origins of the colony, had mercantile connections throughout the community.

The totals for the most frequent investors are impressive almost
to the point of improbability. Belcher invested in 137 vessels and
held altogether, if shares had been equal, over 3,000 tons. Lillie
invested in fewer vessels, but his actual control of shipping
appears to have been greater. He owned outright 42 of the 108
vessels in which he was concerned, representing close to 2,500
tons. Many of his other investments, as will become clear, were in
effect also sole ownerships. The only sudden break in the even
decline of totals comes between Lillie and Clarke, the third listed,
who invested in 39 fewer vessels than Lillie and held some 1,600
tons less. Thereafter the figures decline regularly and slowly, lev-
eling off at the bottom of the list where twelve individuals held
shares in 10 vessels each, with an average total tonnage of approximately 235.

What is known of the personal histories of some of these leading shipowners suggests that the totals were not only high but too
high. Shipping, like trade itself in this period, was full of risks.
There were, to begin with, the risks of the seas which neither
rudimentary forms of locally obtained marine insurance nor expensive and irregularly available foreign underwriting were sufficient to overcome. Perhaps equally important, however, were
those basic conditions of the economy, especially the monetary
shortage and the lack of impersonal financial institutions, that
made it difficult to resolve profits into securities and to maintain
reserves—a difficulty for which the limited amount of urban real
estate was an insufficient solution. Instead of cash payments for
sales, there was a further exchange of goods; instead of securities
for profits, there was a further reinvestment.[11] Both may have
been excellent for the growth of the commercial economy, but
both heaped up dangers for the diligent entrepreneur, who was
logically drawn to involve his full resources in immediate transac-

tions. Reverses could mean disaster. The careers of some of the leading shipowners provide dramatic illustration.

Consider the fate of Samuel Lillie. Linked by marriage to a veritable dynasty of merchant princelings, this prominent shipowner of 1698 continued to pile up investments in vessels, alone and in a great variety of combinations. By early 1707 Lillie was easily the biggest shipowner in the western hemisphere; he probably would have ranked high on any list of European shipping magnates as well. But his investments totaled in Table 5–9 cover not the entire period but only the years before 1707, for in that year he went bankrupt.

The immediate cause of Lillie's downfall was his inability to satisfy his pressing creditors, especially Edward Bromfield and Francis Burroughs, merchants and shipowners of Boston. Once they had brought his credit into question by a court action, Lillie was suddenly overwhelmed with demands for immediate payment of a great variety of obligations. Even his apprentice, Jeremy Condy, joined the crowd, suing his employer for £325 in back wages. Lillie tried to limit the spread of the conflagration by pledges and partial payments, but the blaze was not to be stopped by such measures. He had no choice but to liquidate his fleet of vessels. Threatened with arrest for debt, he gave his wife power of attorney and in the fall of 1708 fled the country, settling in London where he attempted to recoup his fortunes. There is some evidence of his reinvolvement in American trade, but in 1727 he again went bankrupt. He returned to Boston in 1730 "broken in age and infirmities." [12]

To what extent Lillie's failure was due to his own mismanagement and poor judgment cannot be discovered from the records (though his tendency to invest alone, indicated by the figures in the "solely owned" column, is suggestive), but the effect of such personal failings as might have existed was exaggerated by the delicacy of the situation in which security was difficult to attain even for the most affluent and successful. Perhaps it is correct to attribute the collapse of Lillie to incompetence, as one is surely inclined to do in the case of the insolvency of that flamboyant adventurer, that "gay man" and "free liver," Sir Charles Hobby.[13] But must the same be said of Louis Boucher? This leading merchant, associated with a group of influential English and American Huguenots experienced in trade, owned ten vessels outright and invested altogether in fifty-three vessels. He had claims to something like 2,000 tons of shipping. In October 1714, he too declared himself bankrupt.[14]

The systematic difficulty of translating the fruits and enlarged enterprise into security may help explain the character of investment groupings in the period 1699–1714. It will be recalled that the partnership combinations in the 1698 fleet were almost completely *ad hoc*, a situation that may reasonably be explained by the limitation of capital available to any given individual or group of investors and by the need to spread risks. These conditions continued to exist for the great majority of investors; their groupings, therefore, remained varied and highly unstable. The interesting question is whether the leading investors—those who had, at least to some extent, overcome these limitations—had begun to form stable partnerships, shipowning companies, in effect, with permanent forms of organization.

Examination of the investment combinations of the leading shipowners reveals evidence of tendencies in this direction. The biggest shipping magnates increasingly participated in fairly stable investment patterns; but they also continued to draw upon the scattered resources of many small investors. Instances of repeated combinations may now be found. They are, however, still infrequent; those that existed were largely based on personal ties; and they existed side-by-side with a great array of one-time associations.

Thus, Andrew Belcher, for whom success in trade and powerful links to officialdom provided as much security as could be found in the world of colonial commerce,[15] invested with approximately 150 different individuals in the sixteen years after 1698. The vast tangle of his partnerships defies close analysis, but its general characteristics are clear. He shared ownership with most of the leading investors of the time, and also with many of the lesser ones including the masters of his vessels. There is, however, a persistent association among the many combinations Belcher entered. Andrew and his son Jonathan formed what might be called a core partnership that remained constant throughout the period.

Together, the two owned ten vessels; they held eleven others together with one other partner; six with two other partners; and five with three others. Two of the five-man groupings were exact duplicates of each other.

Lillie's investment pattern shows another form of stability. His partnership associations remained highly unstable; though certain names do recur, the most frequently repeated, Penn Townsend and David Jeffries, occur only three and four times, respectively. More important, there is not one single exact duplicate in the entire list of Lillie's partnerships. The sense in which the pattern of his investments may be said to have clarified is that sole ownership became an increasingly important form of investment for him. Between 1699 and 1714 he owned thirty-seven vessels alone. Furthermore, many of his other investments probably came close to exclusive ownership, for in fourteen cases his only partner was the ship's master who had probably received a small share in lieu of wages.

In a different, though also restricted, sense Louis Boucher's partnerships formed a pattern. His main associations were with a group of London Huguenots with whom he joined in a variety of combinations. One strand in this ethnic network was particularly strong. The core partnership in Boucher's case was the one he formed with his London kinsman, the merchant Paul Boucher. With him the Bostonian joined in ownership of five vessels; with him and other London Huguenots, in ever-changing combinations, he shared thirteen others.

Here and there among the hundreds of groupings involving the lesser shipowners there are other repetitions of small partnerships. Thus, for example, Nicholas Roberts of Boston joined with John Shippen of London to finance eight vessels; Roberts also invested in the two other vessels in which Shippen was concerned. Occasionally larger combinations attained at least temporary stability. Thus the four-man partnership of John Colman and Charles Hobby of Boston together with Richard Eyton and Carlton Vanbrough of London owned four vessels totaling 610 tons. The two Londoners and Colman came together also in a fifth case.

To such a limited but still significant extent, then, had the instability of entrepreneurial groupings in the shipping of 1698 given way to fixed shipowning associations in the sixteen years of great expansion that followed. Though important elements of stability may be seen in the patterns of investment, this form of business enterprise was still highly personal, still full of risks, still structured so as to favor a broad popular participation.

Notes

1. The exact proportion is three out of ten. The fact that nine of the Boston investors were women does not affect this figure.
2. Carl Bridenbaugh, *Cities in the Wilderness* (New York: 1938), 143 n.; Evarts B. Greene and Virginia D. Harrington, *American Population Before the Federal Census of 1790* (New York: 1932), pp. xxiii, 19–21; Herbert Moller, "Sex Composition and Correlated Culture Patterns of Colonial America," *William and Mary Quarterly*, II, 3d ser. (1945), 124–126.
3. Bernard Bailyn, *New England Merchants in the Seventeenth Century* (Cambridge, Mass., 1955), chap. vii. esp. pp. 194–195.
4. On the use of Esquire and on titles of prestige in general, see Norman II. Dawes, "Titles of Prestige in Seventeenth-Century New England," *William and Mary Quarterly*, VI, 3d ser. (1949), 69–83, esp. 71–73.
5. John Foster, who was listed simply as a merchant once, as both merchant and Esquire twice, and as Esquire alone twenty-one times, appeared once also as a mariner.
6. The only shipowner resident in Massachusetts who claimed a legal title was Charles Hobby, who was a baronet. His use of the title was irregular. He appears in the Register twice as Baronet, once as both Knight and merchant in the same entry, eight times as Esquire, once as merchant and Esquire combined, and twice simply as merchant.
7. K. G. Davies, "The Origins of the Commission System in the West India Trade," *Transactions of the Royal Historical Society*, 5th ser., II (1952), 89–107.
8. If the relation between investments and tonnage existing in the earlier period had been maintained in the later, the leading 1.5 per cent of the investors would have held not 17.6 per cent as in 1698, but 35.6 per cent of the tonnage registered between 1699 and 1714.
9. The figure in the highest risk category for the 1698 fleet can hardly be used for comparison since there was only one vessel in this category by the end of 1698 and it was owned by a leading investor. Increased concentration in this category of vessel may nevertheless be seen by dividing the later period into four quadrenniums. The percentage of the investments held by leading investors rose from 80 per cent for the year 1699–1702 to 83, 83, and 90 per cent in the subsequent four-year periods.

   It should be pointed out that the definition adopted for isolating the leading investors (ten or more investments throughout the period covered by the Register) precludes absolute comparisons between figures for the 1698 fleet and those for the subsequent sixteen years. By definition a leading investor has a higher probability of appearing in the longer period (1699–1714) than in the shorter (1697–1698). The total figures bear this out: 33 per cent of the 1698 investments were in the hands of leading investors; 40 per cent of the later acquisitions were. It is to be expected, therefore, that percentages would rise somewhat in all cells of the table. The degree of rise and the fluctuations among the cells are what indicate the significant changes in the pattern of ownership.

10. The figures in the lowest risk category represent an exception to the general conclusions from the table. This exception results from the fact that not one of the investments in vessels of this category registered by the end of 1698 was made by a leading investor. The general trend is apparent, however, when the registrations in the years 1699–1714 are divided into four-year periods. In the years 1699–1702, 53 per cent of the investments in this type of vessel were made by leading investors; percentages for subsequent quadrenniums are 43, 11, and 19.

11. Bailyn, *New England Merchants*, pp. 99–100.

12. The intricate tangle of litigation in which Lillie was caught in 1707 and 1708 has been preserved in the Suffolk County Court Files, Boston, Massachusetts. There is a handy guide to these papers in Pierce's *Lillie*, pp. 74–75. The most important set, which includes a large part of the Bromfield-Burroughs suit, is the collection of 58 items listed as File No. 7169. Condy's suit, which contains some remarkably detailed apprenticeship records, may be followed in 7182, 7253, and 7439.

13. Thomas Hutchinson, *The History of . . . Massachusetts-Bay* (Lawrence S. Mayo, ed., Cambridge, Mass., 1936), II, 114; Oliver A. Roberts, *History of . . . the Ancient and Honorable Artillery Company of Massachusetts* (Boston, 1895), I, 341.

14. *Boston News-Letter*, October 11, 1714; May 23 and June 13, 1715.

15. Bailyn, *New England Merchants*, 195–196.

TABLE 5–1

Relation between Residence of Investors and Home Port of Vessels, 1698

HOMEPORT: Residence of Investors	Boston			Other Mass.			Total Mass.			Other New England			Other America		
	People	Investments	Tonn.ᵃ	People	Investments	Tonn.	People	Investments	Tonn.	People	Investments	Tonn.	People	Investments	Tonn.
Boston	186	370	5,456.0	11	16	306.7	193	393ᶜ	5,972.7				1	1	5.0
Charlestown	0	16	142.0	8	8	86.6	14	25ᶜ	233.6				1	1	15.0
Cambridge	1	1	10.0	2	2	30.5	3	3	40.5						
Malden				2	2	7.6	2	2	7.6						
Salem	5	5	41.7	17	37	806.6	19	42	848.3						
Ipswich	1	2	22.0	10	11	84.8	10	13	106.8						
Newbury	1	1	8.6	5	5	77.5	5	6	86.1						
Gloucester	1	1	8.0	3	3	35.0	4	4	43.0						
Beverly	1	1	20.0	5	6	30.0	7	7	50.0						
Lynn				6	6	15.0	6	6	15.0						
Marblehead	1	1	16.9	1	1	5.0	2	2	21.9						
Plymouth	6	6	58.5	1	1	15.0	7	7	73.5						
Weymouth	1	1	5.6				1	1	5.6						
Marshfield	1	2	23.8				1	2	23.8						
Yarmouth	1	1	16.9	2	2	22.5	3	3	39.4						
Sandwich				2	2	20.0	2	2	20.0						
Barnstable				2	2	17.5	2	2	17.5						
Harwich				1	1	10.0	1	1	10.0						
Dartmouth				1	1	7.5	1	1	7.5						
Bristol	5	5	30.2				5	5	30.2						
Nantucket				3	7	64.9ᵈ	3	7	64.9ᵈ						

Footnotes on page 123.

TABLE 5 – 1 (*continued*)

HOMEPORT: Residence of Investors	London			Other Br. Isles			Total Br. Isles			West Indies, etc.			Total		
	People	Invest-ments	Tonn.	People	Invest-ments	Tonn.	People	Invest-ments	Tonn.	People	Invest-ments	Tonn.	People[b]	Invest-ments	Tonn.
Boston	10	10	637.0	4	4	71.0	14	14	708.0	2	2	58.3	203	410	6,744.0
Charlestown													15	26	248.6
Cambridge													3	3	40.5
Malden													2	2	7.6
Salem													19	42	848.3
Ipswich													10	13	106.8
Newbury													5	6	86.1
Gloucester													4	4	43.0
Beverly													6	7	50.0
Lynn													6	6	15.0
Marblehead													2	2	21.9
Plymouth													7	7	73.5
Weymouth													1	1	5.6
Marshfield													1	2	23.8
Yarmouth													3	3	39.4
Sandwich													2	2	20.0
Barnstable													2	2	17.5
Harwich													1	1	10.0
Dartmouth													1	1	7.5
Bristol													6	6	47.7
Nantucket										1	1	17.5	3	7	64.9[d]

Footnotes on page 123.

TABLE 5 – 1 (*continued*)

HOMEPORT: Residence of Investors	Boston			Other Mass.			Total Mass.			Other New England			Other America		
	People	Invest-ments	Tonn.ª	People	Invest-ments	Tonn.	People	Invest-ments	Tonn.	People	Invest-ments	Tonn.	People	Invest-ments	Tonn.
Total Mass.	221	413	5,860.2	82	113	1,642.7	290	534c	7,717.9				2	2	20.0
Other New Eng.	9	10	99.2				9	10	99.2	22	22	207.3			
Other America	3	5	98.4	1	1	10.0	3	6	108.4				3	3	40.0
London	5	5	82.6	1	2	50.5	5	7	133.1						
Other Br. Isles	2	2	27.4				2	2	27.4						
Total Br. Isles	8	8e	130.0	1	2	50.5	8	10e	180.5						
West Indies, etc.	10	12	116.9	1	1	20.0	12	14c	141.9						
Otherf	10	10	142.8	3	3	66.6	10	13	209.4						
TOTALg	261	458	6,447.5	88	120	1,789.8	332	587c	8,457.3	22	22	207.3	5	5	60.0

Footnotes on page 123.

TABLE 5-1 (continued)

HOMEPORT: Residence of Investors	London			Other Br. Isles			Total Br. Isles			West Indies, etc.			Total		
	People	Invest-ments	Tonn.	People	Invest-ments	Tonn.	People	Invest-ments	Tonn.	People	Invest-ments	Tonn.	People	Invest-ments	Tonn.
Total Mass.	10	10	637.0	4	4	71.0	14	14	708.0	3	3	75.8	302	553	8,521.7
Other New Eng.													31	32	306.5
Other America													6	9	148.4
London	33	37	1,471.7	4	4	55.2	36	41	1,526.9				38	48	1,660.0
Other Br. Isles				21	22	261.8	21	22	261.8				23	24	289.2
Total Br. Isles	33	37	1,471.7	25	26	317.0	57	63	1,788.7				62	73e	1,969.2
West Indies, etc.	2	2	46.6	1	1	7.2	2	2	46.6	16	16	739.1	30	32	927.6
Other f	3	4	113.9				4	5	121.1				14	18	330.5
TOTAL g	48	53	2,269.2	30	31	395.2	77	84	2,664.4	19	19	814.9	445	717	12,203.9

a Total tonnage-per-owner figures, computed on the basis of equal shares
b This column does not represent the sum of the figures in the "people" columns.
c Includes investments in vessels listed as coming from "New England."
d All of these investments are in Nantucket vessels which involve "companies."
e Includes one investor whose residence is listed as "England."
f Investors whose residences were either in the Iberian peninsula or unknown.
g Totals of tonnages differ from figures previously given because of rounding errors.

TABLE 5–2

Relation between Residence of Investors and Home Port of Vessels, 1699–1714

Residence of Investors	Boston		Other Mass.		Total Mass.		Other New Eng.		Other America		London
	People	Investments	People	Investments	People	Investments	People	Investments	People	Investments	People
Boston	507	2,015	30	40	518	2,055	9	10	4	4	51
Charlestown	27	63	26	41	41	104			4	4	3
Cambridge	1	1			1	1					
Medford	1	1			1	1					
Dorchester	8	8			8	8					
Roxbury	1	1			1	1					
Hull	5	6	3	3	8	9					
Salem	17	23	46	94	55	117					1
Ipswich	6	7	10	13	14	20					
Newbury	7	8	37	50	39	58					
Gloucester	10	12	17	23	24	35					
Beverly	1	2	3	7	3	9					
Lynn	1	1	7	7	8	8					
Marblehead	10	13	13	15	21	28					1
Manchester			3	4	3	4					
Salisbury			6	6	6	6					
Haverhill			3	3	3	3					
Andover			2	2	2	2					
Boxford			1	1	1	1					
Bradford			1	1	1	1					
Scituate	4	9	11	12	12	21	1	1			

TABLE 5-2 (continued)

Residence of Investors	London Invest-ments	Other Br. Is. People	Other Br. Is. Invest-ments	Total Br. Isles People	Total Br. Isles Invest-ments	W. Ind., etc. People	W. Ind., etc. Invest-ments	Other[a] People	Other[a] Invest-ments	Total People[b]	Total Invest-ments
Boston	85	15	21	58	106	33	46	13	15	544	2,236
Charlestown	4			3	4	3	4	2	2	48	118
Cambridge										1	1
Medford										1	1
Dorchester										8	8
Roxbury										1	1
Hull										8	9
Salem	1	1	1	1	2					55	119
Ipswich										14	20
Newbury						1	1			39	59
Gloucester										24	35
Beverly										3	9
Lynn										8	8
Marblehead										21	28
Manchester	1			1	1					4	5
Salisbury										6	6
Haverhill										3	3
Andover										2	2
Boxford										1	1
Bradford										1	1
Scituate										13	22

Footnotes on page 127.

TABLE 5-2 (*continued*)

Residence of Investors	Boston People	Boston Invest-ments	Other Mass. People	Other Mass. Invest-ments	Total Mass. People	Total Mass. Invest-ments	Other New Eng. People	Other New Eng. Invest-ments	Other America People	Other America Invest-ments	London People
Plymouth	1	1	19	31	19	32					
Marshfield	2	2	9	11	10	13					
Duxbury	1	2	2	2	3	4					
Yarmouth	3	3	6	6	8	9					
Sandwich			4	6	4	6		1			
Barnstable	4	4	11	13	13	17	1				
Hingham	2	2	3	3	4	5					
Eastham	2	2	4	4	6	6					
Harwich			3	3	3	3					
Rochester			1	1	1	1					
Dartmouth	1	1			1	1					
Bristol	1	1	6	6	7	7					
Nantucket	7	8	8	11	13	19					1
Martha's Vineyard			1	1	1	1					
"New England"	2	2			2	2					
Total Mass.	632	2,198	296	420	865	2,618	11	12	8	8	57
Other New England	13	19	4	4	17	23	28	33	1	1	
Other America	8	11	1	1	9	12	1	1	21	24	1
London	62	102	1	1	63	103	1	1			228
Other Br. Isles	14	14			14	14					12
Total Br. Isles	78	118[c]	1	1	79	119[c]	1	1			245
West Indies, etc.	59	69	8	8	67	77	4	4	1	1	2
Other[d]	69	96	12	12	80	108	1	1	1	1	17
Total	859	2,511	322	446	1,117	2,957	45	51	31	34	322

TABLE 5-2 (continued)

Residence of Investors	London		Other Br. Is.		Total Br. Isles		W. Ind., etc.		Other[a]		Total	
	Invest-ments	People	Invest-ments	People	People	Invest-ments	People	Invest-ments	People	Invest-ments	People[b]	Invest-ments
Plymouth							2	2			19	34
Marshfield											10	13
Duxbury											3	4
Yarmouth											8	9
Sandwich											4	7
Barnstable											13	17
Hingham											4	5
Eastham									2	2	8	8
Harwich											3	3
Rochester											1	1
Dartmouth											1	1
Bristol									1	1	8	8
Nantucket	1				1	1					13	20
Martha's Vineyard											1	1
"New England"											2	2
Total Mass.	92		22	16	64	114	39	53	18	20	903	2,825
Other New England											43	57
Other America	1				1	1					30	37
London	305		6	6	233	311	1	1	6	6	275	421
Other Br. Isles	16		220	188	198	236			4	4	210	255
Total Br. Isles	326[c]		226	194	436	552[c]	1	1	10	10	492	683[c]
West Indies, etc.	2		1	1	3	3	102	115	1	1	156	200
Other[d]	17		1	1	18	18			5	9	101	137
Total	438		250	212	522	688	142	169	34	40	1,725	3,939

[a] Vessels from Oporto, Portugal and those whose home ports were not entered in the Register.

[b] This column does not represent the sum of the figures in the "people" columns.

[c] Includes investments by people as resident in "Great Britain."

[d] Investors whose residences were in the Iberian Peninsula, "Archangle, Rousha," or unknown.

TABLE 5-3

Concentration of Ownership in Massachusetts Vessels, 1699–1714

Number of Times Invested	1	2	3	4	5	6	7	8	9	10	11	12	14	15	16	17	18	21	22	25	28	29	31	33	36	38	41	54	58	60	85	101	Total
Number of People Investing	706	193	86	22	17	20	11	7	8	9	4	4	2	4	2	2	1	2	3	1	2	1	1	1	1	1	1	1	1	1	1	1	1,117

Total: 2,957

TABLE 5-4

Concentration of Ownership in Massachusetts Vessels, 1698

	1	2	3	4	5	6	7	8	10	22	23	Total
Number of Times Invested												
Number of People Investing	224	58	23	9	6	7	1	1	1	1	1	332
Total Tonnage Owned [a]	2,731.4 [b]	1,793.4	934.3 [c]	470.1	483.9	553.0	73.7	272.9	221.4	294.5	628.7	8,457.3 [d]
Average Tonnage Per Investment [a]	12.2 [b]	15.5	13.5 [c]	13.1	16.1	13.2	10.5	34.1	22.1	13.4	27.3	14.4

[a] Computed on the basis of equal shares.
[b] Includes one person's investment in a vessel involving "companies." If this is excluded the figures are 2,723.1 and 12.2 respectively.
[c] Includes two people all three of whose investments were in vessels involving "companies." If they are excluded the figures are 877.7 and 13.9 respectively.
[d] This figure differs from total Massachusetts tonnage elsewhere because of rounding errors.

TABLE 5-5

Concentration of Sole Ownership in Massachusetts Vessels, 1699–1714

Number of Vessels Solely Owned	1	2	3	4	9	10	19	20	21	24	26	34	37	Total
Number of People Investing	86	23	10	6	1	1	1	1	1	1	1	1	1	134
Total Tonnage	3,645	1,801	1,422	1,017	670	910	955	753	863[1][a]	1,305	1,388	2,081	2,051[2]	18,861[3]

[a] Numerical superscripts indicate the number of vessels whose tonnages were not entered in the Register.

TABLE 5-6

Concentration of Sole Ownership in Massachusetts Vessels, 1698

	1	2	3	5	Total
Number of Vessels Solely Owned					48
Number of People Investing	27	4	1	2	34
Total Tonnage	740	236	180	475	1,631
Average Tonnage Per Vessel	27.4	29.5	60.0	47.5	34.0

TABLE 5-7

Location of Holdings of Investors in Ten or More Massachusetts Vessels, 1697–1714

	Number of Owners					
	1		2–4ᵃ		5 or moreᵇ	
Tonnageᶜ	1697–1698	1699–1714	1697–1698	1699–1714	1697–1698	1699–1714
100 or Over						
Per Cent of Investments Held by Top Investors	100.0(1)	84.8(33)	28.6(7)	49.2(181)	42.2(116)	37.0(262)
Per Cent of People Who Are Top Investors	100.0(1)	72.2(18)	16.7(6)	31.7(104)	34.6(78)	25.6(160)
31–99						
Per Cent of Investments Held by Top Investors	68.4(19)	75.9(195)	34.4(93)	45.9(896)	32.3(186)	29.1(402)
Per Cent of People Who Are Top Investors	50.0(12)	43.1(72)	26.7(75)	13.3(427)	21.6(139)	16.3(300)
30 or Under						
Per Cent of Investments Held by Top Investors	17.9(28)	47.1(155)	26.6(109)	27.4(716)	0.0(28)	25.3(91)
Per Cent of People Who Are Top Investors	13.0(23)	25.9(85)	19.6(92)	10.3(477)	0.0(28)	24.4(90)

Note—The numbers in parentheses indicate the number of cases on which the percentages are based.
ᵃ Includes investments in ten vessels involving "companies."
ᵇ Includes investments in five vessels involving "companies."
ᶜ Investments in vessels whose tonnages were not entered in the Register are excluded.

TABLE 5-8

Changes in Composition of the Massachusetts Fleet, 1697-1714

	Number of Owners									
	1		2-4		5 or more		Total			
	Per Cent of Vessels	Per Cent of Vessels	Per Cent of Vessels	Per Cent of Vessels	Per Cent of Vessels	Per Cent of Vessels	Per Cent of Vessels	Per Cent of Vessels	Number of Vessels	Number of Vessels
	1697-1698	1699-1714	1697-1698	1699-1714	1697-1698	1699-1714	1697-1698	1699-1714	1697-1698	1699-1714
Tonnage										
100 or Over	0.6	3.0	1.1	5.7	8.2	2.5	9.9	11.2	17	124
31-99	11.1	17.2	18.7	27.8	16.4	6.2	46.2	51.2	79	564
30 or Under	16.4	13.6	24.6	22.5	2.9	1.5	43.9	37.6	75	414
Total	28.1	33.8	44.4	56.0	27.5	10.2	100.0	100.0	171	1,102[a]
No. of Vessels	48	373	76	617	47	112			171	1,102

[a] The tonnages of eleven vessels were not entered in the Register. They fall into the following owner groups: 1 owner, 8; 2-4 owners, 7; 5 or more owners, 1.

TABLE 5-9

Investors in Ten or More Vessels, 1697–1714

Name	Residence	Home Port											
		Massachusetts						British Isles					
		1697–1698		1699–1714		1697–1714		1697–1698		1699–1714		1697–1714	
		No.	Tonn.[b]	No.	Tonn.	No.	Tonn.	No.	Tonn.	No.	Tonn.	No.	Tonn.
Andrew Belcher	Boston	22	294.5	101	2,425.2[e]	123	2,719.7[e]	1	40.0	9	246.5	10	286.5
Samuel Lillie	Boston	23	628.7	85[3d]	3,159.6[e]	108[3]	3,788.3[e]						
William Clarke	Boston	6	82.0	60[1]	2,023.1	66[1]	2,105.1			1	16.7	1	16.7
Samuel Wentworth	Boston			58	2,601.4	58	2,601.4			1	20.0	1	20.0
John Colman	Boston	1	20.0	36	1,560.7[e]	37	1,580.7[e]						
Louis Boucher	Boston	6	71.4	54	2,334.1	60	2,405.5			15	457.1[e]	15	457.1[e]
Benjamin Gallop	Boston	10	221.4	38[1]	1,173.3	48[1]	1,394.7						
David Jeffries	Boston			33	618.0[e]	33	618.0[e]	1	20.0	7	337.4[e]	8	357.4[e]
John Frizell	Boston	1	10.0	41	1,359.0	42	1,369.0						
Gilbert Bant	Boston	2	32.5	28	548.3	30	580.8	1	200.0	2	31.4	3	231.4
John Foster	Boston	5	66.9	29	668.0	34	734.9						
Jonathan Belcher	Boston			28	644.7	28	644.7			5	111.5	5	111.5
James Pitts	Boston	1	16.7	31	493.7	32	510.4			1	25.0	1	25.0
William Harris	Boston	2	25.0	22	478.8	24	503.8			1	20.0	1	20.0
Daniel Oliver	Boston	6	85.6	21	391.6[e]	27	477.2[e]			3	71.7	3	71.7
Nicholas Roberts	Boston	1	50.0	25[1]	1,223.0	26[1]	1,273.0			1	25.0[e]	1	25.0[e]
Charles Chambers	Charlestown	3	22.1	22	377.8	25	399.9						
John Ruck	Boston	4	33.7	22	378.7	26	412.4						
Samuel Phillips	Boston	6	67.2	17	221.5	23	288.7			1	20.0	1	20.0
Thomas Hutchinson	Boston			21	571.9	21	571.9			1	28.0	1	28.0
Charles Shepreeve	Boston			18	299.6[e]	18	299.6[e]			3	126.7[e]	3	126.7[e]
Paul Boucher	London			7	233.0	7	233.0						
John Borland	Boston	6	80.8	15[1]	332.3	21[1]	413.1			14	439.1[e]	14	439.1[e]

Footnotes on page 137.

TABLE 5-9 (continued)

Name	Residence	Other[a] 1699–1714		Solely Owned 1697–1714		1697–1698		Total 1699–1714		1697–1714	
		No.	Tonn.	No.	Tonn.	No.	Tonn.	No.	Tonn.	No.	Tonn.
Andrew Belcher	Boston	4	114.2	22	838.0	23	334.5	114	2,785.9[c]	137	3,120.4[c]
Samuel Lillie	Boston			42[2]	2,381.0	23	628.7	85[3]	3,159.6[c]	108[3]	3,788.3[c]
William Clarke	Boston	2	21.7	26	1,388.0	6	82.0	63[1]	2,061.5	69[1]	2,143.5
Samuel Wentworth	Boston	2	116.7	34	2,081.0			61	2,738.1	61	2,738.1
John Colman	Boston	1	8.0	24	1,305.0	6	71.4	55	2,342.1	61	2,413.5
Louis Boucher	Boston	1	10.0	10	910.0	1	20.0	52	2,027.8[c]	53	2,047.8[c]
Benjamin Gallop	Boston			26[1]	1,008.0	10	221.4	38[1]	1,173.3	48[1]	1,394.7
David Jeffries	Boston	5	140.8	2	66.0	1	20.0	45	1,096.2[c]	46	1,116.2[c]
John Frizell	Boston	1	20.0	19	955.0	1	10.0	42	1,379.0	43	1,389.0
Gilbert Bant	Boston	3	51.7	1	40.0	3	232.5	33	631.4	36	863.9
John Foster	Boston	2	21.0	2	245.0	5	66.9	31	689.0	36	755.9
Jonathan Belcher	Boston	1	16.7	1	35.0			34	772.9	34	772.9
James Pitts	Boston			2	100.0	1	16.7	32	518.7	33	535.4
William Harris	Boston	6	84.5	2	80.0	2	25.0	29	583.3	31	608.3
Daniel Oliver	Boston			1	30.0	6	85.6	24	463.3[c]	30	548.9[c]
Nicholas Roberts	Boston	1	27.5	10	720.0	1	50.0	27[1]	1,275.5[c]	28[1]	1,325.5[c]
Charles Chambers	Charlestown	3	66.7	1	50.0	3	22.1	25	444.5	28	466.6
John Ruck	Boston			1	50.0	4	33.7	22	378.7	26	412.4
Samuel Phillips	Boston					6	67.2	18	241.5	24	308.7
Thomas Hutchinson	Boston			3	210.0			22	599.9	22	599.9
Charles Shepreeve	Boston	1	60.0					22	486.3[c]	22	486.3[c]
Paul Boucher	London							21	672.1[c]	21	672.1[c]
John Borland	Boston			2	72.0	6	80.8	15[1]	332.3	21[1]	413.1

Footnotes on page 137.

TABLE 5-9 (continued)

Investors in Ten or More Vessels, 1697-1714

		Home Port											
		Massachusetts						British Isles					
		1697–1698		1699–1714		1697–1714		1697–1698		1699–1714		1697–1714	
Name	Residence	No.	Tonn.[b]	No.	Tonn.	No.	Tonn.	No.	Tonn.	No.	Tonn.	No.	Tonn.
Edward Martyn	Boston	3	29.3	17	320.8	20	350.1						
Samuel Greenwood	Boston	2	16.7	16[2d]	179.3	18[2]	196.0						
Robert Howard	Boston	5	73.7	12	293.8	17	367.5						
Nathaniel Oliver	Boston	2	120.0	16	481.2[c]	18	601.2[c]						
Benjamin Alford, Sr.	Boston	3	29.0	15	342.0	18	371.0						
Benjamin Marston	Salem	8	272.9	9	188.5	17	461.4						
Jonathan Dowse	Charlestown	3	27.8	11	219.2	14	247.0			2	225.0	2	225.0
Giles Dyer, Sr.	Boston	7	73.7	7	78.7	14	152.4			1	20.0	1	20.0
Arthur Laugharn	Boston			15	484.5	15	484.5						
John Lloyd	London			6	186.3	6	186.3			9	205.5	9	205.5
John Mico	Boston	1	6.3	10	205.1	11	211.4			4	71.5	4	71.5
John Baker	Boston			15	264.3	15	264.3						
Charles Hobby	Boston			14	456.6	14	456.6						
Thomas Palmer	Boston	2	36.7	12	236.2	14	272.9						
John Browne	Salem	3	66.7	11	185.8[c]	14	252.5[c]						
Thomas Savage	Boston			14[1]	195.2	14[1]	195.2						
Florence Maccarty	Boston	4	44.2	10	117.7	14	161.9						
John Pitts	Boston	1	16.9	11	165.4[c]	12	182.3[c]			1	32.5	1	32.5
Benjamin Alford, Jr.	Boston			12	170.3	12	170.3			1	20.0	1	20.0
Andrew Faneuil	Boston	6	65.2	7	124.3	13	189.5						
Jeremiah Allen	Boston	4	46.6	9	113.6	13	160.2						
Samuel Baker	Boston			6	289.0	6	289.0			4	170.0	4	170.0
Thomas Cooper	Boston	2	25.0	10	342.7	12	367.7						
Samuel Browne	Salem	2	36.7	10	202.2	12	238.9						
John Marshall	Boston	3	56.3	9	121.3[c]	12	177.6[c]						
Thomas Marshall	Boston			12	166.3	12	166.3						

TABLE 5-9 (*continued*)

Name	Residence	Other[a] 1699–1714 No.	Tonn.	Solely Owned 1697–1714 No.	Tonn.	1697–1698 No.	Tonn.	Total 1699–1714 No.	Tonn.	1697–1714 No.	Tonn.
Edward Martyn	Boston					3	29.3	17	320.8	20	350.1
Samuel Greenwood	Boston	2	24.5			2	16.7	18[2]	203.8	20[2]	220.5
Robert Howard	Boston	2	57.0	1	110.0	5	73.7	14	350.8	19	424.5
Nathaniel Oliver	Boston			5	330.0	2	120.0	16	481.2[c]	18	601.2[c]
Benjamin Alford, Sr.	Boston			4	200.0	3	29.0	15	342.0	18	371.0
Benjamin Marston	Salem			4	220.0	8	272.9	9	188.5	17	461.4
Jonathan Dowse	Charlestown					3	27.8	13	444.2	16	472.0
Giles Dyer, Sr.	Boston	1	17.0			7	73.7	9	115.7	16	189.4
Arthur Laugharn	Boston			2	102.0			15	484.5	15	484.5
John Lloyd	London							15	391.8	15	391.8
John Mico	Boston					1	6.3	14	276.6	15	282.9
John Baker	Boston							15	264.3	15	264.3
Charles Hobby	Boston							14	456.6	14	456.6
Thomas Palmer	Boston					2	36.7	12	236.2	14	272.9
John Browne	Salem			3	88.0	3	66.7	11	185.8[c]	14	252.5[c]
Thomas Savage	Boston							14[1]	195.2	14[1]	195.2
Florence Maccarty	Boston					4	44.2	10	117.7	14	161.9
John Pitts	Boston					1	16.9	12	197.9[c]	13	214.8[c]
Benjamin Alford, Jr.	Boston			1	15.0			13	190.3	13	190.3
Andrew Faneuil	Boston			1	70.0	6	65.2	7	124.3	13	189.5
Jeremiah Allen	Boston					4	46.6	9	113.6	13	160.2
Samuel Baker	Boston	2	35.0	1	80.0			12	494.0	12	494.0
Thomas Cooper	Boston			3	230.0	2	25.0	10	342.7	12	367.7
Samuel Browne	Salem			2	85.0	2	36.7	10	202.2	12	238.9
John Marshall	Boston					3	56.3	9	121.3[c]	12	177.6[c]
Thomas Marshall	Boston			4	85.0			12	166.3	12	166.3

Footnotes on page 137.

TABLE 5-9 (continued)
Investors in Ten or More Vessels, 1697-1714

		Home Port											
		Massachusetts						British Isles					
Name	Residence	1697-1698		1699-1714		1697-1714		1697-1698		1699-1714		1697-1714	
		No.	Tonn.[b]	No.	Tonn.	No.	Tonn.	No.	Tonn.	No.	Tonn.	No.	Tonn.
Robert Brondson	Boston	5	55.7	7	102.0	12	157.7						
James Gooch	Boston	1	20.0	11	132.5	12	152.5						
Adam Winthrop, Jr.	Boston	1	6.7	10[1][d]	288.1	11[1]	294.8						
Eliakim Hutchinson	Boston	5	130.8	6	134.6	11	265.4						
James Barnes	Boston	3	38.0	8[1]	165.9	11[1]	203.9						
Jeremiah Dummer	Boston	2	21.3	9	177.2	11	198.5						
William Welsteed	Boston			10	159.3[c]	10	159.3[c]			1	20.0	1	20.0
John Ballantine, Sr.	Boston	2	33.8	8	107.0	10	140.8			1	4.3	1	4.3
John Shippen	London			8[1]	360.0	8[1]	360.0			1	25.0[c]	1	25.0[c]
John Oulton	Boston			10	354.9[c]	10	354.9[c]						
Thomas Bannister, Jr.	Boston			10	309.7	10	309.7						
Timothy Harris	Oporto			6	109.3[c]	6	109.3[c]			1	40.0	1	40.0
Ebenezer Wentworth	Boston			10	294.8	10	294.8						
John Desenne	Boston			7	144.1[c]	7	144.1[c]			2	102.3[c]	2	102.3[c]
Peter Butler	Boston	2	25.8	8	150.8	10	176.6						
Grove Hirst	Boston			9	167.3	9	167.3						
John Hobby	Boston	3	64.3	5	71.7	8	136.0						
Penn Townsend	Boston	3	46.7	7	106.2	10	152.9						
David Farnum	Boston	1	5.6	9	120.6	10	126.2						
Nathaniel Henchman	Boston	4	31.6	5	60.0[c]	9	91.6[c]						

Footnotes on page 137.

TABLE 3.3 (continued)

Name	Residence	Other[a] 1699–1714 No.	Other[a] 1699–1714 Tonn.	Solely Owned 1697–1714 No.	Solely Owned 1697–1714 Tonn.	1697–1698 No.	1697–1698 Tonn.	Total 1699–1714 No.	Total 1699–1714 Tonn.	Total 1697–1714 No.	Total 1697–1714 Tonn.
Robert Brondson	Boston					5	55.7	7	102.0	12	157.7
James Gooch	Boston					1	20.0	11	132.5	12	152.5
Adam Winthrop, Jr.	Boston			3	160.0	1	6.7	10[1]	288.1	11[1]	294.8
Eliakim Hutchinson	Boston			4	120.0	5	130.8	6	134.6	11	265.4
James Barnes	Boston			2	85.0	3	38.0	8[1]	165.9	11[1]	203.9
Jeremiah Dummer	Boston					2	21.3	9	177.2	11	198.5
William Welsteed	Boston							11	179.3[c]	11	179.3[c]
John Ballantine, Sr.	Boston					2	33.8	9	111.3	11	145.1
John Shippen	London	1	27.5					10[1]	412.5[c]	10[1]	412.5[c]
John Oulton	Boston			1	25.0			10	354.9[c]	10	354.9[c]
Thomas Bannister, Jr.	Boston			4	145.0			10	309.7	10	309.7
Timothy Harris	Oporto	3	150.0					10	299.3[c]	10	299.3[c]
Ebenezer Wentworth	Boston			3	100.0			10	294.8	10	294.8
John Desenne	Boston	1	8.8					10	255.2[c]	10	255.2[c]
Peter Butler	Boston			4	102.0	2	25.8	8	150.8	10	176.6
Grove Hirst	Boston	1	7.5	1	30.0			10	174.8	10	174.8
John Hobby	Boston	2	20.7			3	64.3	7	92.4	10	156.7
Penn Townsend	Boston					3	46.7	7	106.2	10	152.9
David Farnum	Boston					1	5.6	9	120.6	10	126.3
Nathaniel Henchman	Boston	1	7.5			4	31.6	6	67.5[c]	10	99.1[c]

[a] All entries fall into the 1699–1714 period.
[b] Total tonnage-per-owner figures, computed on the basis of equal shares.
[c] Includes at least one vessel involving "companies."
[d] Numerical superscripts indicate the number of vessels whose tonnages were not entered in the Register.

[a] All entries fall into the 1699–1714 period.
[b] Total tonnage-per-owner figures, computed on the basis of equal shares.
[c] Includes at least one vessel involving "companies."
[d] Numerical superscripts indicate the number of vessels whose tonnages were not entered in the Register.

❦ 6 ❦

Richard L. Merritt

THE EMERGENCE OF AMERICAN NATIONALISM:
A QUANTITATIVE APPROACH

The symbolism of names plays a significant role, not only in the magic of the primitives and the games of children, but in the process of group development and emerging nationalism as well. The designation of a group by a name—a specific name that serves as a symbol under which all would-be members of the group can unite, no less than as a means to differentiate the group from other such groups—is indicative that a group has come of age. In a situation where people are beginning to shift their primary group loyalties, the symbolism of names is particularly important.

Such was the case in the emerging American political community of the eighteenth century. The point at which the colonists stopped considering themselves Englishmen and began more often to think of themselves as Americans was of signal importance in the rise of American nationalism.

If students of the colonial era are fairly unanimous in recognizing the importance of this transitional period, it is not equally true that they agree on when the transition took place. Some writers,

Richard L. Merritt is Associate Professor of Political Science and Research Associate Professor in Communications, University of Illinois. He is author of *Symbols of American Community: 1735-75*, and co-editor of *Comparing Nations*, and of a study on the effects of events on national and international images.
Reprinted from *The American Quarterly*, XVII (1965), 319–335, by permission of the author and the publisher. © 1965, Trustees of the University of Pennsylvania.

such as James Truslow Adams, Michael Kraus, Oscar Handlin and Howard H. Peckham, have suggested that the "Americanization" of the colonists was a gradual and virtually imperceptible process that took place during the whole of the colonial period.[1] A few have associated this transition with specific events. Albert Harkness, Jr., for instance, wrote that the use of the terms "Americans" and "Europeans" to differentiate the colonists from their English contemporaries stemmed from the War of Jenkins' Ear, which began in 1739.[2] And Max Savelle found a growing "national" feeling among Americans during the six years beween the end of King George's War (1748) and the outbreak of the French and Indian War.[3] It was in the forced association of Americans and Englishmen during the latter war that Carl Lotus Becker found the rise of an American community consciousness.[4] More recently Paul A. Varg wrote that "the development of a nascent nationalism" in the colonies found its first manifestation in the fall of 1759 when, "during the celebrations of the conquest of Quebec, the name 'Americans' became something more than a geographical expression."[5] Other historians, including such prominent scholars as Allan Nevins, John C. Miller, Carl Bridenbaugh, Edmund S. Morgan and Bernhard Knollenberg, have argued that the sharp increase in the American sense of community came during the critical decade that began with the passage of the Stamp Act and ended with the creation of the first Continental Congress.[6] And Kenneth C. Wheare and others have asserted that no American sense of nationality really existed until long after formal ties bound the colonies into a single federation.[7]

Such a variety of views leaves the student of American nationalism somewhat bewildered. When *did* the transition to Americanism take place? When did the colonists stop referring to themselves as "His Majesty's subjects" or as "British colonists"—perceptions compatible with membership in a British (or possibly Anglo-American) political community—and start more often calling themselves "Americans"? Did this shift occur in all the colonies at approximately the same time? Did the perceptions of colonists with explicit Tory sympathies differ substantially from those of colonial "Sons of Liberty"? Above all, what was the timing of the transition? Did American nationalism blossom in the space of a few weeks or months, in response, perhaps, to some spectacular event or British pronouncement of policy? Or did the colonists "learn" to become Americans over a much longer period of time?

A useful approach to such questions is the method of communication research known as "content analysis." Now, at first blush, the term seems to imply nothing new. Is that not what we do daily when we "analyze" the "content" of a book, letter, speech or other communication? In the modern social sciences the term "content analysis" has come to mean something much more specific. Quantitative content analysis, in the words of Alexander George, "substitutes controlled observation and systematic counting for impressionistic ways of observing frequencies of occurrence" of content variables.[8] Examples of such content variables include words (or symbols), concepts, images, words in context, sentence lengths or structures, and so forth. Thus content analysis is the systematic tabulation of the frequency with which certain predetermined symbols or other variables appear in a given body of data—newspapers, letters, books, speeches or any other form of recorded communication—covering a specific period of time.

This chapter uses the type of content analysis that concentrates on words or symbols to explore a key aspect of the emergence of American nationalism: the terms used by the colonists to refer to themselves and to the land they inhabited.

Symbol analysis rests on the assumption that the words a person uses in communicating are indicative of or symbolize his attitude. (This is an assumption to which I shall return in later paragraphs.) To some extent the selection of words by a communicator is a conscious process. Novelists frequently seek to describe characters in their stories in a way that will give their readers a set of vivid images. One thinks of Dickens' Mr. Micawber, always painted in gray tones, or Uriah Heep, who everlastingly sought to impress his " 'umility" upon one and all. Similarly, much as the villain in a nineteenth-century melodrama wore (and was expected to wear) a black hat and a mustache, so villains in modern-day propaganda are clothed in "appropriate" garb. It is not the "United States" that communist newspapers discuss, but rather the "monopolistic" or "imperialistic" United States. And not infrequently do American politicians and writers preface the term "communism" with adjectives bearing a pejorative connotation in American symbol usage, such as "atheistic" or "totalitarian." By the same token, the patriot is the "people's hero," the "friend of peace" or the "red-blooded American."

In contrast to this deliberate use of language, designed to create a particular image for its audience, is what might be termed the "style" of a communication—"the subtle *unconscious* patterning of speech, handwriting, posture, and involuntary movements." [9]

But what is meant by the phrase "unconscious patterning of speech"? In one sense the analysis of such unconscious patterns resembles the psychoanalyst's search for the *lapsus linguae*, the "slip of the tongue" that has become such a prominent aspect of the folklore of psychoanalysis. And yet, quantitative symbol analysis does not place much emphasis upon such speech blunders. The intentional or accidental use of a word, such as "immortality" or "immorality," in a speech or in a diary of such a man as John Adams may mean nothing in itself. It would be, we might say, a random element in an otherwise patterned context, a word that might appear once or perhaps twice in any similar speech or diary. [10]

The symbol analyst most often focuses upon the regularities of speech usage. If a word or phrase is used constantly in some form of communication, it ceases to be a random occurrence, and becomes a stylistic pattern itself. In extreme cases, using the example from above, we would say that the speech or diary was preoccupied with "immortality" or "immorality." The songs that Hitler's Stormtroopers sang as they marched through the streets of Germany during the 1930's, for example, dwelled on death and the dead; similarly, such concepts as "nullification" and "abolition" find an especially prominent place in American writing of the mid-nineteenth century.

The symbol analyst is interested less in whether a particular message represents the communicator's style or his deliberate manipulation of symbols than in the frequency with which certain items occur, in frequency changes over time, in variations in frequency patterns in different communication media or in the same

media in different geographic or political areas. He is concerned
not with the intention of the message but with its effect, which in
turn depends far less upon the subtle psychological motivation of
the communicator than upon the qualities of the audience. Taking
an example from colonial history, if a Tory newspaper, such as
the *Massachusetts Gazette*, devoted an increasing share of its
space to American symbols and events as the colonial years
passed, or if it increasingly more often identified its readers as
"Americans" rather than as "His Majesty's subjects" or even
"colonists," we might say that, despite its pro-British point of
view, the latent content of its symbol usage encouraged its readers to think of themselves as members of a distinctly American
community and to turn their thoughts inward toward that American community.

But let us return to the assumption made earlier: that the words
a person uses in communicating are indicative of or symbolize his
attitudes. How can we be sure that this is actually the case? In a
sense, of course, we can never be completely certain whether or
not the communicator is choosing his words carefully to create a
particular effect. There are two points to be noted in considering
this objection. First of all, certain stylistic elements creep into the
person's communication regardless of how hard he may try to
exclude them. The passion for anonymity and unity of style that
attended the writing of *The Federalist* papers has not been completely successful in disguising their authorship.[11] Similarly, matters of style are very significant in differentiating literary, musical
and artistic masterpieces from copies or imitations.

The second point is of a more practical nature. If we do not use
words to symbolize attitudes, what else can we use? Sampling the
mind of the colonial American through public opinion surveys or
through subjective psychological tests is clearly out of the question. Nor is it any more likely, we have learned from psychologists, that a person's actions, while perhaps speaking louder than
words, are any more indicative of his true attitudes than the symbols he uses in communicating. In short, we must use available
analytical techniques, or devise better ones, to explore the meager
data that have come down to us from the colonial era. And, for
the most part, these data comprise words—expressions of opinion,
musings in a diary, outright propaganda, accounts of events by

eyewitnesses, interpretations of these events and of such processes as colonial patterns of behavior or thinking.

The starting place of research using symbol analysis is a grasp of the fundamentals of the analyst's subject of interest: the elaboration of a theoretical framework; the recognition of problems within that framework that are at once significant and subject to analysis; and the framing of questions as well as the selection of adequate means to answer them. But such tasks are not peculiar to symbol analysis research. They find their place in all types of research in the natural and social sciences.

Symbol analysis is useful only when the researcher has questions of a quantitative nature—how often? how much? how many? with what covariance?—that can be answered by counting the appearance of a limited number of symbols in a given body of data. Whether or not the topic that interests the analyst is subject to such a quantitative analysis rests not upon the nature of this research method alone, but upon the theoretical framework within which he is working. Symbol analysis would not be of much value, for instance, in trying to determine when a particular battle took place, or how much trade passed between colonial New York and Philadelphia. It would be considerably more helpful in trying to establish the nature of the colonists' political allegiances.

Once he has decided that a symbol analysis would be feasible and useful, the analyst must frame his questions (or form his hypotheses) so that quantitative data can answer them clearly, directly and simply. Symbol analysis is not merely a counting process, nor is it what might be termed "brute empiricism"—the amassing of statistics in the hope of finding interesting relationships. Effective symbol analysis is designed to test specific hypotheses by establishing a limited universe of relevant items as well as their alternatives, and by establishing their distribution or changes in the frequency of their appearance. On the basis of the evidence the hypotheses can then be accepted or rejected. An example of such an hypothesis might be: "The colonists' sense of group identification shifted from the British political community to a strictly American political community gradually but steadily from 1735 to 1775." This proposition asserts that the colonists

turned away from their British ties in favor of an intercolonial
allegiance; and, further, that a trend line showing the growth of
an American sense of community would be generally linear, that
is, not characteristically marked by sharp shifts in the colonists'
community ties.

With his questions or hypotheses in mind, the symbol analyst
must outline the technical aspects of his project, determining how
to count which symbols in what body of data covering what time
period. Objectivity requires that these technical aspects of the
symbol analysis be specified in advance, and that throughout the
analysis there be strict adherence to the coding procedure. If this
requirement is met, an independent research project should be
able to verify the findings of a symbol analysis by applying the
analyst's coding procedures to the original body of data. If it is
impossible or impractical to analyze all the data, the analyst must
utilize a sampling technique (about which I shall say more later)
designed to produce a representative sample or reproduction in
miniature of the entire body or universe of relevant items. A pre-
test or "dry run" is essential to "indicate whether the prescribed
symbol list, coding rules and recording procedures *actually* will
produce the statistic wanted." [12] After subjecting a small portion
of the sample to analysis, the researcher can often see where he
must eliminate and where he must add categories to his symbol
list, or where he must make changes in his hypotheses or coding
procedures.

How could we test the hypothesis suggested above—that "the
colonists' sense of group identification shifted from the British
political community to a strictly American political community
gradually but steadily from 1735 to 1775"—using symbol analysis? Since one crucial aspect of group identification is the recognition, both by members of the group and outsiders, of the group's
existence apart from other such groups, we can examine the use of
self-referent symbols in colonial newspapers.[13] To return to some
questions suggested above, when did the colonists (or at least
their newspapers) stop referring to themselves as "colonists" or as
"His Majesty's subjects," and begin more often viewing themselves as "Americans"? When did they begin identifying the land
that they occupied as "America" rather than as "British-America"
or the "colonies"? Another aspect of group identification is the

amount of attention paid by the members of the group to one another, in contrast to the attention paid to outsiders. When did the colonists begin devoting more space in their newspapers to local events and occurrences in America than they did to European wars and English court gossip? A simple count of symbols in the colonial press referring to place names throughout the world would give us substantial information about the colonists' focus of attention, and about the changes in this focus as they reached the end of the colonial era.

Clearly a certain amount of expertness in the methodology of symbol analysis—whether, when, what and how to count[14] is important here. Symbol analysis is after all a research tool which, like any other tool or method, has its specific uses, its advantages and its limitations. The analyst must know how to use this research tool, and must be aware of its limitations. This sort of expertness is akin to that of the student of American diplomatic history who, before he can perform competent research, must be familiar with such research aids as bibliographies and dictionaries of biographies; he must be able to evaluate conflicting interpretations of history or of events; he must learn to distinguish between reliable and unreliable sources. The expert symbol analyst, like the expert chemical engineer, strives to clarify his research designs so that even his newest research assistant could carry out at least some of the often tedious testing or counting.

Finally, the analyst must interpret the results of the symbol count in terms of his theoretical framework. That the colonists' use of self-referent symbols changed considerably from 1735 to 1775 is in itself an interesting fact. But where does that fact fit into the development of an American sense of community, the growth of sentiments of separateness from the mother country, the emergence of a desire for independence? It is this relationship —conclusions "formed by means of an inference from observed data to nonobserved continua" [15]—that is the crux of research in the social sciences.

Confronted with the task of analyzing a set of objects or communication media, such as eighteenth-century colonial newspapers, I could follow one of two different procedures. I could, first of all, examine each item individually; or, alternatively, I could use some sort of sampling method to select a few representative items for close examination. The appropriateness of either procedure rests primarily upon the amount and type of information needed to answer my questions about the class of items, as well as upon what economists call the "opportunity cost" of securing a certain amount of information. If I were interested in newspaper reaction to specific events, the Boston Tea Party, for instance, or the Battle of Golden Hill, I would most likely have to analyze every issue of a given number of newspapers for a certain limited time period. But searching for long-run trends in press attitudes or reporting would pose an entirely different research task.

One means of analyzing long-run trends in the press would be to read through every issue published (or extant) for the years in question. This is the time-honored historical method, and has much to commend it. In this manner the alert and insightful scholar can often spot significant relationships in the data that enable him to formulate interesting research problems and to reach useful conclusions.

That his results are important, however, is no guarantee that they adequately represent the actual content of the newspapers. Three critical types of error might have crept into his findings. We may, first of all, ignore the type of error produced by a writer merely searching for statements fitting his preconceived notions about the content of the press. Charlatanism is possible regardless of the research method used. The occurrence of such instances is nonetheless frequent enough to make us wary. A second and more important type of error occurs when the researcher searches through the newspapers for different points of view. It is sometimes difficult to assess the importance of certain ideas or symbols without some sort of frequency count or other measure of intensity. To ignore this is to run the risk of evaluating widely differing ideas or symbols on a par, assigning equal weights to an argument appearing only occasionally and to one appearing constantly.[16] The third type of error falls into the category of simple human failings. To scrutinize every extant issue of the pre-Revolutionary press would consume an inordinate amount of time. The researcher cannot read every word with equal care. He is generally able to do little more than to scan the newspapers, looking for key words or concepts. Even as Homer nodded, so too the modern writer occasionally slips, momentarily gliding by a few words or even paragraphs as the library grows dimmer, the microfilm copy grows fuzzier or the hour grows later. He may judge certain items to be of only marginal interest when in fact their inclusion would be necessary to give a rounded aspect to his final conclusions. Or, still more likely, the categories of items or concepts he considers of marginal interest may vary from day to day.

The alternative is to utilize some method of sampling. The detailed examination of every nth issue of a newspaper, or of a certain number of newspapers selected at random for each year, is as useful in measuring long-run trends in attitude changes as a sampling process is in testing blood or the control of quality on an assembly line. Such a procedure eliminates the necessity of scanning large quantities of newsprint as well as errors of the type mentioned in the previous paragraph. The more we can stratify the sample according to some characteristic of the media, according to political sympathies, for instance, or place of publication, or popularity as indicated by circulation, the more refined it will be. But, at the same time, with increasing refinement comes the need for larger sample sizes and hence added expense in terms of the time and money available for research. Ideally, the sample should be small enough to be manageable, and yet large enough to answer the most important questions about the total class of items.

Whether or not a sample is appropriate also rests upon certain empirical tests. One test would be to compare the analysis of the sample with a complete analysis of the larger set from which the sample has been drawn. Since such a procedure would obviate the need of a sample, it would be efficient only if the sampling technique were to be used in analyzing additional bodies of similar data. More frequently it is sufficient to compare the sample with a second sample drawn independently from the same data. If the variation between the two independent samples is not statistically significant, then either could be used within certain limits of probability in analyzing the data. If the variation is significant, then a larger sample, or perhaps one stratified differently, must be used. In my own work on changes in symbol usage in the colonial press, I have found that a random sample of four issues per year of a newspaper is nine-tenths as good as an independently-chosen random sample of twelve issues per year.[17] But, it must be added, although a sample of four issues per year might well measure yearly changes in symbol usage, it would take a more refined sample to analyze changes within any given year.

As a research method symbol analysis is a lengthy process, costly both in time and research money; and, even worse for the person performing the actual counting, an extensive project may become rather tedious. In this sense symbol analysis resembles a large radar network, which is also expensive, time-consuming and tiresome for the person scanning the radar screens. We know that the payoff of the radar net, in terms of national defense, is important. But why bother with symbol analysis? Is the increment in knowledge—about the development of colonial patterns of group identity, for instance—worth the effort involved?

Intrinsically, of course, any increment in man's knowledge that contributes to an understanding of important events and processes is useful. At the very least a symbol analysis of the colonial press would tell us something about the changing perspectives of their editors. To the extent that these perspectives reflected and helped to shape the perspectives of the politically relevant strata of colonial society, they are useful in analyzing attitude changes in eighteenth-century America.

There is another side to the use of information derived from symbol analyses. In one sense such data are quite different from the standard materials of American history: they are quantitative in nature, based on standard statistical tests of reliability and verification. The information yielded is both impersonal and repeatable, that is, an independent researcher could get similar results by following the same procedures. In another, very important sense, however, this information is not at all dissimilar from any other piece of concrete evidence used in the study of American history. Its usefulness rests upon its interpretation, upon the pattern of events and processes in which the scholar places it. Like customhouse reports on intercolonial shipping patterns, it is evidence that conscientious scholars cannot ignore.

Trend information produced by symbol analysis encourages us to consider history as a continuing process rather than as sets of discrete events in a time series. This fact bears two important implications for research. First of all, trend analyses permit us to fit single pieces of evidence into continuing patterns, giving us a better understanding of the relevance of the single bits of information as well as enriching our understanding of the patterns. In seeking to answer the question, "When did the colonists begin to perceive themselves as Americans rather than as English colonists?" it is often quite tempting to focus upon single documents or single events—occasions upon which the "Americanism" of the colonists was emphasized—and to point to these occasions as the origin of an American sense of nationality. It is an interesting fact, for instance, that documents (letters, battle reports, instructions) written in the Caribbean during the War of Jenkins' Ear frequently used the terms "Americans" and "Europeans" to differentiate colonial from English sailors and marines, but this fact must be considered not in isolation, away from its environment of other relevant information. It is necessary to compare the actual frequency of such usages with the frequency with which common terms were used to refer to colonists and Englishmen alike, and to see how these frequencies changed over time and with the tide of battle. Moreover, the importance of the fact pales if it turns out that the differential usage of nomenclature was restricted to an area of interaction limited in the number of communicators, the time period covered and geographic circumstances. Did the inhabitants of the British Isles or the North American continent adopt such terms? Or were these names like nicknames given one another by children in a summer camp— meaningful at the time, often quite graphic, but soon forgotten when the summer is over? Similarly, how *representative* of more general speech patterns are the statements cited in the writings of others who try to pinpoint in time and place the origin of American nationalism? Did such statements reflect or precede (or even create) a sense of community in the people as a whole? Or were they instances of aberrant or possibly random verbal behavior that found neither basis nor echo in the common language of the day? In sum, an assessment of widely varying points of view about the origins of American nationalism requires adequate information on long-run trends in colonial thinking, the sort of information that symbol analysis can provide.

A second implication for research is that trend data from symbol analyses help us to focus our attention upon years or months of particular importance in the development of American community awareness. If it should turn out that the period during which colonial symbol usage underwent the most radical change was the year 1763 (or, even more specifically, the early summer of that year), then we might do well to commit more of our research resources to an examination of colonial attitudes during that crucial period.

More generally speaking, symbol analysis bears yet another implication for research in the field of colonial history. The training of the top-flight historian, no less so than that of the social psychologist or the political scientist with an interest in communications research, is long and arduous, usually involving a considerable degree of specialization. Can we expect that the historian, having mastered his own trade, will turn to the vast fields of psychology and communications research for further training? There are of course some historians who will do just that. For others, however, the solution may be to encourage interdisciplinary research. The recently developed tools of the social sciences can contribute as much to the study of history as the historian can—by identifying the important and interesting problems in, say, colonial history, as well as the most relevant variables—to contemporary theory in the social sciences.

A systematic analysis of self-referent symbols in the colonial press would tell us much about patterns of nationalism in eighteenth-century America. With this view in mind I examined the news columns of four randomly selected issues per year of newspapers from each of five colonial population centers—Boston, New York, Philadelphia, Williamsburg and Charleston in South Carolina[18]—tabulating each appearance of place-name symbols (such as "Boston," "England," "the colonies," "Americans" or other names of actual places or their inhabitants) during the 41 years from 1735 to 1775. The place-name symbols of particular importance here are self-referent symbols referring collectively to either the colonists or the colonies as a single unit. The tabulation includes both direct symbols (that is, those symbols actually specifying the group or the area, such as "the colonists" or "the colonies") and indirect symbols (those that replace the specific name of the group or area with such terms as "they," "that place" and so forth).

The collective self-referent symbols are categorized in two different ways. One means is by their primary identification content: Do they denote the geographic area that later became the United States, or its population? A second means of categorization is according to the specific label, a so-called secondary symbol, that the self-referent symbols attach when identifying the primary content: Do they associate the land or its population with the British political community or with a distinctly American community? In this respect we can differentiate five groups of such symbols: (1) Symbols of explicit British common identity: "British North America," "the English colonies," "British-America," or "British colonists," "British-Americans," "English provincials"; (2) Symbols of identification with the British Crown: "His Majesty's colonies," "royal colonies" or "crown colonies," "His Majesty's subjects in America," "Royal Americans"; (3) Symbols of implicit British common identity: the "colonies" or "provinces," "our colonies in America" (only when used in articles with British datelines), "colonists" or "provincials"; (4) Symbols of implicit American common identity: the "continent" or "country," the "American colonies" or the "colonies in America," the "United Colonies," the "continentals," "American colonists"; and (5) Symbols of explicit American common identity: "America" or "North America," "Americans" or "North Americans." In this chapter I shall collapse the first three categories into a single one comprising symbols identifying the colonies and colonists as essentially British, and the last two categories into one of symbols identifying the colonial lands and population as American. Elsewhere I have considered the difference it makes if we categorize self-referent symbols according to whether they appeared in articles with American, British or other foreign datelines;[19] here I shall consider the distribution of symbols only in respect to the total image of the American community presented to the newspapers' readers.

The first point to be noted about the distribution of collective

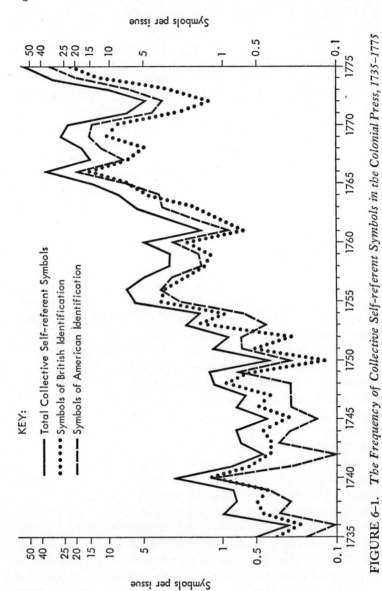

Symbols per issue

50
40
25
20
15
10
5
1
0.5
0.1

1775
1770
1765
1760
1755
1750
1745
1740
1735

KEY:

——— Total Collective Self-referent Symbols

•••••• Symbols of British Identification

– – – Symbols of American Identification

Symbols per issue

50
40
25
20
15
10
5
1
0.5
0.1

FIGURE 6-1. *The Frequency of Collective Self-referent Symbols in the Colonial Press, 1735–1775*

self-referent symbols in the press is that their salience increased dramatically in the years from 1735 to 1775 (see Figure 6–1). In the late 1730's, the newspapers as a whole paid little attention indeed to the colonies or colonists as a collective unit. The average issue contained 0.66 such symbols; that is, in every three issues of a newspaper approximately two self-referent symbols appeared. This figure represented somewhat over 4 per cent of the total number of symbols in the press referring to American place names. The average issue from 1771 to 1775 contained almost 22 collective self-referent symbols, an increase of over 3200 per cent over the 1735–1739 period. During the last five colonial years the press devoted about one-quarter of its news space to collective symbols, another quarter to symbols of place names in the colonies publishing the individual journals, and about one-half of its space to symbols of place names in other colonies. In sum, a concept that was extremely marginal in the late 1730's was quite salient by the early 1770's.

The process by which the salience of the collective concept for the colonial press increased was cyclical. As may be seen in Table 1, the number of collective self-referent symbols per issue fluctuated considerably during the 41 years from 1735 to 1775. The low points of the cycles occurred in 1736 (or possibly earlier), 1745, 1761 and 1772; the peaks were in 1740, 1756, 1769 and 1775 (or later). Two points are of interest here. First, the peaks of the cycles no less than the troughs were on increasingly higher planes as time passed. Second, in general the cycles were of increasingly shorter duration. Thus, despite fluctuations in the curve, the secular trend in the use of collective self-referent symbols was clearly climbing upward at an ever greater rate.

That the salience of the collective concept in the newspapers rose is of course no indication that the colonists were becoming ever more "nationalistic." It is possible that they could merely have been stressing their allegiance to the British political community more often. As it turns out, however, such was not the case. For the period as a whole about six in ten collective self-referent symbols (58 per cent) identified the colonies or colonists either implicitly or explicitly as American. Again the propensity to use American self-referent symbols rose: from roughly 43 per cent in

1735–1739 to about 63 per cent in 1771–1775. In no year after 1755 did less than 50 per cent of these symbols identify the land and people as American rather than British.

Collective self-referent symbols referring to the people appeared in the newspapers far less frequently than did those referring to the land. In fact the latter outnumbered the former by more than five to one. In only one year (1760) before 1765 did the average issue refer collectively to the colonists at least once; the ensuing decade found each newspaper printing an average of 3.7 such symbols, reaching a high point of 10.9 in 1775, the year in which fighting broke out between the Americans and the Redcoats.

It was not until the years after 1764 that the distinction between "His Majesty's subjects" or "British colonists" and "Americans" became a real one in the colonial press. Before then the newspapers were all but unanimous (97.1 per cent) in identifying the colonists with the British political community. By far the most popular terms during these 29 years were those identifying the colonists as subjects of the British Crown—"His Majesty's subjects," "His Majesty's colonists," and, after 1756, the regimental name "Royal Americans"—which together comprised 108 (or 79.4 per cent) of the total of 136 symbols. From 1764 to 1775 almost six in ten (57.0 per cent) of the collective self-referent symbols identified the colonial people as American rather than as British. But even during this period the relative paucity of symbols resulted in wide fluctuations in the distribution of symbols from year to year. If the data for these 12 years are fitted to a linear trend line, however, a clear picture of changing perceptions emerges. The average increase in the use of symbols identifying the colonists as American was 2.3 percentage points per year. The threshold of self-conscious or explicit "Americanism," an imaginary 50 per cent line, was crossed in 1770, although it is true that there were two years before that date when the curve was above the 50 per cent level, and at least two years after 1770 when it was below the halfway mark. (By way of comparison, the linear trend line for symbols identifying the land as American rose 0.8 percentage points per year from 1735 to 1775 and crossed the 50 per cent threshold in 1762, thus suggesting that the perception of the land as being a part of an American rather than a British community clearly preceded a similar perception of the inhabitants of that land.)

As far as newspapers from the individual colonies are concerned, there were some marked differences in their presentation of an image of the American community. The New England prints—the Tory *Massachusetts Gazette* from 1735 to 1764 and, after its level of "Americanism" slipped somewhat, the patriot *Boston Gazette* from 1765 to 1775—led in this respect; the journals of the middle colonies (the *New-York Weekly Journal*, the *New-York Mercury* and the *Pennsylvania Gazette*) lagged until the 1760's; and the southern newspapers (the *Virginia Gazette* and the *South-Carolina Gazette*), after an initial period of rather high awareness of an American political community, seemed to draw closer in their symbol usage to the British political community in the two decades between 1745 and 1764. With the passage of time the individual newspapers not only became more aware of the collective concept, as indicated by the inclusion of an ever larger number of collective self-referent symbols in their columns, but their choice of symbols tended to become quite steady and congruent. Not until the early 1760's, however, did the newspapers of the middle colonies join with the New England prints in a symbol revolution that preceded the outbreak of fighting by more than a decade.

These findings are suggestive of the value of symbol analysis for putting events or specific statements of individuals into a larger time perspective. It becomes clear, for instance, that the "Americanism" that appeared during the War of Jenkins' Ear was not without precedent. Nor did a spirit of American nationalism strike the colonists like a bolt from the blue during the French and Indian War. That spirit was already there. Similarly, the newspapers, which at once reflected and helped to shape the images of the politically relevant strata of colonial society, revealed an upsurge in sentiments of American community during the 1760's. The point, however, is not that such a trend emerged for the first time during the conflicts of that decade. The trend already existed. The crises of the 1760's merely accelerated the pace of that trend toward symbolic separation from the British political community. In short, the changing processes of symbolic identification in the American colonies seem to have been neither revolutionary nor evolutionary in the strictest sense of these terms. Rather, like other learning situations, they were both gradual and fitful, with a few periods of extremely rapid advances (or breakthroughs) interspersed with other periods of more or less mild relapses. Symbol analysis gives us a useful means to examine this process by which the colonists learned to be Americans.

Notes

NOTE: Without wishing to burden them with responsibility for my remarks, I should like to thank Professors Karl W. Deutsch of Harvard University, Edmund S. Morgan of Yale University, Louis P. Galambos of Johns Hopkins University, and Eugene C. McCreary of Lafayette College for their helpful comments on previous versions of this paper; and the Carnegie Corporation for its generous support of this project.

1. James Truslow Adams, *The March of Democracy: The Rise of the Union* (New York and London: 1932), p. 54; cf. pp. 74–75; Michael Kraus, *Intercolonial Aspects of American Culture on the Eve of the Revolution, With Special Reference to the Northern Towns* (New York: 1928); Oscar Handlin, *This Was America: True Accounts of People and Places, Manners and Customs, as Recorded by European Travelers to the Western Shore in the Eighteenth, Nineteenth, and Twentieth Centuries* (Cambridge: 1949), p. 7; Howard H. Peckham, *The Colonial Wars, 1689–1762* (Chicago and London, 1964), pp. 219–21.

2. Albert Harkness, Jr., "Americanism and Jenkins' Ear," *Mississippi Valley Historical Review*, XXXVII (1950), 61–90, esp. 89–90.

3. Max Savelle, *Seeds of Liberty: The Genesis of the American Mind* (New York: 1948), pp. 555, 561.

4. Carl Lotus Becker, *Beginnings of the American People* (Boston, New York, Chicago: 1915), pp. 191–193. In his brilliant essay, "The Spirit of '76," Becker found that the beginning of the American quarrel with Britain was in 1763, but later noted that, as much as his protagonist, Jeremiah Wynkoop, "admired England as the home of political liberty, he was thoroughly American." Carl Becker, J. M. Clark and William E. Dodd, *The Spirit of '76, and Other Essays* (Washington, D. C.: 1927), pp. 10, 14. Cf. also Lawrence Henry Gipson, "The American Revolution as an Aftermath of the Great War for the Empire, 1754–1763," *Political Science Quarterly*, LXV (1950), 86–104.

5. Paul A. Varg, "The Advent of Nationalism, 1758–1776," *American Quarterly*, XVI (1964), 169–181; Varg emphasizes that these sentiments did not begin to crystallize until the 1760's.

6. Allan Nevins, *The American States During and After the Revolution, 1775–1789* (New York: 1924), p. 544; John C. Miller, *Origins of the*

American Revolution (Boston: 1949), p. 22; Carl Bridenbaugh, *Cities in Revolt: Urban Life in America, 1743–1776* (New York: 1955), p. 424; Edmund S. Morgan, *The Birth of the Republic, 1763–89* (Chicago: 1956), p. 101; Bernhard Knollenberg, *Origin of the American Revolution, 1759–1766* (rev. ed., New York: 1961), p. 218.

7. Kenneth C. Wheare, "Federalism and the Making of Nations," in Arthur W. Macmahon, ed., *Federalism, Mature and Emergent* (Garden City, N. Y.: 1955), pp. 33–35; Edward Frank Humphrey, *Nationalism and Religion in America, 1774–1789* (Boston: 1924), pp. 2–4; Esmond Wright, *Fabric of Freedom, 1763–1800* (New York: 1961), pp. 20, 241.

8. Alexander L. George, "Quantitative and Qualitative Approaches to Content Analysis," in Ithiel de Sola Pool, ed., *Trends in Content Analysis* (Urbana, Ill.: 1959), p. 8.

9. Harold D. Lasswell, Daniel Lerner and Ithiel de Sola Pool, *The Comparative Study of Symbols: An Introduction,* Hoover Institute Studies, Ser. C, No. 1. (Stanford, Calif.: 1952), p. 21. They continue: "It is a matter of style when we describe the vocabulary, enunciation or gestures of a speaker; or when we describe the grammatical forms, word choice, and sentence length of a writer" (p. 22). Cf. also Mary McCarthy, in an interview by Elizabeth Niebuhr, *The Paris Review,* No. 27 (Spring 1962), p. 79.

10. More suited to such a task is Alexander George's "qualitative" content analysis, which is interested less in the quantification than in the appearance of key words and phrases, or Philip J. Stone's "General Inquirer" computerized method, which is particularly suitable for the study of psychological variables. See Alexander George, "Quantitative and Qualitative Approaches to Content Analysis," in Ithiel de Sola Pool, ed. *Trends in Content Analysis* (Urbana, Ill.: 1959), pp. 7–32; and Philip J. Stone, Robert F. Bales, J. Zvi Namenwirth and Daniel Ogilvie, "The General Inquirer: A Computer System for Content Analysis and Retrieval Based on the Sentence as a Unit of Information," *Behavioral Science,* VII (1962), 484–498.

11. Cf. Frederick Mosteller and David L. Wallace, *Inference and Disputed Authorship: The Federalist* (Reading, Mass., Palo Alto, Calif., and London: 1964).

12. Lasswell, Lerner and Pool, *op. cit.,* p. 51; italics in the original.

13. For a discussion of the value and limitations of newspapers for analyzing colonial attitudes, and of some of the problems encountered in content analyzing them, see Richard L. Merritt, "Public Opinion in Colonial America: Content Analyzing the Colonial Press," *Public Opinion Quarterly,* XXVII (1963), 356–371.

14. Lasswell, Lerner and Pool, *op. cit.,* pp. 45–63.

15. *Ibid.,* p. 29.

16. For examples of such an error, see Warren H. Goodman, "The Origins of the War of 1812: A Survey of Changing Interpretations," *Mississippi Valley Historical Review,* XXVIII (1941), 171–186.

17. Independent samples of four and twelve issues per year for ten different years were compared, using the nonparametric "Mann-Whitney U Test." In nine of the ten cases, the tests indicated that no significant differences between the two samples existed. More properly speaking, in nine of ten cases (significant at the 0.05 level for a two-tailed test)

the test did not reject a null hypothesis asserting that there was no significant difference between the sample of four and the independent sample of twelve issues.

18. The newspapers were: *The Boston News-Letter* (issues from 1735 to 1775) and *The Boston Gazette, and Country Journal* (1762–1775); *The New-York Weekly Journal* (1735–1751) and *The New-York Mercury* (1752–1775); *The Pennsylvania Gazette* (1735–1775); the various *Virginia Gazettes* (under William Parks from 1736 to 1750, and under William Hunter and his successors from 1751 to 1775); and *The South-Carolina Gazette* (1735–1775).

19. See Richard L. Merritt, *Symbols of American Community, 1735–1775* (New Haven: 1966).

✸ 7 ✸

Lee Benson

AN APPRAISAL OF BEARD'S DESIGN OF
PROOF AND METHOD

Although Beard's most acute insights relate to the unequal power of men to influence opinions and control decisions, he offered almost no evidence to support them. He asserted that men played different roles in the sequence of events that led to the adoption of the Constitution because they occupied different positions in the American social structure, but he did little more than sketch the sequence and suggest the attributes that gave them unequal power. For this set of claims, his treatment was not even "frankly fragmentary." Moreover, he did not indicate how they might be tested.

Beard's main preoccupation becomes evident when we recognize that his design of proof and his method apply only to his claims about the relationships between ideas and interests. They did not actually permit him to test those claims, however, for they both rest upon logically untenable assumptions.

Lee Benson is Professor of History at the University of Pennsylvania. He is author of *The Concept of Jacksonian Democracy: New York as a Test Case* and *Merchants, Farmers and Railroads*.

Reprinted from *Turner and Beard: American Historical Writing Reconsidered* (New York: The Free Press of Glencoe, 1960), pp. 151–174, by permission of the author and the publisher. © 1960 by The Free Press, a Corporation.

The Logical Fallacy in Beard's Design of Proof

Beard's design of proof required him to establish two variable relationships. That is, he proposed first to classify men "as economic beings dependent upon definite modes and processes of gaining a livelihood," and then to ascertain on which "side" of the Constitutional issue they "are to be found." To avoid misunderstanding, a quotation from Beard's first chapter will be repeated here: If men in the same economic group "were equally divided on the matter of adoption or rejection—it would then become apparent that the Constitution had no ascertainable relation to economic groups or classes, but was the product of some abstract causes remote from the chief business of life—gaining a livelihood." But, if "substantially all" members of "groups of personal property interests" and "their professional associates" were pro-Constitution, and "substantially all or the major portion of the opposition came from the nonslaveholding farmers and the debtors—would it not be pretty conclusively demonstrated that our fundamental law was not the product of an abstraction known as 'the whole people,' but of a group of economic interests which must have expected beneficial results from its adoption?" A short answer to that long question is—No.

SELF-INTEREST AND POLITICAL BEHAVIOR

Unless Beard had first demonstrated that perceived self-interest is the only determinant of political behavior, his design of proof was logically untenable. Apart from other considerations, it was logically untenable because it *assumed* what Beard proposed to *demonstrate*.

Beard had no basis for assuming that conscious self-interest is the only aspect of class position that influences political behavior. Apparently, the unresolved dualism in his thought led him to treat the direct effects of self-interest as though they were synonymous with the subtle, complicated, and indirect effects of men's being "dependent upon definite modes and processes of gaining a livelihood." In other words, he confused the concepts of "interest group" and "social class." Certainly, Seligman's version of the economic interpretation of history, which Beard regarded as "nearly axiomatic," did not postulate a direct, one-to-one relationship between self-interest and political behavior. Seligman warned against the fallacies inherent in economic determinism and criticized Loria's "landed" application of it.[1] Thus, even if Beard's description of the divisions of opinion among groups on the Constitution were accurate, he was still logically required to offer additional evidence for his claims about men's motives; he could not infer them from the data required by his design of proof.

IS CLASS POSITION THE ONLY DETERMINANT
OF POLITICAL BEHAVIOR?

The fallacious assumption that self-interest is the only aspect of class position that influences political behavior does not warrant the further assumption that class position is the only determinant of political behavior. Beard revealed the fallacy in his design of proof by making vague, scattered references to the political effects of membership in ethnic and religious groups and of partisan affiliations antedating the Constitutional conflict.[2] If class position were the only determinant of political behavior in 1787–1788, other factors became entirely irrelevant to his interpretation. But, for example, if men's opinions on the Constitution were influenced by their membership in certain ethnic groups, Beard could not test his hypothesis by restricting his attention to their class position.

Stated in somewhat formal terms, Beard's design of proof is logically fallacious because it assumes that the relationship between two variables can be discovered without considering the possible influence of other variables. Or, in positive terms, to discover the relationships between opinion on the Constitution and economic class, it is necessary to consider the effect of other variables (factors) that might also have influenced opinion (e.g., membership in ethnic groups, membership—or lack of it—in religious groups, previous partisan affiliations, level of education). In short, spurious relationships *may* result if attention is restricted to two variables. Two examples—one hypothetical, one substantive —help to clarify the point.

A Potentially Verifiable Hypothesis. To be potentially verifiable, a hypothesis must satisfy at least one set of data that are logically relevant to its claims. (Of course, the likelihood of verifying a hypothesis increases as we see that it satisfies additional sets of relevant data.) In my opinion, voting behavior during the contests for delegates to the state ratifying conventions is the best indicator of men's opinions about the Constitution. Thus, we should regard Beard's hypothesis about why men favored, or opposed, the Constitution as potentially verifiable, if we find it consonant with voting statistics that have been systematically collected, organized, and analyzed.

Suppose we take New York as a test case. To support a judgment that Beard's hypothesis is potentially verifiable, we must show that members of the same class tended strongly to vote for the same party, despite their membership in groups identified by some other attribute than economic class, e.g., small debtor-farmers voted Antifederalist, even though they belonged to different ethnic groups such as Scotch-Irish, English, Dutch, and German. And, to take the same example, if we could show that small debtor-farmers voted Antifederalist irrespective of their membership in groups identified by *any* attribute other than economic class, we would increase the likelihood that Beard's hypothesis was verifiable. No matter how many attributes we consider, the logic of the procedure remains the same. To simplify the example, therefore, we can restrict attention to economic classes and ethnic groups and assume that we have the required data.

To test Beard's hypothesis, we would examine the data to learn the voting behavior of each economic class in each ethnic group, e.g., small debtor-farmers whose ancestry was English, Scotch-Irish, Dutch, and German. Put another way, depending upon the precise nature of our data, in each ethnic group, we would try to learn the voting behavior of men who belonged to the different classes, e.g., men of English ancestry who were small debtor-farmers, landed proprietors, large holders of personal property, merchants, mechanics.

To conclude that Beard's hypothesis was potentially verifiable, we must find a common voting pattern among members of each class. For example, we would not only have to find that most small debtor-farmers voted Antifederalist, but that roughly the same proportion of them tended to vote Antifederalist in each ethnic group. (To simplify the discussion, I am imposing the unrealistic requirement that members of a specified class vote alike in every ethnic group; this enables us to ignore the problem of deciding how much variation among ethnic groups is consonant with Beard's claims about class voting.) Similarly, we would have to find that, in each ethnic group, large holders of personal property gave overwhelming Federalist majorities. The hypothetical table below shows the kind of data that would support the conclusion that Beard's claims were potentially verifiable.

Hypothetical Table: Voting by Class and Ethnic Group,
New York, 1788

	Scotch-Irish		English		Dutch		German	
	Fed. %	Anti. %	Fed. %	Anti. %	Fed. %	Anti. %	Fed. %	Anti. %
Debtor-Farmer	20	80	20	80	20	80	20	80
Landed Proprietor	40	60	40	60	40	60	40	60
Mechanic	75	25	75	25	75	25	75	25
Large Holder, Personal Property	85	15	85	15	85	15	85	15

Suppose we found, however, that small debtor-farmers of Scotch-Irish ancestry held opposite opinions on the Constitution from their English counterparts. And suppose we found that the Scotch-Irish voted strongly Antifederalist irrespective of class, the English voted strongly Federalist, also irrespective of class. Finally, let us suppose that the same homogeneous voting behavior characterized all ethnic groups, i.e., members of the group tended strongly to vote alike, irrespective of class position. We would then be forced to conclude that, insofar as we had tested it, Beard's hypothesis about why men favored or opposed the Constitution was invalid.

I have been trying to show that Beard could not test his hypothesis by restricting attention to the relationships between the two variables, opinion on the Constitution and economic class. *At the minimum*, he was logically required to consider the effects upon men's opinions of one other possible influence, such as their membership in ethnic groups.

Perhaps the logical fallacy in his design of proof is best pointed up by this paradox: We might have to conclude that his hypothesis was invalid, even though we found that most small debtor-farmers voted Antifederalist and most large holders of personal property voted Federalist. In discussing this paradox, let us assume that the following statements are true: The proportion of men who belonged to specified economic classes varied widely according to ethnic group; e.g., a large majority of the Scotch-Irish, but only a small minority of the English, were debtor-farmers. The reverse was true of large holders of personal property, i.e., they constituted a small minority of the Scotch-Irish, a large majority of the English. Irrespective of class, the Scotch-Irish voted strongly Antifederalist, the English voted strongly Federalist. Our final assumption: the large majority of small debtor-farmers were Scotch-Irish; in all other classes, the large majority were not Scotch-Irish.

Under those conditions, although it would be literally true to say that voting patterns showed class differences, it would be thoroughly misleading. For, despite their different class positions, members of the same ethnic group voted alike. Since most small debtor-farmers were Scotch-Irish, as a class they necessarily voted Antifederalist. But the spurious nature of the relationship becomes apparent when we realize that it seems to exist only because of the ethnic composition of the class. Voting behavior was not related to class but to ethnic group; the relationship between opinion and class was a spurious one because it disappeared when another factor (or variable) was considered.

Unfortunately, largely because Beard's design of proof has gone unchallenged to date, the information required by our hypothetical example has never been collected. Thus, to show that it may be possible to collect the information necessary to test his hypothesis about why men favored or opposed the Constitution, as well as to demonstrate further the fallacy in his design of proof, a substantive example from another period in American history will now be given.

Testing Claims about Economic Class and Voting Behavior.
Following Beard's lead, historians of New York politics have
claimed that party divisions in the state essentially followed class
lines. To support their hypotheses, they also used a two-variable
design of proof. But when I examined data about men's membership in groups defined by attributes other than class (e.g., ethnic
and religious), with few exceptions, the alleged relationships became either nonexistent or spurious." [3]

For example, in testing the claim that, during the 1840's, urban
workers in New York strongly supported the Democrats, I considered the possibility that the overwhelming majority of workers
belonged to religious and ethnic groups whose members voted
Democratic *independently of their economic class position.*
Under those conditions, a strong, positive relationship between
workers and the Democratic party might turn out to be spurious;
i.e., their affiliation with the Democrats would be related to their
religious and ethnic affiliations, rather than to their class position.
And, after the relevant data were collected, ordered, and analyzed, that is what I found. With few exceptions, in each economic class, voting tended to vary strongly with membership in
ethnic and religious group, previous political allegiance, local conditions (and numerous other influences). One specific example illustrates the point.

In 1844, about 95 per cent of *Catholic* Irish workers voted
Democratic and about 90 per cent of *Protestant* Irish workers
voted Whig. Yet, because the religious and ethnic groups that
voted overwhelmingly for the Democrats constituted so large a
proportion of the urban workers, the statement that "most workers" voted Democratic is both literally true and completely misleading. They voted that way, not because they were workers,
but because they were Irish Catholics (or members of certain
other groups) and also happened to be workers. Contrary to the
economic determinist interpretation that stemmed from Beard,
during the 1840's, political divisions in New York related more
closely to ethnic and religious groupings than to economic class.

APPRAISING BEARD'S DESIGN OF PROOF

From the examples given above, we can see that neither an economic determinist nor an economic interpretation of politics can be tested by restricting attention to two variables. Beard's design of proof made it impossible for him, therefore, to draw any reasonable inferences about the relationships between class position and opinion on the Constitution. Even if he had devised an adequate system for classifying economic groups, and even if the data he required had been arranged systematically and accurately, it could only be said with confidence that his claims might be correct—and then again, they might not be. When we try to discover the relationships between any two variables, our design of proof must permit us to consider the possible influence of *at least* one other variable. And the more variables we consider, the greater the likelihood of our verifying, or discrediting, a hypothesis. (For convenience, the procedure outlined above will hereafter be referred to as *multivariate analysis*.)[4]

A balanced appraisal of Beard's work, however, must take this consideration into account: In 1913, no useful models existed to inspire him as he tried to devise a design of proof for hypotheses about mass behavior. Here, as elsewhere, he contributed significantly to historiography by recognizing the existence of a problem and beginning the job of solving it. As American history demonstrates, in all fields of endeavor, it is usually the second or third wave of settlers who reap the harvest for which pioneers have broken the ground. And Beard, it is worth remembering, was a pioneer in what he then called "scientific history."

The Logical Fallacy in Beard's Method

Now, if it were possible to have an economic biography of all those connected with its [the Constitution's] framing and adoption—perhaps about 160,000 men altogether,—the materials for scientific analysis and classification would be available.

Since he could not compile those biographies, Beard devised a method that he believed yielded the data required by his design of proof. He divided the 160,000 men into three types, depending upon the roles they played in the framing and adoption of the Constitution: (1) the few who actually framed the Constitution; (2) the somewhat larger number of delegates to the state ratifying conventions; (3) the mass of voters who elected the delegates. He assumed that in all three categories of political activity, men who belonged to the same economic class tended strongly to take the same position on the Constitution, e.g., that roughly the same proportion of large holders of personal property favored the Constitution, whether they were delegates to the Constitutional Convention, delegates to the state conventions, or voters. Thus, according to Beard's assumption, if we learn the group divisions among the delegates to the Constitutional Convention, we can infer the group divisions among the voters.

In his most carefully developed chapter, Beard presented short "economic biographies"—admittedly sketchy and based largely on secondary sources—of the fifty-five delegates who attended the Philadelphia Convention. He conceded that a valid test of his claims also required collection of biographical data about men assigned to the other two categories of political activity. For example, in a later chapter, he observed that:

It would be fortunate if we had a description of each of the state [ratifying] conventions similar to that made [by him] of the Philadelphia Convention; but such a description would require a study of the private economy of several hundred men, with considerable scrutiny. And the results of such a search would be on the whole less fruitful than those secured by the study of the Philadelphia Convention, because so many members of the state-ratifying bodies were obscure persons of whom biography records nothing and whose property holdings do not appear in any of the documents that have come down to us.[5]

Having these data only for Pennsylvania, Beard attempted to buttress his findings with materials "drawn from incomplete sources." For the most part, the sources were secondary works influenced strongly by Turner's adaptation of Loria's "free land" theory of American (and world) history.[6]

Despite the obvious imprecision and fragmentary nature of the data, Beard concluded that collective biographies of the Founding Fathers at Philadelphia and of the delegates to the Pennsylvania ratifying convention—the only one that he studied—supported his claims about the framing and adoption of the Constitution. He based this conclusion on the assumption that his method of compiling collective biographies of men appointed or elected to political assemblies enabled him to discover the class division of opinion. This assumption is logically fallacious. Even if he had compiled accurate and fairly complete collective biographies of delegates to the Constitutional and state ratifying conventions, and even if he had used what we have called multivariate analysis to discover the divisions of opinion among them, he would still have lacked justification for drawing inferences about the class divisions of opinion in the country at large.

DID MADISON INSPIRE THE COLLECTIVE BIOGRAPHY METHOD

Where did Beard get the idea that the compilation of collective biographies of delegates to political assemblies would enable him to discover the divisions of opinion among groups or classes? I suggest that Madison's *Federalist* No. 10 inspired him. At any rate, he based the procedure of compiling collective biographies on the same assumptions that Madison made in the section of that paper dealing with "Legislation by Special Interests"—to use Beard's caption from his edition of *The Enduring Federalist.*

Madison warned that unless a well-designed government system were created to control the "effects" of faction, the will of "the most numerous party . . . must be expected to prevail" in legislative assemblies:

No man is allowed to be a judge in his own cause, because his interests would certainly bias his judgment, and, not improbably, corrupt his integrity. With equal, nay with greater reason, a body of men are unfit to be both judges and parties at the same time; yet what are many of the most important acts of legislation, but so many judicial determinations, not indeed concerning the rights of single persons, but concerning the rights of large bodies of citizens? *And what are the different classes of legislators but advocates and parties to the causes which they determine* [italics added]? Is a law proposed concerning private debts? It is a question to which the creditors are parties on one side and the debtors on the other. Justice ought to hold the balance between them. Yet the parties are, and must be, themselves the judges;

and the most numerous party, or, in other words, the most powerful faction must be expected to prevail. [A number of similar examples follow.] [7]

Whether or not Madison actually inspired Beard's method, their assumptions were identical. For, if it were true that "the different classes of legislators [are] but advocates and parties to the causes which they determine," class divisions of opinion in legislative assemblies might accurately reflect class divisions among the population at large. We have only to substitute the Philadelphia and state ratifying conventions for Madison's legislative assemblies and the parallels with Beard's assumptions and procedures become apparent. But, unless we accept the assumption of economic determinism that all members of the same social class hold the same opinion on issues that affect them, the collective biography method, as used by Beard and implied by Madison, is logically untenable.

Do Public Assemblies Represent the Electorate in Microcosm? Contrary to Madison, delegates (or legislators) belong simultaneously to many different groups (e.g., ethnic, religious, urban). And their ideas of "justice" do influence their opinions—at least to some extent on some occasions. Not all men who belong to the same class or group take the same position on an issue, even if they all perceive that it serves their individual interests. A Liberal Republic is not the same as a Corporate State, and men who belong to one class or group may represent men who belong to classes or groups other than their own. Failure to recognize this possibility, or to weigh it properly, led Beard to devise a method that can demonstrate only how members of public assemblies vote on issues.

The fallacy in Beard's method can be seen most clearly by examining his treatment of the Pennsylvania ratifying convention. Let us make three arbitrary assumptions: (1) membership in an economic group was the only factor that influenced opinion on the Constitution; (2) his system of economic classification was adequate; (3) his information about the delegates' economic interests was accurate and comprehensive. The convention voted 46 to 23 in favor of the Constitution and Beard believed he could accurately classify thirty-eight delegates who favored the Constitution and eighteen who opposed it. His table is given below:

[*Pennsylvania Ratifying Convention—Vote by Economic Group*]

	For the Constitution	Against
Merchants	4	1
Lawyers	8	1
Doctors	2	—
Clergymen	2	—
Farmers	10	13
Capitalists	12	3
Total Classifiable	38	18

Commenting upon his tabulation, Beard argued: "When all allowance for error [in the data] is made, the result is highly significant and bears out the general conclusion that the Constitution was a reflex of personality rather than realty interests." [8] But that conclusion rests on the assumption that the Pennsylvania convention represented the electorate in microcosm, i.e., that the delegates accurately reflected the opinions of the groups to which Beard assigned them. Is that assumption warranted?

For example, can we assume that the five merchant delegates constituted a representative sample of all Pennsylvania merchants? Other considerations aside, the convention delegates were elected to represent *counties*, not *economic classes or interest groups*. Thus, men who happened to belong to the same economic class or group might have been elected to take different positions on the Constitution.

Beard, it should be noted, did not challenge Orin Libby's claim that the "delegates of all the Federal counties . . . [with one possible exception] clearly represented the sentiments of their constituents in their vote in the Convention," and that the "opposition [Antifederalist] section of Pennsylvania, as indicated by the votes of the delegates in convention, seems to have very generally coincided with the avowed sentiments of the majority of the people of the section." [9] If Libby is right, therefore, we do not discover anything about the class divisions of opinion when we learn that the Constitution was favored by 80 per cent of the "merchants" (four of five) at the Convention and by 43 per cent of the "farmers" (ten of twenty-three). It is possible that they reflected accurately the divisions of opinion among all Pennsylvania merchants and farmers; it is also possible that they did not. Since Pennsylvania was overwhelmingly agrarian, Beard's table indicates only that the proportion of delegates at the Convention who were not farmers exceeded their proportion in the population.

Even if we assumed that factors associated with membership in economic groups were the only determinants of opinion, it is still possible to conceive of instances in which Beard's tabulation would misrepresent group divisions on the issue.

Suppose that a small minority of merchants throughout the state favored the Constitution. But, suppose further, that those few merchants were joined by members of other groups favorable to the Constitution, and thus, together, they were able to elect the candidates whom they nominated. In that event, divisions among the mercantile delegates at the Pennsylvania ratifying convention would give a distorted picture of divisions among Pennsylvania merchants generally. For present purposes, it does not matter whether this actually happened; the point is that it could have happened. We must demonstrate, not assume, that members of an elected or appointed public body form a representative sample of a population and accurately reflect its views. But once we know the group divisions of opinion among the population, compilation of the collective biographies of legislators becomes superfluous. At best, it can tell us only what we already know.

The same line of argument applies to the Philadelphia Convention. Beard may have been correct in claiming that the delegates identified themselves with particular economic groups, and that they acted as representatives and accurately reflected the views of those groups. It does not follow, of course, that all *representatives* of a group were actually *members* of that group. Moreover, they may have had diversified interests which made them difficult to classify by the criterion of their occupation or property. Historians are not entitled, therefore, to assume that the compilation of economic biographies automatically reveals which delegates represented what groups at Philadelphia (or at any other convention), or that divisions among delegates assigned by historians to one group accurately reflected divisions among the members of that group. By following Beard's own line of argument about the process of gaining power, we can suppose that a small minority of a specified group may have been able to get its representatives appointed and thereby to prevent the view of the majority from being expressed at the Convention.

In summary: Even if we assume that nothing but conscious self-interest influenced opinions on the Constitution, Beard's method of collective biography cannot provide a short cut to the goal of discovering the group divisions of opinion—no matter how systematically and accurately it is followed.

And yet, it is only fair to say that Beard significantly contributed to the development and application of quantitative methods to historical materials. When we view his work in perspective, we can see that he was trying to find sampling techniques that would facilitate the systematic analysis of group behavior. Beard did not reach his goal, but pioneers rarely do.

RECENT CRITICISMS OF BEARD'S METHOD

Although, in recent years, historians have sharply criticized Beard's use of the method of collective biography, they have not advanced beyond him. Far from questioning his assumptions, they have accepted the essential validity of the method, as he used it. Taken together, they have criticized him on three grounds: (1) his data were inaccurate; (2) his categories of economic groups were inadequate; (3) most important of all, his method, properly used, yielded data that discredited his claims.

Since Forrest McDonald based his critique of Beard's thesis largely upon data gathered by the collective biography method, his assessments of Beard's findings and procedures can illustrate recent criticisms in their most developed and detailed form.[10]

Interest Groups and Voting Behavior. As I read Beard, he wanted to locate men in the social and cultural structure that resulted from the "modes and processes" by which men gained their "livelihood[s]" during the 1780's. To achieve his objective, he tried to devise an index of social class based upon the criteria of wealth, occupation, status, and geographic location.

Convinced that Beard's system of identifying and grouping men was inadequate, Professor McDonald proposed to replace it with a "new system of categories of interest groups," composed of "at least twenty basic occupational groups" and "six basic forms of capital." McDonald would carry the process of atomizing American society even further, for "most of the occupational groups and all the forms of capital may be divided into two to seventy-five subdivisions." Once the requisite data were brought "within the framework of the new system of categories of interest groups presented here [in his book], some assessment may be made of the role of economic forces in the contest over the Constitution." [11] But, in my opinion, if historians abandoned Beard's inadequate system, only to accept the one proposed by McDonald, they still would not be able to assess "the role of economic forces in the contest over the Constitution."

As we have already seen, McDonald accepted Beard's design of proof which rests upon economic determinist assumptions. And, to understate the case, when he proposes to arrange men in an extremely large number of groups with extremely narrow interests, McDonald comes no closer than Beard to a system of classification that would help historians to discover the relationships between social class and political opinion. His "new system," designed to sharpen the theory of economic interpretation, would actually distort it into a theory of atomistic egoism. For McDonald's system derives from the crude version of economic determinism that assumes men behave primarily as members of interest groups that keep a profit-and-loss account of their feelings and calculate the cash value of their political actions.

Conceivably, in the study of some types of political problems, a system similar to the one proposed by McDonald might be appropriate. For example, it might be used to study the history of a tariff bill which directly, immediately, and seriously affected a wide range of narrowly based interest groups, e.g., producers of beet sugar, pottery, steel.[12] From my own work in the politics of railroad regulation, however, I am inclined to believe that, even under those conditions, cash value calculations would at best determine the voting behavior of only a substantial minority of the rank and file members of those groups. On the other hand, such calculations might determine the voting behavior of most of the leaders of those groups.[13] In dealing with problems of this type, therefore, we could profitably use the kind of system that McDonald proposed.

But, whether they are violent or "peaceable," political

revolutions are radically different from battles by pressure groups over tariffs and railroad regulation. Thus, the large number and specific kinds of categories of interest groups, which might be used to study the Smoot-Hawley Tariff and the Interstate Commerce Act, would be grossly inappropriate in a study of the Constitutional revolution.[14] When the system of government of a country is at stake, when fundamental ideas about what constitutes the Good State in the Good Society are in conflict, economic self-interest is only one of many considerations that influence men's opinions and actions. In short, historians can regard ideology as a direct product of self-interest, only by clinging to economic determinist fallacies which, at this late date, need no further exposure.

Ideology always cuts across the lines of interest groups, particularly in a crisis. As a result, some men whose "interests" sharply conflict find themselves in agreement on matters more important to them, or united against other men with whom they have more fundamental conflicts, or both. In studying the battle over the Constitution, we are likely to progress further if we group men, not according to their "economic interests," but according to their social and cultural characteristics (defined by such criteria as class, ethnic group, religious group, residence, education), their formal and informal organizations (e.g., Masonic Order, Order of Cincinnati, political factions), their values, their beliefs, their symbols, their sense of identity.

In general, during the 1780's, with whom did men identify? With whom did they regard themselves as being in conflict? In other words, which side were men for? Which side were they against? With whom were they identified by others? When we learn the answers to these questions, when we learn whom men referred to when they spoke of "us" and "them," we have excellent criteria for classification.

The argument can be summarized briefly: In studying the Constitutional revolution, the problem is not to devise a system of classification based primarily on narrow interest groups that can be precisely defined. The problem is to devise one based on the "broad symbolic groups"—to borrow Daniel Bell's illuminating phrase[15]—that the men of the 1780's knew existed, even though they would have not been able to define them precisely or say exactly whom they included.

As a solution to the problem, Beard's system was seriously inadequate. Yet, with all its deficiencies in conception and execution, it at least pointed in the right direction; that is, it was based upon broad symbolic groups, such as inland "small farmers" and large-scale "landed proprietors." In contrast, the system advocated by his critic would lead historians astray. For if they followed McDonald and used narrowly-based interest groups as guide lines to study the Constitutional revolution, they would march backward and resume the search for "Economic Man."

Did McDonald Advance Beyond Beard? Critical of Beard's categories of delegates to the Philadelphia and state conventions, McDonald proposed new ones and set about gathering the data needed to fill them out. Fortunately for our purposes, his analysis of the Pennsylvania ratifying convention compares directly with Beard's use of the collective biography. McDonald's table, reproduced below, summarized his discussion of "how the delegates lined up for and against ratification, considered from the point of view of their occupations and from the point of view of their investments and security holdings." [16]

Anyone who has compiled the collective biography of a public assembly will appreciate how much work that short table represents, as well as the tremendous amount of work that must have gone into all of McDonald's tables for the Philadelphia and state conventions. Arguing that his categories were more realistic and his data more accurate than Beard's, he claimed to have discredited Beard's findings about the group divisions of opinion in Pennsylvania. Far from dividing along the economic lines, "the delegates on the two sides held about the same amounts of the same kinds of property, and they were engaged in similar occupations." According to McDonald, Pennsylvania was not a unique case, and, he believed, his data for all the conventions demonstrated that "on all counts, then, Beard's thesis is entirely incompatible with the facts." [17]

But once it is recognized that public assemblies cannot be treated as the electorate in microcosm, it becomes clear that McDonald's data no more discredited Beard's claims than Beard's data

[*Pennsylvania Ratifying Convention—Voting by
Interest Groups*]

Economic Classification	Voting Yea		Voting Nay	
	No.	Per Cent	No.	Per Cent
Occupation:				
Merchant	1	2.2	1	4.3
Tradesman	4	8.7	1	4.3
Manufacturing Capitalist	6	13.0	7	30.4
Lawyer	6	13.0	1	4.3
Physician	2	4.3	—	—
Clergyman	2	4.3	1	4.3
Miscellaneous	9	19.6	6	26.0
Farmer	16	34.8	6	26.0
Total	46	100.0	23	100.0
Investments in:				
Commerce	6	13.0	2	8.7
Manufacturing	8	17.4	8	34.8
Vacant Lands	11	23.9	8	34.8
Securities	23	50.0	17	73.9
One or more of the above	39	84.7	21	91.3
Security holdings:	[*dollars*]		[*dollars*]	
Combined, all delegates	67,666		70,852	
Average per holder	2,942		4,167	
Mean per holder	846		1,460	
Average, all delegates	1,471		3,080	

had originally supported them. Suppose we ignore McDonald's commitment to the assumption that only self-interest influences opinion. If we learn that literally one out of two, rather than four out of five, merchants at the Pennsylvania convention voted for the Constitution, can we then conclude that, as a group, the merchants of the state were equally divided on the issue? Can we credibly conclude from the table that 80 per cent of the *members* of his "Tradesman" category favored the Constitution and 20 per cent opposed it? To ask these questions is to answer them. Like his predecessors who had essentially copied Beard's method while trying to discredit his study, McDonald did an enormous amount of work which, because of the logical fallacy on which the method rests, could not yield the data needed to test Beard's claims about the divisions of political opinion among groups.

Failing to recognize the logical fallacies in the design of proof and the method that he copied from Beard, McDonald wound up his book as though its alleged refutation of "Beard's thesis" entitled him to render this judgment:

. . . the whole idea (expounded by Beard and many others) of beginning [historical] research with a system of interpretation and basis of selection, or with a hypothesis, or even with a question, breaks down. However it might be evaluated in terms of philosophy and pure logic, the fact is that it was developed largely for practical reasons, and it is precisely from the practical standpoint that it is weakest. If one guesses wrong, if one investigates a phenomenon in terms of a system of interpretation and selection which proves to be unworkable, all one's efforts may be wasted. An equal amount of effort, applied inductively, might have covered less ground, but it would at least have brought the investigator to a stage at which a more tenable system of interpretation could be induced from the body of particulars, and would *at least have taught him to ask meaningful questions* [italics added].[18]

The errors in that back-to-induction manifesto have long been recognized and exposed. "No systematic thought," A. N. Whitehead observes, "has made progress apart from some adequately general working hypothesis, adapted to its special topic. Such an hypothesis directs observation, and decides upon the mutual relevance of various types of evidence. In short, it prescribes method. To venture upon productive thought without such an explicit theory is to abandon oneself to the doctrines derived from one's grandfather." [19]

Scholars like McDonald who fail to venture forth with theories, hypotheses, and questions fail to recognize that good research designs permit investigators to explore problems by checking, modifying, or abandoning hypotheses and developing new ones as they proceed. Ideally, such designs are not biased in favor of confirming ideas tentatively advanced during the early stages of work. True, the ideal is seldom attained. Time and energy are usually wasted even in well-designed studies that start with interesting questions, hypotheses, and interpretative systems. It is also true that, once committed to a hypothesis or line of investigation, researchers tend to resist recognition of error. "I was wrong" is perhaps the most difficult phrase scholars are ever called upon to pronounce. But this only shows that, in the domain of scholarship and science, as in most others, man has not yet attained perfection.[20]

McDonald to the contrary, perhaps Beard contributed most significantly to American historiography by explicitly rejecting the notion that researchers should venture forth unguided by theory or hypothesis. He recognized that "many pitfalls . . . beset" travelers on the tricky road to interpretation, but he recognized also that Baconian Rules of Induction provide little guidance to historians seeking to avoid those pitfalls. Historians concerned with the "proximate or remote causes and relations" of phenomena, Beard argued, were more likely to reach their goals if they consciously adopted or formulated a theory and a hypothesis than if they set out uncommitted—but blind.[21] That the specific theory he adopted and the specific hypothesis he formulated may be untenable neither discredits his general approach nor detracts from his contribution. After the appearance in 1913 of Beard's book, it was never so easy again for an American historian to ignore theory or hypothesis and proceed to pile up a mountain of "facts," in the hope that, somehow, the mountain itself would move and reveal the truth.

Notes

1. Beard apparently did not grasp the significance of Seligman's assertion that it would "be absurd to deny that individual men, like masses of men, are moved by ethical considerations. On the contrary, all progress consists in the attempt to realize the unattainable—the ideal, the morally perfect. History is full of examples where nations, like individuals, have acted unselfishly and have followed the generous promptings of the higher life. The ethical and the religious teachers have not worked in vain. To trace the influence of the spiritual life in individual and social development would be as easy as it is unnecessary. What is generally forgotten, however, and what it is needful to emphasize again and again, is not only that the content of the conception of morality is a social product, but also that amid the complex social influences that cooperated to produce it, the economic factors have often been of chief significance—that pure ethical or religious idealism has made itself felt only within the limitations of existing economic conditions." *The Economic Interpretation of History* (New York: 1902), pp. 126 and 112–134. Clearly, Selig-

man argued against the fallacy of making conscious self-interest the invariant, primary determinant of human behavior.

2. See, for example, Charles A. Beard, *An Economic Interpretation of the Constitution of the United States* (New York: 1935), pp. 283, 310–312.

3. The material is reported in Lee Benson, *The Concept of Jacksonian Democracy: New York as a Test Case*. (Princeton, N. J.: Princeton University Press, 1961).

4. Historians, no doubt, will find its mathematical passages hard going, but I believe that they can profit considerably from the section, "Multivariate Analysis," in Paul F. Lazarsfeld and Morris Rosenberg, eds., *The Language of Social Research* (Glencoe, Ill.: 1955), pp. 109–199. As defined by Lazarsfeld and Rosenberg, multivariate analysis describes *"the study and interpretation of complex inter-relations among a multiplicity of characteristics."* I do not intend to imply that historians should mechanically imitate procedures developed by nonhistorians. On the contrary, I have deliberately used a nontechnical term, "relationship," instead of "correlation," to avoid the implication that historians must become statisticians in order to use quantitative methods. It is the *logic* of multivariate analysis, not its specific applications in other disciplines, that seems to me to have potential value for historiography.

Scholars who shy away from anything smacking of "scientific" and "statistical" procedures because of concern for literary values might recall that T. S. Eliot developed the method of "objective correlatives," used so effectively by Ernest Hemingway. See Carlos Baker, *Hemingway: The Writer as Artist* (Princeton, N. J.: 1956), pp. 54–58. The "potentially verifiable" concept is discussed in Lee Benson, "Research Problems In American Political Historiography," in Mirra Komarovsky, ed., *Common Frontiers of the Social Sciences* (Glencoe, Ill.: 1957), pp. 118–119.

5. Beard, *Economic Interpretation*, pp. 253–254. "For the purposes of a fine analysis of the economic forces in the ratifying process, it would be of the highest value to have the vote on delegates to the state conventions in each town and county throughout the whole country; but unfortunately no such figures are compiled and much of the original materials upon which the statistical tables could be based have doubtless disappeared." *Ibid.*, p. 243.

6. *Ibid.*, p. 254.

7. Quoted in Charles A. Beard, ed., *The Enduring Federalist* (Garden City, N. Y.: 1948), p. 71. The conjecture that Beard derived the collective biography method from *Federalist* No. 10 is supported by his summarizing the passage quoted above as asserting that "The theories of government which men entertain are emotional reactions to their property interests." *Economic Interpretation*, p. 157.

8. *Ibid.*, p. 273–281. Interestingly enough, members of the "Namier school" of English historiography have employed the collective biography to support conclusions about the absence of class divisions during the English Revolution. For example, see D. Brunton and D. H. Pennington, *Members of the Long Parliament* (London: 1954). I do not know whether Beard inspired the Namier school's use of the method; but, whether it is used to "prove" the presence or absence of class divisions in politics, it is logically fallacious.

9. Orin G. Libby, *The Geographical Distribution of the Vote of the Thirteen States on the Federal Constitution, 1787-8* (Madison, Wisconsin: 1894), p. 82-84.

10. Of course, Beard's critics are legion. But I am concerned here with the four who have specifically employed his method to discredit his conclusions. To my knowledge, the first study of this kind was William C. Pool, "An Economic Interpretation of the Ratification of the Federal Constitution in North Carolina," *North Carolina Historical Review*, XXVII (April, July, October 1950), 119-141, 289-313, 437-461. It was followed by Robert E. Thomas, "The Virginia Convention of 1788: A Criticism of Beard's *An Economic Interpretation of the Constitution*," *Journal of Southern History*, XIX (February 1953), 63-72; Robert E. Brown, *Charles Beard and the Constitution* (Princeton, N. J.: 1956); and Forrest McDonald, *We The People: The Economic Origins of the Constitution* (Chicago, Ill.: 1958). For an illuminating, wide-ranging review of the literature, see Richard B. Morris, "The Confederation Period and the American Historian," *William and Mary Quarterly*, XIII, 3d ser. (April 1956), 139-156.

11. McDonald, *We The People*, pp. 398-399, 358-399.

12. See, for example, the use made of such interest group categories, in E. E. Schattschneider's famous study, *Politics, Pressures and the Tariff* (New York: 1935).

13. See the discussion in Lee Benson, *Merchants, Farmers, & Railroads: Railroad Regulation and New York Politics* (Cambridge, Mass.: 1955), pp. 55-114, 204-246.

14. My thinking about the general problem of devising systems of classification has benefited considerably from Paul F. Lazarsfeld and Allen H. Barton, "Qualitative Measurement in the Social Sciences: Classification, Typologies, and Indices," in Daniel Lerner and Harold D. Lasswell, eds., *The Policy Sciences* (Stanford, Calif.; 1951), pp. 155-192.

15. My ideas have been clarified by discussions with Daniel Bell. The "broad symbolic group" concept will be treated in detail in his forthcoming study, *Communism and the American Labor Movement*.

16. McDonald, *We The People*, p. 181.

17. *Ibid.*, pp. 181-182, 349-357.

18. McDonald, *We The People*, pp. 414, 411-414.

19. Alfred N. Whitehead, *Adventures of Ideas* (New York: 1933), p. 286.

20. A personal note is relevant. The original design of the study which resulted in the present essay called for the compilation of legislative collective biographies. Considerable time and energy was devoted to compiling the requisite data before I became aware of the method's logical fallacy. In fact, in a preliminary paper written in 1954, I confidently asserted that "Beard's main contribution . . . [to American historiography] was not interpretative but methodological. Few would deny that the procedure he outlined and partially demonstrated, constituted a major advance in the investigation of historical problems." Contrary to McDonald's inductionist argument, however, use of a systematic research design eventually helped me to discover the error in my procedures.

21. Beard, *Economic Interpretation*, pp. 3-4.

❧ 8 ❧

Samuel P. Hays

NEW POSSIBILITIES FOR
AMERICAN POLITICAL HISTORY:
THE SOCIAL ANALYSIS OF
POLITICAL LIFE

In recent years American political history has undergone some severe challenges from within the profession. Many have cast aside the traditional study of politics as too concerned with dramatic events and formal institutions, too remote from human experience and values, for a more satisfying economic, intellectual or social history. But these lines of inquiry, although pursued vigorously, have failed to reorient the profession toward the very human qualities of the past they professed to seek. Stressing the formal relationships among ideas, intellectual history has created a past world divorced from human circumstance and situation in which ideas seem to sweep men on through the course of history. Influenced by the abstract quality of theory, economic history has become caught up in the impersonal description of aggregate economic forces. The study of American character has prompted social history to focus on uniform social psychological patterns. Despite advances in these fields, historians still await an approach

Samuel P. Hays is Professor of History at the University of Pittsburgh. He is author of *The First American Conservation Movement 1891–1920*, *The Response to Industrialism: 1885–1914*, and *Conservation and the Gospel of Efficiency: The Progressive Conservation Movement 1890–1920*.

From a paper given before the American Historical Association, December 29, 1964.

which can recapture human experience, thought, values and practice in its variety of situations and circumstances.

These emphases, moreover, have failed to provide an overall context for examining historical change. Remaining separate and compartmentalized, they have fractured history rather than synthesized it. Economic, intellectual and social history have moved further apart from each other, rather than closer together. Each maintains that its facet of human experience is more significant than that of others, but none has brought forward a framework to bring diverse aspects of human life together and provide a substitute for the rejected conceptual unity of political history. Our textbooks have become separate chapters on economic, social and intellectual life, sandwiched in between sections of a traditionally-oriented political history, which remain more akin to separate catalogs of information than integral parts of a single social fabric. Academic log-rolling has predominated over conceptual synthesis and the acquisition of monopoly over specialized pieces of information has prevailed over the intellectual risk of coping with their interrelationships.

The time is now ripe for a new consideration of political life as the major context of historical inquiry, and for its special potential both for focusing on the human quality of the past and integrating its diverse facets. For since political history is concerned with the conflicts among the varied goals and values which arise in society and with the distribution of power which is responsible for the choice of one goal over another, it emphasizes both the particular human situations from which those strivings arise and the larger arena in which the struggle for dominance takes place. It can bring into one context both the fundamental realities of inevitably limited human experience and the larger realm of social choice. But in order to play this role political history must differ radically from its earlier counterpart. It must broaden its conception of the nature of political life from formal institutions to the entire range of the clash of goals in society; it must think more in terms of patterns of human relationships than of isolated people and events abstracted from the fabric of society; and it must be willing to explore both new concepts and new methods of inquiry.

This development is now taking place. Approaches to political history far different from those used previously are under serious exploration.[1] This chapter is an attempt both to articulate these developments more fully and to outline the possibilities which they entail for the revitalization of political life as the central focus of history.

Limitations of Conventional Political History

Traditional political history has come under attack from a number of different sources. In 1948 Thomas C. Cochran criticized the "presidential synthesis," the practice of dividing political history into four-year intervals marked by presidential elections.[2] The ebb and flow of political impulses, he argued, was independent of these formal divisions. Fundamental shifts in political attitudes might well come between presidential elections and last longer than a four-year period, for they reflect changes in attitudes and impulses entirely unconnected in origin with the formal timing of election contests. Cochran's article stressed the distinction between the formal and the informal characteristics of politics, between those more observable and outward conditions of political life and the more underlying impulses for influence and power which arise out of the entire range of human endeavor. The political historian must go beneath the external manifestation and examine the roots of political life.

One example of the traditional political history which Cochran criticized is the tendency to describe the political parties in terms of their formal expressions of policy rather than of the great variety of groups of which they are composed. Parties of the post-Civil War Era are known as high tariff or low tariff, sound money or silver parties, depending upon their platform statements and campaign oratory. Few have gone beyond the high-tariff-big-business image of the Republican party of those years to investigate its internal composition, the characteristics of the delegates to conventions or state executive committees, the composition of its voting support, the voluntary groups associated with it, the different outlooks and voting patterns of different segments of its congressional delegations, the impact of the new Western states admitted in the late 1880's on the intra-party balance, or the patterns of forces within state Republican organizations.[3]

For years historians and political scientists described the distinctions between legislative and executive branches of government, especially on the state and local level, in formal terms. The first makes laws; the second executes them. The city council creates policy; the city manager carries it out. But both executive and legislative branches in state and municipal government are the focal point of political forces; both make political decisions, and, in fact, represent different constituencies. The governor, elected at large, reflects the changing composition of the state's voters; as they become more urban the governor tends to represent the views of the cities.[4] But the legislature, slower to change, represents the views of people in rural areas and small towns. In the city the council members reflect the views of the many and diverse segments of the community in their local and regional interests, while the executive represents the views of those business and professional groups with city-wide interests and perspectives. These distinctions are not apparent through a reading of the formal governmental responsibilities of governors and legislators, but they become clear from an examination of the political impulses which play upon decision-makers and to which those decision-makers look for support.[5]

Movements with the same outward, formal characteristics may often involve vastly different political goals. Joseph Gusfield has recently outlined the variety of impulses in the drive for prohibition.[6] In its pre-Civil War phase the upper class used temperance to protect itself against the stirrings of the "lower orders" of society. In the post-Civil War Era, on the other hand, prohibition involved a middle-class attempt to establish its particular values in the midst of the emphasis on material growth and the leadership of the new industrial elite. The movement which began in the 1890's, far more successful, stemmed from the rural drive to contain and control the growing cultural power of the cities which threatened older, rural ways of life. In all of these instances prohibition or temperance were instruments of social control, but the group which desired control and the group which was to be controlled, the problem to be solved and the group which defined the problem and sought prohibition as the solution to it, all differed.

Political history, then, must go beneath the outward, formal characteristics of political life to investigate the more fundamental impulses of the drive for influence and dominance; these impulses determine the character of political action and should establish the framework of political analysis.

A second criticism of traditional political history has focused on the failure of historians adequately to analyze election returns.[7] Most elections are examined as outcomes of particular campaigns; consequently the margin of victory for one contest is given. But rarely are the results of that contest compared with past elections and even more rarely are the results presented in such a way—percentage strength—that comparisons can be made. The important long-range historical fact about elections is not necessarily the outcome of any one contest, but the degree to which they reveal shifts or continuities in political attitude. It is impossible to determine whether or not a single election deserves analysis without a series of data which indicates the degree of stability or change in voting over time. With such data one can discover that the early 1850's witnessed a revolution in political attitudes which persisted until 1893, that the election of 1883 rather than that of 1884 was the crucial year of Democratic gains; that the Democratic upswing in the early twentieth century was six years in the making and not just a product of the debates of 1909; that the Republican victory of 1918 was often far more crucial than that of 1920 in establishing the new Republican dominance of the twentieth century. Each of these examples concerns a shift or trend in voting which the traditional method of treating elections has failed to emphasize.

Historians have also neglected the disaggregate analysis of elections, the examination of the different patterns of voting by different groups of people which the overall returns do not reveal. How did different ethnic, religious and racial groups or different socioeconomic classes vote? Were ethnocultural factors more powerful than socioeconomic ones in establishing voting patterns? An excellent example of this type of study is an article on German political attitudes in the election of 1860 which demonstrates that Iowa Germans were strongly Democratic.[8] Only with an intensive examination of voting returns and an association of those returns with demographic patterns of all kinds can the different political attitudes of different segments of the population be determined. The overall returns often obscure marked shifts in voting behavior. Historians have begun to stress the significant Democratic urban gains in the election of 1928, despite the Hoover victory, but only after the importance of this shift was emphasized by a political scientist and popularized by a journalist-sociologist.[9] A similar phenomenon took place in 1948 when, in the face of the Truman victory, Dewey scored marked gains in the cities. Such trends as these, which occurred in many elections and which the general returns obscure, await a disaggregate analysis to bring them to light.

Still a third criticism is that the heavy emphasis on the individual and the episodic has obscured the need for investigating the larger structure and processes of political life. Political historians have devoted considerable effort to examining prominent political leaders and dramatic political events. Stimulated markedly by the preservation of personal manuscripts, the study of individual politicians has gone on apace. This has focused political history on the ideas, actions and interrelationships of a few prominent leaders and has diverted attention from the broader composition of political parties and the environment within which both party and leader exist. Political biographies assume, with no rationale for defining the problem, much less resolving it, a particular relationship between the individual and his "times." The impact of a president as a political leader, however, cannot be determined unless one has studied his party, his administrative agencies and his legislatures as thoroughly as the president's personal affairs. Yet, what biographer has done this? James MacGregor Burns, in his treatment of Franklin D. Roosevelt, has moved most fully in this direction.[10]

By the same token, much of our political history is episodic, concerned more with the isolated event than the political context. Legislative history invariably focuses on the drama of the single legislative decision, rather than the network of political forces within which the decision was made. The exciting and colorful struggle over anti-trust legislation in the early twentieth century obscured the contemporary patterns of economic politics and their relationship to public policy. Small businessmen, for example, against whom the Sherman Act had been most effectively used, sought to modify that Act not by strengthening it but by circumventing it through legalized minimum price fixing. The dramatic strikes of the late nineteenth century, as Herbert Gutman has shown, obscured the close relationship between middle and lower classes in instances of industrial strife and the great difficulty, rather than the ease, with which the employers disciplined their labor force.[11] The dramatic controversy over the Supreme Court in 1937 obscured the patterns of political struggle in the first four years of the New Deal which lay behind it, the forces sharpened by executive policies developed under such agencies as the NRA and the PWA and the resulting contest over executive and legislative power.

This emphasis upon the individual and the episodic one might well describe by the phrase "abstracted empiricism," in the same way in which C. Wright Mills used it to describe similar tendencies in sociology.[12] For it conveys accurately the idea that historians have abstracted individuals and episodes from context, examined them apart from that context, and placed them back into the stream of history without regard to that context save for temporal sequence and topical similarity. But historical problems must be defined in terms of the relation of people and events to each other. How important is one episode, for example the election of 1896, in relation to other election episodes? How important is one individual in relation to the human context? How representative is an individual of a broader group? How distinctive is this particular political drive; is it typical of a widespread impulse, or is it atypical? The context of political relationships, whether in space or in time, rather than the frequency of appearance in the historical record or the sensationalism of the event, should determine the particular aspects of political history worthy of study.

The inadequacy of conventional political history is illustrated in even more striking fashion by omissions in the treatment of highly significant problems. The assumptions of political historians have guided them to certain topics and not to others. Now that assumptions about political behavior are changing and more evidence about political life is building up from sociology and political science as well as history, the nature of the problems considered worthy of investigation is changing. Conventional political history appears to have large and almost unexplainable gaps.

Consider, for example, the growth of bureaucracy and administration in the years since the mid-nineteenth century, the elaboration and expansion of systematization which are part of the evolution of the technical-scientific world.[13] Textbooks invariably fail to treat this extensive political change. They will consider it tangentially when discussing the growth of big business or of government. But they do not consider it as a general development: the increase in the size and scope of affairs which are subject to systematization and control; the changing techniques of control; the similarities in public and private bureaucracies in the need for long-range planning, in utilizing experts, in fashioning favorable public relations; the extension of these processes in the mid-twentieth century to our educational system.

An equally striking gap is the failure to consider changes in socioeconomic classes. Some treatment of this occurs for early American history and for the agrarian South. For the most part, however, we know little about the evolution of the upper class in the nineteenth and twentieth centuries, its changing composition and character, the differential movement into it by religious and ethnic groups, its wider public role. The only scholarly historical treatment of this phenomenon is by a sociologist, E. Digby Baltzell in his book *Philadelphia Gentlemen*.[14] We speak blithely of the "middle class" in the nineteenth century, without even investigating its composition. We accept the image, for example, that the urban middle class of small businessmen was overwhelmingly native American, when it appears more likely that the majority were immigrants. Nor do we know much about working-class people and their political attitudes, save their role in organized labor and trade union activity. Cutting across all of these features of class analysis is the problem of social mobility, a process which we assume to have happened, but which we have not examined. Curiously, despite the dominance of liberal historiography, our framework of political analysis has failed to turn our research attention to these socioeconomic dimensions of political life.

An equally striking omission is the role of ethno-cultural factors in politics. Some texts have recognized these factors by incorporating some of Samuel Lubell's ideas into the treatment of the New Deal.[15] But the first full-length treatment of religion and voting in American history appeared only in 1964, and was written by a sociologist, Seymour Lipset.[16] The very great significance of religion and nationality in differentiating the voting patterns of the nineteenth century is apparent to anyone who examines precinct voting returns. They also established a degree of continuity in voting distinctions which constitute one of the most important conditions of American political structure. But the assumptions of our conventional political history have obscured rather than illumined these factors.

Still a fourth example is the conflict between rural and urban areas.[17] We are clearly aware of the significance of this problem, but we have failed to bring it into focus as an historical development. The city has changed our political values, established new contexts for political debate, affected the nature of intra-party struggles and determined the balance of power within state legislatures. All of this should provide one of the major frameworks for the treatment of a whole range of historical phenomena, from ideologies and values through economic policy to the basic struggle for political power. And these conflicts go well back into the nineteenth century. But one can glimpse almost nothing of the entire problem in textbooks save, perhaps, for the decade of the 1920's. Instead, the historian must turn to political science and sociology in such works as *Small Town in Mass Society* by Arthur Vidich and Joseph Bensman[18] to secure insight as to the impact of the wider, metropolitan, technological, scientific society upon an earlier small town and rural America.

One could continue this list of omissions, but these examples establish the point. Conventional political history has been so preoccupied with the outward and formal, the episodic, the unique and the individual that it has failed to draw attention to some of the most significant developments of our political past. The assumptions of that outlook have limited and narrowed our vision rather than illumined and expanded it. They have separated us from the very thing with which we should be most concerned: the determination of those broad patterns of continuity and change which arise out of the network of social relationships established in the course of history.

The Social Analysis of Political History

These concerns, it is apparent, do not involve an interest in new subject matter in political history, the addition of new facts to old, so much as the development of a new perspective and a new set of problems for investigation. For they stress the examination of human behavior itself, its ideology and its practice, rather than its formal products, and of social patterns and social processes which arise from that behavior, rather than the individual and episodic. Implicit in much of the new stirrings in American political history is the desire to understand the impulses and strivings which arise out of human circumstance and situation, the degree to which people hold these in common or in distinction, and the degree to which they persist or change. The emphasis is on human behavior and human relationships, and on the social patterns and social processes to which they give rise. The conceptual framework involved, therefore, can be described by the phrase, the *social analysis* of political history.

This approach requires, first of all, a broader conception of the nature of political life. In the past we have confined political history to political parties and their activities: party organization, the selection of candidates, electoral contests, executive appointments and legislative action. But political life involves the origin, clash and resolution of all value conflicts in society, whether expressed through political parties or not. The context of political analysis must range far beyond the political party to the broader environment of human relationships within which it functions, and which it reflects. This environment is not merely the background to party action, but the context within which political groupings are defined and basic political impulses analyzed and placed in relationship to each other. Other systems of decision-making, such as the administrative process or the give-and-take of nonpartisan interest group action, each of equal importance to the political party as instruments of expressing political goals, function within the same context. The analysis of each rests upon the patterns of human relationships which grow out of economic, social and ideological life; systems of decision-making are the instruments whereby these values and goals are expressed.

The religious composition of voting patterns in the nineteenth century illustrates this problem.[19] Evangelical protestantism found expression in mid-century in the Republican party. The more ritualistic Catholic and Protestant faiths, in reaction, aligned themselves with the Democratic party. The wide clashes over prohibition and Sunday observance, over Sunday schools and revivals as legitimate techniques of instruction and conversion, over the individual soul or the historical institution as the focal point of religious activities—all these took place outside the realm of party politics. They can be observed within the context of denominational decision-making in annual conferences and theological seminary policy, in competition between youth groups such as the Methodists and the Lutherans, in local battles over Sunday baseball games, or in disputation in the religious journals. But they are brought to bear in political party battles which focus all of these value-conflicts into a contest for public policy and political leaders. The final expression of the conflict cannot be separated from all that lay behind it. The one is as legitimate and as essential a part of political history as the other.

Traditional distinctions between political history on the one hand, and ideological, economic, social and cultural history on the other, are artificial. For political life deeply involves the clash of values, the drive for dominance, the resolution of differences in every realm of human affairs. The distribution of the power to secure and disseminate information and ideas; to govern relationships within economic trade groups; to organize and manage economic ventures; to control residential communities against change; to develop, influence and use educational facilities; to establish the policies of religious institutions are in themselves political phenomena. All involve the expression of different goals and values in contexts which are public rather than personal and private; all involve the attempt to control the ideas and practices of other people so that one's own values can be realized more fully. Power and decision-making, therefore, are not isolated segments of the social order, which can be examined separately from ideological, economic, social and cultural affairs, but permeate all realms of life. Our analytical perspective must be equally broad.

Within this context of political history, the social analyst must determine initially the nature of political structure, the groupings of ideas and practices into which the political order can be divided and from which attempts to influence the course of public affairs arise. What distinct political groupings exist among nationality, religious, and racial groups; among occupational and trade groups; among people of different socioeconomic levels; among different geographical sections; among areas of different degrees of urbanization; among people of different educational levels? Survey data secured through polls enable us to develop a fairly complete picture of different voting groups of the past three decades. But we have no such comprehensive view of the period before the 1930's. Our objective, however, should be the same as that of the survey specialist—to secure a broad picture of the significant groupings into which the political order can be divided. Our approach to this problem has been almost casual, as an appendage to the investigation of other matters. It must now be undertaken more thoroughly so that the total range of political groupings for any one time of history can become the context within which political events are understood.

Many current attempts to revise older views of political history consist of a more precise definition of political groups. Some seek to separate more clearly the distinctions among voters in popular elections;[20] others seek to define systematically the groupings among legislators in roll-call votes;[21] still others search for divisions among political leaders.[22] Some define more precisely for distinct divisions among bankers in the Jacksonian Era, or the divisions in the contest over the currency in the Greenback Era.[23] Such studies as these have advanced our knowledge of political groupings significantly. But they are only beginnings. Since most of them describe the patterns of groups which form around specific issues, they do not provide a view of the full range of groups in the political structure and the total pattern of the peculiar distribution power. Yet it is in the direction which such studies as these have outlined that we must turn for a more satisfactory treatment of political structure.

An example of this approach is contained in Robert Wiebe's book on businessmen and reform in the Progressive Era.[24] Wiebe seeks to understand the struggle over banking policy and the formation of the Federal Reserve Act by sorting out the segments of the banking community and relating their conceptions of what policy should be to their position in the structure of the banking world. The eastern banker, dominant in the banking community, wished a currency based upon federal and railroad bonds and a centralized banking system. The regional bankers, led by those in Chicago, sought an assets currency and a regionally based organization. But the country bankers wanted land-mortgage paper to be included as a base for issuing currency and an organization resting upon local clearing houses. Each of these groups within the banking community lived in a different banking world and as a result formulated different ideas about public policy. The history of every legislative enactment should provide as complete a treatment of the structure of relevant political groupings.

From what particular segment of the political structure does a particular political impulse arise? This is one of the most fundamental questions in political analysis. Does it come from one socioeconomic group or another, from one ethnocultural group or another, from leaders or from the grass roots, from one geographical section or another? The peculiarities of a political movement are rarely observable from the political ideology, whether it be federalism, states rights, anti-trust or socialism. They can be determined, however, from the way in which the people involved in that movement differ from others in the political structure. From what particular religious denominations or segments of denominations did anti-slavery impulses in the pre-Civil War years spring? Was there any connection between these particular groups and the particular segments from which the Republican party drew its initial strength? It is doubtful whether an extensive description of anti-slavery ideology can answer these questions. They can be dealt with, however, by tracing the peculiar geographical location of those segments of the Presbyterian or Methodist churches, for example, from which the demand for anti-slavery pronouncements came and by observing the peculiar sources of Republican party voting strength at the precinct level.

In defining the source of a political impulse, it is especially important to be able to determine not only that it came from a particular segment of the political structure, but that it did not come from other segments. The peculiarities of a phenomenon grow not only from its own characteristics, but more significantly from the ways in which it differs from other phenomena. Some attempts at the social analysis of political history have gone astray because they sought to associate distinctive political behavior with groups which themselves were not different from other groups. One must know, for example, not only who anti-slavery leaders were, but also how they differed from slavery apologists; not only who New England Mugwumps were, but how they differed from Republicans who did not bolt the party or from Democrats who were their new associates in 1884; not only who the Progressive Era reformers were, but how they differed from their political opponents.[25]

Fundamental to the social analysis of political history, therefore, is an understanding of the group character of politics, not simply in the sense of active, organized interest groups impinging directly on the legislative process, but in the sense of shared attitudes, ideas, situations and goals which produce uniformities in political thought and practice. The dramatic episodes and personalities, the products of legislation and party conventions provide at best only a superficial context of political relationships. Political structure, instead, grows out of the persistent, on-going, day-to-day relationships established among people in their work, their community life, their religion, recreation and education, and out of the patterns of dominance and subordinance which these activities generate. Historians have not devoted their energies extensively to the determination of political structure; yet political history cannot be understood even in its most elementary form without knowledge of the characteristics of that structure and the peculiar origins of political impulses within it.

The social analysis of political life requires an understanding of political process as well as political structure. How do the patterns of political forces change? With time new political groups emerge and others decline; groups formerly subordinate may become more influential. The context of ethnocultural politics in the late eighteenth and early nineteenth centuries which involved establishment and disestablishment gave way in the mid-nineteenth century to a context of evangelical protestantism and the reaction to it.[26] The old commercial-agrarian political leaders of the pre-1850 years gave way to the new industrial political elite which formed effective ties with the urban masses.[27] Economic groups, organized along trade lines, began in the late nineteenth century to establish a new, nonpartisan system of economic politics not known before. The socioeconomic background of urban political leaders in the early twentieth century shifted from working and lower middle class to upper middle class.[28]

One of the most useful devices for determining the timing of political change is the analysis of election data. By arranging party percentages of the total vote in a time series, one can observe the shifts and stabilities in popular voting sentiment over a long period of time.[29] An index of party strength in Congress, for example, indicates that since 1874 the greatest shift in political sentiment took place in 1894 (32 percentage points), the next greatest in 1890 (23 points) and the third greatest in 1932 (20 points). Since the two most drastic changes took place in off-presidential years and in elections which historians have hardly mentioned, such an approach indicates the extent to which the use of quantitative data can direct attention to changes not customarily observed. The election of 1896, for example, continued a voting pattern first established in 1894; to understand the vote in 1896, therefore, one must first understand the causes for the revolutionary change of 1894. Traditional evidence has obscured the fact that the dramatic election of 1896 was a contest of ideology and leadership; the voting realignment which lay behind it had already taken place.

The analysis of political history would be greatly enhanced if we knew precisely when major changes took place in different segments of the political structure. When, for example, did shifts occur in the occupational background of legislators? In the percentage of eligible voters which actually voted? In the balance of political power between rural and urban areas as revealed, for example, in the constituencies of state legislators? In the upward shift in the location of decision-making from smaller to larger units of government? In the relationships between lower- and middle-class groups from cooperation in the nineteenth century to hostility in the twentieth? In the balance of power within the Democratic party against the South in the twentieth century? Data about the changing backgrounds of those elected to city councils and school boards, for example, raise several questions.

Why, at certain points in history, did city councilmen from the old patrician upper class give way to those of the newer entrepreneurial groups, and why in turn did these give way later to lower- and middle-class groups? Why, in the twentieth century, was this tendency reversed in some cities? Not all changes can be described in quantitative terms. But the observation of change is a major starting point for some of the most significant historical investigations.

Observation of the location of change is as important as observation of its timing. For change may not take place uniformly throughout a society. If it is greater in one geographical area than another, analysis is facilitated by the attempt to associate that particular change with characteristics peculiar to that area. The Populist movement took place in areas other than those where the Granger movement had been strong; it can be understood, then, through an analysis of the conditions peculiar to the trans-Missouri West and the South as distinct from the changing economy of the old Granger areas. The massive changes in electoral behavior in the 1890's took place primarily in the North and East. Over two-thirds of the congressional seats which changed hands between 1890 and 1898 came in areas north and east of the centers of agrarian unrest. To understand these changes, therefore, one must investigate the North and East rather than, as has been done, concentrate almost exclusively on the South and West. The rise of the Democratic party in the decade after 1904 was peculiarly located in a belt of states from Illinois to New Jersey; why? In the late 1840's, and early 1850's, the Republican party made particularly heavy inroads into former Democratic areas in a belt of counties beginning in southern New York and northern Pennsylvania and extending west in the same latitude. Why? Understanding of why change takes place, therefore, is greatly facilitated by pinpointing where it takes place.

Soon computations for all county election data for President, governor, congressman and United States senator since 1824 will be readily available. From this data we can secure a complete picture of the timing and distribution of changes in election behavior throughout the entire United States over a period of 140 years. As a result, a host of problems for analysis will come to the fore. We will be able to pinpoint precisely not only all changes over time and all peculiarities of distribution of those changes over space, but will also be able to distinguish between those changes of greater and of lesser magnitude. The effect of such a catalog of changes will be to bring into focus many problems for analysis which have heretofore escaped our attention. It will lead to studies which will provide a far more comprehensive picture of both political structure and political process, and stimulates the social analysis of an increasingly wider range of historical evidence.

Situational Analysis

The social analysis of political history, the examination of both structure and process, focuses on the human situation. Human experience and action are not universal but limited, and from such limited rather than universal existence grow limited rather than universal patterns of thought and behavior. Each group has a particular "situation" in society, with a distinctive consciousness of the world, distinctive goals, values and behavior, all of which are understandable only in terms of that situation. Knowledge of the world is circumscribed by the extent of the world with which one comes into contact. The person whose consciousness is limited to a local community from which he does not move physically or psychologically has a limited and circumscribed set of values and behavior. Those whose contacts and experiences are geographically broad and varied have an altogether different, yet also limited, pattern of thought and action. The blue-collar workingman views the world differently from the white-collar clerk, the lower-income group differently from the upper, the Catholic from the Jew or the Protestant, the Italian immigrant from the Mexican, the New Englander from the Southerner—all because the circumstances in which they live are different and the context in which their ideas and attitudes develop are peculiar to those circumstances.

The initial question to be asked of any historical problem is: what particular people, at what particular time, in what particular place thought and acted in what particular way? Every historical question is a question concerning human behavior; it should be referred back not to a general scheme or idea, but to people who are thinking and acting in a particular situation. Instead of intellectual history, there is the history of people who have ideas; instead of economic history the history of people who organize production or consume; instead of political history the history of those who seek influence to make their goals and values prevail. Historical analysis has a tendency to move to higher grounds of broad forces conceptualized in supra-human terms, sweeping men on through time. Social analysis is a healthy antidote to this tendency, for it forces one to think in terms of the peculiarities of the human situation, and to modify constantly the broader outlines of history in terms of the limitations of human consciousness and experience. Each historical question, then, is traced back to the human situation from which it arises, and is understood in terms of that situation.

The failure to adopt such an approach has severely limited the analysis of those movements in American history variously called "reform," "progressive," or "liberal." These are presumed to have arisen from universal impulses of "progress," from the gradual realization in political life of the forces of reason, enlightenment or good will. But such an approach does not facilitate more precise analysis. Only particular groups sought these changes, and examination of these groups demonstrates that their interest arose from their particular circumstances rather than from general conditions of "progressiveness." Why, for example, were some professional groups rather than others interested in changes in municipal government in the Progressive Era? [30] Why civil engineers rather than mechanical, electrical or chemical? Why ministers from upper-class parishes rather than from parishes of other income levels? Why schoolteachers from the more well-to-do school districts rather than from the school system as a whole? Why particular groups of lawyers rather than others? Why doctors concerned with communicable disease rather than surgeons? Why architects who designed large structures, such as office buildings and churches, rather than those who designed residences? These particular groups of people became involved in municipal reform because of desires peculiar to the goals and values of the particular segment of the profession in which they worked.

The patrician liberals of the latter half of the nineteenth century have been described as an example of the "reform" movement. But the limited treatment of this group, already carried out by Ari Hoogenboom in his study of civil service reform and Geoffrey Blodgett in his treatment of the Mugwumps and the Democratic party in Massachusetts, indicates that patrician liberals can be understood only in terms of their particular situation.[31] The whole problem awaits a full-length treatment. It should take the form of a collective biography of several hundred members of the group and a complete picture of their historical situation: their competition for leadership with the new industrial entrepreneurs, the changes experienced in their residential communities as they underwent in-migration from other socioeconomic groups, the challenge to their intellectual world of literature and art by new ideas, their relationship to the new political leaders arising in the Republican party. The patrician liberals form a fairly coherent political movement; one must understand their political role not in terms of the sweep of reform in general but of their unique historical situation in particular.

Two different approaches are possible in situational analysis. The first starts with the results of behavior, with institutions, public policies, movements, ideas, or broad social changes, and traces these back into the human situation from which these emerged so as to determine their roots in human behavior. What, for example, was distinctive about the particular people involved in a particular political party or faction, such as the Gold Democrats or the Anti-Masons, and how were they different from those involved in other parties. How were Federalists different from anti-Federalists; Bull Moosers from regular Republicans? What particular groups were adversely affected by the "distribution revolution" at the turn of the twentieth century and how did they, as a result, react? What precise groups were helped and what were hurt by the NRA codes; which ones wanted restrictions on the work day and which did not, which higher minimum wages and which lower? Who supported the prohibition movement and who opposed it? Which particular groups in local, provincial America accepted cosmopolitan ideas and thereby changed their patterns of life and which ones resisted these innovations? Who were involved in the social gospel emphasis or the anti-trust movement in the Progressive Era? Who interpreted the post-1929 innovations in public affairs as socialism and who did not? In each of these cases a product of human behavior, whether it be ideological, economic or political, is traced back to its situational roots.

The direction of analysis can be reversed by starting with the human situation and determining the peculiar types of resulting conceptions, values and action. In the pre-Civil War years did the economic leaders of the East behave differently from those in the newer, trans-Appalachian areas? Did Lutherans from the eighteenth-century migrations to Pennsylvania react differently to anti-slavery agitation from those in the nineteenth-century migrations to the Midwest? How did the value-orientation in the sectarian college in New York and Michigan in the latter nineteenth century differ from that in the new state universities? What were the peculiar views and objectives of small businessmen in the twentieth-century world of mammoth corporations? Did academics in small and relatively isolated colleges in the mid-twentieth century behave differently from those in large, cosmopolitan universities; those in New England institutions differently from those in the Midwest in the Progressive Era? Did the rural and small-town American view the world and behave differently from the city-dweller? Was the economic outlook of New England in 1910 different from that of the Midwest, the South, the Mountain and Far West? Did Negroes vote in distinctive patterns in the 1930's? What distinctive approach to public affairs was manifested by the Eastern European émigré who came to the United States after World War II?

It should be clear, once more, that I am not speaking about formally organized groups alone. Such groups may exist in the form of country clubs, trade associations, the Sons of Italy, labor unions, professional education organizations, or associations to protect civil liberties. But social groupings may be informal as well as formal, growing out of common circumstances and shared attitudes. To the social analyst these patterns of life are just as important, and perhaps even more important, than formal groups. The latter are more easily observable, but they are not necessarily more significant; they serve as clues to patterns of group behavior rather than exhaustive descriptions of it. Social data which describe income levels, occupations, places of residence, religion, nationality, education or race help to define continuing and persistent shared attitudes which are above and beyond the formal organizations themselves. The explicit assumption is simply that societies are not homogeneous, but heterogeneous, and that the values and behavior of each subdivision are understandable in terms of the particular characteristics and experience, the particular situation of the people involved.

It should also be clear that in relating behavior to situation I am not referring to a "self-interest" type of thought and action which is so prevalent in the liberal analysis of history and popular thought. To argue that the ideas or actions of a group cannot be understood apart from their particular circumstances and conditions of life is not to argue that the group deliberately weighs each action in terms of calculable benefits. Each group inevitably relates broad questions of public affairs to its own particular experience; it is impossible for it to act otherwise. This is especially true of the "disinterested" person, so common on the "good" side of the traditionally-defined liberal-conservative political struggle. For the "disinterested" person's definition of the public good is inevitably a limited one, understandable in terms of his own particular experience and his own particular conception of the good society which arises from that experience. That view may differ widely from the views of others. Groups act not from "self-interest," but from "limited perspectives," from conceptions of their society and themselves which are bounded by their own experience and therefore directly related to it.

Leaders of the conservation movement in the Progressive Era, for example, clearly did not act from "self-interest" in the usual sense of the term.[32] They did not self-consciously calculate benefits to themselves. Yet they most assuredly sought to define public policy in their own terms. The assumptions of science and technology bounded their world. This prompted them to define ultimate values in terms of efficiency, and "progress" as the degree to which the goals of efficiency were realized. It made them favor manipulative decision-making by experts and suspicious of the give and take of a more pluralistic political system. It caused them to define democracy in terms of equality of benefits rather than equality of political power. Their world view was limited and circumscribed by the world within which that view was formed and such a view, rather than bringing them more closely in touch with other segments of the political order, actually alienated them from it. They must be described, therefore, not as the instruments of universal impulses, but as particular people with particular experiences proposing particular policies. Their behavior involved not "self-interest" but "limited perspectives."

The rationale for a situational analysis of politics lies in a focus on man's conscious life, an attempt to understand human perspectives and human conceptions of the world and to relate political life to those particular perspectives. One of man's most basic motives is the search for clarity and understanding of the world around him, to be secure ideologically within that world, and to exercise influence over it. The mere drive for understanding is a political drive, because understanding is a prerequisite for control. But such an impulse for understanding does not take place within either a vacuum or a context of universal experience of reason, spirit or good will. It occurs within particular environments, in situations peculiar to the experience of a particular group of men. And the particular perspective of particular people can be understood most fully in terms of the particular situation in which it develops and is played out. The context of such an approach is that of an active, creative, searching mind, formulated and working within the framework of an inevitably limited human experience.

Evidence and Conceptualization

The social analysis of American political history has been retarded by the historian's unimaginative preoccupation with traditional types of evidence and his consequent failure to conceptualize in working with that evidence. Historians are empiricists *par excellence* to a degree which distorts rather than clarifies the past. By feeling that they cannot "go beyond the evidence" they in fact permit the weight of historical evidence, without discrimination, to impose itself on their studies and to determine the categories of historical description. Evidence may well distort history because that which is readily available may not be significant and that which is highly significant may be entirely unavailable or

difficult to secure and organize in usable form. Too often historical studies are chosen simply because evidence is at hand and can
be worked up into a coherent study within a relatively short period of time. Such studies may not be high in a scale of significance and frequently impose upon the author a difficult burden of
demonstrating, often in a final chapter and often with considerable strain, their larger relevance.

Progress in any field of knowledge comes from constant interaction between conceptualization and evidence. The initial definition of a problem may well come through being impressed with
the nature of particular evidence, but it might well also come
through exposure to a concept derived from a more theoretical
work, a contemporary study, or treatment of an entirely different
geographical area. Such ideas might direct one's attention to
facets of history and types of historical evidence never before
encountered. Evidence may then modify the original concept
considerably, but the concept has played a significant role in
providing insight into a heretofore unobserved facet of the past.
Too complete immersion in evidence may well dull the historical
imagination so as to obscure other possible ways of looking at the
past, and require a complete shift from evidence into more abstract concepts in order to free one's imagination for a fresh set of
observations. These concepts may prove to be false, but far more
is gained by testing an hypothesis which may be either true or
false than by accumulating evidence which does not provide significant historical understanding.

Several types of evidence have distorted the study of American
political history. Each implicitly involves assumptions about the
nature of society or social change which limits the historian's
angle of vision or fixes his attention upon particular facets of society and obscures others. More important for our purposes, this
evidence encourages a way of looking at history quite different
from that involved in social analysis and in fact predisposes the
historian to turn away from an examination of political structure,
political process, and the human situation. It becomes, therefore,
an impediment rather than an aid to research.

Much evidence is institutional evidence. It is the product of a
particular institution such as a church, business, trade union, nationality groups, government agency, professional society, college,

university or public welfare association. Whether in the form of published reports or newspapers and news magazines or more ephemeral descriptions of activities, this evidence is produced to establish the image which the institution feels desirable to maintain before its contemporary public. The limitations in its use by historians, however, lie in the fact that institutions and their participants are frequently not explicitly self-conscious about many of the social processes in which they are involved. The very factors in which a social analyst is most interested might also be unexpressed assumptions or privately discussed conditions which are not explicitly recorded in "external evidence." Some of these might be self-consciously discussed in "internal" evidence available in private manuscripts, but others might be observable only in indirect ways.

The history of education, for example, is intimately interwoven with changing political values and perspectives.[33] But this connection is not made clear so long as the history of education focuses primarily on the growth in numbers of students, teachers and schools and in amount of financial support; the changing policies and practices of pedagogy; or the changing relationships between local, state and federal educational administration. These problems occupy the attention of the historian primarily because they are the matters about which "external" evidence, readily available, is concerned. But education reveals far more about social structure and social change than this evidence would suggest. For it plays a significant role in vertical social mobility on the part of both students and teachers; in horizontal geographical mobility from local and restricted communities into more cosmopolitan and varied environments; in elaborating the administrative structure of modern systematization, its reliance upon trained experts and its division of groups between the managers and the managed; and in either transmitting or modifying values and culture from one generation to the next.

These facets of the history of education concern social structures and processes of change which are rarely made explicit by those involved in education. Relevant evidence, therefore, is not directly available in those sources which institutions produce. Hence historians have rarely investigated them. Yet the sensitive analyst, either by a more acute attention to the indirect implications of formal institutional evidence, or by the discovery of new and more appropriate sources, can find material relevant to these problems. Consciousness of significance of those questions, however, will arise only insofar as the student develops through his own imagination or through ideas from other disciplines concepts about social mobility, local-cosmopolitan relationships or administration as a process of decision-making.

Without such conceptual imagination, moreover, the connection between education and political life remains obscure. Once the conceptual framework is shifted to types of human relationships involved in education, then the connection becomes clear and the possibilities of exploring common types of relationships become sharper. The upward social mobility of both students and teachers is closely related to the changing political attitudes which social mobility produces. The systematization in the administrative process in education is an integral part of the entire process of systematization which pervades almost every realm of modern society.[34] The parochial or cosmopolitan character of educational institutions are specific examples of the same dimension in political life. The social analysis of political life in its broadest scope, therefore, requires a more imaginative set of concepts, freed from the limitations of institutional evidence.

Ideological evidence has been as powerful a factor as institutional evidence in limiting our range of historical vision. Traditional political history has been severely narrowed by a preoccupation with evidence about the ideas expressed in party platforms, by candidates in campaign speeches, and by legislators in congressional debate. For the political historian works under a powerful impulse to organize his evidence into logical categories of ideas and then to assume that these categories can be applied directly to the nonideological world. If the political protagonists argued that the political world was divided primarily between the business community on the one hand and the mass of the people on the other, then this was so. Almost unconsciously the historian of ideas is tempted to transfer his conceptions about the structure of ideas to assertions about the structure of society. Such a process has drastically limited rather than expanded the possibilities of understanding society and social change by diverting attention from nonideological conceptual frameworks which relate more to what people did rather than what they said.

The "people versus the interests" framework of liberal historians, which has dominated the interpretation of the years since mid-nineteenth century, is a major case in point. It has obscured such plausible hypotheses that the Republican party was during the years from 1850 to 1893 a cultural entity rather than an instrument of big business, that the tariff was an understandable and natural product of working-class demands rather than an imposition upon them by employers, that the post-Civil War years were rich with grass-roots political conflict rather than decades of sterile shadow-boxing in the spirit of nineteenth-century "me-tooism," that the major question concerning the elections of the 1890's is why the Republican party secured such enormous gains in 1894 and held the loyalty of these voters for over a decade and a half, that the "public" regulation of private business is most often a case of certain segments of private business seeking to use government to control other segments of private business, that reforms in municipal government came not from the lower and middle classes, but from the dominant business and professional elements of the community.

The liberal ideological framework which has dominated the treatment of this period of political history has, like a "steel chain of ideas," bound our historical imagination to a limited set of problems. One of the major tasks of the social analysis of political history now is to break through this limited vision by means of looking at new types of evidence and delving into new conceptual alternatives. We need especially to understand the sharp difference between ideology and practice, between what people say they do and what they do. This is not to say that ideology is unimportant; it is, of course, a powerful factor in any historical situation. It is merely to say that the categories derived from ideological evidence are no safe guide to an understanding of political practice.

The personal record is a third type of evidence which is abundant to the point of being overwhelming and which by its very weight unconsciously distorts the writing of history. Biographies, memoirs and personal manuscripts are some of the most widely used sources of political evidence. Yet these sources give rise to a conception of political history as a network of personal relationships among a few leaders and party politics as a process of interpersonal maneuvering. Such a focus precludes attention to the wider structure of political life or to political process. It draws attention away from such evidence as popular voting, legislative roll-calls, or the data about hundreds of political leaders who left few manuscripts but about whom statistical information is available. In recent years the history profession has not considered political studies to be adequate unless they are based upon a wide coverage of personal manuscript sources. At the same time, however, it has not demanded equal use of these other types of evidence. The great concern with personal manuscripts has channeled interest into a narrow range of evidence, and, consequently, into a narrow range of problems. It has created a weight of interest and preoccupation, a climate of opinion, which is relatively unreceptive to the social analysis of political history.

The impact of individuals upon larger events may well be great, but it cannot be demonstrated and the precise interaction between individuals and larger affairs cannot be determined merely by observing the behavior of individuals or recounting their public actions or their reputations. For decision-makers work within persistent patterns of social relationships which establish an environment of action not readily manipulable by individual decisions. Concentration upon personal manuscripts has almost precluded a concern for the reconstruction of these social patterns. This is not so much a product of explicit and deliberate choice in social theory but of almost accidental immersion in a particular type of evidence which by its own weight establishes the historian's assumptions concerning social theory and the limits of his vision. Preoccupation with any type of evidence can so dull the historical imagination. It can be overcome only if one is willing to conceptualize at some distance from the evidence, look at new and different types of data, and then select evidence to test particular hypotheses.

Perhaps the most significant and widespread type of evidence which limits the historical imagination is that represented by sensational events. The historian's attention is almost naturally drawn to those events which gave rise to dramatic newspaper coverage or which aroused some unusual degree of sensationalism. If they were in the headlines, they were in the minds of most people, it is argued; their prominence in the historical record indicates accurately their prominence in the consciousness of people in society as a whole. Such episodes provide a clue to the preoccupations of the "average man," who is the object of study in "social history," and therefore to the more fundamental processes of political life.

The sensational event, however, provides few such clues. Surely our picture of the history of workingmen in the latter part of the nineteenth century, as one historian has recently pointed out, has been distorted by concentration upon the sensational labor upheavals of the railroad strikes of 1877, the Haymarket riot, the Pullman strike and the Homestead strike.[35] Far more significant features of that period of history are to be found in the less public, less sensational records, in reports of industrial commissions, in judicial proceedings, in local newspapers and in the census returns. Without these the meaning of the event is impossible to determine. Moreover, preoccupation with event and episode produces a picture of relationships over time which are sequences of isolated incidents tied together purely by chronology rather than continuing patterns of human relationships. The sensational event provides few clues as to the nature of social structure or process, or the kinds of groups into which a society is divided, their interconnections and their changes over time. The sensational event dictates a certain structure to history which is almost structureless, save the accidental juxtaposition of those events in a time sequence. Those who become immersed in event history, in fact, by the very weight of their preoccupation are prone to deny the existence of systematic human relationships, and to distrust conceptualizations about social structure and social process.

The social analysis of political history requires a new formulation of the problems of political history, and this, in turn, requires that the historical imagination be freed from the limitations within which traditional evidence has confined it. Instead of being overcome by the weight of evidence, of merely organizing it into logical categories, one should define the elements of political structure and political process which are important to investigate and then search for evidence which has a bearing on those problems. This approach, in fact, will lead the political historian to vast amounts of evidence, abundantly available, which he has never tapped. For lying in unused archival sources there are innumerable records with which the social analyst can reconstruct political history in a sharply new and different way.

Quantitative Data

The most promising current methodological innovation in the social analysis of political history lies in the use of quantitative data. This data is far more plentiful than we have been accustomed to think. In a host of scattered archives are masses of information about popular voting, legislative voting, demography and thousands of political leaders who left no papers. This evidence is bulky and difficult to use because of the enormous task of compiling and presenting it in manageable form. But it is, nonetheless, of enormous value. Moreover, there is not only an increasing desire to use it, but a growing ability to cope with it through new techniques of data compilation, storage and retrieval.

One of the most important types of this evidence is popular election data, which constitutes the only comprehensive information in documentary sources approximating a record of public opinion. Much of this data has been published in state manuals,[36] and often in the form of precinct as well as county returns, but much also is available in a variety of state reports, city directories or city council minutes, and an enormous amount lies in state and local archives and newspapers. Investigations have made clear that a very high percentage of past election returns are extant in one form or another and that the task of making these available for use is only a matter of time, effort and funds.[37]

Many other types of quantitative data are also available. Substantially complete legislative voting data at the federal and state levels has been published in the *Congressional Record* and its predecessor volumes and in state Senate and House journals. Newspapers and city council proceedings contain the votes on issues in city councils. A vast amount of demographic data concerning economic, religious, educational and ethnic characteristics of counties and even wards is available in federal, state and local censuses, in municipal and county archives, and in the compilations of private associations.[38] The microfilm publication of the federal manuscript population schedules, especially those from 1850 to 1880, presents untold opportunities for the political historian. For here is information concerning every individual in the United States, by name, where he lives (in cities even the precise street and house number), his age, his occupation, where he was born, where his mother and father were born, and in some years the value of his personal and real property. Several students have already used this material to determine patterns of social mobility; it can be used with equal value in describing the ethnocultural and socioeconomic composition of voting subdivisions.

The scattered but extensive information in county and municipal archives is formidable to use, but can provide far more insight into the dynamics of social change than we have had in the past. Economic records of taxes, real estate assessments and value of personal property have been used in the study of early American history. There is no reason, save that of time and cost, why the same kind of data should not be used far more extensively in investigating the nineteenth and twentieth centuries. An excellent example of the possibilities is the study by Sam Warner, Jr., of the process of suburbanization in Boston, *Street-Car Suburbs*.[39] Through the examination of 23,000 building permits issued for Roxbury, West Roxbury and Dorchester, Massachusetts, between 1870 and 1900, Mr. Warner has presented the first precise picture of the process of urban outward migration and vertical mobility from blue to white collar occupations. His study is a model in the imaginative use of local quantitative records for the analysis of social processes.

Equally extensive is the source material concerning individual political leaders. Historians have only recently undertaken studies of groups of political leaders—as contrasted with individuals—in order to determine patterns in the origin and nature of political leadership. For the most part confined to national figures, these studies have relied heavily upon information drawn from existing biographical compilations or from personal manuscripts. They have, therefore, been limited in coverage. But information is available in great abundance about tens and hundreds of thousands of political leaders at the state and local level. City directories indicate the occupation and address of every adult inhabitant; they reveal changes in both occupation and residence within and between generations and therefore demonstrate patterns of social mobility. Social registers provide ample information about upper-class groups to examine fully a facet of political life hardly investigated. Manuscript census returns, both federal and state, provide sources which permit an extensive analysis of political leadership for some years. Such sources make available an almost unbelievable amount of information about individual political leaders which permits types of collective biography analyses hardly even imagined in the not-too-distant past.

From these types of evidence one can reconstruct the characteristics of communities at the grass-roots level. This can be done especially with ward and precinct data. For although counties are rarely homogeneous in either social or economic characteristics, many wards and precincts are relatively so. At this level one is able to isolate communities of German Catholics, of coal miners, of lumbermen, of the upper class, of Quakers, or of Scotch Highland Presbyterians, to name only a few. Since election data is available for these same ward and precinct units, the analysis of voting patterns can be made fairly precise. At the same time, the abundant personal data enables one to establish family ties and family relationships from one generation to the next. Patterns of social mobility, intermarriage, and occupational and educational changes can be observed within specific contexts so that the resulting generalizations are fairly exact.

Because such studies are possible, the increased use of quantitative data should give rise to a renewed interest in both local history and genealogy by professional historians. Mr. Warner has amply illustrated the possibilities that urban local history holds for the analysis of broad social change. The genealogical compilations in the eastern states pertaining to families of the seventeenth and eighteenth centuries have provided an enormous amount of information for those who wish to undertake more detailed studies of early American history. Similar genealogical collections for the trans-Appalachian region are badly needed. The more traditional political historian is well aware of his indebtedness to the editor of personal manuscripts of political leaders. Perhaps in the future we will have as kind a regard for the person who undertakes the equally thankless task of compiling basic data about local communities or painfully constructs family histories.

The major problem with which this material confronts historians is the task of making it usable, of reducing vast amounts of data to comparable quantitative units and of presenting it in forms which facilitate analysis. Although perhaps 90 per cent or more of all popular election data ever recorded is still available, little is collected in one place and even less is available in the form of percentages. Researchers have neither the time nor the facilities to bring the data together in proper form and although studies of relatively small geographical areas over very short periods of time are feasible, larger ones covering more election units and defining longer trends, or comparative studies of different types of electorates, are now impossible to undertake. But the development of new technologies, and the increasing interest in financing their use, provide an opportunity for solving some of these problems. A project is now under way to do this for popular voting; if successful, as it appears it will be, the same approach can be applied to other data.

Some three years ago several historians and political scientists formally requested the Social Science Research Council to take up the project of collecting, computing and making available historical popular election data. The Council, in turn, asked W. Dean Burnham, who had compiled county returns for presidential elections in the nineteenth century, to survey the problem. This investigation, in the summer of 1962, revealed the vast extent of the available data and the Council in turn provided funds for Mr. Burnham to make a more extensive and precise determination of the sources of data. This he did during the 1963–1964 academic year from his location at the Survey Research Center at the University of Michigan. The work moved so well that by the fall of 1963 attention turned to the actual collection and computation of data.

At the same time the Survey Research Center expressed an interest in popular election data. Established originally to collect survey data through interviewing and questionnaire techniques, the Center began to collect documentary census data as well, and the extension into historical election data seemed to be a natural

evolution of its concerns. This development tied in closely with
the Center's changing role in the academic world. In 1961 it
helped to create the Consortium for Political Research. It invited
academic institutions to join in annual financial support of the
new institution and in turn receive political data which it would
collect in its library and participate in summer training seminars
at the University of Michigan. Originally established for the use
of political scientists, the Consortium could readily draw in those
in other disciplines interested in political research.

In late 1963 these two developments began to converge. The
transfer of data to Ann Arbor was tackled by historians themselves. In January 1964 the American Historical Association established the Ad Hoc Committee to Collect the Basic Quantitative Data of American Political History. Within three months
committees in 46 states were photocopying materials in their own
states to be sent to the Consortium. The original project called for
election returns since 1824 at the county level for the races of
president, governor, United States senator, and Congress, as well
as other state-wide races in years when these elections were held.
The project is now over 90 per cent complete. The response from
historians has been gratifying for it reveals a considerable interest
long felt to exist but finally confirmed. Meanwhile, the Consortium secured $144,000 from the National Science Foundation to
process the data and to support a project director. It seems feasible, therefore, to anticipate that the county data now being collected will be computed, processed, stored and available for research in about a year.

The success of the initial project has encouraged the AHA
Committee to move on to other tasks. It plans to collect data concerning county elections prior to 1824, primaries of all kinds and
state referenda. It will provide for the collection of minor civil
division returns—ward, township, precinct—not on a comprehensive scale but where it is needed for specific research projects. It
has under way discussions which will lead to the collection of the
demographic data needed to interpret election returns—nationality, race, religion, production, employment, income, communications, education, transportation, and degree of urban or rural
population. Steps have been taken to bring together congressional
roll-call votes, both those already tabulated in earlier projects and

those not yet tabulated, and to make them available to researchers through modern data processing techniques. An integral part of this project will involve more extensive and more readily accessible biographical information about legislators. It is hoped that legislative data for states can be developed as well, although on a more selective basis, in response to immediate research needs.

With this large amount of quantitative data available to us, we can be optimistic about the degree to which our knowledge of both political structure and political process will be advanced. At the same time, however, let us make no claims that the millennium is around the corner. Much needed quantitative data will not be available, many facets of political life, highly important for social analysis, cannot be investigated through its use. Moreover, quantitative data will often lead to confusion rather than clarity simply because, like other data, it will be used to disprove more than to prove, to qualify and hedge, and render conclusions which the methodological purists will disavow. Despite all this, the fact remains that the use of quantitative data constitutes at the present time one of the most promising opportunities for political historians, and the social analysis of political history, in which that data will be of considerable aid, is the area in which we can currently make the largest gains in our knowledge of the political past.

A further word of caution. As the collection of quantitative data increases and as support for and popularity of its use grows, we must approach it with discrimination. It is as fruitless to accept as important every piece of quantitative data as to accept every piece of nonquantitative data. Statistics can become as dead a weight, as distorting an influence, as can the mass of personal manuscript evidence in our archives. No matter of what kind, evidence must be used selectively, and unless the criteria of selection, the conceptual framework which defines the problem, is defensible, the evidence will not be selected with adequate discrimination. As it is not justifiable to write a biography because a man's papers are easily available, so it is not justifiable to devote resources and energy to the analysis of statistical data because funds are available and it is the thing to do. The basic element in any methodology is to make sure that it is relevant to the task at hand. Methodology should follow from rather than dictate the nature of the problem to be studied.

Comparative Analysis

The social analysis of political history facilitates and stimulates comparative study, the examination of apparently similar phenomena under different circumstances or of differences in the incidence of those phenomena. As a method of analysis comparative study sharpens distinctions which are otherwise not apparent. A more traditional and formal approach fails to identify such comparisons and contrasts because it does not give rise to analytical categories with respect to which distinctions and similarities can be observed. An emphasis on structure and process, however, focusing on patterns of human relationships, brings such common categories into sharp relief and permits comparative analysis.

The phenomena of human migration illustrate these possibilities. For decades historians have studied both the westward movement and immigration from Europe, but rarely has anyone even suggested that these might fruitfully be analyzed comparatively. Even more rarely has anyone suggested that they both might be explored in relation to other migrations. For American history has witnessed four major types of human migration: from the east to the west, from Europe to America, from rural to urban America, and from the central city to the suburb. All of these have in common the element of physical movement of people, but all of them also involve social processes. Who migrated and why? What was the impact of migration on the community from which it came? What effect did the process of migration have upon the social organization of the migrants? To what degree did migration involve an attempt to preserve a past social organization, to create a new one, or to escape from confining social patterns? What kinds of new social organization did the migrants create in their new residence? Insight into any of these questions would be enhanced by observing the same process in different migration contexts.

A comparative study of migrations in terms of their impact on political structure and political process would shed considerable light upon our political history. The political complexion of many communities depends upon the political attitudes formed by migrants in their previous location. Yet, the nature of the migration produces different effects. The stability of party affiliation in many areas of the country in the nineteenth century grew out of the stability of ethnic and cultural attitudes transplanted and preserved in new areas; this, in turn, depended upon the ability of migrating groups to maintain their social and therefore political attitudes from erosion in a more rational-secular society. Some migrations, however, involved individuals rather than groups, a process of breaking away from traditional patterns and considerable vertical as well as horizontal mobility in which the individual went through a rapid transformation of his values, sought to achieve a higher class position and developed different political attitudes. This might well have been the case with migration from rural America to cities and migration from the central city to the suburbs. These speculations suggest some of the possibilities of a comparative study of migration for political history.

A second possibility for comparative study lies in the political impact of depressions. The two most violent depression-caused political upheavals about which we know anything at all are those of 1893 and 1929.[40] Both have striking similarities. That of 1893 had a more dramatic and sudden impact, the voting shifts it produced being confined to the elections of 1893 and 1894. The 1929 depression, on the other hand, did not produce its full effect on the voting public in 1930 or even in 1932, but came over a period of a half-dozen years. Both were violent reactions to the party in power, the Democrats in 1893 and the Republicans in 1929. Both led to long-term shifts in voter preferences, toward the Republicans in the 1890's and the Democrats in the 1930's.

Each of these political changes went through a similar three-phased process. The Democratic gains of the 1930's involved initially a shift of ethnic voters in 1928 under the leadership of Al Smith. As a result of the depression, however, a second phase took place, involving a shift of all voting groups toward the Democratic party, and extending further the urban majorities which Smith established. By 1934 still a third stage developed in which lower-than-median income groups shifted even more strongly Democratic, and more-than-median income groups moved back toward their more Republican leanings. A similar sequence took place in the 1890's, but with different parties being the beneficiaries of the shifts in stages one and two. The Democrats in 1890 made major congressional and state gains. These seem to have arisen from the intense cultural conflict of the preceding decade which came from reaction against the political activities of evangelical protestantism in such forms as anti-foreign-language and prohibition laws. In 1892 this shift was a major element in Cleveland's victory. When the 1893 depression inaugurated a second stage, a massive revolt against the party in power, it reversed rather than continued the political trend of four years earlier, producing a sharp break in the pattern rather than a cumulative effect. The election of 1894 corresponded to the election of 1932 in that voters of all kinds shifted sharply toward the party out of power. And the election of 1896 corresponded to that of 1934 in that a marked polarization of voting took place, with a major segment of voters continuing to shift toward the dominant party, the Republicans, while another large segment reverted back toward its previous loyalties.

The political impact of other depressions is not clear because the effect of such crises as those of 1819, 1837, 1857 and 1873 on voting patterns is known only in the most general way. The shifts might have been less dramatic or might not have involved the juxtaposition of both ethno-cultural and socioeconomic changes in close temporal proximity. Therefore, one cannot now define the kinds of comparative problems which would arise from such an approach to these earlier elections. But the similarities and differences in the depressions of 1893 and 1929 suggest what could be done.

Urban political structure might well be still a third possibility for comparative analysis. The political leadership of upper classes, for example, differed in different cities. In the nineteenth century Eastern seaboard city, upper classes played a major role in political life. Although some aspects of this phenomenon have been studied, such as in Ari Hoogenboom's work on civil service reformers, its development as an extensive political movement has not. More important, the contrast between these cities and those west of the Alleghenies, such as Buffalo, Pittsburgh, Cleveland and Cincinnati, has not been explored. Here the upper class was not deeply involved in either the Liberal Republican movement, civil service reform, or other manifestations of Eastern genteel reform.

Here the upper class probably had more shallow roots, weaker traditions of civil leadership and fuller appreciation of the role of the new industrial labor force than was the case in the seaboard cities.

Reforms in the structure of municipal government around the turn of the twentieth century could also be better understood through comparative study. In all cities there appears to have been an upward shift in the location of decision-making. For systematization and organization in industrial society gave rise to integration in political, economic and ideological life.[41] Business and professional leaders who carried out these processes in their private affairs were in the forefront of the movement to systematize government and to shift decision-making into the hands of fewer people with more expert technical advice. This entire movement reveals processes of social integration in the evolution of cities and especially in the evolution of political relationships. Did these occur in the same way in cities in different geographical locations, of different size, of different degrees of cultural homogeneity? What different forms did the drive for political integration take? Did political integration proceed in roughly the same degree in all cities? Comparative study of this kind should create far more insight into the larger processes of urban social organization.

One of the most significant larger comparative studies concerns the origins and nature of the different systems of decision-making which have arisen in the course of American history. Three of these could come under study: the political parties which grew up in the late eighteenth century; the nonpartisan economic politics which developed in the late nineteenth century; the systematized, administrative decision-making which emerged at about the same time. Each of these is a distinct political system, each involving different processes by which decisions affecting large numbers of people are made. Each grew up to express political forces which other systems could not adequately express. Each involves different political clienteles, different environments for operation and different methods, and distinct conceptions of what a political system is and should be.

In *Political Parties in a New Nation*, William Chambers develops a scheme for analyzing the functions of political parties which could be applied to other political systems as well.[42] The political party must mobilize large numbers of voters for the election of national leaders; this new setting of national decision-making greatly broadened the scope, the problems and the tactics of political action. It required the development of a political ideology, for example, as the only way in which many diverse groups could be communicated with and focused on a single goal.

This method of decision-making became a millstone around the necks of those specialized economic groups in labor, industry and agriculture, who in the late nineteenth century wished to stress a particular legislative policy. Both their clientele and their objectives were more limited. They did not wish to be drawn into a political party in which many diverse groups vied for expression, in which their own goals would be watered down and their resources dissipated for political aims in which they had no direct interest. These groups, therefore, established political forces resting largely upon their economic organizations—trade unions, trade associations, farm cooperatives—which gave them economic bases from which to finance and organize political representation. Their clienteles were now disciplined through their economic organizations, rather than approached through ideology, and their tactics were attuned to legislative in-fighting rather than mass-voter appeal.

The administrative process involved a still different clientele and a different method of decision-making.[43] It arose from an attempt to coordinate and systematize, to bring together a great variety of factors for a single end. Those involved in it considered both the representative system of political parties and the log-rolling of economic groups to be wasteful and ineffective, incapable of providing the required centralization of decision-making. The administrative system, therefore, needed to develop no ideology or method of give-and-take compromise for its immediate functioning. It served to draw an ever-widening range of factors into a single orbit of influence and a single point of control, and to establish an orderly flow of influence between individuals in the hierarchy from the top down, on a person-to-person basis. Its tactics changed when it could not incorporate into its orbit of decision-making factors it wished to control. Thus, it often bargained with labor on equal terms, and fashioned ideology through the medium of public relations to influence public opinion. These processes, however, were viewed only as extensions of a tightly-knit, centralized system of decision-making into a larger arena. Examples of questions which are susceptible of comparative analysis could be multiplied manyfold. They include such specific problems as the legislative behavior of moderate and conservative Republicans since the 1930's; the impact of new immigrant workers on the political life of rural raw-material producing communities, communities along developing lines of transportation, or cities; the leadership of Whigs and Democrats in the 1840's; the voting patterns of Germans in Pennsylvania and Germans in Missouri in the years after 1850; the different political environment of the South and the West in the late nineteenth century. Or it could involve more general concerns such as the relationships between political ideology and political practice at different times, the interaction between grass-roots and national-level strata of political activity within the political parties, or the relationship between political elites and political masses. However specific or general, such comparative studies can be defined far more easily and thoroughly through the social analysis of politics. For political relationships are far more susceptible of comparison and contrast than are isolated episodes and events or formal characteristics. The social analysis of political history, therefore, brings into focus a host of comparative problems which under a more conventional treatment remain almost totally obscure.

History and the Social Sciences

The social analysis of political history involves a close relationship between history and the social sciences. Both concepts and methods developed in the social sciences are extremely useful to any historian who wishes to undertake political analysis within the guidelines proposed in this paper. Yet history is not a social science and the relationship between the two should be one of mutual cooperation rather than fusion. The social analysis of historical change requires not only that the historian be willing to borrow from the social sciences, but that he be clear about what he should borrow and what he should not. For political history has suffered from too much influence by the social sciences in some respects, as well as from too little in others. The social sciences are cast in an entirely different framework from the study of history and the two should approach each other with a willingness to cooperate when their interests dovetail and an acceptance of disagreement when their interests diverge.

By failing to utilize the social sciences, historians have been hampered in carrying out the very task which they presume to pursue. For the study of history is the attempt to reconstruct the process by which societies change over time. The emphasis is on society as a whole, not isolated segments of it, and broad changes over time, not episodes. The social sciences have developed more conceptual frameworks through which these problems can be approached than have historians. Examples of such works, in addition to those cited in previous pages, include Daniel Lerner, *The Passing of Traditional Society;* Dwight Waldo, *The Administrative State;* Gerhard Lenski, *The Religious Factor;* William Kornhauser, *The Politics of Mass Society;* Ferdinand Tonnies, *Community and Society;* Seymour Lipset, *Political Man;* Robert and Helen Lynd, *Middletown;* Robert Dahl, *Who Governs?;* Maurice Stein, *The Eclipse of Community;* and scores of others.[44] Studies of the process of modernization in the non-Western world, as some of these references indicate, can be especially useful for the development of concepts about both political structure and political process.

The historian can also benefit extensively from the healthy interest in quantitative data displayed in the social sciences. The historical record contains enormous amounts of quantitative data. Its use involves no esoteric or mysterious statistical methods, but only the simplest forms of quantification, the use of absolute and relative figures, the observation of changes in relative values over time, and simple correlations. These elementary devices one would hardly dare to glorify by the term statistics. Their use involves only a willingness to take the fullest advantage of quantitative data as a major type of historical evidence.

From the social sciences, then, we can secure both ideas and techniques as to how to undertake the systematic analysis of human situations and human relationships. We can become aware of the fact that political values and political actions are not fleeting and capricious, but patterned in both space and time. We can develop a sensitivity to the various ingredients of political systems, to the relationship between political leaders and political followings, the interaction between ethnocultural and socioeconomic political structures, the relationship between ideology and practice, the interaction between levels of political life within political parties, the roles of parties, nonpartisan economic politics and administration as different types of political systems, and the relationship between parochial and cosmopolitan political life. Historical scholarship in the United States has not generated, by itself, a sensitivity to these facets of social relationships despite the fact that history professes to be concerned with society and social change. Our major current task in history is to develop this sensitivity, and one of the most effective ways it can be done is through a judicious exposure to the social sciences.

Despite all this, however, history is not a social science, for the context within which it pursues social analysis is quite different from that of the social sciences. The social sciences seek to understand the present and history the past. The concepts of the former, therefore, are intended to analyze a relative static society, while history must develop concepts to understand change over long periods of time. As economics, sociology and political science drift further away from their earlier historical interests the role of history as the discipline focusing on change over time becomes sharper. As historians borrow from the social sciences, in fact, they often find common cause with those apparent minorities in the social sciences who seek to use their discipline to understand long-run change. Within a favorable climate, however, it is relatively easy to translate concepts used to analyze contemporary society into concepts which relate to change over time. The constant interest in the time-dimension, therefore, makes it imperative that the historian borrow from rather than accept fully the framework of the social sciences.

The social sciences are interested not only in understanding the present, but also in prediction and control. Their spirit is reformist. They seek to determine the present so as to change the future. They are guided by normative concepts which involve such values as the most efficient use of resources, the involvement of more citizens in the political process as informed voters, the reduction of social tension, the promotion of social welfare or public health, or the creation of a different balance between population and resources. Their major framework of analysis often is not one of how society changes, but of how certain impediments to desirable change can be overcome. The public health specialist, for example, becomes interested in the social sciences because it might help explain, and thus better to counteract, resistance to desirable public health measures. The political scientist seeks to understand how legislative decisions are made so that legislatures can function more in accordance with his conception of what is desirable. The economist seeks to understand the urban economy so as to counteract more effectively those forces which retard economic growth.

This normative spirit has influenced the study of American political history which has long been closely associated with political economy and sociology. Studies by political economists of the tariff, labor, or trusts, of governmental regulation or governmental reform, and by social workers of immigration, poverty and slums, serve as major historical source materials. In using them, historians have unconsciously accepted their implicit normative definition of political relationships. The tariff involves a political struggle between what is good for the public—the economist's conception of the most efficient allocation of resources—and the selfish "interests"—those who would compromise the ideal economy. The contest for municipal reform involved the public interest—the ideal government of the political scientist—in conflict with the selfish interests of the pressure group or machine. This transfer of a normative framework into a descriptive framework, the attempt to apply concepts derived from thinking about what ought to be to concepts about what was, has long restricted the imagination of the political historian. The social analysis of political history will not proceed fully unless it is set loose from this normative framework to conceptualize freely within the context of change over time alone.

Finally, history differs markedly from the social sciences in its approach to quantitative data and statistical method. For in the attempt to claim membership in the scientific world the social scientist has become less sensitive to problems of social analysis which those techniques cannot reach. The historian is far more aware than is the social scientist that the significance of a problem does not depend upon its susceptibility of statistical treatment. Despite the vast advances that can be made by using quantitative data, many problems in political history cannot be reached in this way. It would be tragic if historians failed to take the fullest possible advantage of the new opportunities which quantitative data and its related technology make available to us. It would be equally tragic if political historians confined themselves to such problems alone. Historical investigation should be guided by the degree to which it enhances understanding of political structure and political process rather than by the techniques of utilizing evidence. The re-creation of the past involves the construction of a mosaic in which perhaps only 25 per cent of the pieces are known. With the quantitative evidence now at our disposal we can add significantly to those available pieces, but it will raise the total to scarcely more than the 50 per cent level. We must still interpolate, fill in the gaps by inference and be willing to paint a total picture with insufficient pieces. This involves an attitude toward evidence which today is not received with open arms in the social sciences.

Political history offers a rich opportunity for the study of the past. Its concern for the variety of perspectives and values which contend for dominance inevitably draws it toward an understanding of different human situations which are limited by the finite scope of human perspective. At the same time it seeks to determine the patterns of relationships, of dominance and subordinance which develop among these groups. Since every area of human life involves the desire of some to influence others and inequalities in the distribution of the ability to command that influence, the range of political life is as broad as the scope of society itself, rather than limited to particular institutions. Political history, thus conceived, can well restore itself as the major integrative context of history. But it cannot perform this function unless it undergoes profound changes. It must greatly broaden its perspective to encompass the full range of value conflicts throughout society; it must develop concepts concerning structure and process and focus more directly on patterns of human relationships; and it must be willing to use the vast store of available quantitative data. With these shifts in perspective, the future holds bright possibilities, indeed, for the study of American political history.

Notes

1. For two convenient compilations of work in this vein see Thomas C. Cochran, *The Inner Revolution* (New York: Harper & Brothers, 1964); and Edward N. Saveth, *American History and the Social Sciences* (Glencoe, Ill.: 1964).
2. Thomas C. Cochran, "The Presidential Synthesis in American History," *American Historical Review*, LIII (July 1948), 748–759.
3. A recent study, relying heavily on a formal approach to political history, is Stanley L. Jones, *The Presidential Election of 1896* (Madison, Wis.: 1964).
4. V. O. Key, *American State Politics* (New York: 1956), p. 76.
5. For a critique of older views of municipal government see Lawrence J. R. Herson, "The Lost World of Municipal Government," *American Political Science Review*, LI (June 1957), 330–345.
6. Joseph R. Gusfield, *Symbolic Crusade* (Urbana, Ill.: 1963).
7. Lee Benson, "Research Problems in American Political Historiography," in Mirra Komarovsky, ed., *Common Frontiers in the Social Sciences* (Glencoe, Ill.: 1957), pp. 113–183; *The Concept of Jacksonian Democracy* (Princeton: 1961).
8. George Daniels, "Immigrant Vote in the 1860 Election: The Case of Iowa," *Mid-America*, XLIV (July 1962), 146–162. See also Arthur Gorenstein, "A Portrait of Ethnic Politics," *Publication of the American Jewish Historical Society*, L (March 1961), 202–238; and Robert P. Swierenga, "The Ethnic Leaders and Immigrant Voting," (forthcoming, *Civil War History*).
9. Samuel J. Eldersveld, "Influence of Metropolitan Party Pluralities on Presidential Elections," *American Political Science Review*, LXIV (1949), 1189–1206; Samuel Lubell, *The Future of American Politics* (New York: 1952), pp. 28–57.
10. James MacGregor Burns, *Roosevelt, the Lion and the Fox* (New York: 1956).
11. Herbert Gutman, "The Worker's Search for Power: Labor in the Gilded Age," in H. Wayne Morgan, ed., *The Gilded Age* (Syracuse, N. Y.: 1963), pp. 38–68.
12. C. Wright Mills, *The Sociological Imagination* (New York: 1959), pp. 50–75.
13. Dwight Waldo, *The Administrative State* (New York: 1948); Barry Karl, *Executive Reorganization and Reform in the New Deal* (Cambridge: 1963).
14. E. Digby Baltzell, *Philadelphia Gentlemen* (Glencoe, Ill.: 1958).
15. Lubell, *op. cit.*
16. Seymour Lipset, "Religion and Politics in the American Past and Pres-

ent," in Robert Lee and Martin E. Marty, eds., *Religion and Social Conflict* (New York: 1964).

17. See Gordon E. Baker, *Rural Versus Urban Political Power* (New York: 1955); Donald Kirschner, "Conflict in the Corn Belt: Rural Responses to Urbanization, 1919–1929," doctoral dissertation, University of Iowa, 1964.

18. Arthur J. Vidich and Joseph Bensman, *Small Town in Mass Society* (New York: 1960).

19. This analysis is based upon voting patterns in Iowa between 1887 and 1920.

20. Benson, *The Concept of Jacksonian Democracy.*

21. Joel Silbey, "Congressional Voting Behavior and the Southern–Western Alliance, 1841–1852," doctoral dissertation, University of Iowa, 1963.

22. See, for example, recent literature on the 1780's, such as Forrest Mac-Donald, *We The People* (Chicago: 1958); Jackson Turner Main, *The Anti-Federalists* (Chapel Hill, N. C.: University of North Carolina Press, 1961).

23. Robert Sharkey, *Money, Class and Party* (Baltimore, Md.: 1957).

24. Robert Wiebe, *Businessmen and Reform* (Cambridge: Harvard University Press, 1962), pp. 62–65.

25. For studies which fail to take this precaution, see George Mowry, *The California Progressives* (Berkeley and Los Angeles: 1951), pp. 86–104; and Alfred D. Chandler, Jr., "The Origins of Progressive Leadership," in Elting Morrison *et al.*, eds., *The Letters of Theodore Roosevelt* (Cambridge: 1951–1954), Vol. VIII, Appendix III, pp. 1462–1464. Two studies which use a more satisfactory method are Eli Daniel Potts, "A Comparative Study of the Leadership of Republican Factions in Iowa, 1904–1914," Master's thesis, State University of Iowa, 1954; William T. Kerr, Jr., "The Progressives of Washington, 1910–12," *Pacific Northwest Quarterly,* LV (January 1964), 16–27.

26. Lipset, *op. cit.*

27. Ari Hoogenboom, "An Analysis of Civil Service Reformers," *The Historian,* XXIII (November 1960), pp. 54–78.

28. Samuel P. Hays, "The Politics of Reform in Municipal Government in the Progressive Era" (forthcoming, *Pacific Northwest Quarterly*).

29. These conclusions are based upon an examination of the party affiliations of each member of Congress since 1874.

30. These observations are based upon several studies under way at the University of Pittsburgh of the role of professional groups in municipal reform in the city of Pittsburgh during the Progressive Era.

31. Hoogenboom, *op. cit.*; Geoffrey Blodgett, "The Gentle Reformers: Massachusetts Democrats in the Cleveland Era," doctoral dissertation, Harvard University, 1961.

32. Samuel P. Hays, *Conservation and the Gospel of Efficiency* (Cambridge: Harvard University Press, 1959), pp. 1–4, 261–276.

33. An excellent approach to the history of education is Bernard Bailyn, *Education in the Forming of American Society* (Chapel Hill, N. C.: University of North Carolina Press, 1960).

34. Raymond E. Callahan, *Education and the Cult of Efficiency* (Chicago: 1962).

35. Gutman, *op. cit.*

36. For a bibliography of state manuals see Charles Press and Oliver Williams, *State Manuals, Blue Books and Election Results* (Berkeley, Calif.: 1962).

37. Walter Dean Burnham, "Pilot Study: Recovery of Historical Election Data," (mimeo) prepared for the Committee on Political Behavior, Social Science Research Council (1962). See also Walter Dean Burnham, "Sources of Historical Election Data: A Preliminary Bibliography," Bibliographic Ser. No. 10, Institute for Community Development and Services (East Lansing: Michigan State University, 1963).

38. A bibliography of state censuses is Henry J. Dubester, *State Censuses*, (Washington: U. S. Government Printing Office, 1948).

39. Sam B. Warner, Jr., *Street-Car Suburbs* (Cambridge: 1962).

40. I am indebted to Mr. Paul Kleppner for the development of data concerning the 1894 and 1896 elections.

41. Hays, "The Politics of Reform."

42. William N. Chambers, *Political Parties in a New Nation* (New York: 1963).

43. Waldo, *op. cit.*

44. Daniel Lerner, *The Passing of Traditional Society* (Glencoe, Ill.: 1962); Dwight Waldo, *The Administrative State* (New York: 1948); Gerhard Lenski, *The Religious Factor* (New York: 1961); William Kornhauser, *The Politics of Mass Society* (Glencoe, Ill.: 1959); Ferdinand Tonnies, *Community and Society* (East Lansing, Mich.: 1957); Seymour Lipset, *Political Man* (New York: 1960); Robert and Helen Lynd, *Middletown* (New York: 1929); Robert Dahl, *Who Governs?* (New Haven, Conn.: 1961); Maurice Stein, *The Eclipse of Community* (Princeton, N.J.: 1960).

✢ 9 ✢

Richard P. McCormick

NEW PERSPECTIVES ON JACKSONIAN POLICIES

The historical phenomenon that we have come to call Jacksonian democracy has long engaged the attention of American political historians, and never more insistently than in the past decade. From the time of Parton and Bancroft to the present day scholars have recognized that a profoundly significant change took place in the climate of politics simultaneously with the appearance of Andrew Jackson on the presidential scene. They have sensed that a full understanding of the nature of that change might enable them to dissolve some of the mysteries that envelop the operation of the American democratic process. With such a challenging goal before them, they have pursued their investigations with uncommon intensity and with a keen awareness of the contemporary relevance of their findings.

A cursory view of the vast body of historical writing on this subject suggests that scholars in the field have been largely preoccupied with attempts to define the content of Jacksonian democracy and identify the influences that shaped it.[1] What did Jacksonian democracy represent, and what groups, classes, or sections gave it its distinctive character? The answers that have been given to these central questions have been—to put it succinctly—bewildering in their variety. The discriminating student, seeking the

Richard P. McCormick is Professor of History and university historian at Rutgers University. He is author of *Experiment in Independence: New Jersey in the Critical Period, The History of Voting in New Jersey, New Jersey from Colony to State*, and the *Second American Party*.

Reprinted from *American Historical Review*, LXV (1960), 288–301, by permission of the author and the publisher.

essential core of Jacksonianism, may make a choice among urban workingmen, southern planters, venturous conservatives, farm-bred *nouveaux riches,* western frontiersmen, frustrated entrepreneurs, or yeoman farmers. Various as are these interpretations of the motivating elements that constituted the true Jacksonians, the characterizations of the programmatic features of Jacksonian democracy are correspondingly diverse. Probably the reasonable observer will content himself with the conclusion that many influences were at work and that latitudinarianism prevailed among the Jacksonian faithful.

In contrast with the controversy that persists over these aspects of Jacksonian democracy, there has been little dissent from the judgment that "the 1830's saw the triumph in American politics of that democracy which has remained pre-eminently the distinguishing feature of our society." [2] The consensus would seem to be that with the emergence of Jackson, the political pulse of the nation quickened. The electorate, long dormant or excluded from the polls by suffrage barriers, now became fired with unprecedented political excitement. The result was a bursting forth of democratic energies, evidenced by a marked upward surge in voting.[3] Beard in his colorful fashion gave expression to the common viewpoint when he asserted that "the roaring flood of the new democracy was . . . [by 1824] foaming perilously near the crest. . . ." [4] Schlesinger, with his allusion to the "immense popular vote" [5] received by Jackson in 1824, creates a similar image. The Old Hero's victory in 1828 has been hailed as the consequence of a "mighty democratic uprising." [6]

That a "new democracy, ignorant, impulsive, irrational" [7] entered the arena of politics in the Jackson era has become one of the few unchallenged "facts" in an otherwise controversial field. Differences of opinion occur only when attempts are made to account for the remarkable increase in the size of the active electorate. The commonest explanations have emphasized the assertion by the common man of his newly won political privileges, the democratic influences that arose out of the western frontier, or the magnetic attractiveness of Jackson as a candidate capable of appealing with singular effectiveness to the backwoods hunter, the plain farmer, the urban workingman, and the southern planter.

Probably because the image of a "mighty democratic uprising" has been so universally agreed upon, there has been virtually no effort made to describe precisely the dimensions of the "uprising." Inquiry into this aspect of Jacksonian democracy has been discouraged by a common misconception regarding voter behavior before 1824. As the authors of one of our most recent and best textbooks put it: "In the years from the beginning of the government to 1824, a period for which we have no reliable election statistics, only small numbers of citizens seemed to have bothered to go to the polls." [8] Actually, abundant data on pre-1824 elections is available, and it indicates a far higher rate of voting than has been realized. Only by taking this data into consideration can voting behavior after 1824 be placed in proper perspective.

The question of whether there was indeed a "mighty democratic uprising" during the Jackson era is certainly crucial in any analysis of the political character of Jacksonian democracy. More broadly, however, we need to know the degree to which potential voters participated in elections before, during, and after the period of Jackson's presidency as well as the conditions that apparently influenced the rate of voting. Only when such factors have been analyzed can we arrive at firm conclusions with respect to the dimensions of the political changes that we associate with Jacksonian democracy. Obviously in studying voter participation we are dealing with but one aspect of a large problem, and the limitations imposed by such a restrictive focus should be apparent.

In measuring the magnitude of the vote in the Jackson elections it is hardly significant to use the total popular vote cast throughout the nation. A comparison of the total vote cast in 1812, for example, when in eight of the seventeen states electors were chosen by the legislature, with the vote in 1832, when every state except South Carolina chose its electors by popular vote, has limited meaning. Neither is it revealing to compare the total vote in 1824 with that in 1832 without taking into consideration the population increase during the interval. The shift from the legislative choice of electors to their election by popular vote, together with the steady population growth, obviously swelled the presidential vote. But the problem to be investigated is whether the Jackson elections brought voters to the polls in such enlarged or unprecedented proportions as to indicate that a "new democracy" had burst upon the political scene.

The most practicable method for measuring the degree to which voters participated in elections over a period of time is to relate the number of votes cast to the number of potential voters. Although there is no way of calculating precisely how many eligible voters there were in any state at a given time, the evidence at hand demonstrates that with the exception of Rhode Island, Virginia, and Louisiana the potential electorate after 1824 was roughly equivalent to the adult white male population.[9] A meaningful way of expressing the rate of voter participation, then, is to state it in terms of the percentage of the adult white males actually voting. This index can be employed to measure the variations that occurred in voter participation over a period of time and in both national and state elections. Consequently a basis is provided for comparing the rate of voting in the Jackson elections with other presidential elections before and after his regime as well as with state elections.[10]

Using this approach it is possible, first of all, to ascertain whether or not voter participation rose markedly in the three presidential elections in which Jackson was a candidate. Did voter participation in these elections so far exceed the peak participation in the pre-1824 elections as to suggest that a mighty democratic uprising was taking place? The accompanying data (Table 9-1) provides an answer to this basic question.[11]

In the 1824 election not a single one of the eighteen states in which the electors were chosen by popular vote attained the percentage of voter participation that had been reached before 1824. Prior to that critical election, fifteen of those eighteen states had recorded votes in excess of 50 per cent of their adult white male population, but in 1824 only two states—Maryland and Alabama —exceeded this modest mark. The average rate of voter participation in the election was 26.5 per cent. This hardly fits the image of the "roaring flood of the new democracy . . . foaming perilously near the crest. . . ."

There would seem to be persuasive evidence that in 1828 the common man flocked to the polls in unprecedented numbers, for the proportion of adult white males voting soared to 56.3 per cent, more than double the 1824 figure. But this outpouring

TABLE 9-1

Percentages of Adult White Males Voting in Presidential Elections, 1824–1844

%	Year	State	1824	1828	1832	1836	1840	1844
62.0	1812 g	Maine	18.9	42.7	(66.2)*	37.4	(82.2)*	(67.5)*
80.8	1814 g	New Hampshire	16.8	76.5	74.2	38.2	(86.4)*	65.6
79.9	1812 g	Vermont	—	55.8	50.0	52.5	74.0	65.7
67.4	1812 g	Massachusetts	29.1	25.7	39.3	45.1	66.4	59.3
49.4	1812 g	Rhode Island	12.4	18.0	22.4	24.1	33.2	39.8
54.4	1819 †	Connecticut	14.9	27.1	45.9	52.3	(75.7)*	(76.1)*
41.5	1810 g	New York	—	(70.4)*	(72.1)*	(60.2)*	(77.7)*	(73.6)*
71.8	1808 p	New Jersey	31.1	70.9	69.0	69.3	(80.4)*	(81.6)*
71.5	1808 g	Pennsylvania	19.6	56.6	52.7	53.1	(77.4)*	(75.5)*
81.9	1804 g	Delaware	—	—	67.0	69.4	(82.8)*	(85.0)*
69.0	1820 †	Maryland	53.7	(76.2)*	55.6	67.5	(84.6)*	(80.3)*
25.9	1800 p	Virginia	11.5	(27.6)*	(30.8)*	(35.1)*	(54.6)*	(54.5)*
70.0 #	1823 c	North Carolina	42.2	56.8	31.7	52.9	(83.1)*	(79.1)*
62.3	1812 c	Georgia	—	35.9	33.0	(64.9)*	(88.9)*	(94.0)*
74.4	1820 g	Kentucky	25.3	70.7	73.9	61.1	74.3	(80.3)*
80.0	1817 g	Tennessee	26.8	49.8	28.8	55.2	(89.6)*	(89.6)*
34.2	1812 g	Louisiana	—	(36.3)*	24.4	19.2	(39.4)*	(44.7)*
96.7	1819 g	Alabama	52.1	53.6	33.3	65.0	89.8	82.7
79.8	1823 g	Mississippi	41.6	56.6	32.8	62.8	(88.2)*	(89.7)*
46.5	1822 g	Ohio	34.8	(75.8)*	(73.8)*	(75.5)*	(84.5)*	(83.6)*
52.4	1822 g	Indiana	37.5	(68.3)*	(61.8)*	(70.1)*	(86.0)*	(84.9)*
55.8	1822 g	Illinois	24.2	51.9	45.6	43.7	(85.9)*	(76.3)*
71.9	1820 g	Missouri	20.1	54.3	40.8	35.6	(74.0)*	(74.7)*
—		Arkansas	—	—	—	35.0	86.4	68.8
—		Michigan	—	—	—	35.7	84.9	79.3
		National Aver.	26.5	56.3	54.9	55.2	78.0	74.9

Highest Known Percentage of Adult White Males Voting before 1824

* Exceeded pre-1824 high
g Gubernatorial election
p Presidential election
Estimate based on incomplete returns
c Congressional election
† Election of legislature

shrinks in magnitude when we observe that in only six of the twenty-two states involved were new highs in voter participation established. In three of these—Maryland, Virginia, and Louisiana —the recorded gain was inconsiderable, and in a fourth—New York—the bulk of the increase might be attributed to changes that had been made in suffrage qualifications as recently as 1821 and 1826. Six states went over the 70 per cent mark, whereas ten had bettered that performance before 1824. Instead of a "mighty democratic uprising" there was in 1828 a voter turnout that approached—but in only a few instances matched or exceeded—the maximum levels that had been attained before the Jackson era.

The advance that was registered in 1828 did not carry forward to 1832. Despite the fact that Jackson was probably at the peak of his personal popularity, that he was engaged in a campaign that was presumably to decide issues of great magnitude, and that in the opinion of some authorities a "well-developed two-party system on a national scale" had been established,[12] there was a slight decline in voter participation. The average for the twenty-three states participating in the presidential contest was 54.9 per cent. In fifteen states a smaller percentage of the adult white males went to the polls in 1832 than in 1828. Only five states bettered their pre-1824 highs. Again the conclusion would be that it was essentially the pre-1824 electorate—diminished in most states and augmented in a few—that voted in 1832. Thus, after three Jackson elections, sixteen states had not achieved the proportions of voter participation that they had reached before 1824. The "new democracy" had not yet made its appearance.[13]

A comparison of the Jackson elections with earlier presidential contests is of some interest. Such comparisons have little validity before 1808 because few states chose electors by popular vote, and for certain of those states the complete returns are not available. In 1816 and 1820 there was so little opposition to Monroe that the voter interest was negligible. The most relevant elections, therefore, are those of 1808 and 1812. The accompanying table (Table 9–2) gives the percentages of adult white males voting in 1808 and 1812 in those states for which full returns could be found, together with the comparable percentages for the elections of 1824 and 1828. In 1824 only one state—Ohio—surpassed the highs established in either 1808 or 1812. Four more joined this list

in 1828—Virginia, Maryland, Pennsylvania, and New Hampshire
—although the margin in the last case was so small as to be incon-
sequential. The most significant conclusion to be drawn from this
admittedly limited and unrepresentative data is that in those states
where there was a vigorous two-party contest in 1808 and 1812
the vote was relatively high. Conversely, where there was little or
no contest in 1824 or 1828, the vote was low.

TABLE 9–2

*Percentages of Adult White Males Voting in
Presidential Elections*

State	1808	1812	1824	1828
Maine	Legis.	50.0	18.9	42.7
New Hampshire	62.1	75.4	16.8	76.5
Massachusetts	Legis.	51.4	29.1	25.7
Rhode Island	37.4	37.7	12.4	18.0
New Jersey	71.8	Legis.	31.1	70.9
Pennsylvania	34.7	45.5	19.6	56.6
Maryland	48.4	56.5	53.7	76.2
Virginia	17.7	17.8	11.5	27.6
Ohio	12.8	20.0	34.8	75.8

NOTE: No complete returns of the popular vote cast for electors in Kentucky or Tennessee
in 1808 and 1812 and in North Carolina in 1808 could be located.

When an examination is made of voting in other than presidential elections prior to 1824, the inaccuracy of the impression that
"only small numbers of citizens" went to the polls becomes apparent. Because of the almost automatic succession of the members of the "Virginia dynasty" and the early deterioration of the
national two-party system that had seemed to be developing
around 1800, presidential elections did not arouse voter interest as
much as did those for governor, state legislators, or even members
of Congress. In such elections at the state level the "common
man" was stimulated by local factors to cast his vote, and he frequently responded in higher proportions than he did to the later
stimulus provided by Jackson.

The average voter participation for all the states in 1828 was
56.3 per cent. Before 1824 fifteen of the twenty-two states had
surpassed that percentage. Among other things, this means that
the 1828 election failed to bring to the polls the proportion of the

electorate that had voted on occasion in previous elections. There was, in other words, a high potential vote that was frequently realized in state elections but which did not materialize in presidential elections. The unsupported assumption that the common man was either apathetic or debarred from voting by suffrage barriers before 1824 is untenable in the light of this evidence.

In state after state (see Table 9–1) gubernatorial elections attracted 70 per cent or more of the adult white males to the polls. Among the notable highs recorded were Delaware with 81.9 per cent in 1804, New Hampshire with 80.8 per cent in 1814, Tennessee with 80.0 per cent in 1817, Vermont with 79.9 per cent in 1812, Mississippi with 79.8 per cent in 1823, and Alabama with a highly improbable 96.7 per cent in its first gubernatorial contest in 1819. There is reason to believe that in some states, at least, the voter participation in the election of state legislators was even higher than in gubernatorial elections. Because of the virtual impossibility of securing county-by-county or district-by-district returns for such elections, this hypothesis is difficult to verify.

Down to this point the voter turnout in the Jackson elections has been compared with that in elections held prior to 1824. Now it becomes appropriate to inquire whether during the period 1824 through 1832 voters turned out in greater proportions for the three presidential contests than they did for the contemporary state elections. If, indeed, this "new democracy" bore some special relationship to Andrew Jackson or to his policies, it might be anticipated that interest in the elections in which he was the central figure would stimulate greater voter participation than gubernatorial contests, in which he was at most a remote factor.

Actually, the election returns show fairly conclusively that throughout the eight-year period the electorate continued to participate more extensively in state elections than in those involving the presidency. Between 1824 and 1832 there were fifty regular gubernatorial elections in the states that chose their electors by popular vote. In only sixteen of these fifty instances did the vote for President surpass the corresponding vote for governor. In Rhode Island, Delaware, Tennessee, Kentucky, Illinois, Mississippi, Missouri, and Georgia the vote for governor consistently exceeded that for President. Only in Connecticut was the reverse true.[14] Viewed from this perspective, too, the remarkable feature of the vote in the Jackson elections is not its immensity but rather its smallness.

Finally, the Jackson elections may be compared with subsequent presidential elections. Once Jackson had retired to the Hermitage, and figures of less dramatic proportions took up the contest for the presidency, did voter participation rise or fall? This question can be answered by observing the percentage of adult white males who voted in each state in the presidential elections of 1836 through 1844 (Table 9–1). Voter participation in the 1836 election remained near the level that had been established in 1828 and 1832, with 55.2 per cent of the adult white males voting. Only five states registered percentages in excess of their pre-1824 highs. But in 1840 the "new democracy" made its appearance with explosive suddenness.

In a surge to the polls that has rarely, if ever, been exceeded in any presidential election, four out of five (78.0 per cent) of the adult white males cast their votes for Harrison or Van Buren.[15] This new electorate was greater than that of the Jackson period by more than 40 per cent. In all but five states—Vermont, Massachusetts, Rhode Island, Kentucky, and Alabama—the peaks of voter participation reached before 1824 were passed. Fourteen of the twenty-five states involved set record highs for voting that were not to be broken throughout the remainder of the ante bellum period. Now, at last, the common man—or at least the man who previously had not been sufficiently aroused to vote in presidential elections—cast his weight into the political balance. This "Tippecanoe democracy," if such a label is permissible, was of a different order of magnitude from the Jacksonian democracy. The elections in which Jackson figured brought to the polls only those men who were accustomed to voting in state or national elections, except in a very few states. The Tippecanoe canvass witnessed an extraordinary expansion of the size of the presidential electorate far beyond previous dimensions. It was in 1840, then, that the "roaring flood of the new democracy" reached its crest. And it engulfed the Jacksonians.

The flood receded only slightly in 1844, when 74.9 per cent of the estimated potential electorate went to the polls. Indeed, nine states attained their record highs for the period. In 1848 and 1852 there was a general downward trend in voter participation, followed by a modest upswing in 1856 and 1860. But the level of voter activity remained well above that of the Jackson elections. The conclusion to be drawn is that the "mighty democratic uprising" came after the period of Jackson's presidency.

Now that the quantitative dimensions of Jacksonian democracy as a political phenomenon have been delineated and brought into some appropriate perspective, certain questions still remain to be answered. Granted that the Jacksonian electorate—as revealed by the comparisons that have been set forth—was not really very large, how account for the fact that voter participation doubled between the elections of 1824 and 1828? It is true that the total vote soared from around 359,000 to 1,155,400 and that the percentage of voter participation more than doubled. Traditionally, students of the Jackson period have been impressed by this steep increase in voting and by way of explanation have identified the causal factors as the reduction of suffrage qualifications, the democratic influence of the West, or the personal magnetism of Jackson. The validity of each of these hypotheses needs to be reexamined.

In no one of the states in which electors were chosen by popular vote was any significant change made in suffrage qualifications between 1824 and 1828. Subsequently, severe restrictions were maintained in Rhode Island until 1842, when some liberalization was effected, and in Virginia down to 1850. In Louisiana, where the payment of a tax was a requirement, the character of the state tax system apparently operated to restrict the suffrage at least as late as 1845. Thus with the three exceptions noted, the elimination of suffrage barriers was hardly a factor in producing an enlarged electorate during the Jackson and post-Jackson periods. Furthermore, all but a few states had extended the privilege of voting either to all male taxpayers or to all adult male citizens by 1810. After Connecticut eliminated its property qualification in 1818, Massachusetts in 1821, and New York in 1821 and 1826, only Rhode Island, Virginia, and Louisiana were left on the list of "restrictionist" states.[16] Neither Jackson's victory nor the increased vote in 1828 can be attributed to the presence at the polls of a newly enfranchised mass of voters.

Similarly, it does not appear that the western states led the way in voter participation.[17] Prior to 1824, for example, Ohio, Indiana, and Illinois had never brought to the polls as much as 60 per cent of their adult white males. Most of the eastern states had surpassed that level by considerable margins. In the election of 1828 six states registered votes in excess of 70 per cent of their adult white male populations. They were in order of rank: New Hampshire, Maryland, Ohio, New Jersey, Kentucky, and New York. The six leaders in 1832 were: New Hampshire, Kentucky, Ohio, New York, New Jersey, and Delaware. It will be obvious that the West, however that region may be defined, was not leading the "mighty democratic uprising." Western influences, then, do not explain the increased vote in 1828.

There remains to be considered the factor of Jackson's personal popularity. Did Jackson, the popular hero, attract voters to the polls in unprecedented proportions? The comparisons that have already been made between the Jackson elections and other elections—state and national—before, during, and after his presidency would suggest a negative answer to the question. Granted that a majority of the voters in 1828 favored Jackson, it is not evident that his partisans stormed the polls any more enthusiastically than did the Adams men. Of the six highest states in voter participation in 1828, three favored Adams and three were for Jackson, which could be interpreted to mean that the convinced Adams supporters turned out no less zealously for their man than did the ardent Jacksonians. When Van Buren replaced Jackson in 1836, the voting average increased slightly over 1832. And, as has been demonstrated, the real manifestation of the "new democracy" came not in 1828 but in 1840.

The most satisfactory explanation for the increase in voter participation between 1824 and 1828 is a simple and obvious one. During the long reign of the Virginia dynasty, interest in presidential elections dwindled. In 1816 and 1820 there had been no contest. The somewhat fortuitous termination of the Virginia succession in 1824 and the failure of the congressional caucus to solve the problem of leadership succession threw the choice of a President upon the electorate. But popular interest was dampened by the confusion of choice presented by the multiplicity of candidates, by the disintegration of the old national parties, by the fact that in most states one or another of the candidates was so overwhelmingly popular as to forestall any semblance of a contest, and possibly by the realization that the election would ultimately be decided by the House of Representatives. By 1828 the situation had altered. There were but two candidates in the field, each of whom had substantial sectional backing. A clear-cut contest impended, and the voters became sufficiently aroused to go to the polls in moderate numbers.

One final question remains. Why was the vote in the Jackson elections relatively low when compared with previous and contemporary state elections and with presidential votes after 1840? The answer, in brief, is that in most states either Jackson or his opponent had such a one-sided advantage that the result was a foregone conclusion. Consequently there was little incentive for the voters to go to the polls.

This factor can be evaluated in fairly specific quantitative terms. If the percentage of the total vote secured by each candidate in each state in the election of 1828 is calculated, the difference between the percentages can be used as an index of the closeness, or one-sidedness, of the contest. In Illinois, for example, Jackson received 67 per cent of the total vote and Adams, 33; the difference—thirty-four points—represents the margin between the candidates. The average difference between the candidates, taking all the states together, was thirty-six points. Expressed another way this would mean that in the average state the winning candidate received more than twice the vote of the loser. Actually, this was the case in thirteen of the twenty-two states (see Table 9–3).[18] Such a wide margin virtually placed these states in the "no contest" category.

A remarkably close correlation existed between the size of the voter turnout and the relative closeness of the contest. The six states previously listed as having the greatest voter participation in 1828 were among the seven states with the smallest margin of difference between the candidates. The exception was Louisiana, where restrictions on the suffrage curtailed the vote. Even in this instance, however, it is significant that voter participation in Louisiana reached a record high. In those states, then, where there was a close balance of political forces the vote was large, and conversely, where the contest was very one sided, the vote was low.

Most of the states in 1828 were so strongly partial to one or another of the candidates that they can best be characterized as one-party states. Adams encountered little opposition in New England, except in New Hampshire, and Jackson met with hardly any resistance in the South. It was chiefly in the middle states and

TABLE 9–3

Differential between Percentages of Total Vote Obtained by Major Presidential Candidates, 1828–1844

State	1828	1832	1836	1840	1844
Maine	20	10	20	1	13
New Hampshire	7	13	50	11	19
Vermont	50	10	20	29	18
Massachusetts	66	30	9	16	12
Rhode Island	50	14	6	23	20
Connecticut	50	20	1	11	5
New York	2	4	9	4	1
New Jersey	4	1	1	4	1
Pennsylvania	33	16	4	1	2
Delaware	—	2	6	10	3
Maryland	2	1	7	8	5
Virginia	38	50	13	1	6
North Carolina	47	70	6	15	5
Georgia	94	100	4	12	4
Kentucky	1	9	6	29	8
Tennessee	90	90	16	11	1
Louisiana	6	38	3	19	3
Alabama	80	100	11	9	18
Mississippi	60	77	2	7	13
Ohio	3	3	4	9	2
Indiana	13	34	12	12	2
Illinois	34	37	10	2	12
Missouri	41	32	21	14	17
Arkansas	—	—	28	13	26
Michigan	—	—	9	4	6
Average Differential	36	36	11	11	9

the older West that the real battle was waged. With the removal of Adams from the scene after 1828, New England became less of a one-party section, but the South remained extremely one sided. Consequently it is not surprising that voter participation in 1832 failed even to match that of 1828.

Here, certainly, is a factor of crucial importance in explaining the dimensions of the voter turnout in the Jackson elections. National parties were still in a rudimentary condition and were highly unbalanced from state to state. Indeed, a two-party system scarcely could be said to exist in more than half of the states until after 1832. Where opposing parties had been formed to contest the election, the vote was large, but where no parties, or only one, took the field, the vote was low. By 1840, fairly well-balanced parties had been organized in virtually every state. In only three states did the margin between Harrison and Van Buren exceed twenty points and the average for all the states was only eleven points. The result was generally high voter participation.[19]

When Jacksonian democracy is viewed from the perspectives employed in this analysis, its political dimensions insofar as they relate to the behavior of the electorate can be described with some precision. None of the Jackson elections involved a "mighty democratic uprising" in the sense that voters were drawn to the polls in unprecedented proportions. When compared with the peak participation recorded for each state before 1824, or with contemporaneous gubernatorial elections, or most particularly with the vast outpouring of the electorate in 1840, voter participation in the Jackson elections was unimpressive. The key to the relatively low presidential vote would seem to be the extreme political imbalance that existed in most states as between the Jacksonians and their opponents. Associated with this imbalance was the immature development of national political parties. Indeed, it can be highly misleading to think in terms of national parties in connection with the Jackson elections. As balanced, organized parties subsequently made their appearance from state to state, and voters were stimualted by the prospect of a genuine contest, a marked rise in voter participation occurred. Such conditions did not prevail generally across the nation until 1840, and then at last the "mighty democratic uprising" took place.

Notes

NOTE: The present study was made possible by a grant from the Social Science Research Council.

1. For a concise survey of the literature on the topic, see Charles G. Sellers, Jr., *Jacksonian Democracy* (Washington, D. C.: 1958) or his "Andrew Jackson versus the Historians," *Mississippi Valley Historical Review*, XLIV (March 1958), 615–634. For the most recent treatment of the period, see Glyndon G. Van Deusen, *The Jacksonian Era, 1828–1848*, in Henry Steele Commager and Richard B. Morris, eds., *The New American Nation Series* (New York: 1959).

2. Sellers, *Jacksonian Democracy*, p. 1.

3. For representative examples of this viewpoint, see Charles A. and Mary R. Beard, *The Rise of American Civilization* (2 vols. in 1, New York: 1933), pp. 540, 546, 550; Wilfred E. Binkley, *American Political Parties: Their Natural History* (New York: 1943), pp. 101, 108, 111, 115, 121; John D. Hicks, *The Federal Union* (2d ed., Cambridge, Mass.: 1952), pp. 351, 363–364; William MacDonald, *Jacksonian Democracy, 1829–1837* (New York: 1906), pp. 3, 42, 311; Richard Hofstadter, *The American Political Tradition* (New York: Vintage ed., 1954), pp. 50–52; John Bach McMasters, *A History of the People of the United States* (8 vols., New York, 1883–1913), Vol. V, p. 518; Marvin Meyers, *The Jacksonian Persuasion: Politics and Belief* (Stanford, Calif.: 1957), pp. 4, 11; E. E. Robinson, *The Evolution of American Political Parties* (New York: 1924), p. 101; E. H. Roseboom, *A History of Presidential Elections* (New York: 1957), p. 91; Arthur M. Schlesinger, Jr., *The Age of Jackson* (Boston: 1947), pp. 12–15, 36.

4. Beard, *American Civilization*, p. 550.

5. Schlesinger, *Age of Jackson*, p. 36.

6. Frederick A. Ogg, *The Reign of Andrew Jackson* (New Haven, Conn.: 1919), p. 114.

7. Roseboom, *Presidential Elections*, p. 91.

8. Richard Hofstadter, William Miller, and Daniel Aaron, *The American Republic* (2 vols. New York: 1959), Vol. I, p. 391.

9. The only states in which property qualifications were a factor in restricting voting in presidential elections after 1824 were Virginia and Rhode Island. New York did not completely abolish property qualifications until 1826, but the reform of 1821 had resulted in virtually free suffrage. In Louisiana, where voters were required to be taxpayers, the nature of the system of taxation operated to confine the suffrage to perhaps half of the adult white males. See Joseph G. Tregle, "Louisiana in the Age of Jackson: A Study in Ego Politics," doctoral dissertation, University of Pennsylvania, 1954, pp. 105–108. To be perfectly accurate, estimates of the size of the potential electorate would have to take into account such factors as citizenship and residence requirements and, in certain states, the eligibility of Negro voters.

10. After 1840 when the proportion of aliens in the population increased markedly and citizenship became an important requirement for voting, the adult-white-male index becomes less reliable. In order to calculate

accurately the number of qualified voters in 1850, the alien adult white males would have to be deducted in those states where citizenship was a qualification for voting. Unfortunately, federal census data on aliens is not obtainable prior to 1890, except for the censuses of 1820 and 1830. In the latter year there were only 107,832 aliens out of a total population of nearly thirteen millions, a fraction so small as to be insignificant. But by 1850, according to one calculation, adult male aliens may have amounted to one-twelfth of the total voting population. J. D. B. De Bow, *Statistical View of the United States* (Washington, D. C.: 1854), p. 50. In certain eastern states the proportion of aliens was higher than the national average. In New York, for example, 18.5 per cent of the total population in 1855 were aliens; the proportion in 1835 had been only 3.79 per cent. Franklin B. Hough, *Census of the State of New York for 1855* (Albany: 1857), pp. xiv, xliii.

11. The figures on voter participation have been computed from a compilation I have made of returns of state-wide elections covering twenty-five states over the period from 1800 to 1860. For the post-1836 years the returns may be consulted in the *Whig Almanacs* and *Tribune Almanacs* issued by Horace Greeley and, for presidential elections, in W. Dean Burnham's *Presidential Ballots, 1836–1892* (Baltimore, Md.: 1955). For the period prior to 1836 the best general sources are the official manuals of certain states, the legislative journals, and the contemporary newspapers. For several states, among them Massachusetts, Connecticut, New Jersey, Maryland, Virginia, North Carolina, and Georgia, it is necessary to use the manuscript sources. The estimate of the adult white male population was computed for each decennial year from the federal census, and the figure for the particular election year was obtained by interpolation. I have computed for each gubernatorial and presidential election in the twenty-five states admitted to the Union by 1836 (exclusive of South Carolina) the percentage of adult white males voting.

12. Charles G. Sellers, Jr., *James K. Polk: Jacksonian, 1795–1843* (Princeton, N. J.: 1957), p. 166. See also Meyers, *Jacksonian Persuasion*, p. 11.

13. It may be suggested that it is invalid to compare voter participation in each state in the presidential contests of 1824, 1828, and 1832 with the highs, rather than the average participation in each state prior to 1824. The object of the comparison is to ascertain whether the Jackson elections brought voters to the polls in unprecedented numbers, as has so often been asserted. Moreover, it is hardly feasible to compare average participation in elections before and after 1824 in many states because of the changes that were made in the methods of electing governors and presidential electors or—in certain instances—because the state had only recently entered the Union. However, among those states in which average voter participation was obviously higher before 1824 than it was in the three Jackson elections were Alabama, Connecticut, Georgia, Massachusetts, Mississippi, New Hampshire (1809–1817), Pennsylvania, Rhode Island, Tennessee, and Vermont (1807–1815).

14. These summary statements are based upon an analysis of the compilation referred to in footnote 11.

15. It can be calculated that the total of adult white males in the twenty-five states was 3,090,708. The total popular vote was 2,409,682. In the presidential election of 1896 the total vote approximated 80 per cent of the

potential electorate. In 1940 and 1952 the comparable figures would be 63 per cent and 65 per cent respectively. These percentages have been calculated on the assumption that the potential electorate in 1896 included all adult male citizens and in 1940 and 1952 all adult citizens.

16. There is no reliable study of suffrage qualifications, but the standard account is Kirk H. Porter, *A History of Suffrage in the United States* (Chicago: 1918). Porter erred in stating that New Jersey retained a property requirement until 1844; it was replaced in 1807 by taxpayer suffrage. See my *The History of Voting in New Jersey: A Study of the Development of Election Machinery, 1664–1911* (New Brunswick, N. J.: 1953), p. 100. Porter's statement that a freehold property requirement existed in Tennessee under the 1796 constitution is based on a misreading of that document. Porter, *Suffrage*, pp. 24, 80; Francis N. Thrope, *Federal and State Constitutions, Colonial Charters, and Other Organic Laws* (7 vols., Washington, D. C.: 1909), Vol. VI, p. 3418.

17. See Table 9–1.

18. The index figures in the table represent the difference between the percentages of the total popular vote secured by the two major candidates in each state. For the election of 1832, the figures represent only the difference between the votes obtained by Clay and Jackson.

19. Careful analysis of the data in Table 9–3 will suggest that there were three fairly distinct stages in the emergence of a nationally balanced two-party system. Balanced parties appeared first in the middle states between 1824 and 1828. New England remained essentially a one-party section until after Adams had passed from the scene; then competing parties appeared. In the South and the newer West, a one-party dominance continued until divisions arose over who should succeed Jackson. Sectional loyalties to favorite sons obviously exerted a determining influence on presidential politics, and consequently on party formation, in the Jackson years.

✤ 10 ✤

David Donald

THE CONGRESSIONAL EQUATION

When Mrs. Julia Ward Howe, already famous for her "Battle Hymn of the Republic," visited Washington during the Civil War, she felt snubbed because her old friend Charles Sumner failed to call on her. Accidentally encountering her on the street, the Senator showed no remorse for his neglect but remarked languidly that he had "been engrossed so long by grand public questions" that he had "quite lost all interest in individuals." Promptly Mrs. Howe retorted that she was glad to hear of his progress, for she had not known that even the Almighty had "reached that point yet."

For generations historians have chuckled over Mrs. Howe's wit, but, without attempting to emulate Sumner's detachment in every way, I suggest that his attitude has some value for the student of Reconstruction. Perhaps we have all been too much interested in individuals. Recognizing that the road to reunion was surveyed by the Republicans in Congress, historians have devoted much attention to the individual leaders of that body. There has been

David Donald is Harry C. Black Professor of American History at Johns Hopkins University and Director of The Institute of Southern History. He is the author of *Charles Sumner and the Coming of the Civil War*, which won the Pulitzer Prize in 1961, of *Lincoln Reconsidered, Divided We Fought, Inside Lincoln's Cabinet*, and other books. He has edited *Why the North Won the Civil War*, is co-author of the second edition of *The Civil War and Reconstruction*. Professor Donald is also general editor of *Making of America* and of the *Documentary History of the American People*.

Reprinted from *The Politics of Reconstruction 1863–1867* (Baton Rouge: Louisiana State University Press, 1965), pp. 26–52, by permission of the author and the publisher.

much pen-swinging about even the most personal and eccentric aspects of their behavior—Thaddeus Stevens' alleged fondness for a mulatto mistress; Zachariah Chandler's demonstrable passion for liquor; Benjamin F. Butler's supposed gravitational attraction for silver spoons; and all the rest. Biography has its value, but the biographies of these Reconstruction leaders do not add up to any consistent interpretation of the age. From them, as we have seen, no historian has been able to construct a tenable thesis which will serve to distinguish Radical Republicans in terms of personality, ideology, geographical origins, or social and economic status from their Moderate counterparts.

Once we leave this circle of well-known and much-studied leaders, we confront the fact that the majority of the members of Congress, the men who actually passed the laws which determined the Reconstruction process, are almost total blanks: George W. Anderson, of Missouri; Abraham A. Barker, of Pennsylvania; John Bidwell, of California; and the rest of the dreary roll call. Lest this be read as a plea for graduate students to do more and more research on less and less consequential politicians, let it be said at once that not even the most enthusiastic state or local historian can resurrect most of these disembodied spirits. We cannot even rely upon the proverbial loquacity of congressmen for further light on these forgotten men. During the four months in 1864 while the House of Representatives was considering the Davis Reconstruction bill (later the Wade-Davis bill), which surely posed most acutely the dilemmas of Reconstruction and the difficulties that lay ahead between executive and legislative branches of the government, only forty-one congressmen of both parties even opened their mouths about the measure.

Since the leaders fall into no discernible pattern and since the followers are almost unknown, perhaps the time has come for the Reconstruction historian to emulate Sumner's olympian remoteness and to cease being concerned with individuals. In studying Republican factionalism it might be helpful to forget about personality, rhetoric, motives, and popular repute of individual congressmen. Instead, we may hope to find significance in their objective behavior patterns—i.e., in the way they voted—and to explain this behavior in terms of political forces.

I

It is not, as we have seen, easy to find objective criteria for separating Radical from Moderate Republicans during the Civil War years. During the Reconstruction period the party situation became more complex, because a few Republicans, like Edgar Cowan, James R. Doolittle, and Henry J. Raymond, became identified with President Johnson's policies and formed a separate, clearly recognizable group of Conservatives, falling somewhere between the Democrats and the Republicans. But their defection did little to make the line between Moderate and Radical Republicans in Congress clearer. The final votes even on such controversial measures as the Second Confiscation Act, the bill for the readmission of Arkansas, the 1866 Civil Rights bill, and the 1867 Reconstruction Act reveal only monolithic Republican solidarity in both houses. But, by working carefully through the congressional proceedings, we can point to preliminary roll calls on some of these measures, where the caucus rules were not in force, where the party whip was held in abeyance, and where it was thought permissible for Republicans to express their differences and to divide along factional lines.

The following roll-call analysis is confined to votes taken in the House of Representatives. In thus apparently neglecting the Senate, I have no desire to minimize the importance of that body, whose debates I have studied with care if not with pleasure, or to deny the existence of Republican factionalism there. But Senators are such prickly and egotistical persons that alliances among them tend to be short-lived. Moreover, the most important business of the upper house was often transacted in the secret meetings of the Republican caucus, of which no minutes were kept, and the public record of Senate proceedings published in the *Congressional Globe* is decidedly unrevealing. Finally, since the members of the Senate were indirectly elected for long terms, the upper house is not the best place to test the effect of constituents' influence upon legislative action.

I have found no one vote during the Civil War years which will serve as a clear-cut test of Radicalism, but during the sessions of the Thirty-Eighth Congress in 1864 and 1865 there were six House roll calls, often on small and even procedural matters, which, taken together, show patterns of bloc voting. Doubtless another historian might select a somewhat different series of preliminary test votes, but these six, all relating directly to Reconstruction issues, seem to me most sharply to define the factions:

(1) The vote, on May 4, 1864, on a proposal, sponsored by acknowledged Radicals, to add a preamble to the Davis Reconstruction bill (later the Wade-Davis bill) to the effect that Confederates had "no right to claim the mitigation of the extreme rights of war" and announcing that none of the states of the Confederacy could "be considered and treated as entitled to be represented in Congress, or to take any part in the political government of the Union." Moderate Republicans allied with Democrats to defeat the preamble (76–57).

(2) The vote, on December 13, 1864, on a motion to remove a bill for the reconstruction of Louisiana from the fairly Moderate House judiciary committee and give it to the special committee on the rebellious states, headed by the arch-Radical, Henry Winter Davis. The vote was a tie (66–66), with many abstentions, and the Speaker broke it by recording his vote against the proposal.

(3) The vote, on January 17, 1865, to postpone for two weeks further consideration of a Radical-sponsored bill for the reconstruction of Louisiana and other Southern states. Moderate Republicans joined Democrats to secure the delay (103–34).

(4) The vote, on February 21, 1865, to table this Reconstruction bill favored by the Radicals. Moderate Republicans and Democrats united in an attempt to kill the bill (91–64).

(5) The immediately subsequent roll call to table a motion to reconsider this vote on the general Reconstruction bill. Again the Radicals were defeated (92–57).

(6) The vote, on February 22, 1865, to table a bill providing that constitutional conventions in the Confederate states should be elected by loyal whites and Negroes who had served in the Union armies, to the exclusion of all Southern whites who had held civil or military office "under the rebel usurpation" and of all who had "voluntarily borne arms against the United States."

Once again the Radicals were defeated by a Moderate-Demo-cratic alliance (80–65).

No one of these votes, it should be repeated, is a sure index of a congressman's identification with one faction or another. Even a composite tabulation has to be used with care, for indubitable Radicals, like Thaddeus Stevens and George W. Julian, sure that all the Reconstruction proposals before the Thirty-Eighth Congress were milk-and-water measures and confident that the Thirty-Ninth Congress would impose more rigorous conditions upon the South, had voting records on these six measures rather like those of conservative Northern Democrats. Nevertheless, the six votes taken together do select out a considerable number of House Republicans who favored congressional, rather than presidential, control over the Reconstruction process and who looked toward punitive action against the Southern rebels. Ten House Republicans voted the Radical line on all of these six measures. Twenty-nine others agreed with the Radical position on all but one of these votes, and eleven more disagreed with the Radicals on only two of the votes. These fifty congressmen, then, may be taken as the core of Republican Radicalism in the House of Representatives during the last year of the Civil War.

To determine party and factional groupings in the House of Representatives during the Reconstruction period, I have made roll-call tabulations of every vote, however apparently trivial or technical, recorded during the second session of the Thirty-Ninth Congress (1866–1867) on all resolutions or bills relating to the reorganization of the South. Of these six proved significant:

(1) The vote, on December 4, 1866, which approved the resolution offered by John M. Broomall, of Pennsylvania, requiring the committee on territories to look into the expediency of reporting a bill that would establish territorial governments, with universal manhood suffrage, in all the former Confederate states except Tennessee. Since the resolution asked only for an inquiry and not for specific action, it was supported by 106 Radical and Moderate Republicans and by one Democratic; 8 Conservatives joined 29 Democrats in opposing it.

(2) The vote, on January 28, 1867, to refer a drastic Recon-

struction bill urged by Thaddeus Stevens, who would have disfranchised most Southern whites and given the vote to the Negroes, back to the Joint Committee of Fifteen on Reconstruction, where it would in all probability languish until the end of the Thirty-Ninth Congress. John A. Bingham, of Ohio, the leading Moderate Republican in the House, sponsored the motion to refer, and fifty other Moderate Republicans and Conservatives joined him in voting with the Democrats to defeat the Stevens proposal (88–65).

(3) The vote, on February 11, 1867, on ordering the main question—i.e., on cutting off further debate and moving toward a final vote—on the bill introduced by Thomas D. Eliot, of Massachusetts, to provide for the reconstruction of Louisiana. Eliot's proposal was drastic, and it had strong Radical backing, but since the provisional government of Louisiana had shown itself so unable or unwilling to protect its Negro citizens, many Moderate Republicans supported the measure. Twenty-one Moderate Republicans and Conservatives joined with the Democrats in an effort to protract the debate, but the motion was carried over their opposition (84–59).

(4) The vote, on February 13, 1867, on ordering the main question—again cutting off further debate and delay—on James G. Blaine's Moderate proposal to refer the military Reconstruction bill, which Stevens was now advocating, to the committee on the judiciary, where Moderate amendments would be added. Moderate Republicans, Conservatives, and twenty Democrats favored cutting off debate; fifty-seven other Republicans followed Stevens in joining the remaining Democrats in an effort to prolong the debate. The Moderates won (85–78).

(5) The subsequent vote, on the same day, on Blaine's motion itself. Fifty-two Moderate Republicans and Conservatives joined with seventeen Democrats to send the military bill to the judiciary committee for amendment, but they were defeated by a coalition of seventy-one Radical Republicans and twenty-three Democrats (69–94).

(6) The final vote, also taken the same day, on the adoption of the Stevens version of the military Reconstruction bill. Thirteen Conservatives joined the Democrats in opposing final passage, but

they were overwhelmed by the united Moderate and Radical Republican vote (109–55).

Taken together, these six votes select out seventy-two Republican Representatives in the Thirty-Ninth Congress who could be generally relied upon to support Radical legislation directed at the South.[1]

II

To study these fifty Republican Radicals of 1864–1865 and these seventy-two Republican Radicals of 1866–1867 in the way historians usually analyze groups is thoroughly disheartening. No obvious personal or social characteristics united them or distinguished them from other Republican congressmen. They were not notably different in ethnic background, geographical origin, previous political affiliation, or age from the non-Radical Republican Representatives in the same Congress. Far too little is known, and can be known, about most of these Radicals to warrant any generalization as to their social-economic status or personality type, but the few who have been studied by historians fall into no single pattern.

Voting together on measures relating to the South, the Negro, and Reconstruction was the one bond which held these Radicals together. They tended consistently to vote together on such issues over a considerable period of time. Of the fifty Radicals of 1864–1865, forty-one were still serving in the House of Representatives two years later, and three out of four of them continued to vote Radical (see Table 10–1). Since in the 1860's the Representative's term of service tended to be short and precarious, this record of continuity inevitably provokes the speculation that there might be some connection between the relative degree of security which these congressmen felt in their office and their Radical voting record.

A study of the election returns proves that, in fact, the fifty Radicals in the Thirty-Eighth Congress (1864–1865) were elected by overwhelming majorities, having received on the average 58.3 per cent of the vote in their districts even in 1862, the disastrous

TABLE 10-1

*Votes of Radical Congressmen of 1864–1865
on 1867 Reconstruction Legislation*

Of 10 Republicans who voted Radical on all 6 test roll calls in 1864–1865:
   7 voted with the Radicals in 1867
   1 voted with the Moderates in 1867
   1 joined no recognized faction in 1867
   1 was not re-elected (replaced by another Republican who voted Radical in 1867)

Of 29 Republicans who voted Radical on 5 of 6 test roll calls in 1864–1865:
   18 voted with the Radicals in 1867
   3 voted with the Moderates in 1867
   1 voted with the Conservatives in 1867
   1 was an absentee in 1867
   6 were not re-elected (replaced by 2 Radicals, 1 Moderate, 2 Democrats, and 1 absentee in 1867)

Of 11 Republicans who voted Radical on 4 of 6 test roll calls in 1864–1865:
   6 voted with the Radicals in 1867
   1 voted with the Moderates in 1867
   1 joined no recognized faction in 1867
   1 was an absentee in 1867
   2 were not re-elected (replaced by 1 Moderate and 1 Democrat in 1867)

---

year when military defeats and Lincoln's emancipation policies nearly cost the Republican party control of the House. Their districts continued to be heavily Republican long after 1862, since all but three of them elected these same Representatives or other Republicans in both 1864 and 1866. It is tempting to derive from such figures a new formula to explain Republican factionalism: Radicalism was a function of party strength. Or, to put it less technically, one might predict that the more heavily a district voted Republican, the more surely its Representative would support Radical measures in Congress.

It would be gratifying to report that my analysis of voting statistics, which I have calculated for every congressional district for every election during the Civil War and Reconstruction era, confirms this simple formula, but, unfortunately, such is not the case. The seventy-two Republicans who can be identified as Radicals in the 1866–1867 Congress had been elected in 1864 by an average vote of 59.3 per cent[2]—but the thirty-two recognizable

Moderate Republicans in the same session had received an average vote in that election of 59.2 per cent. On first trial, therefore, a definition of Radicalism in terms of constituency strength seems no more successful than the economic, geographical, psychological, or other interpretations of Republican factionalism.

But, upon reflection, perhaps I should have expected to encounter what V. O. Key used to call "melancholy experience with the eccentricities of data," which resolutely refuse to fall into a simple pattern. It would be unreasonable to hope that all election data in a country so broad and diverse as the United States would conform to a single formula. Moreover, that formula implies a degree of correlation between constituents' attitudes and a congressman's voting that is contrary to our everyday experience. We know that many Representatives—in the 1860's as well as in the 1960's—owed their seats not to their votes or speeches on great national issues but to their skill in securing federal contracts for factories in their districts, in winning appropriations to improve local rivers and harbors, and the like. Other congressmen were elected because of their ethnic or religious affiliations. In still other cases districts chose Representatives for none of these reasons but because they were war heroes.

No doubt many of even these congressmen did try to make their votes on Reconstruction issues conform to the wishes of the voters in their districts, but it was hard always to know what those wishes were. Since the Civil War so closely and directly affected most Northern families, there was an unusual amount of public interest in the general issues of Reconstruction, but only a minority of voters could have held decided opinions on specific legislative proposals—say, on the merits of James M. Ashley's proposed Reconstruction plan as compared with those of Thaddeus Stevens' bill. Though a congressman tried to learn both the desires of this articulate minority and the general preferences of his constituents by reading his mail, by studying the newspapers published in his district, and by talking with the voters on his occasional visits home, he could never be really sure he was reflecting the will of the majority.

For some congressmen the opinions of their constituents were not a major consideration. Many of the Representatives who voted on the 1867 Reconstruction Act were lame-ducks, congressmen who either had not stood for re-election the previous fall or who had been defeated. These, it would be only reasonable to expect, would care less about what the voters back home wanted than did the congressmen who had just been re-elected and who might hope for additional terms of office in the future. It is significant that of the Republicans who supported Bingham's Moderate resolution in 1867, which sent Stevens' Radical Reconstruction bill to its death in committee, one in four was ending his service in the House, while only one in eight of the Radicals was retiring. Even more instructive is the fact that three-fifths of the twenty-five Republican Representatives who abstained from voting in this clear test of factions had not been re-elected; they had the independence of judgment which can be exhibited by the politicians who aspire to nothing.

A Representative who hoped for higher political office might also show himself indifferent to the voice of his constituency. If James A. Garfield, re-elected in 1866 by 71.3 per cent of the votes in his Ohio district, or Nathaniel P. Banks, chosen by 74.9 per cent of his Massachusetts constituency, hoped to become President or Vice President, he had to reckon with the same pressure that had pushed both Lincoln and Johnson into a Moderate, or even a Conservative, position. No man could hope to gain the Republican nomination for national office, much less to win the election itself, unless his record was Moderate enough for independents and some Democrats, who together formed the majority of the nation's voting population, to support him.

Because of these considerations, which can only be evaluated on a local level, it is best to study the relationship between Republican factional affiliation and voting strength in individual states, or regional groups of states. From the critical state of New York, where the Democrats elected the governor in 1862 and won seventeen of the state's thirty-one seats in the House of Representatives, there were only two Radicals in the 1864–1865 Congress. Both of these had been elected, even in the black year of 1862, by over 57 per cent of their districts' voters. By 1864, with the worst of the war over, voters began returning to their normal allegiances, and Republicanism was resurgent in New York. Even though the two parties were closely balanced in voting for national and state-wide offices, the Republicans regained a majority of the congressional delegation, in many instances by very large majorities. Radicalism increased along with Republican voting strength, and by 1866–1867 three New York Representatives belonged to the Radical faction, while five were Moderates and three were Conservatives.

A graph of the voting record of these individual New York districts (see Figure 10–1) strikingly shows that Radicals usually represented the most heavily Republican districts in the state, that Moderates came from marginal districts where some Democratic support was necessary for victory, and that Conservatives were the temporary congressmen from districts whose normal affiliation was Democratic. A chart showing the average vote received by Republican candidates in these three kinds of districts (see Figure 10–2) even more impressively reinforces this thesis.

Pennsylvania election returns (see Figure 10–3) generally fall into the same pattern as those of New York. The Ninth Pennsylvania District, which consistently cast the highest percentage of Republican votes throughout the era, sent none other than Thaddeus Stevens himself to Congress, while the two Moderate districts were always marginally Republican. There was, however, an important difference between the pattern of Pennsylvania and New York voting. The former was a notably Radical state, and congressmen from many of its weaker Republican districts tended to support Radical measures. Representative Leonard Myers, for example, received on the average only 51.1 per cent of the votes in his Third Pennsylvania District, but he stalwartly voted alongside Thaddeus Stevens. In New York, one can hardly doubt, such a congressman would have been a Moderate, or even Conservative. The key to the difference lies in the fact that the Democratic organization in Pennsylvania was feebler than that in New York, while Pennsylvania Republicans were well organized, disciplined, and financed. As a result, the Republican congressman from the Keystone State felt a greater security in office than did his New York counterpart. Nine of the Pennsylvania districts elected Republican Representatives in every election from 1862 to 1868, and seven others chose Republicans in all but one of these elections. Representative Myers' margins might be small, year after year, but he could have a high degree of confidence that he would be repeatedly returned to office.

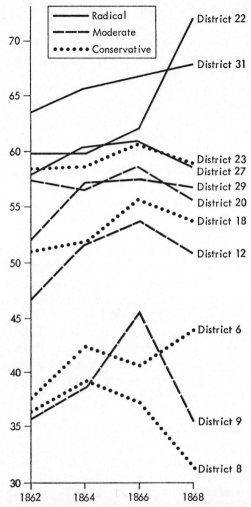

FIGURE 10-1. *Percentage of Votes Received by Republican Candidates in New York Congressional Districts, 1862–1868* *

* Districts are classified according to votes of their Representatives in the 1866–1867 session of Congress. Districts whose Representatives were not identified with any Republican faction, who were absentees, or who were Democrats in 1867 are not shown.

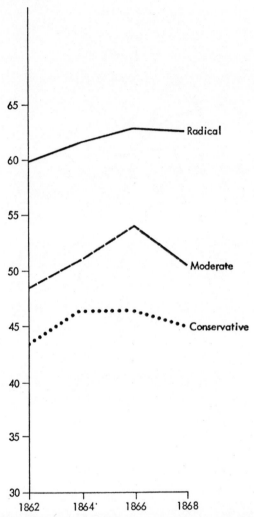

FIGURE 10–2. *Average Percentage of Votes Received by*
Republican Candidates in Radical, Moderate, and Conservative
New York Districts, 1862–1868 *

* Districts are classified according to votes of their Representatives in the 1866–1867 session
of Congress.

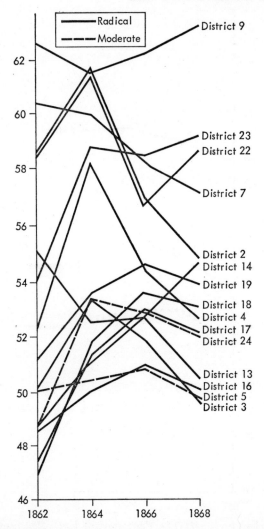

FIGURE   10–3. *Percentage of Votes Received by Republican Candidates in Pennsylvania Congressional Districts, 1862–1868* *

* Districts are classified according to votes of their Representatives in the 1866–1867 session of Congress. Districts whose Representatives were Democrats or who were Republican abstainers are not shown.

The election returns from the states of the Middle West (Ohio, Indiana, Illinois, Michigan, Wisconsin, Minnesota, Iowa, and Kansas) generally correspond to those of New York and Pennsylvania. Since most of these were strongly Republican states, one would expect to find a strong preponderance of Radicals among their congressmen. In fact, fifteen of the fifty Radicals of the 1864–1865 Congress came from this region, as did thirty-one of the seventy-two in the 1866–1867 session, which contained only twelve Moderates from the Middle West and only four Conservatives. These three groups of Middle Western Republican congressmen received strikingly different degrees of support in the 1864 elections. The successful Radical candidate in that year won, on the average, 57.8 per cent of the total vote in his district; the Moderate received 55.7 per cent;[3] and the Conservative had only 51.7 per cent.

Within any single Middle Western state the symmetry of this pattern is likely to be marred because of circumstances peculiar to individual districts and to individual candidates, yet a glance at the Indiana Republican election percentage for 1864 (see Table 10–2) shows that, in a rough way, Radical congressmen from that

TABLE 10–2

*Percentage of Votes Received
by Indiana Republican Representatives in 1864*

	Percentage
Radicals in 1867	
G. W. Julian	68.7
Ebenezer Dumont	63.4
G. S. Orth	52.2
J. H. Farquhar	50.1*
Moderate in 1867	
Ralph Hill	51.8
Conservatives in 1867	
T. N. Stillwell	53.8
J. H. Defrees	51.0
Representatives not voting on	
4 or more of 6 test roll calls	
Schuyler Colfax (*Speaker*)	52.6
H. D. Washburn	50.0

* Farquhar can best be characterized as an Independent Radical. Though he sometimes supported Radical positions, he voted for J. A. Bingham's motion on January 28, 1867.

state tended to come from areas of great Republican constituency strength, while Representatives from doubtful districts were usually Moderates or Conservatives.

It is, at first thought, rather a surprise to find that votes in the New England states reflect this same tendency. They were, after all, securely Republican and had few marginal districts. Massachusetts, for example, elected only Republicans to Congress from 1862 through 1870, and the weakest Republican in 1864 received 62.3 per cent of the votes in his district. Yet, aside from Banks, who had presidential aspirations, the Massachusetts Representatives with the strongest constituency support were Radicals, while those with the least voted Moderate (see Table 10–3). It would be misleading to consider the three Moderate Massachusetts seats doubtful in the same sense that districts were marginal in New York or Indiana, yet two of them, which included the city of Boston, gave Lincoln only a minority vote in 1860 and supported a Democratic gubernatorial candidate two years later. In these districts there seems to have been much crossing of party lines in the congressional elections by Democrats who realized that their party had little chance to win and who, therefore, supported Republicans known to be Moderates.

Thus, though there were a great many individual and local eccentricities, voting behavior in New England, the Middle States,

TABLE 10–3

Percentage of Votes Received
by Massachusetts Representatives in 1864

Radicals in 1867	Percentage
T. D. Eliot	82.7
W. B. Washburn	81.4
J. B. Alley	75.8
John Baldwin	74.8
G. S. Boutwell	68.9
Moderates in 1867	
H. L. Dawes	64.7
Samuel Hooper	64.0
A. H. Rice	62.3
Conservative in 1867	
N. P. Banks	80.0

and the Middle West conformed to a general pattern. When a district, over a long series of elections, showed itself to be doubtful or only marginally Republican, its Representative frequently tended to vote with the Moderate or Conservative blocs in Congress. But when there was a consistent degree of high Republican strength in a district, its congressman usually belonged to the Radical faction of the party.

III

It is not hard to account for this ratio between security in office and Radicalism. A congressman from a stalwartly Republican district or state was aware that he owed little to his national party and less to the President. In many cases he had joined the Republican party before Abraham Lincoln, and he generally ran ahead of the presidential candidate in both 1860 and 1864. In his view Andrew Johnson, a life-long Southern Democrat, was even less entitled than Lincoln to set policy for the party which he accidentally headed.

To be sure, even a congressman from a safely Republican district or state looked to the President for patronage, but in the early months of his administration Lincoln tied his own hands by requiring that Representatives be consulted about appointments in their own districts and he later extended this rule to cover the small army of internal revenue appointees created under the tax law of 1862. In any case, after 1862, most of the choice jobs had already been distributed, and the congressman's insatiable appetite for new patronage triumphed over his transient memory of past favors. The advent of Andrew Johnson did little to make him more dependent upon the White House. Severely limited by his need to keep the National Union coalition intact, Johnson, as we have seen, made few removals for political reasons in 1865–1866, and those few served more to insure the bitter hostility of the displaced than the loyalty of the new officeholders.

The secure Republican congressman, in short, felt more certain of his base of power than did the President. Unless he aspired to national office, he had no need to be Moderate, for he required no support from the independents or the Democrats. Nor did he have any need to follow the President's course, for his own power stemmed from his seniority on important congressional committees. To be sure, not all congressmen from overwhelmingly Republican districts desired to flout the President's will or to espouse harsh Reconstruction measures. A Representative like Thomas A. Jenckes, whose Rhode Island district voted 99.0 per cent Republican in 1865 and 97.7 per cent Republican in 1867, was so well entrenched that he could follow his own ideas, without much regard to possible disaffection of constituents. But most of the leading Radicals in both houses occupied unassailably secure Republican seats—Charles Sumner, Thaddeus Stevens, Zachariah Chandler, George W. Julian, and the rest.

Very different was the lot of the Republican congressman from the doubtful district. Where the vote was almost evenly divided, he had to eschew Radicalism, whatever his own personal wishes and beliefs. The most thoughtful exponent of the Moderate position in the House was John A. Bingham, who was fully aware that his Ohio district could easily go Democratic, since his own average vote in the elections from 1862 through 1870 was only 50.6 per cent of the total. Bitterly he protested against Radical proposals "for universal suffrage among . . . women and colored citizens, and for confiscation, banishment, and the disfranchisement of all others without trial—and for the removal of the President by Joint Resolution." Begging his fellow Republicans not to commit "an act of political Suicide," he warned: "Any such folly on our part will inevitably throw the whole country into the hands of the opposition alias the late rebels."

Even had there been no pressure from his own district, such a Representative would have felt obliged to support the President, who, as we have seen, was compelled to be a Moderate. The congressman from the doubtful district often had only a brief tenure, and he could not normally expect to have much power in the House committees. His continuance in office often depended upon presidential backing, sometimes by way of the suppression of hostile newspapers or even the use of Federal troops to keep his Democratic opponents from the polls. Powerful too for such congressmen was the pull of the presidential coat-tail. In New York, for instance, Lincoln's race for re-election in 1864 helped both Radical and Moderate Republican candidates in the same degree,

but, as Table 10–4 shows, the increase in strength was only a welcome addition to large majorities for the Radicals while to many
Moderate candidates it made the difference between success and
failure.

TABLE 10–4

Average Percentage of Votes
Received by New York Republican Candidates
for Congress, 1862 and 1864 *

Year	Conservatives	Moderates	Radicals
1862	43.3	48.6	60.3
1864	46.6	51.0	61.8

* Districts classified according to Representatives' position on 1867 legislation.

The need for the marginal Republican congressman to look to
the President, therefore, overruled considerations of personality
or ideology. The case of Representative Owen Lovejoy of Illinois, the brother of an early antislavery martyr, is instructive.
During the 1850's there had been few Republicans in the House
more vituperative toward the South and more positive that the
social system of that region had to be radically reorganized. But
after the 1860 census, Illinois, like many other states, was redis-
tricted, and Lovejoy's once safe seat became doubtful. Fright-
ened, the Illinois congressman put aside his fear that President
Lincoln was too slow, too lenient, too soft on the South and,
through a friend, made a "delicate request" for Presidential endorsement. "He has a fierce battle in his district," the intermedi-
ary wrote Lincoln on October 21, 1862, "but thinks that a line
which he might not use in the newspapers but to exhibit to a few
of your friends would do him great service." With the President's
backing Lovejoy won re-election in 1862 by a majority of only
fifty-six votes, and he became one of the President's most stalwart
supporters in the House, although he continued from time to time
to urge faster action. In Professor Williams' carefully documented compilation of Radical assaults upon the President, the
last anti-Lincoln item from Congressman Lovejoy is dated June
1862; thereafter, the facts of political life controlled and he became Lincoln's man. When Lovejoy died in 1864, the President

praised him as his "most generous friend," who deserved to be enduringly remembered "in the hearts of those who love liberty, unselfishly, for all men."

Other Republicans from marginal districts felt the same pressures toward moderation on issues of slavery and Reconstruction. Isaac N. Arnold, who, next to Lovejoy, received the smallest majority of any Illinois Republican candidate for Congress in 1862, became one of the few congressmen who early and enthusiastically urged Lincoln's re-election, and after the assassination he wrote a warmly admiring biography of the President. Bradley F. Granger, elected to Congress in 1860 by the smallest majority of any Republican candidate in Michigan, sought vainly to avert defeat in his re-election campaign by becoming one of the few Republican Representatives to vote against confiscation measures. More successful was Joseph H. Defrees, who, after the Tenth Indiana District went Democratic in 1862, recognized that a Republican could win only if he attracted support outside of his party regulars. Though Indiana Radicals from their safe seats scorned him as an old fogy, his Conservative views won him election in 1864.

In the Reconstruction years as well leading Moderates and Conservatives came from marginal and doubtful districts. The case of John A. Bingham has already been noted. Even more striking is that of Henry J. Raymond, the editor of the *New York Times*, who became Andrew Johnson's chief spokesman and defender in the House. The fact that Raymond was elected in 1864 only because New York Democrats in his Sixth District were divided and that no Republican candidate for Congress received more than 47 per cent of the vote in that district in any election from 1860 through 1870 explains much about the sources of Conservative Republicanism.

IV

In arguing that a congressman's Radicalism during Reconstruction varied in proportion to his political security in his district, I am, of course, making an implicit judgment that most Republican voters were themselves Radicals, in the sense that they desired the abolition of slavery, the reorganization of Southern society, and the perpetuation of Republican control of the national government. No student who has studied the Republican newspapers of the period and the unpublished correspondence of Republican leaders can doubt that this was the case, at least up to the time when Johnson was impeached. It would be easy to compile an anthology of letters in the same vein as that of a Ravenna, Ohio, Republican to Representative Garfield in February 1867: "The delay of Congress in coming to any agreement is trying the patience of the people very much. The masses sympathize with Stevens more than men in Washington think. . . . Don't be afraid of the people. They are ahead of Congress now, as they were during the war, when the administration of Mr. Lincoln was timidly halting, and afraid to touch the *hallowed* institution of slavery!" Regardless of their personal convictions, therefore, those congressmen repeatedly elected by Republican votes alone were pushed by their constituents into becoming increasingly Radical.

On the other hand, if the Moderate Republican congressman's course during Reconstruction can be related to his need to secure broader support in his doubtful district, it is legitimate to ask whether he really disagreed on issues and principles with the Radicals in his party or whether he was subordinating his true beliefs to expediency. To this question no definitive answer can be given, for we know, and can know, much too little about what most congressmen truly believed. Doubtless in many cases a circular process was at work: doubtful districts ran Republican candidates known to have Moderate views, in order to secure Democratic support; congressmen from such districts supported Moderate positions because they had to woo marginal voters.

It is perhaps permissible to speculate that, had all Republicans been equally free from the necessity of playing to a bipartisan constituency, the ideological differences between Moderates and Radicals might not have amounted to a great deal. Certainly historians have tended to polarize these differences to an unwarranted extent. It is instructive to remember that Moderate Senator William Pitt Fessenden, of Maine, objected to the final version of the 1867 Reconstruction Act because, he said, "it did not go far enough." The "gentlemen who glory in the name of radical," he took waspish pleasure in pointing out, "are not quite so radical on

THE CONGRESSIONAL EQUATION

that subject as I am. . . ." Similarly, it is chastening to note that Bingham's adherence to the Fourteenth Amendment as a truly Moderate plan of Reconstruction had some decidedly Radical overtones. Asked how, in view of Southern refusal to accept that amendment, it could become part of the Constitution, Bingham replied that there was no need for it to be ratified except "by three fourths of the organized and represented States"—i.e., by the North and the West, without consulting the South; this was precisely the position maintained by Radical Charles Sumner in the Senate. But when colleagues suggested to Bingham that the Supreme Court might not sustain such a partial ratification of an amendment, the Ohio Moderate took a breath-taking step even beyond the most Radical in his party by suggesting that Congress should first curtail the Court's jurisdiction and then procure "a further constitutional amendment . . . , which will defy judicial usurpation by . . . the abolition of the tribunal itself."

Certainly as Republican voting strength increased between 1862 and 1864, the number of Radical Republicans in Congress, as we have noted, grew proportionately. There were further additions to the Radical ranks after the elections of 1866, when Southern failure to guarantee minimal rights to the Negroes and Johnson's ill-conceived "swing around the circle" in support of his policy resulted in larger Republican majorities throughout the North. In the case of individual congressmen the transformation from Moderate to Radical was neither immediate nor complete, but it is suggestive that Bingham, who thought the Civil Rights bill of 1866 unconstitutional and took his stand on the Fourteenth Amendment, came out for Negro suffrage in 1867 and the year after became one of the seven House impeachment managers at Andrew Johnson's trial. There was, therefore, a certain warped wisdom in Montgomery Blair's view that Republican factional fights, such as those which led up to the adoption of the 1867 Reconstruction Act, were all play acting, part of a plan to throw dust in President Johnson's eyes "by having Bingham . . . *pretending* to make war on Stephens [*sic*]."

But the factional war within the Republican party was, in fact, no pretense, even if the basis of the factions was political necessity rather than ideology. Moderates had to check extreme Radical proposals or be defeated in the districts they represented. To the

Radicals, on the other hand, the Moderates seemed a dead weight, the more onerous because these fellow party members ought to know better. The history of Reconstruction legislation is the story of the tug of war between these two groups, and, like the basis of factionalism, it can best be analyzed in quantitative, almost mechanistic, terms.

Notes

1. Since my purpose here is to develop a general explanation of factionalism, I have in the following pages discussed these Radicals as a single group. One can distinguish three subcategories of Radicals—Independent Radicals, Stevens Radicals, and Ultra Radicals—but the differences among these were over relatively minor, tactical matters.
2. In a few states congressmen were chosen in odd, rather than even, years, and in these cases I have used 1865 election returns.
3. The votes of James A. Garfield and J. F. Farnsworth have been omitted from this calculation. In the 1864–1865 Congress Garfield voted with the Radicals, but two years later he was thinking of state or national offices and felt compelled to be a Moderate. Farnsworth's voting record was erratic. Though he supported Bingham's motion on January 28, 1867, in most other respects he agreed with the Radicals.

❦ 11 ❦

Merle Curti
Judith Green
Roderick Nash

ANATOMY OF GIVING:
MILLIONAIRES IN THE LATE
NINETEENTH CENTURY

The proliferation of large-scale philanthropic institutions in twentieth-century America has encouraged, in the past few years, interest in the history of voluntary giving. Long before this writers, without benefit of either quantitative studies of American giving or of careful comparative analyses of philanthropic behavior in the United States and in other countries, maintained that generosity had been an important and indeed a distinguishing aspect of the national character.[1]

These generalizations, which rested on impressions, can be illustrated by representative examples. James Bryce, writing in 1888, declared that "in works of active benevolence, no country has

Merle Curti is Frederick Jackson Turner Professor of History at the University of Wisconsin. He is author of the *American Peace Crusade, American Philanthropy Abroad, American Scholarship in the Twentieth Century, The Great Mr. Locke, America's Philosopher, The Growth of American Thought, Young America,* and many other books. He is co-author of *An American History,* and together with Roderick Nash of *Philanthropy in the Shaping of American Higher Education.*

Reprinted from *American Quarterly,* XV (Fall 1963), pp. 416–435, by permission of the authors and the publisher. © 1963, Trustees of the University of Pennsylvania.

surpassed, and perhaps none has equalled, the United States. Not only are the sums collected for all sorts of philanthropic purposes larger relatively to the wealth of America than in any European country, but the amount of personal effort devoted to them seems to a European visitor to exceed that he knows at home." [2] Informed observers and scholars have largely supported Bryce's judgment. In 1953 a leading authority on American history wrote that successful Americans "shared their money with others almost as freely as they made it, returning at least part of their substance to channels of social usefulness through munificent gifts and bequests. This philanthropic streak in the national character, an index of the pervasive spirit of neighborliness, appeared early and has in our own day reached fabulous proportions." [3] Some years later a scholar competent in the economic history of both Europe and America concluded that, despite the inadequacy of the statistical record, "the best data available indicate that philanthropic contributions in Western Europe, for all purposes—education, social work, religion, scientific research, and art—amount to less than one-half of one per cent of the annual national income, whereas in the United States they amount to some two per cent of the national income." [4]

While several studies lend support to the thesis of outstanding generosity on the part of Americans in the past,[5] we have nothing comparable to the elaborate and detailed quantification that marks the notable work of W. K. Jordan for British philanthropy in the Tudor and Stuart periods.[6] The work of F. Emerson Andrews, to be sure, is admirable in its statistical base and methodology, but it is largely confined to the recent period.[7] The extent to which the American reputation for generosity is valid over time has been one of the many inquiries that has concerned the University of Wisconsin Project on the History of American Philanthropy, defined as private and voluntary giving for public purposes.

Many other questions might and ought to be asked concerning the activities of American donors and the Wisconsin Project has tried to fill some of the gaps. What, for instance, are the fields that have received the most support from donors, and what trends are discernible over a period of time? How much philanthropy has been in the form of lifetime gifts rather than bequests? Are gifts and bequests more likely to be made by those with few or no dependents or survivors than by those with many? Was there any marked difference between men and women donors in the causes chosen for philanthropy? What part does religion, educational background, means of acquisition of fortune, and occupation play in philanthropic giving? On the assumption that philanthropy reflects social trends, can an analysis of American giving reveal any definite trends?

Widespread concern during the 1890's and early years of the twentieth century over the creation of million-dollar fortunes and the uses of great wealth resulted in the publication of several relevant articles and studies. This interest was reflected in and stimulated by the compilation of two nation-wide lists of millionaires. The more important appeared as a supplement of the *New York Tribune* and was the work of Roswell G. Horr, a financial editor of the paper.[8] The report listed 4,047 men and women reputed to be millionaires. The list was arranged state by state, city by city. The kind of economic activity thought to be the major factor in the creation of each fortune was indicated. The *Tribune*'s financial editor claimed to have consulted 1,500 merchants, bankers, commercial agents, lawyers, surrogates of counties, trustees and other citizens all over the country in a position to know the facts. The concentration on major cities and on the Eastern section of the country may have resulted in some exaggeration of the proportion of millionaires in this region. The *New York Tribune*'s commitment to protective tariffs may also have resulted in a slight bias in minimizing the importance of protected industries in the growth of great fortunes. Yet scholars who have studied the compilation believe that it was carefully and honestly done.[9] In 1902 the *New York World*, a staunch advocate of income and inheritance taxes and a vigorous opponent of protective tariffs, made a comparable list of millionaires for that year.[10]

These lists of millionaires were only one factor in explaining the increasing discussion of the origins and uses of great wealth around the turn of the century. As evinced by a rash of book and periodical publications many Americans were pondering the Spencerian concept of social Darwinism and the gospel of wealth as enunciated by Andrew Carnegie. The sharp debates over trusts, tariffs and income taxes, together with the growing strength of Populism, also accentuated the issue of the sources of great fortunes and the uses to which they were put. Moreover, a series of notable gifts for philanthropic purposes attracted a good deal of attention. These included Rockefeller's 1886 gift of $600,000 to resuscitate the defunct University of Chicago and Stanford's to the West Coast institution bearing that name; Armour's bequest of $100,000 for the establishment of a mission for poor Chicago youngsters, which was a start toward the technical institution bearing the family name; the Drexel endowment of a similar school in Philadelphia; and the donations for libraries associated with the names of Pratt, Newberry and Crerar. Most spectacular of all benefactions were those of Andrew Carnegie for public libraries and other educational institutions. These implemented the thesis advanced in his famous essay, "The Gospel of Wealth," which first appeared in the *North American Review* for June 1889. Carnegie argued, in secular terms, for a vast extension of the ancient doctrine of stewardship. A man of wealth was obligated to society to spend all but a minimal part of his fortune for desirable social purposes which did not properly engage the public treasury and which did not undermine individual initiative and self-reliance.[11] In the context of all these things it was natural to raise questions concerning the reputation of millionaires for benevolence and to make the *New York Tribune* list a point of reference.

Within a few months after the appearance of this list the *Review of Reviews* published an article entitled "American Millionaires and Their Public Gifts." [12] It was unsigned but may have been written by the editor, Dr. Albert Shaw, who was known to have been interested in the general problem. The author observed that it would be interesting if the millionaires enumerated by the *Tribune* could be separated into givers and nongivers and if, further, the list had included men worth less than a million dollars, many of whom were known to be generous contributors to philanthropic causes. In preparation for the article the writer had consulted knowledgeable men in several cities regarding the local reputation for benevolence of the millionaires listed. The New York contingent included 1,003 men and women, but the writer of the article found that this number was too large to classify. No estimates were available for Philadelphia, and the correspondent from Boston had a low opinion of that city's philanthropic habits.

Although 200 millionaires were listed, there were no great benefactions: Henry Lee Higginson's support of the Boston Symphony Orchestra was an exception. Of Eastern cities, Baltimore enjoyed an especially favorable record: half of its 55 millionaires were checked as generous. The correspondent in Cleveland noted that of 68 millionaires in that city 28 were considered "to a moderate extent at least, mindful of their public opportunities and duties." [13] Of the 67 millionaires listed for Cincinnati, 21 were checked as being comparatively liberal givers. At least 12 of Detroit's 42 millionaires enjoyed a reputation for benevolence. The St. Louis correspondent checked 10 out of 45 persons listed in his city. In St. Paul, nine of the 28 millionaires had a reputation for giving, James J. Hill being the best known, while in Minneapolis, 14 out of 44 were so regarded. The California respondent felt that the millionaires of his state were not reasonably mindful of their responsibilities despite the examples of James Lick, Darius O. Mills, Edwin Searles and Serranus C. Hastings.

Desiring, perhaps, more complete data on the giving habits of men and women of wealth than the fragmentary and imprecise estimates revealed by the article in the *Review of Reviews*, George J. Hagar, a member of the staff of *Appleton's Annual Cyclopaedia*, began in 1893 to collect figures on gifts and bequests during the year for religious, charitable and educational purposes. He decided to exclude all gifts or bequests under $5,000 in money or material, all national, municipal and state appropriations, and all ordinary contributions to churches and missionary societies. "The result of the first year's quest," Hagar later wrote, "was such a grand tribute to the humanity of the American men and women" that he continued to make similar investigations through the year 1903. In that year Hagar summarized and commented on the figures he had collected, which he believed to prove "a stalwart unselfishness, a willingness of favored ones to promote the welfare of the less favored, and particularly a growing tendency on the part of men and women of large means to administer personally a fair share of their estates to aid the educational, religious and philanthropic activities of the country." [14] Table 11–1 shows in round numbers the amounts of gifts and bequests that were made or that became legally available. No claim was made for their completeness. In fact the compiler was certain that the total contributions

in the eleven-year period must have been at least $250,000,000
more than his record indicated.

TABLE 11-1

*Annual Contributions in Gifts and Bequests 1893-1903 According to
Investigations of George J. Hagar of* Appleton's Annual Cyclopedia

1893	Over	$29,000,000
1894		32,000,000
1895		32,800,000
1896		27,000,000
1897		45,000,000
1898		38,000,000
1899		62,750,000
1900		47,500,000
1901		107,360,000
1902		94,000,000
1903		95,000,000
	TOTAL	$610,410,000

As one might expect, the figures reflected the general financial
condition of the country. In 1896, when almost every business
was depressed, the total contributed was the lowest in the record.
In 1898 benevolence tended to meet the immediate demands of
war relief, with the result that contributions to religious, charitable and educational purposes dropped. The high-water mark in
1901 was explained by the fact that in that year Carnegie's gifts
aggregated more than $31,000,000, but even so more than $75,-
000,000 were contributed by other benefactors. In 1903, 19 persons gave or bequeathed more than $65,000,000. Gifts and be-
quests ranging from $5,000 to $25,000 aggregated nearly $2,-
000,000, and those from $25,000 upward composed the sum of
more than $87,000,000. Hagar added somewhat ambiguously that
in the great majority of cases the money came, "not from those
considered rich in the present meaning of the word, though the
acknowledged wealthy contributed the bulk of the total." [15]

Suggestive as these contemporary reports are, the light thrown
on the larger questions under discussion leaves much to be desired. To find out whether an application of quantitative methods
would be helpful in further illuminating the problem of the alleged generosity of Americans of great wealth, the authors con-

ducted two related investigations of philanthropic activities. Our emphasis, as the study proceeded, was on the allocation of gifts and bequests to particular philanthropic areas, but where possible we also assembled data on factors which may have influenced motivation. The period chosen was that between 1851 and 1913.

For our first project we undertook a detailed study of the philanthropic habits of a sample from the 1892 list of 4,047 reputed millionaires compiled by the *New York Tribune*. Our sample, chosen by using Tippet's Table of Random Numbers, included 124 names. By means of a careful numerical analysis of this sample we hoped to establish the patterns of philanthropy among a class which, as we have shown, enjoyed in some quarters the reputation of fulfilling voluntarily and privately the welfare functions which in many countries are the charge of religious and political institutions. All but one of our sample are deceased so it was possible, within the limits of available data, to survey their life-long giving habits. Our quantitative study affords, we feel, a more reliable indication of certain conditions in American philanthropy and trends than do prevailing impressions based merely on general surveys and biographies.

Our procedure was to collect personal and philanthropic data on the 124 subjects, record the coded data on IBM cards, and then tabulate and analyze the information with the aid of a mechanical sorter. Only a few in the sample bore such familiar names as Crerar, Widener, Fahnestock and Frelinghuysen. But the wealth of many men and women in the sample often secured them a local reputation, so we were able to learn a good deal about them through correspondence with local libraries, historical societies, and surrogate courts. On our numerical analysis data sheets we recorded such biographical data as family background, education, religion, occupation or source of wealth, and philanthropic gifts and bequests amounting to more than $5,000. These donations were assigned to eleven categories: social welfare and health, religion (including missionary activities), civic improvement, liberal arts education, vocational and technical education, libraries and adult education, research in natural sciences, research in social sciences and humanities, the arts, aid abroad, and movements for peace and international understanding. All gifts and bequests for each category were then lumped together for each individual.

TABLE 11-2

Recorded Gifts and Bequests above $250,000
(New York Tribune *Sample*)

Name	Gift or Bequest	Field	Amount
Barber, Ohio C., born 1841	G	Vocational-Technical	$3,000,000
	B	Education	417,000
Crerar, John R., 1827	B	Libraries	2,000,000
	B	Religion	750,000
	B	Voc.-Tech. Ed./Civic	300,000
Drexel, Joseph, 1833–	G	Welfare	600,000
Fahnestock, Harris C., 1835-	B	Welfare	505,000
Phelan, James, 1824–	B	Art	310,000
	B	Welfare	1,175,000
Proctor, John C., 1822–	G	Welfare	500,000
	B	Welfare	1,590,000
	B	Civic	300,000
Ralston, William C., 1826–	G	Art	300,000
Rose, Chauncy, 1794–		Voc.-Tech. Ed.	350,000
Thorn, John, 1811–	G	Civic/Welfare	500,000
Webb, William H., 1816–	G	Voc.-Tech. Ed.	250,000
	G	Welfare	250,000
Widener, Peter A. B., 1834–	G	Lib. Arts Ed.	1,000,000
	G	Voc.-Tech. Ed.	6,000,000
	G	Libraries	1,000,000
	B	Art	2,500,000

We had hoped to ascertain fairly accurately at least the major amounts donated by millionaires and to correlate type and magnitude of gifts with biographical variables. Three major problems, however, required us to limit our plan severely. First, despite sustained effort, virtually no data concerning the presence or absence of philanthropic activity were found for 68 of the 109 men and 15 women in the sample. Second, we had reason to believe that many donations were given anonymously. This prevented our making even the relatively simple distinction between "givers" and "nongivers" for the names in the sample. Finally, the records frequently did not specify amounts of gifts, particularly for repeated donations to the same institution; some donations were simply labeled "generous" or "liberal." [16] In other words it was, within our experience, impossible to discover records of lifetime giving comparable to the detailed and comprehensive ones which Professor W. K. Jordan found for his study of philanthropy in Tudor and Stuart England in accessible and carefully kept records at central depositories.

Records on bequests were the most reliable, but for 53 millionaires no testamentary information could be found at all. Consequently, attempts to analyze statistically dollar amounts even in the bequest category were effectively frustrated. Table 11–3 summarizes our over-all findings:

TABLE 11–3

Methods of Giving and Summary of Knowledge about the Sample of 124 Millionaires from the New York Tribune *1892 Listing*

	Men	Women	Total
Donors			
Gifts only	15	2	17
Gifts and Bequests	23	1	24
Bequests but no information on possible gifts	5	1	6
Gifts but no information on possible bequests	8	1	9
TOTALS	51	5	56
Unknown			
Absence of bequests ascertained but no information on possible gifts	24	1	25
No information	34	9	43
TOTALS	58	10	68

We decided, therefore, to limit any conclusions to those 51 men and five women for whom we had some evidence of philanthropy and to consider in the main only the number and intent, not the sketchily reported dollar amounts of gifts and bequests.[17] The factors of anonymity and unspecific reporting are fairly constant among the categories of philanthropy, and we assumed that discrepancies in reporting donations to the various categories would roughly balance out among the 56 donors. This enabled us tentatively to establish correlations and noncorrelations between biographical categories and philanthropic habits for the *New York Tribune* sample.

The most salient aspect of the patterns of recorded giving among the millionaires is their provincialism. *Virtually all giving was directed toward the local community.* With the exception of missionary activities there was little or no "world consciousness" among the donors, even those of foreign birth. Hospitals, museums and vocational schools might serve a small region, but the givers extended their horizons only for institutions of higher education. Nor did millionaires feel responsible for extending intellectual horizons into new fields. In strong contrast to our contemporary donors, those of the *Tribune* sample *gave virtually nothing directly to further research in either the social or natural sciences.* Funds given to vocational, technical and liberal arts education may have had an indirect effect on the sciences and humanities, but the zest for research had not yet intrigued the American benefactor.

Education in the broad sense rivaled health and welfare in the competition for the largest share of contributors' dollars. Aid to liberal arts, technical and vocational education, libraries, adult education and the arts accounted for slightly over a third of the philanthropic categories chosen by the millionaires. Relief to the poor, sick and aged likewise took another third. Our evidence indicates that these funds usually were given to institutions rather than individuals, but many of the donors were reported to have made informal gifts to individuals which did not appear on the record. Religious organizations ranked next in the minds of contributors and received about a quarter of the donations. Less than a tenth went to civic improvement, chiefly to public buildings, monuments and parks.

On the whole, *the millionaires did not alter their lifelong philanthropic preferences when they included charitable and educational bequests in their wills.* Although our evidence shows some individual variations, the over-all allocations of gifts and bequests were virtually identical. Since it was impossible to determine the net worth of most of the estates, the relative weight of philanthropic and other bequests could not be reliably calculated in three out of four cases. But we found that while 54 per cent of the donors made some bequests, at least 30 per cent made none at all. It was impossible to find wills for the remainder. Table 11–4

summarizes the allocations of gifts and bequests to seven of the
eleven philanthropic categories, the only ones which received attention from donors:

TABLE 11-4

*Allocation of Gifts and Bequests in Relation to
Philanthropic Categories**

	Welfare		Religion		Civic		Lib. Arts Ed.		Voc.-Tech. Ed.		Libraries		Art		Totals*	
	No.	%	No.	%	No.	%	No.	%	No.	%	No.	%	No.	%	No.	%
Gifts only	40	36	24	22	9	8	11	10	9	8	13	12	5	4	111	100
Bequests only	19	33	15	26	4	7	4	7	5	9	5	9	6	9	58	100

* These figures and percentages give only a rough indication of the areas which interested
philanthropists. The table gives no indication of actual dollar amounts or of proportion
of dollar amounts.

*Our figures suggest that women were more interested than men
in donating to religious organizations and welfare activities.* They
were also possibly less interested in vocational and technical education. But since there are only five women in our sample, we
cannot draw any really significant conclusions about their habits
of philanthropy. Table 11–5 may, however, be regarded as suggestive of a general tendency.

TABLE 11-5

Allocation of Gifts and Bequests in Relation to Sex
(51 men, 5 women)

	Welfare		Religion		Civic		Lib. Arts Ed.		Voc.-Tech. Ed.		Libraries		Art		Totals*	
	No.	%	No.	%	No.	%	No.	%	No.	%	No.	%	No.	%	No.	%
51 men	42	3	27	21	11	8	12	11	12	8	17	12	10	8	131	100
5 women	4	30	4	30	1	8	2	15	—	—	1	8	1	8	13	100

* In these and some subsequent tables percentage components do not add to total because
of rounding.

Ten of the givers were of foreign birth, but this had no discernible effect on their allocations to fields of philanthropic interest.
Place of residence, on the other hand, seems to have had a slight
influence on allocations. Those living in New England and the

Middle Atlantic states tended somewhat to emphasize welfare and health, while those in the old Northwest were more interested in libraries. For the West we have a much smaller number of millionaires to work with, but they tended to fall below the average in welfare and above it in gifts to civic improvements and to liberal arts education. Table 11–6 gives the breakdowns:

TABLE 11–6

Allocation to Philanthropic Categories Compared with Residence
(all gifts and bequests integrated for each individual)

	Welfare		Religion		Civic		Lib. Arts Ed.		Voc.-Tech. Ed.		Libraries		Art		Totals	
	No.	%	No.	%	No.	%	No.	%	No.	%	No.	%	No.	%	No.	%
New Eng. and Mid. Atlantic states (34 philanthropists)	29	39	16	21	4	5	7	9	5	7	8	10	6	8	75	100
Old N. W. and Middle West (16)	13	28	10	22	4	9	3	7	5	11	8	17	3	7	46	100
Mountain and West Coast (5)	3	15	4	20	4	20	3	15	2	10	2	10	2	10	20	100
South (1)	1		1				1								3	100
TOTALS:	46		31		12		14		12		18		11		144	

It appears clear from our study *that residence did not greatly affect the propensity to give*. The proportion of millionaires definitely identified as donors was 44 per cent in both areas—Northeast and Middle West—for which we had a sizable number of millionaires. The very small number of millionaires in the South and Southwest that turned up in our sample was too small to make comparisons between donors and nondonors in these regions meaningful. We cannot be at all sure that "nondonors" including unknowns really gave nothing (unlikely), but if we assume that the amount and reliability of our data on individuals were fairly constant for all parts of the country (a fair assumption), then the closeness of these percentages indicates that the proportion of donors to nondonors was also constant even if we cannot establish definitely the numbers of these two classes.

Since the religious affiliation of 70 millionaires in the sample of 124 could not be identified, no over-all conclusions could be drawn about the proportion of contributors in each group. Among those that could be identified, the 27 Protestants gave slightly more often than the average to religious activities. The six unaffiliated and "liberal" Protestants (Unitarians, Universalists and members of the Ethical Culture Society) ranked slightly lower in giving to religion and to technical and vocational education but gave more than the average for libraries. Tables 11–7 and 11–8 present our findings:

TABLE 11-7

The Religious Pattern of Givers and of Unknowns in the
124 Tribune *Sample*

Religion	No. of Givers	No. of 124	Percentage of Givers
Catholic	2	3	67
Protestant	27	39	44
Jewish	3	5	60
No affiliation or Liberal	6	7	86
Unknown	18	70	21
TOTAL	56	124	

TABLE 11-8

Allocations to Categories Compared with Religion

	Welfare		Religion		Civic		Lib. Arts Ed.		Voc.-Tech. Ed.		Libraries		Art		Totals	
	No.	%	No.	%	No.	%	No.	%	No.	%	No.	%	No.	%	No.	%
2 Catholics	1	14	2	29	1	14	1	14	1	14			1	14	7	100
27 Protestants	25	32	23	29	7	9	7	9	5	6	8	10	4	5	79	100
3 Jews	3	43	2	29			1	14					1	14	7	100
6 no affiliation or Liberals	3	28	2	18	1	9	1	9			3	28	1	9	11	100
18 unknown	14	35	2	5	3	8	4	10	6	15	7	18	4	10	40	100
TOTALS:	46		31		12		14		12		18		11		144	

To our surprise *no very meaningful relationships could be discovered between the number of dependents or survivors and propensity to donate.* Those without children, however, tended to give less frequently to welfare and health. Table 11–9 summarizes our findings.

TABLE 11–9

Dependents and Philanthropy

	Welfare		Religion		Civic		Lib. Arts Ed.		Voc.-Tech. Ed.		Libraries		Art		Totals	
	No.	%	No.	%	No.	%	No.	%	No.	%	No.	%	No.	%	No.	%
80% (45) had children	37	33	23	21	9	8	11	10	8	7	14	12	10	9	112	100
18% (10) had no children	8	25	8	25	13	3	10	4	4	13	4	13	1	3	31	100
2% (1) family unknown	1	10													1	100
															144	

The level of education attained by the millionaires seems to have had no regular or logical effect on their philanthropy, although no conclusions could be drawn with any confidence since the education of almost half could not be established. But on the basis of available data *those who had no more than secondary education seem to have done more for charitable, educational and other philanthropic causes than those with either elementary or higher education*, while the proportion of donors with elementary and with college educations (excluding graduate, professional and business schools) was approximately the same.

Among the donors, however, one notices that those with only elementary education apparently gave somewhat more often to liberal arts education and somewhat less to welfare and health. Those with secondary education tended in their giving to be more generous to libraries and less generous to religion. Those with higher education tended to emphasize religion and to slight vocational and technical education.

Only those with college and graduate professional school education omitted categories in their choices of fields for philanthropy. No donors in either group gave to vocational and technical education. The graduate and professional school donor likewise did not give to liberal arts education or to art. Table 11–10 presents the over-all picture.

In our sample *neither sex, place of birth or residence, religion, family or education had more than a slight relationship to the decision of millionaires to donate to philanthropic causes.* A composite millionaire contributor would be male, native-born, resident in the Northeast, Protestant, head of a family and educated at only the elementary level. But these characteristics also describe a nonphilanthropic millionaire.

TABLE 11–10

Allocation to Categories Compared with Education

% No.	Welfare No. %	Religion No. %	Civic No. %	Lib. Arts Ed. No. %	Voc.-Tech. Ed. No. %	Libraries No. %	Art No. %	Totals No. %
21 (12) Elementary	10 25	8 20	4 10	6 15	5 13	4 10	3 8	40 100
16 (9) Sec. public	8 32	4 15	1 3	2 7	3 12	6 24	2 7	26 100
13 (7) Sec. private	7 35	4 20	2 10	1 5	2 10	2 10	2 10	20 100
18 (10) College	6 33	6 33	1 6	2 11		1 6	2 11	12 100
11 (6) Grad. & prof.	4 50	2 25	1 13			1 13		8 100
7 (4) Bus. school	4 27	3 20	2 13	2 13	1 7	2 13	1 7	15 100
14 (8) Unknown	7 40	4 24	1 6	1 6	1 6	2 12	1 6	17 100
100 (56) TOTALS:	46	31	12	14	12	18	11	138

The only variable which seems to have had a pronounced influence on the propensity of a millionaire to be a philanthropist was the method by which he acquired his fortune. *The "self-made men" in the sample were much more philanthropic than were those who inherited their wealth.* There were 56 per cent more known philanthropists in the "self-made" category (Table 11–11, line 4) than in the other acquisition group (line 1), although there were twelve more subjects who inherited their money. Among those who inherited their fortunes, we found that 46 per cent of those gainfully employed became donors. Only 22 per cent of those who were not so employed or who held only minor jobs were philanthropists. Of the 27 subjects not gainfully employed (line 3) only six could even tentatively be called donors and this gives the benefit of the doubt to Hugh Baxter, contributor of the prize for the "Baxter Mile" in a New York City track meet. The remaining five nonemployed, endowed philanthropists were all women, and this number, out of a total of 15 woman millionaires, is relatively close to the average for the entire sample, 56:124. On the other hand, 80 per cent of the subjects known to be entirely responsible for their own wealth were philanthropists (line 5). The few subjects who worked for their money but inherited a position, such as the presidency of a company, (line 6) were less generous than those entirely self-made but more so than the inheritors of wealth.

Source of fortune usually made no difference in allocation to specific fields of philanthropy, which approximate the general average (see Table 11–4). The sole exception was the sharp drop in donations to vocational and technical education among the 34 per cent who had inherited their million. Table 11–11 shows the major results of asking our data the question, "What relation did source of fortune have on philanthropy?"

A more meaningful expression of the relation between self-made men and heirs as philanthropists may be arrived at by computing the "generosity ratio" for each group. Dividing the ratio of self-made donors (line 4) to endowed donors with jobs (line 2) or 28:12 by the ratio of self-made nonphilanthropists (line 4) to their endowed counterparts (line 2) or 7:14 gives the "generosity ratio" between these groups, which is 14:3. In other words the propensity of a self-made millionaire's being a donor was more than four times greater than that of a man who inherited his wealth but was also employed. *It would seem, therefore, that the most significant differences in philanthropic habits existed between the possessors of self-made and inherited wealth.*

One factor in making the self-made millionaire more philanthropically inclined than those who inherited their wealth or position was the opportunity his lowly start gave him to become acquainted firsthand with conditions on the lower social and economic levels. The problems he himself faced, and overcame,

TABLE 11-11

Philanthropy and Acquisition of Wealth

	Identified Givers		Nongivers, Unknowns		Totals	
	No.	%	No.	%	No.	%
1. *Inherited Wealth*	18	34	35	66	53	100
A. (20%) own work and/or position, *i.e.*, starting with family connections	12	46	14	54	26	100
41% B. (21%) no work or minor jobs only	6	22	21	78	27	100
2. *Self-Made Wealth*	32	78	9	22	41	100
A. (28%) own work only	28	80	7	20	35	100
33% B. (5%) own work plus position	4	67	2	33	6	100
3. *Source of Wealth Unknown*	6	20	24	80	30	100
26%						
100% TOTALS	56		68		124	

were constant reminders of the needs philanthropy could serve. Such a man was also aware of the importance of providing the less fortunate individual with access to education, books, medical care, works of art and fresh air. With such opportunities the chances of his improving his condition were increased. To the self-made man, philanthropy did not dampen initiative but provided an incentive to self-improvement. His benefaction helped open the door of success to more of his kind. Conversely, those born with the proverbial silver spoon had difficulty seeing beyond its handle or, if they could, were less sensitive to the problems of the needy than those responsible for their own success.

Another factor in the philanthropic habits of those who worked for their wealth and those who inherited it was the nature of the responsibility engendered by the possession of a million dollars or more. The self-made man was less apt to take his wealth for granted. Having made his money actively and, as it were, taken it from society, he was highly susceptible to influence by the concept of stewardship of wealth. Like Carnegie, he was inclined to feel that after providing for his family he owed society a debt that could be paid with philanthropy. Merely to pass his money on to his heirs was a violation of the trust great wealth entailed. Society had a claim to his fortune of which the self-made million- aire was sometimes apt to be aware.[18] As an example of this atti- tude, George F. Peabody, generous American philanthropist to many causes, once made a forceful statement of the motives which impelled him to give:[19]

Twenty-five years ago I realized that I had considerable wealth and it dawned upon me that the money was the result of other men's labors. I had been a banker for a quarter of a century and during that time I fear that I had forgotten that the only way a dollar can be actually produced is by real work. But when I came to see that the money which I had amassed was the work of others, I then and there decided to retire from business and become my own executor, to administer for the people that which rightfully belonged to them.

Of course not all rich Americans agreed with Peabody, but his statement suggests that for a self-made man the claims of society to his fortune could have a special meaning.

It is also likely that some self-made men found it desirable to give to respectable and worthy causes in order to improve their own social status. Concern for one's standing in the community certainly figured in the mental outlook and behavior of some men who had come up the hard way from humble beginnings, and although quantification is obviously impossible, biographical data suggest that status considerations entered into the complex mo- tivation of many donors, including Andrew Carnegie.

On the other hand, many of these considerations were irrele- vant to the man who inherited his million. He owed only his ben- efactor, most probably his parents, for this fortune. Of course at one time someone must have made the money with his own hands, but the beneficiary was less conscious of any debt to society that may have existed. Stewardship of wealth was not a pressing obli- gation. After all, his father, not his God, had given him his money. Moreover, being wealthy was something he took for granted, a commonplace with which he had usually grown up. The man who was given his money often felt a responsibility to *his* heirs and was inclined to pass it on to them rather than to the public, thereby perpetuating the pattern from which he bene-

fited. Obviously, too, status considerations were much less important among those who inherited their fortunes than among many
self-made men.

Our second project was an analysis of large-scale gifts and bequests in the *New York Times*.[20] We checked every year from
1851 through 1879 but were forced by reason of the newspaper's
greatly increased coverage to limit our study to only four years in
the subsequent two decades. We chose 1885, 1887, 1890 and 1897
as years least likely to be affected by cataclysmic events such as
depressions and wars. We then studied the *Times* for 1913 to see
whether the trends continued to the dislocations of World War I
and the income tax authorized by the Sixteenth Amendment to
the Constitution.

Working through the *New York Times* index we assigned all
reported gifts and bequests to the eleven categories used in the
New York Tribune study of millionaires. The results of our
study of long-range trends in philanthropy through the *New
York Times* study were disappointing. We had hoped that the use
of a single, reasonably reliable source would yield a fair basis for
comparing philanthropic habits of a broader category than millionaires over a long period. Regrettably, the daily exigencies of
newspaper publishing and changes in editorial policy over the
years had distorting effects for which we could not compensate.

On the one hand, a donation might have been considered news-
worthy one day but might be slighted the next. Then, the coverage of the *Times* was naturally heavier for New York City and
the metropolitan area; only the most important or impressive donations from other sections of the country were reported. The
proportion of gifts to the field of welfare, for example, was much
heavier for New York, while that for universities and other regional and national institutions was greater in the rest of the country. Furthermore, as the *Times* became larger and more national
in scope, habits of reporting donations to the several fields of
philanthropy changed also.

A few tentative conclusions may, however, be drawn. *The
fields of welfare and liberal arts education dominated the attention of American philanthropists in this period.* Outside of general
contributions to education, interest in scholarly research was negligible in the nineteenth century. Research in natural science grew

to 10 per cent of the total donations by 1913, but then only five contributors (3 per cent) accounted for the $2,573,000 contributed to this field. Support for research in the social sciences was also negligible, for in the entire period we found only one contributor in the 1860's of $150,000 and two in 1913 of $108,000. With the exception of missionary activities, donations to areas outside the country were higher in 1896 and 1913 but still small both in number of contributors and amounts given. The dollar amounts of gifts to libraries apparently hit a peak in the 1860's, with $1,057,000 or 18 per cent of the total amount contributed and 8 per cent of the total number of donations. Philanthropic interest in libraries declined for the rest of the century and were only 1 per cent of the total number of donations in 1913.

The *New York Times* study uncovered some data on benefactions to Negro education. Although it is known that many churches and missionary societies in the North contributed to this cause, in the South after the Civil War one would have to generalize that interest in this cause was slight if one depended on the *New York Times* record alone. In the decade after Appomattox a New Haven Negro laundress bequeathed her life savings of $5,000 to the Yale Theological School for a scholarship for a Negro student. This decade also witnessed a gift of $50,000 to Fisk University. Since our study included only two years in the 1880's (1885 and 1887), the $1,000,000 gift of John Slater in 1882 for Negro education in the South did not come into the range of the *New York Times* data. Mrs. John Jacob Astor bequeathed $25,000 to Hampton in 1886 and the 1897 survey yielded two bequests, one of $40,000 to a girls' school and one of $100,000. The Rosenwald gift of $202,000 in 1913 was, of course, only a small part of what one generous philanthropist did for the Negro.

The proportion of numbers and amounts of gifts to religion were comparatively high but no trend was noticeable. Gifts to social welfare and health, on the other hand, increased in the depression years clustered between 1870 and 1885 and thereafter replaced the liberal arts in numbers of donations.

In the field of education, the *New York Times* study indicated that donations to vocational and technical institutions increased somewhat irregularly up to the 1880's and 1890's, *while the general interest in liberal arts education fell off after a high in the*

1870's of 35 per cent both in amount and numbers of donations.
Important exceptions to this general trend in liberal arts education
were the endowments of three universities established in the
1880's: Stanford ($20,000,000), Clark ($1,500,000), and DePauw
($1,250,000), accounting for 60 per cent in amounts given in that
decade.

In concluding the summary of the *New York Times* study it
may be useful to include a list of the three leading philanthropies
for each decade both with respect to dollars given and number of
contributors (Table 11–12):

TABLE 11-12

*Top Three Philanthropies by Percentage of Dollar Amounts
and Total Number of Contributors*

Time span	Per cent of dollars		Per cent of numbers	
1850's	Liberal Arts Ed.	59	Liberal Arts Ed.	19
	Religion	12	Civic	19
	Civic	9	Welfare	14
1860's	Liberal Arts Ed.	36	Liberal Arts Ed.	29
	Libraries	18	Welfare	21
	Welfare	14	Religion	18
1870's	Liberal Arts Ed.	35	Liberal Arts Ed.	35
	Welfare	27	Welfare	26
	Religion	12	Religion	21
1885, 1887	Liberal Arts Ed.	61	Welfare	32
	Welfare	10	Religion	26
	Libraries	9	Liberal Arts Ed.	11
1890, 1897	Religion	30	Welfare	28
	Welfare	23	Religion	26
	Liberal Arts Ed.	21	Liberal Arts Ed.	20
1913	Liberal Arts Ed.	24	Welfare	42
	Voc.-Tech. Ed.	20	Religion	22
	Art	20	Liberal Arts Ed.	17

Because of statistical difficulties involved in both the *New York
Times* and the *New York Tribune* studies it is difficult to make
any really valid comparison between the findings of the two studies. Nonetheless, our investigation led us tentatively to believe

that *the interests of philanthropic millionaires, despite the prefer-ences of a few for liberal arts education, the arts and civic im-provement, was not substantially different from those of most donors of their time.*

In retrospect, the study we made might have proved more posi-tively revealing had it been undertaken and executed along differ-ent lines. It might, for example, have been more profitable to have made an exhaustive investigation, in terms of the total universe or by random sample, of wills probated in one city. Or, had we chosen to study a period later than the one we did choose, it might have been possible to have obtained permission from the Commissioner of Internal Revenue to examine the estate tax rec-ords available at the Federal Records Center at Alexandria, Vir-ginia, for some part of the period since 1916 when the Federal estate tax first went into effect. But this study, while it might have yielded more positive results, would have thrown no light on the earlier period in which the generosity of millionaires was under special discussion. It is precisely this early period for which we have hitherto had no quantitative study in which an effort was made to control variables. It is nevertheless to be hoped that the path broken by F. Emerson Andrews and Frank Dickinson in quantitative studies of philanthropy in the period since 1916 may be followed back to the nineteenth and twentieth centuries. Whether it is possible to project into the period before that date an investigation such as we undertook and succeed better than we did depends on the ability to uncover a complete record of the lives and philanthropic habits (or lack of them) for a group of Americans. This we found an extremely difficult task despite the use of available research tools including personal investigation in and hundreds of written inquiries to the surrogate courts, histori-cal societies and libraries of the communities in which our sample of millionaires lived and in some cases gave. The effort might nev-ertheless be worth pursuing, for our results, limited though they are in many respects, do suggest that the available impressionistic writings, biographies, and even the efforts of a more systematic sort made by the *New York Tribune,* the *New York World* and *Appleton's Cyclopaedia* leave a great deal to be desired in precise knowledge. Moreover, our study has yielded significant results on the anatomy of the giving habits of a random sample of millionaires. It has given the first precise information on the categories of philanthropic causes which millionaire donors favored. It is also clear that sex, religion, family, education and place of birth and residence did not have more than a slight relationship to the decision of millionaires to donate to philanthropic causes; on the other hand, contrary to expectations, the self-made men were much more philanthropic than those who inherited their wealth. Hopefully we may some day know whether these generalizations hold for both men and women of wealth in other periods, and whether the same factors figure in the giving habits of the less well to do, and of how the anatomy of giving in America compares with that of other countries.

Notes

NOTE: In every sense, this project was a cooperative one. Dr. Margaret Wooster Curti helped to plan the project. My colleague, Professor Irvin G. Wyllie, offered helpful suggestions during the planning stage. Charles Strickland, a research assistant in the University of Wisconsin History of Philanthropy Project, gave valuable aid in planning the layouts and in collecting and coding biographical material. Professor and Mrs. Burton Fisher, while in no way responsible either for planning procedures or for our interpretations, have given us valuable criticisms and suggestions.

1. For examples see Merle Curti, "American Philanthropy and the National Character," *American Quarterly*, X (Winter 1958), 420–437.
2. James Bryce, *The American Commonwealth* (3rd ed.; 2 vols.; New York: 1909), II, p. 723.
3. Arthur M. Schlesinger Sr., "The True American Way of Life," *St. Louis Post-Dispatch*, December 13, 1953, Part II, 3.
4. Shepard E. Clough, "Philanthropy and the Welfare State in Europe," *Political Science Quarterly*, LXXV (March 1960), 87.
5. For example, the completed and recently published book-length study of American giving overseas by Merle Curti and the investigation in progress on the impact of philanthropy on American colleges and universities by Curti and Roderick W. Nash; Jesse B. Sears, *Philanthropy in the History of American Higher Education*, Department of Interior, Bureau of Education, Bull. No. 26 (Washington: 1922); Robert Bremner, *American Philanthropy* (Chicago: 1960); Merle Curti, "Tradition and Innovation in American Philanthropy," *Proceedings of the American Philosophical Society*, V (April 1961), 146–156; Edward C. Jenkins, *Philanthropy in America* (New York: 1950); and Arnaud C. Marts, *Man's Concern for His Fellow Man* (New York: 1961).
6. W. K. Jordan, *Philanthropy in England, 1480–1660* (New York: 1959); *The Charities of London, 1480–1660* (London: 1960); and *The Charities of Rural England, 1480–1660* (New York: 1962).

7. F. Emerson Andrews, *Philanthropic Giving* (New York: 1950), *Corporation Giving* (New York, 1952), *Attitudes toward Giving* (New York: 1953), and *Philanthropic Foundations* (New York, 1956). The study of American philanthropy sponsored by the National Bureau of Economic Research similarly concentrates on the fifties.

8. "American Millionaires: The Tribune's List of Persans Reputed to Be Worth a Million or More," *Tribune Monthly*, IV, No. 6 (June 1892). Sidney Ratner has reprinted the *New York Tribune* list and discussed it in an informing introduction: *New Light on the History of Great American Fortunes: American Millionaires of 1892 and 1902* (New York: 1953).

9. George P. Watkins, "The Growth of Large Fortunes," *Publications of the American Economic Association*, VIII, 3d ser. (1907), 875 ff. For other favorable judgments on the care with which the *Tribune* list was compiled and on its general reliability see Ratner, *New Light on the History of Great American Fortunes*, p. xix.

10. The *New York World's* list of 3,561 millionaires living in 1902 is also included in the Ratner volume.

11. For a recent edition of this and other essays bearing on the problem of wealth see Andrew Carnegie, *The Gospel of Wealth*, Edward C. Kirkland, ed. (Cambridge: 1962).

12. *Review of Reviews*, VII (February 1893), 48–60.

13. Attention was called to the generosity of several Cleveland millionaires to Western Reserve University, to the $1,000,000 gift of William J. Gordon for a park and to the donations of Mrs. Samuel Mather and her late husband for several public causes.

14. George J. Hagar, "Magnitude of American Benefactions," *Review of Reviews*, XXIX (April 1904), 464–465. The yearly totals as well as an itemized listing of the contributions appeared in *Appleton's Annual Cyclopaedia and Register of Important Events* under the heading "Gifts and Bequests" from 1893 to 1902. Hagar's figure for 1903 appears only in his article.

15. Hagar, *Review of Reviews*, XXIX, 465.

16. It seems not improbable that the records for outstandingly large gifts (and bequests) are fairly complete. See Table 11–2 which presents figures which may have some general interest.

17. For what limited value it may have, the authors compiled a table of dollar amounts for their own reference which is on file at the Wisconsin Project on the History of American Philanthropy.

18. Hagar (*Review of Reviews*, VII, 49) argued in 1893 that millionaires are the product not only of their own efforts but of "the unearned increment in expanding land values, the productive value of railway and other franchises, and the other forms of wealth that arise out of conditions which Society itself creates. . . ." For this reason, he concluded, the wealthy should give generously to public purposes.

19. *New York Times*, July 26, 1931.

20. We appreciate the careful and time-taking work of Sharon Smith and John Tomsich, research assistants on the University of Wisconsin Project, in collecting data on donations as reported in the *New York Times* in selected years.

☙ 12 ☙

Fred I. Greenstein

NEW LIGHT ON CHANGING
AMERICAN VALUES: A FORGOTTEN
BODY OF SURVEY DATA

Abstract. The hypothesis that Americans have come to value personal achievement less in the past half century has been supported by impressionistic arguments and by indirect measures of value change such as Lowenthal's content analysis of trends over the years in heroes of magazine biography. Lowenthal's findings are juxtaposed with a forgotten body of historical survey data on children's choices of exemplars since the turn of the century. The survey data suggest that indirect indices such as magazine biographies are not adequate measures of values. In general, the value change hypothesis is not supported.

The values held by Americans are commonly believed to have undergone a radical change since the turn of the century. Americans, it is said, have come increasingly to prize leisure over work, accommodation to their fellows over individual achievement, in general, passivity over activity. The best known statement of the many variations on this theme is probably that of David Riesman and his associates. Riesman's thesis was presented in terms of changes in social structure and "social character"; changes from an "age of production" to an "age of consumption," which he

Fred I. Greenstein is Professor of Government at Wesleyan University. He is the author of *Children and Politics*, and *The American Party System and the American People*.

Reprinted from *Social Forces*, XLII (1964), 441–450, by permission of the author and the University of North Carolina Press.

believed had been accompanied by a shift from "inner-" to "other-direction" in the sources of Americans' "modes of conformity."[1] William Whyte's well-publicized comments on "The Declining Protestant Ethic" parallel Riesman's assertions at many points.[2]

The views of Riesman and Whyte are widely accepted. Clyde Kluckhohn reaches similar though not identical conclusions on the basis of a "massive" review of several hundred "empirical and impressionistic writings on American culture and especially American values by social scientists and others."[3] Much of the literature Kluckhohn was able to find had been "produced by writers . . . who based their reflections on their own experience rather than upon specifically pointed and systematic research."[4] Granting that these observations did not meet satisfactory standards of evidence, Kluckhohn nevertheless was impressed by the amount of broad agreement with Riesman and Whyte, although he felt it necessary to point to "the possibility that the consonance derives from Zeitgeist or from parrotings—with variations—of a few popular formulations."[5]

In addition to impressionistic accounts of changing American values, Kluckhohn was able to draw upon several studies which presented "hard" data—analyses of various indirect indices of value change, such as the variations over the years in the content of the lyrics of popular songs, best selling novels, and religious literature. The findings of a number of these studies seem to support the assertions of Riesman and Whyte. For example, after observing differences in the types of individuals who served as topics of popular magazine biographies between 1901 and 1941,[6] Leo Lowenthal concluded that contemporary audiences were being exposed to "idols of consumption" (e.g., film stars) rather than the "idols of production" (e.g., business magnates) of earlier years. Lowenthal's findings were drawn upon by Riesman to support the thesis of *The Lonely Crowd*. A more recent example of the analysis of value changes in cultural products is the study by de Charms and Moeller of a century-and-a-half of grade school textbooks.[7] Noting that "achievement imagery" in children's readers had declined consistently after the 1880's, de Charms and Moeller concluded that their findings "correspond very well" with those of Riesman and other commentators.

Lately, however, objections have been raised to the argument that one of the major twentieth century developments has been the supplanting of the Protestant Ethic with what Whyte calls "the Social Ethic." Lipset, for example, after a detailed examination of comments on the United States by nineteenth century foreign visitors, asserts that the "traits of the other-directed man have to a considerable extent always existed in the American character and that the values of achievement and individualism persist in American Society." [8] Parsons and White argue that the American "value-system has . . . remained stable . . ." and that "a major part of the phenomena that form the center of the analyses of Riesman, Kluckhohn, and others" consists merely of "new *specifications* of the [unchanged] general value system, in relation to new structural and situational conditions." [9]

Ideally one would hope to resolve such disagreements by direct observation of trends over the years in people's values (a research tactic which is becoming increasingly practical as historical survey data accumulate), rather than by impressionistic reports or indirect indices of value change. As Riesman and Glazer comment, referring to questionnaires which have been devised to test Riesman's hypotheses, "we wish there were ways of finding out how nineteenth-century young people might have responded to such questionnaires . . . but history buries its dead. . . ." [10]

A Forgotten Body of Survey Data

The present article analyzes a forgotten body of survey data going back to the 1890's. Between 1896 and 1910, students of education conducted numerous investigations of the "ideals" of children and adolescents—i.e., of their statements about "what person you would most like to resemble." In later years a number of additional studies of children's exemplars were carried out, one in the 1920's and several since 1944.[11] Thus evidence is available over a 50-year period on trends in juvenile heroes and hero-worship. These data, which are probably the longest time series of reasonably reliable and comparable questionnaire findings, have the merit of providing us with a direct index of values in the general population. In view of the emphasis by Riesman, among others, on changing socialization practices as one determinant of value changes, it is especially interesting that the data are on the values of young people.

Several factors make possible the use of these data from a period before acceptable standards for survey research had been developed. First, although not based on random sampling, the studies draw on exceedingly large and diversified populations of children. For both the pre-World War I and the post-1944 periods (which are most important for our purposes) several studies are available from widely dispersed geographical areas, and for both periods there is enough impressionistic information about respondents' social characteristics to make it clear that the populations studied were broadly heterogeneous. Second, raw data are available from five of the studies—two from the early period, one from the 1920's, and two from the later period—making possible secondary analysis in terms of categories which are more revealing than those used in the original studies. In these five studies complete or nearly complete inventories of all the individuals referred to by the respondents were reported. Therefore re-analysis was possible once the identities of some of the more obscure names (ranging from turn-of-the-century congressmen to silent screen performers) were established and a number of minor estimates were made to fill in slight gaps. Finally, the pattern of findings emerging from all the studies, a pattern which, as we shall see, supports the thesis that values have *not* changed markedly in the directions suggested by Riesman, is sufficiently clear-cut and internally consistent to eliminate doubts about the representativeness of the data.

Since the studies are of hero-worship it is useful to juxtapose them with Lowenthal's findings on changing heroes of popular biography and to discuss them in the context of both Lowenthal's and Riesman's interpretations of the former's findings.

Lowenthal and Riesman on Changing Values

Lowenthal's conclusion that "idols of consumption" had taken the place of "idols of production" was based on rather striking differences in the occupations of magazine biography subjects before and after World War I. Three major changes were found in "the professional distribution of . . . 'heroes' "; changes which Ries-man saw as fitting snugly into the conclusions of *The Lonely Crowd:*

1. Perhaps the most clear-cut change followed close upon the growth in the second decade of the century of spectator sports and the mass entertainment industry. During the period before the Great War, 77 per cent of the biographies of entertainers were of representatives of "serious arts" (i.e., literature, fine arts, music, dance, theater). For each successive time period sampled there was a consistent shift in the direction of representatives of athletics and of what Lowenthal refers to as "the sphere of cheap or mass entertainment," until by 1940–1941 "serious artists" made up only 9 per cent of the entertainers about whom biographies were written. In all, entertainers ("serious" and "non-serious") accounted for only a fourth of the pre-World War I biographies as opposed to one-half of the post-war biographies. Lowenthal concluded that "the [contemporary] idols of the masses are not, as they were in the past, the leading names in the battle of produc-tion, but the headliners of the movies, the ballparks, and the night clubs." [12]

2. The over-all decline in biographies of leaders "in the battle of production" was not as sharp as the overall increase in biogra-phies of entertainers. Leaders of production made up 28 per cent of the pre-1914 biographies and an average of about 17 per cent of the biographies in the three later time-periods sampled by Lowen-thal. But here also the differences were greater if one took ac-count of the degree to which the biographical subjects repre-sented the "serious side" of life. Early biographies were of bankers and railroad executives; the later ones concentrated on such figures as the owner of a vacation resort, a man who had organized a roadside restaurant chain, and a professional model.

3. Finally, consistent with the assertion in *The Lonely Crowd* that with the advent of other-direction politics increasingly has become a passive spectator activity rather than an arena in which to vent intense feelings,[13] biographies of political leaders were less common after World War I. Forty-six per cent of the early biog-raphies were of people in political life; less than 30 per cent of the later biographies were of politicians.

Both Lowenthal and Riesman interpret the shifts in biographical heroes since the turn of the century in terms of a decline in popular aspiration levels. Biographies during the early period were "to be looked upon as examples of success which can be imitated," Lowenthal suggests. Taking note of the rhetoric in the biographies as well as the individuals who were their subjects, he concludes that during the early period such magazine articles served as "educational models." They reflected a period of "rugged individualism . . . characterized by eagerness and confidence that the social ladder may be scaled on a mass basis." The later biographies, on the other hand, "seem to lead to a dream world of the masses who no longer are capable or willing to conceive of biographies primarily as a means of orientation and education." [14]

Riesman agrees that biographies during the early period served as models which were within the aspirations of their readers, whereas today the individual "cannot imagine himself in the work role of the president of the United States or the head of a big company." However, he suggests that the contemporary biographies also are models; but these are new, other-directed models of taste, life-style, and leisure-time pursuit—"the frontiers on which the reader can himself compete. . . ." [15]

Besides using the data on trends in children's exemplars to determine whether Lowenthal's content analysis findings are valid indicators of changes in "the idols of the masses," they also may be used to establish whether one other shift in the type of exemplar chosen by children which might be anticipated from speculations in *The Lonely Crowd* has taken place.

4. Riesman suggests that identification with national heroes served an important function in the socialization of children during the period when society was "dependent on inner direction."

[In] the George Washington myth . . . [N]ot only are the little boys told in the period of inner direction that they may grow up to be president but they are given scales by which to measure and discipline themselves for the job during boyhood. If they do not tell lies, if they work hard, and so on—if, that is, they act in their boyhoods as the legendary Washington acted in his—then they may succeed to his adult role.[16]

TABLE 12-1

Per Cent of Children and Adolescents Choosing Various Classes of Public Figures as Exemplars: 1902–1958 *

Exemplars	Place, Approximate Date of Field Work, and Investigator				
	1902 New Castle, Penna.	1910 Nashville, Tenn.	1928 Birmingham, Montgomery, Mobile, Ala.	1944 Springfield, Mass.	1958 New Haven, Conn.
	Chambers	Hill	Hill	Stoughton, Ray	Greenstein
Entertainment					
"Serious"	4.1	4.1	5.1		1.8
"Non-Serious"	0.6	0.3	10.4	8.1	36.1
Business	1.6	1.0	1.0		0.6
Contemporary Political					
Incumbent President	3.3	0.9	0.2	2.7	3.3
Other	9.2	1.4	2.2	0.4	3.0
National Hero					
Washington	29.2	22.0	19.9	4.9	3.2
Lincoln	3.4	0.6	2.4	1.5	3.6
Other	3.0	9.6	5.1	4.6	3.6
Miscellaneous Figures from Wider Environment	17.2	20.6	15.6	33.4	14.8
Immediate Environment Figures	22.4	39.5	33.8	44.4	2.0
No Response or Invalid Response	6.0		4.3		28.0
TOTAL	100.0	100.0	100.0	100.0	100.0
Ages Included in Present Tabulation	7–16	7–15	6–20	9 & 11	9–15
Number of Cases	2333	1431	8813	259	659

* A number of the percentages in Table 12-1 are estimates of the percentages which would have resulted if certain minor gaps in the data did not exist. All estimates are between a fraction of a per cent and about three per cent of what would have been found if full data were available, with the exception of the 1902 statistic for "other national heroes," which is—to some unknown degree—larger than the 3 per cent indicated in the table. In each case where an estimate has been made the estimate is conservative with respect to the interpretation of the table in the text, so that any other estimate would have further strengthened the conclusions. (For example, the highest possible estimate is used for "other contemporary political figures" in 1902, and the lowest possible estimate in 1944.) Further information about the five studies summarized here, along with a discussion of the techniques of retabulation and estimation, is contained in a mimeographed technical appendix available from the author. The "miscellaneous figures from wider environment" category is residual. It includes, among others, scientists, inventors, military leaders, religious figures, and characters from fiction, as well as a small number of responses which could not be classified because the names of the exemplars were not listed or were unidentifiable.

Invalid responses (e.g., references to an occupation rather than an individual; illegible questionnaires; etc.) were eliminated from the 1910 study prior to analysis. These made up about three per cent of the original 1910 sample. There is no discussion of invalid re-

Although Riesman does not explicitly state that the use of national heroes as childhood models has declined over the years, this conclusion is consistent with this discussion.

Trends in Children's Heroes
since the Turn of the Century

In addition to drawing on the five studies (summarized in Table 12–1) which were suitable for retabulation, the following analysis makes impressionistic use of other internal evidence from the studies, including lengthy but not exhaustive inventories of children's statements about why they chose to be like their hero, and additional studies which did not supply sufficiently comparable or detailed data for retabulation. We shall be concerned with (1) whether the direct questionnaire data confirm the trends in "hero-worship" suggested by Lowenthal's indirect data, and (2), more fundamentally, with whether the pattern of findings in the various direct studies of children is consistent with the belief that popular aspiration levels have declined.

The first four studies summarized in Table 12–1 (as well as the other early studies referred to in the text and notes) employed the following item, or some slight variation thereof: "Of all persons whom you have heard, or read about, or seen, whom would you most care to be like or resemble? Why?" [17]

The fifth study used a somewhat different question: "Name a famous person you want to be like." [18]

The earlier item produced references to figures from the immediate environment by between about one-fifth and two-fifths of the respondents; the item used in 1958 produced very few such references. Therefore the latter wording may inflate the proportion of children referring to public figures, although in 1958 fail-

sponses or of failures to respond in the 1944 study, and none are reported. The 1944 study was of second grade (age 7), fourth grade (age 9), and sixth grade (age 11) children; I have retabulated the percentages, eliminating the second grade subsample in order to bring the mean age closer to that of the other studies. Even after retabulation the mean age of this sample is still somewhat lower than that of the other samples. This evidently accounts for the greater tendency of 1944 respondents to refer to immediate environment exemplars. The size of the residual "miscellaneous" category in this study is a function partly of war-time references to military heroes and partly of a somewhat larger number of unidentified exemplars.

ure to respond is much more common than in the earlier studies. As will be seen, the variation in item and response pattern is not a serious drawback for the analysis.[19]

1. ENTERTAINERS

Following Lowenthal, I have defined "entertainer" in "the broadest sense of the word" to encompass not only popular performers such as film stars and professional athletes, but also all representatives of literature and the arts. Included are figures from the past (e.g., Longfellow and even Mozart) as well as those who were living at the times of the various studies.

The long-run trends in children's responses are generally consistent with Lowenthal's findings. In particular, the change he observed in the ratio of "serious" and "non-serious" artists is clearly evident. Before World War I both the percentages in Table 12–1 and the authors' discussions of their findings indicate that children rarely referred to popular performers. By 1928, the proportion of popular figures referred to (e.g., Clara Bow, Rudolph Valentino, Ty Cobb, Paul Whiteman) is double that of "serious" artists; in the post-1944 samples, references to the latter category virtually disappear.[20] Because the decline of "serious artists" is accompanied by an increase in "non-serious" artists and because of the possibility that the phrasing of the 1958 item "increased" the frequency of reference to entertainers, it is not possible to determine with certainty whether over-all references to entertainers have increased.

2. BUSINESSMEN, INDUSTRIALISTS, FINANCIERS

Lowenthal's procedure was to combine business and professional occupations into a single category, the latter including such disparate types as a college president and an inventor of gadgets. Then he further analyzed the occupations in terms of whether they were "serious" or "non-serious" and whether they represented production or consumption spheres of life.

In Table 12–1, I have reported only the proportion of references to "captains of industry" (industrialists, financiers, and businessmen in general). This avoids a great many troublesome coding decisions about whether a profession is "serious" and at the same time provides a clear-cut test of whether veneration of "idols of production" has declined.

The findings summarized in Table 12–1 cast serious doubt on the assumption that the frequent pre-World War I magazine biographies of captains of industry were an accurate indication of mass aspirations at the time. If such goals were prevalent in the population, it is difficult to believe that they would not have been reflected in children's statements about who they would "care to be like or resemble." But only a minute proportion (less than 2 per cent) of the children in the early studies referred to men like Carnegie, Rockefeller, and Morgan as their "ideals." It is true that still fewer contemporary children make such choices (none seem to have in the 1944 study). But the decline is within an exceedingly small range.

3. CONTEMPORARY POLITICAL FIGURES

The incumbent president and other living politicians have been placed in this category, plus individuals who were active during the adult lifetimes of parents of the children studied. Thus for the 1958 respondents, Franklin D. Roosevelt is treated as "contemporary"; Woodrow Wilson and Theodore Roosevelt have the same status for the 1928 children.

The data on contemporary political figures also cast doubt on the adequacy of Lowenthal's index. During all periods very few children chose the incumbent president. The proportion of 1902 references to Theodore Roosevelt, for example, is virtually identical with the proportion of 1944 references to Franklin Roosevelt, and in general there is no significant variation over the half-century in references to the chief executive. Studies of children's occupational goals, which were conducted around the turn of the century, further support the finding that children of that period rarely developed presidential aspirations.[21]

At first glance there seems to be partial support for Lowenthal's thesis in the finding that "other contemporary political figures" were chosen by about 9 per cent of the 1902 respondents, in contrast to less than 3 per cent of the respondents in later studies. But two-thirds of the "other" 1902 references were to the recently assassinated President McKinley and there is evidence that during the period immediately after his death, McKinley's "martyrdom" led to a widespread idolization of him on the part of children, as well as adults.[22]

4. NATIONAL HEROES

Riesman's discussion of the erstwhile role of national heroes in children's socialization leads us to expect that references to the *dramatis personae* of American patriotic lore will have declined. And this indeed is the case. Over 35 per cent of the 1902 responses and only about 10 per cent of the post-1944 responses fell in this category. In the first of the reports on children's exemplars, Darrah's 1896 study of 1440 St. Paul, Minnesota, and San Mateo County, California children, references to Washington and Lincoln alone (by far the most frequently mentioned patriotic figures in all of the studies) were made by 40 per cent of the ten-to-sixteen-year-old respondents.[23] The breakdown of national heroes reported in Table 12–1 leads to a further observation: one individual—George Washington—seems to account for the entire declining trend in references to national heroes.

To recapitulate, the direct data on children's exemplars are consistent with only one of the three trends reported by Lowenthal. The ratio of popular over "serious" entertainers has increased over the years in roughly the same way that the content of magazine biographies has shifted. But changes in magazine biographies of "heroes of production" and of political leaders are not reflected in the direct observations of public exemplars. The direct data also support Riesman's hypothesis that contemporary children are less likely than their predecessors to identify with national heroes. We may now consider the implications of these findings.

Discussion

In general, the body of "forgotten" data discussed here provides little if any support for the notion that Americans have placed a declining value on achievement. It is true that when one compares "official" emanations (for example, addresses to high school and college graduating classes) of the past with those of today "the decline of the Protestant ethic" seems plentifully evident. But this comparison may merely confound *fin de siècle* rationalizations with reality.[24] De Charms and Moeller find that between 1880 and 1910 "achievement imagery" in children's textbooks was about twice as common as it is in the contemporary period. This, they imply, indicates that achievement values were more prevalent then than now, a factor which they feel helps to explain industrial growth during those years.[25] Yet, in view of the consistently low rate of choice of businessmen as exemplars, it is difficult to believe that turn-of-the-century young people exceeded contemporary youths in the desire to excel in economic enterprise. The absence of business exemplars is especially striking in the face of what, on Lowenthal's showing, seems to have been a concerted attempt in the media to display businessmen as models for popular emulation.[26]

Similarly, rhetoric suggesting that "every boy is a potential President of the United States" abounded 60 years ago. Consider, for example, the statement by the author of one of the early studies that this "feeling . . . is one of our prized possessions. Our school literature is full of it; no address before children is complete which fails to remind them that each is on his way to the presidential chair." [27] As we have seen, the rhetoric seems to have had little impact on children's felt aspirations—choice of the incumbent president as an exemplar was exceedingly rare.

The two classes of exemplar which *did* shift over the half-century—entertainers and national heroes—are quite ambiguous indicators of aspiration levels. There is no *a priori* reason for assuming that the individual who wants to be like Enrico Caruso or Lily Pons is more driven to succeed than someone who sets up Frank Sinatra or Debbie Reynolds as an "ideal." The reverse could as easily be true. The decline in reference to national heroes (or, more precisely, references to Washington) is equally difficult to interpret. One hypothesis, which at first seems credible, is that identification with a hero such as Washington serves to channel a child's aspirations in the direction of political achievement. This seems to have been Riesman's assumption in the passage quoted above about the function of the George Washington myth in the period "dependent upon inner direction." His remarks continue:

"The [presidential] role, moreover, by its very nature, is a continuing one; somebody is always president. . . . In fantasy the little boy not only identifies with the young Washington in the French and Indian wars but also with the adult role of president. . . ." [28] If this were the case we would expect—contrary to the present findings—that populations which were high in identification with figures such as Washington also would be high in reference to incumbent presidents.[29]

Unfortunately, in the early studies respondents' explanations of why they chose to be like their exemplars were not presented exhaustively. Therefore they cannot be retabulated. However, the extensive quotations which are given also fail to support the Riesmanian conception of an era in which the socialization process instilled in children lofty aspirations—*ad astra per aspera*.[30]

The responses reported in the early studies are not couched in the language of personal striving, nor do they carry the implication that the child expected personally to assume the role of the individual to whom he referred. The largest proportion of statements seem simply to ascribe to the child's hero what one of the early writers called "rather vague moral qualities." [31] ("I want to be like George Washington because he was good.") Other responses stress the fame of the child's exemplar, his wealth (but without the implication that by emulating his hero the child expects personally to obtain riches), his physical appearance.

Even the earliest of the studies (1896) contains quotations which, with slight alterations in prose style, might have served as epigraphs for chapters in *The Lonely Crowd* on the other-directed way of life. For example, a fifteen-year-old boy explained shortly before the election of 1896 that he wanted to be like William Jennings Bryan because Bryan "is well proportioned and well built, a good looking gentleman, and one of the smartest men in the United States . . . and is, without an exception, the greatest orator on the face of the globe.[32] In the same study, a fourteen-year-old boy selected as his idol a man he wanted to resemble "because he has not very hard work, and he has a good time and plenty of money. . . ." [33]

The assumption that achievement values have changed may, as Lipset's remarks suggest, simply be the result of inaccurate conceptions of nineteenth century America. Writers who emphasize the passivity of contemporary Americans usually at least tacitly picture a much more vigorous, optimistic, upwardly striving folk who populated what Lowenthal calls the "open-minded liberal society" at the beginning of the century. But commentators on the present often find it tempting to idealize the past.[34] Certain mistaken notions about structural changes in American society in the present century probably have contributed to the widely held belief that American aspiration levels have declined. For example, until recently it was widely assumed that upward occupational mobility has diminished in the United States. This assumption has been severely challenged by recent research.[35] Similarly, questionable assertions about the debilitating effects of contemporary "mass society" may have predisposed observers to accept oversimplified, if not erroneous, hypotheses about value change.[36]

Summary

A secondary analysis of trends in children's exemplars over a period of approximately 60 years fails to support the hypothesis that American values have changed in the directions suggested by such commentators as David Riesman. Identifications with business leaders and political leaders are rare today, but were equally rare at the turn of the century. Children are less likely today to choose national heroes; more likely to choose popular entertainment figures. However, there is no reason to interpret these changes as evidence of declining aspiration levels. In general, examination of this body of studies suggests that commentators who point to the increasing passivity of contemporary Americans are able to do so only by idealizing the American past.

Notes

NOTE: Helpful comments on earlier drafts of this chapter were made by a number of readers, including Arthur J. Brodbeck, Jurgen Herbst, Elton F. Jackson, Robert E. Lane, Stanley Lebergott, Nelson Polsby, Josef Silverstein, Vladimir Stoikov, and Barbara and Raymond Wolfinger.
1. David Riesman with Nathan Glazer and Reuel Denney, *The Lonely Crowd: A Study of the Changing American Character* (New Haven,

Conn.: Yale University Press, 1950), hereafter attributed for the sake of brevity to the senior author. A number of commentators on Riesman's work have pointed out that his discussion is less of changing character than of changing values and practices. See, for example, the articles by Sheldon L. Messinger and Burton R. Clark and by Robert Gutman and Dennis Wrong in Seymour M. Lipset and Leo Lowenthal, eds., *Culture and Social Character: The Work of David Riesman* (New York: The Free Press of Glencoe, 1961).

2. *The Organization Man* (New York: Simon and Schuster, 1956).

3. "Have There Been Discernible Shifts in American Values During the Past Generation?" in Elting E. Morison, ed., *The American Style* (New York: Harper and Brothers, 1958), pp. 145–217.

4. *Ibid.*, p. 148.

5. *Ibid.*, p. 182.

6. Leo Lowenthal, "Biographies in Popular Magazines," in Paul F. Lazarsfeld and Frank N. Stanton, eds., *Radio Research 1942–43* (New York: Duell, Sloan and Pearce, 1944), pp. 507–548.

7. Richard de Charms and Gerald H. Moeller, "Values Expressed in American Children's Readers: 1800–1950," *Journal of Abnormal and Social Psychology*, LXIV (1962), 136–142.

8. Seymour M. Lipset, "A Changing American Character?" in Lipset and Lowenthal, *op. cit.*, p. 140.

9. Talcott Parsons and Winston White, "The Link between Character and Society," in Lipset and Lowenthal, *op. cit.*, p. 103. Also see Winston White, *Beyond Conformity* (New York: The Free Press of Glencoe, 1961).

10. David Riesman with the collaboration of Nathan Glazer, "*The Lonely Crowd*: A Reconsideration in 1960," in Lipset and Lowenthal, *op. cit.*, p. 429.

11. This paper draws mainly on the studies indicated with asterisks below. Following each in parentheses is the estimated or actual date of field work. In the text of the paper, these studies are indicated by date of field work rather than date of publication.
   * Estelle M. Darrah, "A Study of Children's Ideals," *Popular Science Monthly*, LIII (May 1898), 88–98 (Field work 1896); Earl Barnes, "Type Study on Ideals," *Studies in Education*, II (1902), 36–42, 78–82, 115–122, 157–162, 198–202, 237–242; * Will G. Chambers, "The Evolution of Ideals," *The Pedagogical Seminary*, X (March 1903), 101–143 (Field work ca. May 1902); * David S. Hill, "Comparative Study of Children's Ideals," *Pedagogical Seminary*, XVIII (June 1911), 219–231 (Field work ca. 1910); * David S. Hill, "Personification of Ideals by Urban Children," *Journal of Social Psychology*, I (August 1930), 379–393 (Field work ca. 1928); * M. Louise Stoughton and Alice M. Ray, "A Study of Children's Heroes and Ideals," *The Journal of Experimental Education*, XV (December 1946), 156–160 (Field work ca. 1944); Robert J. Havighurst, et al., "The Development of the Ideal Self in Childhood and Adolescence," *Journal of Educational Research*, XL (December 1946), 241–257; J. B. Winkler, "Age Trends and Sex Differences in the Wishes, Identifications, Activities, and Fears of Children," *Child Development*, XX (1949), 191–200; * Fred I. Greenstein, Children's Political Perspectives: A Study of the Development of Political Awareness and Preferences Among Pre-

Adolescents, unpublished doctoral dissertation, Yale University Library, 1959, pp. 77–102 (Field work January through March, 1958).

Chambers, *op. cit.*, presents a bibliography of a number of additional early studies. Not considered in the present discussion are several early studies of the "ideals" of foreign children, most of which are cited in Chambers' bibliography, and a study of parochial school children by Sister Mary Inez Phelan, *An Empirical Study of the Ideals of Adolescent Boys and Girls* (Washington, D. C.: Catholic University of America, 1936). A discussion of the findings in several of the early studies with respect to sex differences appears in Herbert Hyman, *Political Socialization* (Glencoe, Ill.: The Free Press, 1959), pp. 30–31. I am indebted to Hyman's book for bringing these studies to my attention.

12. Lowenthal, *op. cit.*, p. 517. In a brief aside, Lowenthal raises the possibility that the subjects of magazine biographies were representative merely of the "ideology" of the time, *ibid.*, p. 513. Riesman, however, seems to assume that they represent attitudes in the general population. ("Surveys of content in the mass media show a shift in the kinds of information about business and political leaders that audiences ask for.") *The Lonely Crowd, op. cit.*, p. 237.

13. *The Lonely Crowd, op. cit.*, Chap. 8.

14. Lowenthal, *op. cit.*, p. 517.

15. *The Lonely Crowd, op. cit.*, p. 273.

16. *Ibid.*, p. 96.

17. This is the wording used by Hill, "Personification of Ideals by Urban Children," *op. cit.* The item was worded as follows in the other studies: "What person of whom you have heard or read would you most like to be? Why?" Chambers, *op. cit.;* "Which person (among those you have seen, or thought of, or heard of, or read about) would you most like to resemble? Why?" Hill, "Comparative Study of Children's Ideals," *op. cit.;* "Of all the persons whom you have known, or heard about, or read about, whom would you most wish to be like? And why do you like this person?" Stoughton and Ray, *op. cit.*

18. Greenstein, *op. cit.*, p. 76.

19. When no response and immediate environment categories in Table 12–1 are dropped and percentages are computed for all studies on the basis only of responses to wider environment exemplars, there is no change in the findings discussed below.

20. Evidently none of the 1944 children referred to "serious" artists. The findings of Havighurst et al., although presented in categories which are not strictly comparable to the present ones, provide supporting evidence that children have tended to choose popular entertainers as their exemplars in recent decades. Their study, which was of nine different populations of children and adolescents—most of them Midwesterners—seems to have been conducted in 1944 or 1945. The total number of respondents is 1,147. Havighurst et al. present a category of exemplars labeled "glamorous adults," including "people with a romantic or ephemeral fame, due to the more superficial qualities of appearance and behavior; e.g., movie stars, military figures, athletes," as well as "characters in comic strips or radio dramas." Their discussion suggests that most of the references coded in this category were to popular entertainers. In three of the populations they studied, references to "glamorous adults" ex-

ceeded 30 per cent and in four they exceeded 20 per cent. In the remaining two the percentages were 14 and 2. The item used in this study permitted references both to individuals personally known by the respondents and to imaginary "composite characters," as well as to public figures. The inclusion of the "composite" category (numerous responses were classified under this heading) presumably reduces references to figures in the wider environment and therefore makes Havighurst's estimate of the frequency of "glamorous" exemplars conservative.

21. If log cabin-to-White House mythology ever had much of an impact on children's aspirations, this must have been in the period before the 1890's, judging from the early occupational preference studies. For example, in a study of the responses of 1,065 five through 16-year-old Brooklyn, New York, Long Branch, New Jersey, and Melrose, Mass., children to the question, "What would you like to be when you grow up?" only 11 references to the presidency emerged. Adelaide E. Wyckoff, "Children's Ideals," *The Pedagogical Seminary*, 8 (December 1901), pp. 482–492. In another early study, in which the field work took place in 1893, 1,234 Santa Rosa and San Jose, California, public school children were read an anecdote describing a group of children expressing their occupational preferences. Included in the occupations listed was president. Some children made this choice, but apparently too few to be included in a table which lists occupations referred to as infrequently as six times. Hatti M. Willard, "Children's Ambitions," *Studies in Education*, 1 (January 1897), pp. 243–253. The discussions of two other early studies, neither of which presents tabulations, also suggest that when children in the 1890's were asked "What would you like to be?" few of them mentioned the presidency. Will S. Monroe, "Vocational Interests of Children," *Education*, 18 (January 1898), pp. 259–264, a study of 1,755 eight to 16-year-old school children from a number of Connecticut River Valley communities in Massachusetts; and J. P. Taylor, "A Preliminary Study of Children's Hopes," *Forty-Second Annual Report of the State Superintendent for the School Year Ending July 31, 1895*, Vol. II, State of New York Department of Public Instruction, pp. 987–1015, a study of 2,000 school children from various New York State communities. These occupational preference studies present extensive quotations of children's responses and therefore are of considerable impressionistic interest. Unfortunately, they are not suitable for systematic secondary analysis.

22. A few weeks after McKinley's assassination, Earl Barnes asked 1,800 seven through 17-year-old Long Branch, New Jersey, and Winfield, New York, children to write essays on the topic, "Would you wish to be like Mr. McKinley? Why?" Ninety-two per cent of the responses were positive and the remaining eight per cent apparently consisted not of personal rejections of McKinley, but rather of statements such as "I would not like to have the care he had on his mind all the time." Earl Barnes, "Political Ideas of American Children," *Studies in Education*, II (1902), 25–30. Barnes' discussion of his findings makes it clear that the positive responses were in the nature of vague, eulogistic statements about McKinley's character; they were not assertions of the child's desire some day to become president.

23. Darrah, *op. cit.*, p. 94.

24. For one likely intellectual source of such rationalizations, see Richard Hofstadter, *Social Darwinism in American Thought: 1860–1915* (Philadelphia: University of Pennsylvania Press, 1944). Cf. also R. Richard Wohl, "The 'Rags to Riches Story': An Episode of Secular Idealism," in Reinhard Bendix and Seymour M. Lipset, eds., *Class Status and Power* (Glencoe, Ill.: The Free Press, 1953), pp. 388–395.

25. De Charms and Moeller, *op. cit.*, pp. 193 and 141. For additional uses of children's textbooks as indices of achievement motivation see David C. McClelland, *The Achieving Society* (Princeton, N. J.: Van Nostrand, 1961).

26. Further research would be desirable to determine whether the two magazines sampled by Lowenthal, *Saturday Evening Post* and *Collier's*, were representative of other periodicals of the time.

27. Barnes, "Political Ideas of American Children," *op. cit.*, p. 27.

28. *The Lonely Crowd, op. cit.*, p. 96.

29. We might also expect that age breakdowns would show identifications with Washington to be common among young children and to decline among older children, accompanied by a compensatory increase in reference to the incumbent president. Fragmentary evidence from the two earliest studies summarized in Table 12–1 suggests that references to Washington did indeed decrease with age, but that there was no age variation in the infrequent identifications with the incumbent president.
    The discussion of trends in references to entertainers and national heroes carries no implication that the changes reported in Table 12–1 are irrelevant to understanding shifts in American values; it *is* being suggested that the trends do not support the thesis that there has been a shift in the direction of greater mass passivity. In explaining the changes in children's exemplars, at the very least one would have to take account of the enormously great visibility of popular entertainers to contemporary Americans as a consequence of technological change in mass communication, and of curricular changes in public education, including the advent of "social studies" as a substitute for history. On the latter see Wilhelmina Hill, *Social Studies in the Elementary School Program* (Washington, D. C.: Department of Health, Education, and Welfare, 1960), p. 24.

30. *The Lonely Crowd, op. cit.*, pp. 118–120.

31. Barnes, "Political Ideas of American Children," *op. cit.*, p. 28.

32. Darrah, *op. cit.*, pp. 90–91.

33. *Ibid.*, p. 92. Similar statements may be found in the numerous quotations of children's reasons for preferring occupations reported in the studies cited in footnote 21.

34. It is interesting to compare Lowenthal's characterization of turn-of-the-century American society with the following observation by one of the early students of children's occupational preferences: "The small number of extravagant impossible hopings [among the respondents] seems quite remarkable. The apparent contentment with the lot nature has given them, the genuine delight with which the poorer children look forward to the severe monotonous labors that the future holds in store, the glad willingness to share the heavy burdens of supporting their father's family, all are witnesses to the triumph of childhood's hope and idealism over the toil and pain of the world." Taylor, *op. cit.*, p. 999. Children

during this period doubtless were not devoid of mobility aspirations. Cf. the comparisons of Massachusetts children's occupational preferences with parental occupations by Monroe, *op. cit.*, which suggest, for example, that children of unskilled laborers tended to aspire toward skilled trades.

35. Natalie Rogoff, *Recent Trends in Occupational Mobility* (Glencoe, Ill.: The Free Press, 1953); Seymour M. Lipset and Reinhard Bendix, *Social Mobility in Industrial Society* (Berkeley and Los Angeles: University of California Press, 1959).

36. Cf., for example, Daniel Bell, "America as a Mass Society: A Critique," *Commentary*, XXXII (July 1956), 75–83; Scott Greer and Peter Orleans, "Mass Society and Parapolitical Structure." *American Sociological Review*, XXVII (1962), 634–646.

E. Digby Baltzell

RELIGION AND THE CLASS STRUCTURE

> Hardly a generation ago when business men were establishing themselves and making new social contacts, they encountered the question: "To what church do you belong?" . . . Evidently it was never asked accidentally.
>
> MAX WEBER

Commenting on the mores of the carriage trade, Ralph Waldo Emerson once remarked that "no dissenter rides in his coach for three generations; he invariably falls onto the Establishment." This chapter will attempt to show how the members of the American metropolitan upper class, deeply rooted though their ancestors were in the Calvinism of New England or the Quaker faith of Philadelphia, gradually returned to the Anglican communion of the Protestant Episcopal Church. Before discussing this Episcopalian upper class, especially Philadelphia's Quaker-turned-Episcopal gentry, a word should be said about religion and the class structure as a whole in America.

Religion and the American Class Structure

"However much details may differ," writes Liston Pope of the Yale Divinity School, "stratification is found in all American communities, and religion is always one of its salient features." [1] The middle classes in America have been traditionally Protestant,

E. Digby Baltzell is Professor of Sociology at the University of Pennsylvania. He is author of *The Protestant Establishment* and *Philadelphia Gentlemen*.

Reprinted from *Philadelphia Gentlemen* (Glencoe, Ill.: The Free Press, 1958), pp. 223–261, by permission of the author and the publisher. © 1958 by the Free Press, a Corporation.

while labor, especially the unskilled, has tended to be Catholic. Historical circumstance, rather than the "Protestant ethic" alone, has been the most important factor in the American situation. On the whole, throughout our history, the earliest arrivals have constantly been thrust upward in the social and economic structure as each new wave of immigrants has taken its place at the bottom of the occupational hierarchy. Colonial stock in this country was primarily Protestant; even as late as the first census in 1790, for example, Catholics made up less than 1 per cent of the population. But the Irish who came in the 1840's and 1850's, and the millions of immigrants from southern and eastern Europe who flooded these shores at the turn of the century, were more likely to belong to the Catholic and Jewish faiths.

During a famous and bitter coal strike in 1902, when George F. Baer, then president of the Philadelphia and Reading Railroad, spoke out in defense of the "men and women to whom God in His infinite wisdom has entrusted the property interests of this country," he was referring, no doubt, to a Protestant elite. Certainly the more than 150,000 men and boys striking for better working conditions in the anthracite mines of Pennsylvania at the time, many of whom had been brought to America as contract laborers after the Civil War, were predominantly good Catholics from Poland, Lithuania, Czechoslovakia, or Italy. The fabulous railroad baron, James Hill, took a realistic view of the Catholic church in American society. Hill, himself a Protestant, when asked why he had suddenly donated a million dollars for the establishment of a Roman Catholic theological seminary in St. Paul, Minnesota, quickly replied: "Look at the millions of foreigners pouring into this country to whom the Roman Catholic Church represents the only authority they fear or respect." [2]

One of the important consequences of the Reformation has been the fact that whereas the Catholic Church traditionally ministered to all social strata, the numerous Protestant sects and denominations have been divided along class lines virtually from the beginning. Today, while each individual Protestant congregation tends toward class homogeneity, the Catholic parish, larger in size and geographically organized, ministers to the whole community. The differential segregation of races as between Protestantism and Catholicism serves as a dramatic clue to the one-class-church policy within Protestantism. In 1953 it was reported, for instance, that over *one-third* of the Catholic Negroes in America, as against almost *none* (less than one-tenth of 1 per cent) of the Negro Protestants, attend mixed churches.[3] Liston Pope, in *Millhands and Preachers*, found that the Catholic Church was not popular in the mill towns of North Carolina because, as the mill hands say with a chuckle, "Catholics use the same church for both white people and niggers." [4]

Although the Catholic Church appeals to the whole community, due to historical circumstance in America, it has been predominantly the church of the urban industrial masses. The business and professional community, on the other hand, has been dominated by Protestantism which, in turn, is subtly stratified along denominational lines. On the whole, while the educated elite tend to worship in Presbyterian or Episcopalian churches, the Lutheran, Methodist, and Baptist congregations appeal to the urban middle classes and rural farmers. At the same time, of course, certain smaller denominations—Congregationalists, Unitarians, Christian Scientists, and Quakers—tend toward elite or middle-class status, depending on local conditions. Finally, the Protestants within the laboring classes, disenchanted with the middle-class smugness which characterizes the major denominations, often prefer the more radical sects—the Jehovah's Witnesses, for example, or the Four Square Gospel Churches, or the Adventists. The relationship between religion and the class situation in America has been amusingly summed up by a Jesuit friend of the author's: "The average American is born the son of a Baptist or Methodist farmer; after obtaining an education, he becomes a businessman in a large city where he joins a suburban, Presbyterian church; finally, upon achieving the acme of economic success, he joins a fashionable Episcopal church in order to satisfy his wife's social ambitions; in a materially secure old age, of course, this unusually successful American is converted to the Catholic Church as a hedge against failure in the after life."

The Episcopalian Upper Class in America

John Calvin was the spiritual father of the union of *Bourse* and Bible which has long been recognized as an important characteristic of Western civilization. Thus the opening paragraph in Max Weber's classic essay, *The Protestant Ethic and the Spirit of Capitalism*, reads as follows: "A glance at the occupational statistics of any country of mixed religious composition brings to light with remarkable frequency a situation which has several times provoked discussion in the Catholic press and literature, namely, the fact that business leaders and owners of capital . . . are overwhelmingly Protestant." [5]

The "Protestant ethic" of hard work and worldly asceticism paid dividends in a business civilization. In both Europe and America, most of the great Victorian capitalists were faithful Protestants, while many of them, including Cecil Rhodes and E. H. Harriman, grew up in the pious homes of Protestant clergymen. John D. Rockefeller, who always led the simple life and taught Sunday school for many years, quite naturally felt that "God gave me money." Even the notorious Daniel Drew was founding a Methodist theological seminary and faithfully attending prayer meetings when he was not printing bogus shares and devising techniques for watering stock. It was no wonder that a leading Protestant spokesman could declare in an American religious periodical in the 1870's, "that there is no sleeping partner in any business who can compare with the Almighty." [6]

Following its reverence for British traditions of all sorts, members of the American upper class of second- and third-generation wealth quite naturally prefer the Episcopal Church to the more aggressively Protestant denominations. In the "good taste of its architecture, the dignity and breeding of its clergy, and the richness of its ritual," the Episcopal Church reflects the values of the cultivated classes in this country.

Clarence Day, a graduate of fashionable St. Paul's School and Harvard University, once began an analysis of his father's religious convictions as follows:

My father's ideas of religion seemed straightforward and simple. He had noticed when he was a boy that there were buildings called churches; he had accepted them as a natural part of the surroundings in which he had been born. He would never have invented such things himself. Nevertheless they were here. As he grew up he regarded them as unquestionably as he did banks. They were substantial old structures, they were respectable, decent, and venerable. They were frequented by the right sort of people. Well, that was enough.

As to creeds, he knew nothing about them, and cared nothing either; yet he seemed to know which sect he belonged with. It had to be a sect with a minimum of nonsense about it; no total immersion, no exhorters, no holy confession. Since he was a respectable New Yorker, he belonged to the Episcopal Church.[7]

In 1907 the General Convention of the Protestant Episcopal Church met in Richmond, Virginia. One of the most eloquent speakers there, George Wharton Pepper, recalls in his autobiography that this was the three hundredth anniversary of the establishment of "English Christianity" in the New World.[8] Thus the Anglican Church first achieved its aristocratic position in America among the tidewater squires of Virginia where it was the established church until late in the eighteenth century. As with the abolition of entail and primogeniture, Thomas Jefferson, deist and democrat, played a leading role in disestablishing the Anglican Church in 1786. Although the separation of church and state in America has been official doctrine ever since the founding of the Republic, "the affiliation of George Washington and other Virginia patricians with the Episcopal Church, and the fact that after the inauguration he, the Vice-President, cabinet officers, and many senators and representatives repaired to St. Paul's Chapel in Broadway where Doctor Provost invoked the blessings of God upon the Administration, lent a new semi-official character to the Church."[9] Today, the National Cathedral on beautiful Mount St. Albans, towering above both the Capitol and the Washington Monument, symbolizes the semi-official character of the Episcopal Church. For many years, Philadelphia's George Wharton Pepper was the leading fund-raiser and supporter of the Cathedral, which was appropriately designed by a British architect in the Gothic tradition.

In contrast to the Virginia cavaliers, most of the oldest first-families in the other colonies along the eastern seaboard were, of course, not originally Anglicans. In the course of the second half of the eighteenth century, however, many fashionable descendants of Puritan, Dutch Reformed, Quaker, and Huguenot families in Boston, New York, Philadelphia, and Charlestown, gradually returned to the Anglican communion. In *Cities in Revolt*, a study of American urban life during the second half of the eighteenth century, Carl Bridenbaugh writes that "the spread of Anglicanism in the Northern colonies was one of the most significant religious and social developments of the period." [10] The opening of King's Chapel in Boston for worship in 1754 symbolized the social triumph of Anglicanism there, and similarly, St. George's Chapel in New York was opened in 1752 to relieve the pressure on Trinity Church. At the same time, "the most fashionable religion" gained control of King's College (Columbia University) in 1754, and the ardent Anglican, William Smith, was made Provost of the College of Philadelphia (University of Pennsylvania) in the same year. Even in Charlestown many Huguenots "changed over to the modish liturgy," and a new Anglican Church was completed in 1751.

After the turn of the nineteenth century, the Protestant Episcopal Church soon absorbed many members of the newer planter aristocracy which grew up in the Deep South during the five decades preceding the Civil War. These romantic cotton aristocrats, primarily of Scotch-Irish Presbyterian descent, lost no time in absorbing the manners and values of the Virginia gentry.[11]

Of all the northern colonists, the original Quaker families in Philadelphia were the first to return to the church of their Anglican ancestors. By the time the Protestant Episcopal Church in America was founded in 1789 at Christ Church, in Philadelphia, most of the city's wealthier citizens had gone over to the Anglican Church.[12] President Washington had his own pew in Christ Church as well as in St. Peter's, which was erected in 1758 to take care of the swelling congregation at Christ Church (for many years both churches were under the same rectorship). The elite, or semi-official, status of the Episcopal Church in the "Quaker City" during the early years of the new republic is indicated by the fact that Robert Morris, James Wilson, John Penn, Payton Randolph, Francis Hopkinson, Benjamin Rush, Generals Charles and Jacob Morgan of the Continental Army, Commodores Truxton, Bainbridge and James Biddle of the Navy, and even the famous deist, Benjamin Franklin, are all buried in the churchyard of Christ Church.[13]

There were, of course, important exceptions to this trend toward upper-class Episcopalian uniformity in America. In Boston, for instance, a hard core of top-drawer families have retained their Unitarian or Congregationalist convictions to this day; many Proper Baltimorians, in the Calvert and Carroll tradition, have remained loyal to Catholicism, and even the hardest riders out in "The Valley" are seen at early Mass on Sunday after a Hunt Ball; and, finally, the Creole aristocrat in New Orleans has never seen any reason why he should forsake the Catholicism of his ancestors. Even in Philadelphia there are a few fashionable weddings held in the quaint suburban Friends' meetinghouses. The fashionable Friends, however, do not as a rule attend meeting regularly, nor do they participate in the intricate web of Quaker institutions, such as the American Friends Service Committee, which do good works throughout the world.

On the eve of the Civil War, then, with certain exceptions—Baltimore and New Orleans, for instance—the Episcopal Church was firmly established among the planter aristocracy throughout the South. Although perhaps to a lesser extent, this same pattern prevailed among the upper classes in the northern commercial cities.

After the Civil War the Episcopal Church experienced another period of rapid growth when fashionable Episcopalian congregations in the northern cities were flooded with converts from the ranks of the new plutocracy. Jay Cooke, the financier of the Civil War, eventually gave up his Methodist affiliations and became a devout Episcopalian. Philadelphia's greatest financial genius, Cooke, in addition to teaching Sunday school, supporting struggling young ministers, and organizing adult Bible classes, also built beautiful St. Paul's Protestant Episcopal Church near his celebrated mansion, "Ogontz," in the Old York Road area.[14] The affinity between the gentleman-businessman of the "Gilded Age" and the Episcopal Church is illustrated in the career of Henry Clay Frick, the "Coke King" from Pittsburgh. Mr. Frick, who was "the child of Pennsylvania Dutch ancestors, ended by departing from the plain Lutheran faith of his fathers and 'later in life' attended the Protestant Episcopal Church whose form of service appealed more strongly to his sense of dignity, harmony and beauty." [15] Perhaps the conversion of other new-rich gentlemen like Henry Clay Frick and Jay Cooke helped to swell the Episcopal Church from 160,000 communicants in 1866 to 720,000 in 1900.[16]

Apparently, the members of America's new industrial elite were only too eager to conform to the customs of the class to which they aspired. The fashionable New England boarding schools, many of them first established in the "Gilded Age," were educating the sons of the new elite in an Episcopalian atmosphere. Young Endicott Peabody, for example, returned from an English education at Winchester and Cambridge to establish the Groton School in 1884.[17] In response to an increasing demand, St. Paul's School went through its period of most rapid growth during the last two decades of the nineteenth century. "Never forget," the first rector, Henry Coit, once said to a St. Paul's parent, "that in the life to come the Presbyterians will not be on the same plane as the Episcopalians." [18]

Proper Boston also changed. After the Tories' exodus during the Revolution, fashionable King's Chapel (Anglican), in Boston, became the first Unitarian church in America. Under the leadership of such "priestly men of letters" as Emerson and Channing, Proper Boston became staunchly Unitarian, as did Harvard College. In 1836, for example, of the fifty-one churches in Boston, thirteen were Unitarian, eleven were Congregationalist, and only six were Episcopalian.[19] As Lyman Beecher put it: "All the literary men were Unitarians; all the trustees of Harvard College were Unitarians; and all the elite of fashion and wealth crowded the Unitarian Churches." [20] But after the Civil War Proper Boston also underwent an Episcopalian renaissance.

Henry Adams, whose *Education* was a pessimistic analysis of post-Civil War America, drifted away from his family's Unitarian faith into an urbane skepticism with leanings toward the Roman Catholicism of *Mont Saint-Michel and Chartres*. At the same time, many of his contemporaries reverted to an Anglo-Catholicism which reflected an aesthetic revival in America and a Europeanization of the leisured classes. While men of enterprise unleashed their acquisitive instincts on the western frontier, those of a more sensitive and critical mind turned to Europe for spiritual and aesthetic enrichment. After the Civil War, the artists flocked abroad as usual. More important, however, was the birth of the modern American tourist in the seventies. A wave of art treasures, bric-a-brac, and a new respect for European culture soon rolled westward across the Atlantic.

Proper Boston, rooted in Anglophilia, responded to this aesthetic revival with its first Museum of Fine Arts, founded in 1870; young men of decided ability, such as Ralph Adams Cram, developed rigid High Church views, founded a "Medieval Academy of America," and dreamed of a new scholasticism in stone, the American cathedral; Mrs. Jack Gardiner, who combined an interest in art with High Church Anglicanism, ostentatiously scrubbed the steps of the Church of the Advent before the Good Friday services; and, finally, Trinity Church, rebuilt in 1877 by Richardson with the aid of John La Farge, Stanford White, and the sculptor Saint-Gaudens, became the decisive symbol of this aesthetic and Episcopalian revival. Boston had buried its Puritan past.[21]

Phillips Brooks was the clerical leader of Boston's Episcopalian renaissance. A very Proper Bostonian, who had already made a name for himself in the Church as the rector of Holy Trinity on Philadelphia's Rittenhouse Square, young Phillips Brooks was called to fashionable Trinity Church in Boston in 1869. Born a Unitarian and a direct descendant of John Cotton, the founder of Calvinism in New England, Phillips Brooks became a Boston institution in the course of the seventies and eighties. A handsome man whose preaching rivaled the great Henry Ward Beecher's, he was especially successful with Proper Boston's females: "With ringing rhetoric from his Trinity Church pulpit, Brooks soon had even such staunch Unitarian feminists as the daughters of James Russell Lowell, and Dr. Oliver Wendell Holmes proudly referring to him as 'our bishop.' "[22] Aristocratic Bostonians had traveled a long way from the Puritan convictions of Cotton and Increase Mather when they turned to the teachings of the Right Reverend Phillips Brooks, Bishop of Massachusetts, who was once referred to by a Philadelphian as "an Episcopalian—with leaning toward Christianity."[23] When he died in 1892, Phillips Brooks' funeral attracted the largest crowd in Boston's history.[24]

Throughout the nineteenth century, the leading bishops of the Protestant Episcopal Church were intimately allied by birth and breeding with the eastern seaboard aristocracy: "The social as well as apostolic succession was unbroken through such bishops of blue blood as William Ongreham Kip, Mark Anthony De Wolfe Howe, and William Heathcote De Lancey." [25] Many of the Church's greatest leaders were, like Phillips Brooks, recent converts to the Episcopal Church. Of the twenty Presiding Bishops of the Church, from the first bishop, William White of Philadelphia, through Henry Knox Sherrill, who took office in 1947, only eight were of Episcopalian lineage.[26]

Frederick Dan Huntington, for instance, a graduate of Harvard and a Unitarian, was appointed Plummer Professor of Christian Morals and preacher in the Harvard College Chapel in 1855.[27] A contemporary Congregationalist review stated that "Professor Huntington occupies a public position of incalculable power over the religious convictions of the American people." [28] Although his father was a Unitarian clergyman, and his grandfather had been a staunch Calvinist, in 1860, he resigned from his position at Harvard, joined the Episcopal Church, and eventually became bishop of the newly created diocese of central New York in 1869.

Similarly, the Right Reverend Alonso Potter, the third Episcopal bishop of Pennsylvania, was the first of a great family of the cloth.[29] Although himself the son of a Quaker farmer, in Dutchess County, New York, he was confirmed an Episcopalian by Bishop White in Philadelphia, and elected Bishop of Pennsylvania in 1845. His brother, Horatio Potter, also became an Episcopalian clergyman and eventually Bishop of New York. His wife was the daughter of Dr. Eliphalet Nott, the great Presbyterian preacher and president of Union College. Of their six sons, two entered the Church. One son, Eliphalet Nott Potter, became president of Episcopalian Hobart College, and the other, Henry Codman Potter, succeeded his uncle, Horatio Potter, as Bishop of New York. Bishop Henry Codman Potter, generally considered to be New York's first citizen at the turn of the century, was very proud that "English visitors often pronounced him to be 'a typical mid-Victorian Bishop,' and was never happier than when officiating at the titled marriage of a Vanderbilt or a Goelet, or travelling to a church convention in the private car of J. P. Morgan." [30]

The great Episcopalian bishops, of course, usually officiated at the more important marriages which allied America's new-rich heiresses with many an impecunious European nobleman, thus helping to create an international Victorian aristocracy. The era of international marriages began when Jennie Jerome, the daughter of a New York broker and sportsman, married Winston Churchill's father, the Duke of Marlborough, in 1874. Between that date and 1909, more than 500 American women married titled foreigners; an estimated $22 million followed them to Europe.[31] Bishop Henry Codman Potter cemented the most celebrated international alliance of the era when he blessed the marriage of Consuelo Vanderbilt and the ninth Duke of Marlborough in 1895 at St. Thomas's Church on Fifth Avenue. St. Thomas's, one of Ralph Adams Cram's more well-known Gothic creations, "contains two significant details inserted by a waggish young architect in Mr. Cram's employ—a dollar-sign worked into the tracery over the Bride's Door, and three money-bags initialed 'J. P. M.' carved above the choir-stalls."[32]

In many ways the elder Morgan, who collected the autographs of Episcopal bishops in his youth, was a symbol of the close relationship between the Episcopal Church and America's business aristocracy.[33] In addition to being a constant contributor to various church causes, he was on the original board of Groton School (along with his close friend, Bishop Lawrence), the senior warden of fashionable St. George's Church on Stuyvesant Square, and the leading lay figure at every general convention of the Protestant Episcopal Church. In 1907, for example, "two special cars took him and his guests—who included three American Bishops and the gaitored Bishop of London—to Richmond, where they took up residence in the Rutherford House on Grace Street, which Morgan had engaged for the occasion, with Louis Sherry once more serving as Major-domo."[34]

While attending the Richmond convention J. P. Morgan first heard of the approaching panic of 1907. The ominous messages and telegrams received by Mr. Morgan during the last days of this auspicious gathering of bishops and prosperous laymen of the Episcopal Church seem somehow symbolic of the shallow confidence and optimism of wealthy Americans in the "Gilded Age." Outside the calm Victorian drawing-room, the two decades prior to 1907 were marked by unrest and revolt: the tragic Haymarket Riot, for example, shook the nation in the spring of 1886 and the

American Federation of Labor was formed the following December; the "Gay" nineties, ushered in by the Sherman Act, witnessed the Homestead and Pullman strikes, the populist revolt, and the march of "Coxey's Army" on Washington; and, finally, at the end of this gay decade, Andrew Carnegie, a former immigrant boy, was enjoying an *income*, according to Frederic Lewis Allen, of something like $15 *million* a year (the income tax had been declared unconstitutional in a test case in 1895), while the mass of unskilled workers in the North received less than $460 a year in wages—in the South the figure was less than $300.[35]

If their congregations were saturated with upper-class complacency and conformity, it is true, nevertheless, that many Episcopalian clergymen were vitally concerned both with the corruption at the top of society and the cruel living and working conditions of the urban masses. In one of the most popular novels of its day, *Inside of the Cup*, novelist Winston Churchill dramatized the struggle of a young Episcopalian minister with corrupt "pillars of the church" within his congregation. The elder Morgan's rector, Dr. Rainsford, was surely morally concerned about the role of the Episcopal Church among the poor of New York City. Although he never carried out his threat, J. P. Morgan almost resigned as the senior warden of his beloved St. George's when Dr. Rainsford placed a member of the working class on the parish board (Admiral Mahan did resign as a result of the rector's democratic ways). Mr. Morgan summed up his position as follows: ". . . The rector wants to democratize the church, and we agree with him and will help him as far as we can. But I do not want the vestry democratized. I want it to remain a body of gentlemen whom I can ask to meet me in my study." [36] Dr. Rainsford, who came to this country in 1880, was an enthusiastic supporter of Kingsley's "muscular Christianity" and admired the work of the English church among the poor. As the once-fashionable mansions on Stuyvesant Square gradually became tenements, he eventually built up St. George's from 200 to 4,000 communicants. Although Morgan certainly never understood Dr. Rainsford's brand of Christianity, he continued to admire him and took care of him for life in the form of a legacy.

Allied with the reforming clergymen were many laymen of second- and third-generation wealth who were overly sensitive to the crude materialism so characteristic of the new-rich in the "Gilded Age." In *A Hazard of New Fortunes*, for example, William Dean Howells shows how Conrad Dryfoos, the son of a crude, new-rich millionaire, and his old-family friend, Margaret Vance, both High Church members, become interested in the rights of labor through the Episcopal Church. In the end, Miss Vance enters an Episcopal religious order and Dryfoos, symbolically enough, is accidentally killed in the course of a streetcar strike.

The Episcopal Church was the first Protestant denomination to recognize the right of labor to organize for its own protection. In an age when the Protestant churches, especially the Calvinist pulpits, regarded poverty as a sin, Bishop Henry Codman Potter of New York repeatedly stated in public: "It is because they have helped to teach the lesson of fellow service that modern civilization may well thank God—however impatient capitalists or the public may from time to time have been of them—for trade unions." [37]

The two leading reform organizations within the Protestant Church in America—The Church Association for the Advancement of the Interests of Labor (CAIL) and the Christian Social Union (CSU)—were founded and led by Episcopalians in the last part of the nineteenth century.[38] Father James Otis Sargent Huntington, founder of the Order of the Holy Cross and a member of the old Knights of Labor, was the first Protestant clergyman to devote his life to the labor question. After the Haymarket tragedy, Father Huntington and other church leaders founded the CAIL in 1887. Bishop Huntington, Father Huntington's father, was the first president of the CAIL, and Bishop Henry Codman Potter, a seasoned and respected arbitrator of strikes and lockouts, became the second president in 1904 upon the death of Bishop Huntington. The Christian Social Union, an American branch of the British organization of the same name, was founded in 1891, with Bishop Huntington as president, and the economist and lay Episcopalian, Richart T. Ely, as secretary. All through the nineties and until World War I, these two organizations took the lead in the American social gospel movement.

It was often difficult for contemporary church leaders to understand why "the Church of wealth, culture, and aristocratic lineage" was leading the way. The fashionable clergymen in America, however, were strongly influenced by the Christian socialism of their British cousins. In his *Protestant Churches and Industrial America*, Henry F. May explains the leadership of the Episcopalians in the American Social Gospel movement:

> The most obvious explanation of Episcopalian social emphasis is the influence of English Christian Socialism, which all Episcopalian progressives and radicals heartily acknowledged. Perhaps a more fundamental explanation is the persistence of authoritative, disciplined, "church" tendencies in the American as well as in the English Episcopal tradition. Episcopalianism had never lost touch completely with the medieval dream of society guided and led by the church.
>
> Significantly, many of the most outspoken Episcopalian Social Gospel leaders belonged to the High Church wing of the denomination, and thus had an especially lofty conception of their own status as priests. The fact that Bishops Huntington and Potter consistently backed the C.A.I.L. made it difficult for even the most conservative Episcopal laymen to believe it altogether bad. Similarly, Morgan yielded not to Rainsford's arguments but to his priestly authority.[39]

In an age when the great capitalist entrepreneurs were unifying the nation and even the world with trusts and giant corporation structures, leading bishops of the Protestant Episcopal Church became the moral spokesmen of this new national upper class in America. Bishop Henry Codman Potter, the "first citizen of New York," was not only a national but an international leader of his age. As his biographer put it: "He was called, indeed, to be the pastor of the rich. In Boston and New York he was brought into intimate relations with the most privileged people. Wherever he went, he entered naturally, as by right, into the best society. It was as a matter of course that at Baden-Baden he walked with the Prince of Wales, and that in London, even while he was a parish minister, content with 'humble lodgings,' he was sought out by the Archbishop of Canterbury." [40] Steeped as they were in the ideas of British Christian socialism, on the other hand, these great men of the cloth took the concept of *noblesse oblige* much more seriously than the business gentlemen who conscientiously filled the pews of the more fashionable churches on Sunday mornings. When Bishop Potter died in 1908, for example, Samuel Gompers, on behalf of the American Federation of Labor, wrote: "A movement for the social betterment of all the people had no stauncher advocate nor more earnest worker than Bishop Potter. His every work, his every act, was an effort and an appeal for a higher and better life for all." [41]

In the course of the twentieth century, the Episcopalianization of the American business aristocracy has been a continuous process. One was reminded of this never-ending process by the recent marriage of the first John D. Rockefeller's great-granddaughter at St. Paul's Episcopal Church in Tarrytown, New York.[42] The Suffragen Bishop of New York performed the ceremony. The bride, a great-granddaughter of the wealthiest Baptist of his day, was also a great-granddaughter of both E. W. Clark, Philadelphia banker and founder of the first Unitarian Church in Germantown, and George B. Roberts, fifth president of the Pennsylvania Railroad, whose good Quaker ancestors had owned land in the "Welsh Barony" since the seventeenth century.

Proper Philadelphia: Quaker-Turned-Episcopal Gentry

In accord with most studies reporting on the relationship between religion and educational and economic position in America, the Philadelphia elite in 1940 was predominantly Protestant (Table 13–1).

While the Presbyterians and Episcopalians in Philadelphia were about equally represented in *Who's Who*, the Episcopalians were definitely more likely to be listed in the *Social Register*. Before proceeding to a detailed discussion of Philadelphia's Episcopalian upper class, something should be said about the Presbyterians. In 1940 there were vigorous Presbyterian congregations in all the fashionable suburbs of the city as well as the downtown residential areas around Rittenhouse Square. On the whole, however, the parishioners of these churches were less inclined to participate in the city's fashionable social life than were their neighbors in the Episcopal churches. There were a few exceptions: for example, Henry S. Drinker (the brother of Catherine Drinker Bowen, biographer and historian), descendant of the Quaker merchant, Henry Drinker, who was exiled to Virginia along with Pembertons and Norrises in 1777, was both a Calvinist and a very Proper

TABLE 13-1

Philadelphia in Who's Who *in 1940—Religious Affiliations as Related to Social Class*

Religious Affiliation	Social Class						Per Cent in Social Register
	Social Register		Non Social Register		Who's Who Total		
	No.	%	No.	%	No.	%	
Episcopalian	95	(42)	75	(14)	170	(22)	56
Presbyterian	30	(13)	107	(20)	137	(18)	22
Quaker	7	(3)	15	(3)	22	(3)	32
Baptist	2	(1)	22	(4)	24	(3)	8
Methodist	0	(—)	26	(5)	26	(10)	—
Other Protestant	10	(5)	70	(12)	80	(10)	13
Catholic	2	(1)	25	(5)	27	(4)	7
Jewish	1	(—)	26	(5)	27	(4)	3
No information	79	(35)	178	(32)	257	(33)	31
TOTAL	226	(100)	544	(100)	770	(100)	29

Philadelphian. He was senior partner of Drinker, Biddle, and Reath, one of the city's leading law firms, a member of the Philadelphia Club, a trustee of the University of Pennsylvania, and on the board of the Philadelphia Savings Fund Society.

More representative of the Presbyterians, however, was J. Howard Pew, also listed in both *Who's Who* and the *Social Register*, and head of one of the newer Proper Philadelphia families. President of the family-owned Sun Oil Company since 1912 and one of the most influential Republicans in Pennsylvania and in the nation, J. Howard Pew was not interested in conforming to the mores of Proper Philadelphia's inner circles (he belonged to the Union League rather than the Philadelphia Club). His wide civic interests included the chairmanship of the board and principal benefactor of Grove City College, a Presbyterian college in the western part of the state, presidency of the board of the Presbyterian Church, and chief benefactor of his local Main Line Presbyterian church. The Calvinist ethic was still strong, at least in this generation of the Pew family.

Perhaps the career of Henry Pitney Van Dusen, president of Union Theological Seminary, best reflects the difference between

the Episcopalian and Calvinist traditions in America. Van Dusen
grew up in Chestnut Hill before World War I, where he attended
St. Paul's Episcopal Church (he is still a nominal member in good
standing). After attending Penn Charter School, he went on to
Princeton. As an undergraduate he captained the debating team,
headed the undergraduate council, was class valedictorian, Ivy
Orator, Phi Beta Kappa, and an active member of the Student
Christian Association. During his summers he served as a counse-
lor in a Princeton-run camp for underprivileged boys. Maintaining that the system of exclusion was "undemocratic and un-Chris-
tian," he joined a boycott of the Princeton eating clubs.

After Princeton, although there was a strong family tradition in
the law (his father was a Philadelphia lawyer; his uncle was a
Supreme Court Justice from 1912 to 1922), Henry Pitney Van
Dusen finally chose the ministry as his career. Although a communicant at St. Paul's—his mother was a devout Presbyterian—he
chose the Presbyterian Church. "I wasn't keen about the liturgical
emphasis in the Episcopal Church," he once said. "I also thought
it contained more charming Christians than any other. I missed its
lack of moral drive. My religious motivation is primarily moral,
and always will be. I didn't have to read Reinhold Niebuhr to
know about original sin. The forces of evil are always gaining
ground, and must be stopped again and again. This is a continuous
battle." [43]

While members of most of the Protestant denominations were
represented in the *Social Register* in 1940, a detailed analysis of
the historical development of Philadelphia's Anglo-Catholic gentry is necessary for an understanding of the city's upper-class traditions and values.

The Colonial Period

The spirit of tolerance which prevailed in Penn's City from the
very beginning, and the absence of an established church, drew
settlers of diverse religious beliefs, or of no faith at all, to the
Quaker colony. Although one of the last colonies to be established in the New World, Philadelphia grew rapidly and pros-
pered.

During the first three decades of the eighteenth century, the Society of Friends gradually lost its numerical superiority in Philadelphia. The steady stream of Englishmen to Pennsylvania, for example, was stepped up by a wave of Scotch-Irish Presbyterians in the 1720's. A flood of Germans arrived during the 1730's. The Society's failure to proselytize, and its frequent expulsion of members for "marrying out of meeting" or for "disunity," contributed to its failure to keep pace with the city's growth. By 1750, Philadelphia was the Quaker City in name only; less than one-fourth of its inhabitants were members of the Society of Friends.[44]

In spite of their loss of numerical superiority, however, "wealthy God-fearing Quakers" formed the backbone of the city's merchant elite throughout the first half of the eighteenth century. Friends who had come to the New World "to do *good* ended up by doing extremely *well.*" When the Philadelphia Contributionship for the Insurance of Houses from Loss by Fire, America's oldest fire insurance company, was founded in 1752, all the twelve original directors save three—one of them Benjamin Franklin—were members of the Society of Friends (of the three non-Friends on the board, one Amos Strettell had only recently been read out of meeting for "disunity").[45]

After accumulating fortunes in trade and finance, the vigorous Quaker aristocrats built large country houses, collected books for their libraries (paintings were discouraged), laid out fine formal gardens, and founded such civic and intellectual institutions as the Pennsylvania Hospital and the American Philosophical Society. Of the nine founders of the American Philosophical Society, five were Quakers.[46] The Pennsylvania Hospital, the first in the New World, was financed and run by the Quaker elite in its early years. Of the twelve original managers, nine were Quakers. At the time the hospital was founded, the Quaker majority in the Assembly had blocked all appropriations for the military defense of the frontier. It was said that the generosity of the wealthy Quaker merchants toward the hospital was calculated to show that "when they are not restrained by principle they can be as liberal as others." [47]

The Quaker merchant oligarchy was no closed aristocratic circle. There were great opportunities for advancement in the world of trade for diligent Quakers like the first Samuel Powel, carpenter, who accumulated enough capital to launch his own mercantile ventures, buy up quantities of valuable real estate, and, finally, to leave a sizable fortune to his children. The ethic of the meetinghouse was congenial to success in the countinghouse. Long before Poor Richard made Benjamin Franklin famous as the "first Bourgeois," William Penn was advising his children to "think only of present Business . . . First, it is the way to Wealth: *The diligent Hand makes Rich . . . Seest thou a Man diligent in his Business he shall stand before Kings.*" [48] The way to wealth in early colonial Philadelphia is nicely documented in the following passage by a Quaker historian:

> The history of John Bringhurst (1691–1750) may be taken as a representative Philadelphia Quaker success story. Son of a London printer, he was apprenticed at the age of ten to a cooper in Philadelphia, whither his mother had brought him. After serving out his time and working for a few years as journeyman cooper, he concluded, in hopes of faster advancement, to go to sea. Shipping first as a cooper, he learned navigation, and made several voyages to Barbados, Curacua, and Surinam as mate. Having accumulated about forty pounds, he decided to remain ashore and resume the cooperage business. "Under Providence," he recorded, "I got beforehand and Carried on a Trade of Merchandise with a small Stock which helped me forward into a good way of getting." Beginning to be recognized as a Friend of some weight in the affairs of the meeting, he was made an Overseer of the Poor in 1728 and two years later an Overseer of the Friends School. By 1736 he was able to purchase a one-third share in the brigantine *Joseph* which made numerous voyages to Barbados, Lisbon, and Madeira, freighted with provisions. Within a few years he was also half owner of the sloop *James*, which carried pipestaves and beeswax to the Wine Islands. Two years before he died, he was named an Elder of the meeting. His three sons engaged in mercantile undertakings and amassed considerable wealth; James, the second son, was to be styled "gentleman" in the city Directory.[49]

The "Protestant ethic" may be especially congenial to the *parvenu*. Quaker convictions, however, have never endorsed the more conspicuous forms of worldly display so dear to the hearts of the aristocratic classes. Small wonder that many of the more elegant and urbane members of the Quaker elite, especially those of second- and third-generation wealth, preferred the ritual and drama of the Anglican Church and the more worldly social life of its members to the plain living and high thinking of the meeting-house. After William Penn died in 1718, the province passed to his sons who hardly shared their father's strong Quaker convic-tions: John attended meeting only infrequently; Richard joined the Anglican Church at an early age; and Thomas openly avowed his lack of sympathy with the Society of Friends, although he delayed in joining the Church until the 1750's.[50] John Penn, grand-son of William, was a pew-holder at both Christ Church (1778–1781) and St. Peter's (1782–1792).[51]

Toward the middle of the century, it was said in Philadelphia that one could be a Christian in "any church, but not a gentleman outside the Church of England." After 1750, "Quakerism had to share wealth and influence with the Church of England. Though never so numerous as the Friends, Presbyterians, or even the Lu-therans, the Anglicans became definitely the congregation of wealth, fashion and position." [52] Samuel Powel III—last colonial mayor of Philadelphia, patron of artists such as Benjamin West, trustee of the College of Philadelphia, and the city's most elegant host—provides an excellent example of the city's Quaker-turned-Anglican gentry. After inheriting the largest Quaker fortune in Pennsylvania and graduating from the College in 1760, young Samuel Powel "found ready welcome among a group, made up principally of young Quakers, who called themselves the Society Meeting Weekly in the City of Philadelphia for Their Mutual Improvement in Useful Knowledge." [53] Perhaps the earnest ethics of the Friends, so useful to the *parvenu*, bored the young Quaker aristocrat? At any rate, he soon sailed for England "to begin a quest for European culture and experience that was to last for seven years."

After several years spent in the best of London Society, and the usual Grand Tour of the continent which included a reception with Voltaire at Verney and a familiar conversation with the Pope, the sophisticated young Quaker returned to Philadelphia in 1767. How far he had traveled was soon demonstrated "when shortly he was baptized by the city's most fashionable prelate and became a communicant of St. Peter's Church." [54] Undoubtedly the Church of England provided this cultivated young Philadel-phian with a comfortable compromise between the provincial

Protestantism of the New World and the pagan and Catholic world view opened up to him by the great Renaissance art of Italy.

In the 1750's Christ Church, the only Anglican church in the city, began to feel the pressure caused by the rising tide of wealthy and fashionable converts: "The long tramp through filthy muddy streets to the very overcrowded Christ Church was becoming more and more distasteful to these fine gentlemen and beautiful belles, in damasks and brocades, velvet breeches and silk stockings, powdered hair and periwigs." [55] To take care of the overflowing congregation at Christ Church, Robert Smith, the designer of Carpenter's Hall, the famous Walnut Street prison, and Nassau Hall at the College of New Jersey, produced his masterpiece in St. Peter's, the second Anglican church in the city. Situated on Pine Street, around the corner from the Powel and Bingham mansions on Third Street, St. Peter's was conveniently located in the midst of the Society Hill district, where many prominent merchants then lived.[56] The new church was opened in 1761, with Provost Smith of the College preaching the first sermon to the city's most distinguished congregation.

It was significant that St. Peter's should have been founded at the close of the 1750's. During this decade, the Quaker oligarchy finally lost control of Philadelphia and the Colony of Pennsylvania. In 1755, the Pennsylvania Assembly, deadlocked in a contest for power with the governor, failed to appropriate adequate funds for Braddock's expedition to Fort Duquesne. With Braddock's defeat, conditions deteriorated on the frontier, and, after three-quarters of a century of peace with the Indians, Pennsylvania found itself at war in 1755. The Quaker leadership in the Assembly ("The Norris Party") had held up appropriations partly because of pacifist convictions and partly because of opposition to placing money at the disposal of the governor. At any rate, after war was declared, six of the leading Quakers in the Assembly resigned. As they put it, "the present Situation of Public Affairs calls upon us for Services in a Military Way, which, from a Conviction of Judgement, after mature Deliberation, we cannot comply with." [57]

Pacifist convictions plagued the Quakers right through the Revolutionary period. Gallantry on the battlefield, of course, has been the mark of the aristocrat in all ages. During the Revolution, the "Fighting Quakers" included many young men such as Owen and Clement Biddle, and Samuel and Anthony Morris, whose descendants became the core of the city's Episcopalian upper class. The Philadelphia Troop of Light Horse, now the First City Troop, was organized by aristocratic young Philadelphians in 1774. As we have seen, Quaker Sam Morris, "Christian Sam," was Captain of the Troop and served at Princeton, Brandywine, and Germantown, while his brother, Anthony Morris, gave his life at Princeton. Other Quaker blades formed their own company of light infantry: "Notwithstanding their endeavors to keep aloof from the contest," writes Alexander Graydon in his memoirs, "a good many Quakers swerved from their tenets, and, affecting cockades and uniforms, openly avowed themselves fighting men. They went so far as to form a company of light infantry . . . which was called the *Quaker Blues*, and instituted a spirit of competition with the *Greens*, as they were sneeringly styled, the *silk stocking company*, commanded by Mr. John Cadwalader, and which, having associated early, had already acquired celebrity." [58] Finally, the Board of War, instituted in 1777, included such prominent Friends as Owen Biddle, Samuel Morris, Sr. (Captain Sam's uncle), and Samuel Cadwalader Morris.

Anglican communicants in America also went through a soul-searching period during the Revolution. Unlike King's Chapel in Boston, which became a Unitarian Church after its Tory communicants fled from the city during the war, most of the parishioners of Christ Church and St. Peter's remained Whigs and loyal supporters of the Revolution.[59] Several Anglicans who had held important posts in the King's colonial government, however, were temporarily arrested as Tories during the scare which preceded Howe's march on Philadelphia (John Penn and Benjamin Chew were among those arrested and placed on parole, forbidden to go more than six miles from their houses).[60] The patriotic position taken by most Philadelphia Anglicans can partly be explained by their opposition to the Quakers' record of pacifism.

Although most of the prominent Anglican laymen supported the war, Jacob Duché, the Rector of the United Churches (Christ Church and St. Peter's), finally chose the Tory position after some vacillation. In 1774 and 1775 Duché had served as the official chaplain to the first and second Continental Congresses (Sam Adams, the crafty patriot from Boston, nominated him for the job because he thought it "prudent" to have the rector of such a prominent congregation on the side of rebellion).[61] After the Declaration of Independence was signed in 1776, Duché again showed his patriotism by omitting the prayers for the King at both Christ Church and St. Peter's on Sunday, July 7 (these were the first Anglican churches in America to make this omission). Three months later, however, Duché reversed his position and resigned as Chaplain to Congress because of the "State of his health." Although now no longer in charge of the United Churches, he remained in Philadelphia during Howe's occupation and finally fled to England.

After the Revolution, William White, who had served as a chaplain with Washington's army at Valley Forge, became the leading Anglican clergyman in the New World. In 1787 he was consecrated a bishop of the Anglican Church by the Archbishop of Canterbury, assisted by the Archbishops of York, Bath, and Peterborough. After returning to Philadelphia, he took the lead in founding the Protestant Episcopal Church in America at Christ Church in 1789. William White was the ideal leader of the Episcopal Church which has been closely associated with Philadelphia's gentry from its inception. He was a leader of both inherited and acquired position. His father, who had practiced law at the Maryland bar representing the Lord Proprietary, was a great landowner, who left 7,772 acres of taxable land in Baltimore County alone when he died in 1779.[62] William White, brother-in-law of Robert Morris, took an active part in all aspects of Philadelphia life. He was one of the founders of the Protestant Episcopal Academy and at the age of twenty-six became a trustee of the College of Philadelphia, a post which he held for sixty-two years.

By the end of the eighteenth century, then, the Episcopal Church was clearly the church of the aristocratic elite in the Quaker City. The Philadelphia Contributionship, which was founded only a half century earlier by a dominant Quaker elite, was, by 1782, virtually an Anglican gentleman's club which it has continued to be to the present day.[63] Even the skeptical deist, Benjamin Franklin, who was amused to find that most Europeans considered him a good Philadelphia Quaker, was a pew-holder at

Christ Church (No. 59) between 1778 and 1790.[64] Many distinguished Americans of this period are buried at Christ Church.

In the early years of the new republic, St. Peter's was probably the most fashionable church in the city. Among its pew-holders were Samuel Powel and William Bingham, two of the wealthiest men in the city, Robert Morris and Thomas Willing, financiers of the Revolutionary period, the artist, Charles Wilson Peale, Chief Justices of the Supreme Court of Pennsylvania, Benjamin Chew and Edward Shippen, Doctors Benjamin Rush, John Morgan (founder of the medical school at the college) and Thomas Bond, and General John Cadwalader, colonel of the "Silk Stocking" Battalion (Cadwalader, Shippen, Morgan, Bond, and Powel all had fathers who were birthright Friends). George Washington, who usually attended Christ Church, used the Powel-Willing pew (No. 41) at St. Peter's during the entire winter of 1781–1782, after renting a house nearby.[65]

There were probably several reasons why so many leading citizens of the Quaker City returned to the Anglican Church at the end of the colonial period and during the founding of the new republic. The drabness of Quakerism hardly suited a mercantile aristocracy bent on modeling itself after the Georgian gentlemen of England. Even the descendants of such staunch Quakers as the two Israel Pembertons were not immune to the fashionable trend. Joseph Pemberton, for example, was the son of Israel, Jr., who had been exiled to Virginia during the Revolution because of his moral convictions: "Though both Joseph Pemberton and his wife came of strict Quaker families," writes John W. Jordan, in his *Colonial Families of Philadelphia*, "they appear to have renounced the plain dress of their ancestors, as attested by two handsome oil paintings of them now in the possession of their grandson, Henry Pemberton, which showed them attired in the height of the mode of their day. It was in their time, too, that the name of Pemberton first appeared on the list of the Philadelphia Dancing Assemblies." (One can usually gauge the dates of old Quaker family conversions to Anglicanism by noting when they first appear on the Assembly lists.)[66]

As this is primarily a sociological analysis of stratification, we have naturally stressed the congeniality of the Anglican ritual to the aristocratic mind. But sociological causation should not be overemphasized. The moral conflict surrounding the extreme pacifist position, which even James Logan, the leading Quaker in Penn's young city, could not abide, was unquestionably an important factor in causing the decline of the influence of the Society of Friends in Philadelphia after 1750. This position on war, of course, was but one aspect of a consistent and extreme form of Protestantism which, perhaps inadvertently, tended to institutionalize an irresponsibility toward the state which, in modern society, must always include military power. Philadelphia Quakers took no part in the Revolution or the founding of the republic. To have refrained from participating in the series of stirring events which took place in Philadelphia between 1776 and 1787 was to have missed one of the greatest opportunities for statesmanship in world history. In fact, it may be argued that the attitudes of Proper Philadelphians toward governmental service down through the years, and the fact of their relatively small number of distinguished public servants, are deeply rooted in their Quaker heritage. Traditions die hard, and the extreme withdrawal from the world so characteristic of eighteenth- and early-nineteenth-century Quakerism has left a definite mark on even the contemporary Proper Philadelphia mind.

This is not the place to discuss theological matters. A brief mention of the "Keith Controversy," however, will provide a theological balance to our more worldly analysis. The fact that Rufus Jones, distinguished Quaker philosopher and member of the Philadelphia elite in 1940, could sum up the controversial career of George Keith in the following words testifies to the existence of legitimate doubts about the tenets of Quakerism among sincere Friends in the seventeenth and eighteenth centuries. "The writings of George Keith," Rufus Jones wrote,

both before and after his repudiation of Quakerism, are marked by an excellent style, an earnest spirit, much clearness in thought, and moderation of temper. . . . Had he died in 1690, they would have ranked high as Quaker classics. . . . He was intellectually a great man. His changes from Presbyterianism to Quakerism, from this, after nearly thirty years' advocacy, to Independency, and from this again to Episcopalianism, necessarily made many enemies and required many explanations. His biographies have been mainly written by his opponents who emphasize his faults and his apostasy.[67]

*The Victorian Age: The Church on Rittenhouse
Square*

The Protestant Episcopal Church in Philadelphia continued to
grow throughout the nineteenth century. The most fashionable
churches in the city and its suburbs are shown in Table 13–2.
Soon after the turn of the century, St. James' on Seventh Street
just north of Market Street, became part of the United Churches
under the rectorship of Bishop White. The building of the
church was "projected in the year 1806 to supply the want of
church accommodation in what was then the western part of the
city." [68] St. James', St. Peter's, and Christ Church, under the leadership of Bishop White until his death in 1836, took care of the
spiritual needs of fashionable Philadelphians during the first four
decades of the nineteenth century. During this period, St. Mary's
Church (1827) was built west of the Schuylkill River in Hamilton Village, a small rural community near the "Woodlands," the
famous mansion built by the family of Andrew Hamilton, the
Philadelphia lawyer in the Peter Zenger case.[69]

As the population of Philadelphia expanded, the upper classes
moved westward, and St. Mark's (1848) and the Church of the
Holy Trinity (1857) were built in the newly fashionable "West
End," in the neighborhood of Rittenhouse Square. At this same
time, across the river in the elite neighborhood of West Philadelphia, some parishioners of St. Mary's, Hamilton Village, established the Church of the Savior (1852), at Thirty-Eighth and
Chestnut, just down the street from the Drexel colony. A. J.
Drexel and his family were members of the parish from the beginning; he was a vestryman between 1856 and 1889 and accounting
warden from 1889 until his death in 1893.[70]

After the Civil War, as the figures in Table 13–2 illustrate, the
Victorian gentry filled the three churches in the Rittenhouse
Square neighborhood. In addition to St. Mark's and Holy Trinity,
St. James' finally followed the fashionable westward trend and
moved to Twenty-Second and Walnut streets in 1870.[71] The fact
that these three churches had an increase in communicants of

over 300 per cent (see Table 13-2) between 1860 and 1900 is indicative of the growing influence of the Episcopal Church upon the Victorian upper class. Christ Church and St. Peter's also held their own during this period as many old families remained loyal to their family traditions. "The present John Cadwalader, Senior, has been a vestryman for forty years," wrote a St. Peter's historian in 1923. "In his pew three generations of John Cadwaladers are represented each Sunday." [72] Even as late as 1940, Cadwaladers were still associated with St. Peter's.

The Rittenhouse Square parishes not only increased in size but also in wealth during the prosperous Victorian period. The Parochial Reports of St. James' Church between 1833 and 1899 are revealing: [73] Whereas the total annual offerings of the parish never exceeded $3,000 during the 1830's, $4,000 during the 1840's, and only twice exceeded $5,000 in any one year during the 1850's, things were quite different after the Civil War. During the 1860's, for instance, even though most of the parishioners had already moved away and "had to depend on their carriages and ultimately on street cars for reaching their place of worship," the annual offerings only once fell below $5,000 and were usually between $8,000 and $10,000 per year. Finally, after removal of the church to the fashionable "West End" in 1870, the annual offerings at St. James' remained between $20,000 and $60,000, most often nearer the higher figure, for the remainder of the century.

The list of vestrymen at St. James' during the nineteenth century included many ex-Quaker family names. Dr. Edward Shippen (vestryman 1879–1895), for example, recalls the Quaker merchant of the same name who owned the "biggest house and the biggest coach in Philadelphia" at the end of the seventeenth century; Senator Pepper's grandfather, George Mifflin Wharton, himself a birthright Friend and the son of the wealthy Quaker merchant, William Fishbourne Wharton, served as a vestryman between 1837 and 1870; finally, James C. Biddle, grandson of Owen Biddle, a leader of the "Free" or "Fighting" Quakers during the Revolution, served St. James' between 1834 and 1839. The old Episcopalian Cadwaladers and the newer Episcopalian Biddles were nicely blended in the person of Mr. Cadwalader Biddle, vestryman and accounting warden at St. James' in the 1880's. It is said that the Biddles and Cadwaladers are to Philadelphia what the

TABLE 13-2

Fashionable Episcopal Churches in Philadelphia: Number of Communicants, 1860-1940

		1860	1880	1900	1920	1940	1860-1900	1900-1940
Urban Churches								
Old Philadelphia								
Christ Church	(1695)	353	392	566	492	509		
St. Peter's	(1761)	502	754	931	825	637		
		855	1146	1497	1317	1146	+75%	−24%
Rittenhouse Square								
St. James'	(1810)	250	400	944	1118	546		
St. Mark's	(1848)	294	850	1627	1520	720		
Holy Trinity	(1857)	268	900	988	1789	1091		
		812	2150	3559	4427	2357	+338%	−34%
West Philadelphia								
St. Mary's	(1827)	104	311	544	479	261		
The Savior	(1852)	110	452	1221	1807	914		
		214	763	1765	2286	1175	+725%	−33%
Suburban Churches								
Chestnut Hill-Whitemarsh								
St. Paul's	(1856)	54	122	306	625	1198		
St. Martin's	(1884)			368	473	605		
St. Thomas'	(1710)	98	110	220	375	846		
		152	232	894	1473	2649		+197%

TABLE 13-2 (*continued*)

		1860	1880	1900	1920	1940	1860–1900	1900–1940
Main Line								
Redeemer	(1852)	29	150	318	601	831		
Good Shepherd	(1871)		121	200	471	699		
St. Asaph's	(1888)			261	480	644		
St. Martin's	(1887)			77	152	290		
St. David's	(1715)	80	52	130	116	390		
		109	323	986	1820	2854		+189%
Old York Road								
St. Paul's	(1861)		155	257	418	836		+225%
Summary:								
Urban Communicants		1881	4059	6821	8030	4678	+263%	−31%
Suburban Communicants		261	710	2137	3711	6339	+719%	+196%
Total Communicants		2142	4769	8958	11741	11017	+318%	+23%
Population: Philadelphia County:		565,529	847,170	1,293,697	1,823,779	1,931,334	+130%	+49%

Source: Journals of the Annual Conventions of the Protestant Episcopal Church in the Diocese of Pennsylvania: 1861, 1881, 1901, 1921, 1941.

Cabots and Lowells are to Proper Boston: While the "Cabots speak only to Lowells and the Lowells speak only to God," as the saying goes, "when a Biddle gets drunk, he thinks he's a Cadwalader."

St. Mark's Church, on Locust Street just east of Rittenhouse Square, is the finest example of Gothic church architecture in the city. Founded by men who were vitally concerned with the Oxford movement in England (the Oxford movement was founded to combat the various attempts to disestablish the Church after the Reform Bill of 1832), the High Church services at St. Mark's closely resemble the form of the Anglican communion.[74] The building and furnishing of St. Mark's over the years suggest the nostalgia for Europe, the Anglophilia of the American Victorian gentry. The plans of the church, "suggested by an old abby, were drawn up by the Ecclesiological Society of London," and executed by John Notman, leading Society architect, who also designed the Church of the Holy Trinity, and the first brownstone-front house in the Square area.[75] St. Mark's was decorated "in the style which prevailed in the last quarter of the Fourteenth Century, a period when Gothic architecture attained its highest point of perfection and beauty." [76]

Like Henry Adams, the parishioners of St. Mark's dreamed of the days of Mont St. Michel and Chartres. "Love for the church in the Middle Ages," a new rector told his parishioners in the nineties, "led people not only to build and adorn beautiful churches but to store them with costly vessels and vestments. The churches were possessed of great treasures of gold, silver, and precious stones, the work of the most celebrated artists of the time. In our time churches too often suggest cheapness rather than simplicity." [77]

Rodman Wanamaker, the son of Philadelphia's most famous department store merchant and devout Presbyterian, John Wanamaker, was St. Mark's greatest single benefactor. A man of exquisite taste, Rodman Wanamaker had represented the family interests in Europe for many years. When his wife died in 1900, he donated the Lady Chapel at St. Mark's, including many priceless furnishings gathered from all over Europe. His gift of a silver altar was the chief treasure of St. Mark's: "This altar is without doubt the greatest work of English ecclesiastical art in twentieth century America," writes the Church's historian, "and the first such example since the Fifteenth Century, when one was made in Florence by Pallajuolo (1429–1498) and his associates." [78] The altar was, of course, designed in London "by Messrs. Barkentin and Krall of Regent Street." The American merchant prince, the spiritual cousin of the Medici of Renaissance Italy rather than the knight of the Middle Ages, certainly would have been extremely cramped by the style of the Quaker meetinghouse.

The installation of the bells at St. Mark's, cast in 1875 by the Whitechapel Bell Foundry in London, the same firm which had cast the bells of Christ Church and St. Peter's, was responsible for one of the most curious cases in the history of American jurisprudence. According to the best historical opinion, the steeple at St. Mark's was so low that the sound of the new bells was a definite nuisance in the community. Although the following account by the church's historian of the bell controversy at St. Mark's in the seventies may be overdrawn, it does illustrate the typical tenacity of Proper Philadelphians in defending their creature comforts:

In January, 1875, while the bells were being cast, nineteen over-imaginative neighbors remonstrated to the vestry concerning the proposed installation of the bells. They said their nervous systems could not be shocked by sharp, sudden, or loud noises, such as chimes being rung. They estimated their properties would decrease in value to the extent of $5,000 apiece, if St. Mark's installed the bells. . . .

On Whitsunday, 1876, the four bells arrived from London. . . . Protests began anew. Philadelphia society was rent in twain. Matrons had to select their dinner guests, all of whom either favored or opposed the bells of St. Mark's. The Centennial Exposition and the Pennsylvania-Princeton football game were nearly eclipsed.

A bill for injunction was finally filed against St. Mark's. The case came up for hearing in February, 1877, in Court of Common Pleas No. 2, Judge Hare, presiding. Philadelphia lawyer was arrayed against Philadelphia lawyer—P. Pemberton Morris and George W. Biddle for St. Mark's and William Henry Rawls and R. C. McMurtrie for the plaintiffs. The latter averred that the environs of the Sixteenth and Locust Streets were replete with handsome and expensive residences which were enhanced by their supposed immunity from nuisances. However, the present bell ringing was harsh, loud, high, sharp, clanging, discordant, and the noise was an intolerable nuisance. The bells shook the very walls of the houses, made conversation impossible in the immediate vicinity of the tower, disturbed the sleep of infants and children, distracted the mind from serious employment, and destroyed social and domestic intercourse and much of all that goes to make up the peace and happiness of home life. All this was so increased in summer that departure from the city was necessary. (It is hard to imagine any of these gentle folk staying in town during the summer. To do so would have been very unfashionable.) The nuisance became much intensified for those who were ill. Property values were depreciating in the neighborhood because of bell ringing. This action of the defendants was not a secular work carried on for private profit nor was it part of the necessary apparatus or machinery by which a great city had its wants supplied. It certainly was not a work of benevolence, charity, or education. The fact that for the last quarter century the prosperity of the defendants had increased, during all of which time they had not a single bell, showed that bell ringing was neither essential to their worship nor their worldly welfare. Dr. S. Weir Mitchell, probably influenced by his more affluent patients, testified that "medical treatment of the neighborhood had to be regulated by the hours of the defendants' bell ringing." Thus ran the curious reasoning of the complainants, many of whom were Episcopalians. Apparently their belief in the Holy Catholic Church was on the condition of personal convenience.[79]

The plaintiffs won their case, and the bells of St. Mark's rang no more. The day following the court's decision, a ballad appeared in the Philadelphia *Sunday Dispatch*:

IN STATU QUO ANTE BELLUM

No more the clanging sound of bells shall fright the quiet air;
No more the tolling "country chimes" will agitate the fair;
And drowsy Cit may sweetly doze upon his easy chair.
No chiming now for brownstone folks
Who live in St. Mark's square.

At midnight now the soldier "swell" from club may safely reel,
And, pausing at his lofty door, for friendly latch-key feel;
His morning nap is all secure—his dream's his own affair.
No matin-bell for brownstone folks
Who live in St. Mark's square.

To Justice—sweet and noble maid, with balances so true,
Who blindly weighs the good and bad—our thanks are warmly due;
But loftier, greater, grander, still is Equity so rare,
Who guards the nerves of brownstone folks,
Who live in St. Mark's square.[80]

General George Gordon Meade was one of St. Mark's most famous parishioners. After his sudden death from pneumonia in

1872, his funeral was held in the church and was attended by federal, state, and city officials, a host of relatives and friends, and the President of the United States, Ulysses S. Grant. Born to one of the city's most distinguished Catholic families, Meade had been baptized in the parish of "Nuestra Senora del Rosario," at Cadiz, Spain. According to parish records, he had been confirmed at St. Mark's in 1855 at the age of forty.[81]

Across the Square from St. Mark's, on Walnut Street, the Church of the Holy Trinity ministered to Low Church fashionable Philadelphians. Simple in ritual and decor, Holy Trinity became the leading Philadelphia congregation under the great Phillips Brooks.[82] After graduating from the Virginia Theological Seminary, the most fashionable in the Episcopal Church, Phillips Brooks began his ministry in 1859 at a rather poor parish, the Church of the Advent, in North Philadelphia. He attracted citywide fame in a very short time and was called to Holy Trinity in 1860. Phillips Brooks' influence on Philadelphia is described here by a contemporary observer:

The costly, spacious Church of the Holy Trinity, in Rittenhouse Square, was always filled, crowded in all weathers, whenever it was known that he was going to preach. And yet to the breathless multitudes who came and went under the spell of his unique eloquence as certainly as the tides, he stood an insoluble puzzle and wonder. Perhaps there never was developed in any pulpit a parallel experience. Here were thousands crowding the pews and standing room of the Holy Trinity Church, Sunday after Sunday, and year after year. . . .[83]

In 1869 Phillips Brooks left Philadelphia to become the famous rector of Trinity Church in Boston. In a memorial service for Dr. Alexander Hamilton Vinton, a Proper Bostonian and his predecessor at Holy Trinity in Philadelphia, Phillips Brooks summed up his impressions of the Philadelphia upper class:

Philadelphia is a city where the Episcopal Church is thoroughly at home. Side by side with the gentler Puritanism of that sunnier clime, the Quakerism which quarrelled and protested, but always quarrelled and protested peacefully, the Church of England had lived and flourished in colonial days, and handed down a well-established life to the new Church which sprang out of her veins at the Revolution. It was the temperate zone of religious life with all its quiet richness. Free from antagonism, among a genial and social people, with just enough internal debate and difference to insure her life, enlisting the enthusiastic activity of her laity to a degree which we in Boston know nothing of, with a more demonstrative if not a deeper piety, with a confidence in herself which goes forth in a sense of responsibility for the community and a ready missionary zeal, the Church in Philadelphia was to the Church in Boston much like what a broad Pennsylvania valley is to a rough New England hillside.[84]

The fashionable Philadelphians on Rittenhouse Square were unquestionably a devout and charming people whose well-regulated social world included firm religious habits. Cordelia Drexel Biddle, who grew up on Rittenhouse Square and attended Holy Trinity, recalls in her chatty biography of her father that grace was always said at the Biddle table and that "all the Philadelphia families we knew were strict about daily prayers, regular church attendance, and spiritual duties." [85] George Wharton Pepper, a vestryman and warden at St. Mark's for over half a century, attended the 7:45 A.M. service daily when he lived in the neighborhood of Rittenhouse Square. Always an advocate of action and the cultivation of worth-while habits as a defense against doubt-producing introspection, Senator Pepper records in his autobiography that "it is not in analysis but in actual experience that the power of the Sacrament is to be found." [86]

Anthony J. Drexel Biddle, Cordelia Biddle's father, was perhaps Holy Trinity's most colorful parishioner. An intimate friend of pugilists, from Jack Lawless to Gene Tunney, and of revivalists such as Billy Sunday, Tony Biddle built the men's Bible class at Holy Trinity from a feeble three participants into a thriving enterprise.[87] His "Athletic Christianity" movement, started at Holy Trinity, eventually spread all over the world. With only a minimum of formal education, Tony Biddle published several books and hundreds of articles during his active and busy life. He was an officer in the United States Marine Corps during both wars and a special consultant to the Federal Bureau of Investigation (as specialist in the art of self-defense) until his death in 1948. Needless to say, he was one of the most interesting Proper Philadelphians listed in *Who's Who* in 1940.

Despite the popular notion that high prestige accrues to the businessman in America, men such as the Biddles and Cadwaladers—

military and professional men, not businessmen—have always out-ranked, in the minds of the public, men more adept in the affairs of money. Charming, romantic, cerebral rather than acquisitive, and always with an eye on a chance for glory and adventure, the Biddle family have never been conspicuous money-makers. Nevertheless, they seem to have had the happy faculty, in the tradition of the British gentleman, of marrying well. Anthony J. Drexel Biddle, Senior, as his name suggests, was the great Philadelphia banker's grandson. Even more spectacular wealth was absorbed by the family, however, when Anthony J. Drexel Biddle, Jr., Franklin Roosevelt's ambassador to most of the exiled governments of Europe during World War II, married into the Duke fortune. His charming sister, Cordelia, married her brother's new brother-in-law, Angier Duke, six months later. Both marriages eventually ended in divorce.[88]

Divorce was not acceptable to Rittenhouse Square society at the height of its glory. Both the Protestant Episcopal Church, which stands nearer to Rome on the matter of divorce than the other Protestant denominations, and the rules of the dancing Assembly, foster and defend the sanctity of the Proper Philadelphia family. Thus the Episcopal Church does not sanction the marriage of a divorced person, and invitations to the annual Assembly Balls are never sent to divorced persons who have taken a second spouse. The power of the Assembly in regulating upper-class mores is suggested by the ex-Philadelphian, Cordelia Biddle, who recalls that "any family not getting a bid might as well jump from the City Hall dome." [89]

While the upper-class mores included a rigid code of personal morality, no one on Victorian Rittenhouse Square would ever have thought of questioning the essential rightness of the social structure. The conscientious parishioners of Holy Trinity, St. Mark's, and St. James' certainly felt it their duty to help those less fortunate than themselves and responded generously to the founding of slum parishes and city missions as well as a multitude of other charitable causes. Any suggestion, however, that the basic institutional pattern needed reforming, generally found the Proper Philadelphian either indifferent or adamantly in opposition. Even the great Phillips Brooks, who had vigorously preached the cause of anti-slavery from the Holy Trinity pulpit, felt that the Church should deal with private spiritual problems rather than the social question. He did not approve of the "fact that the English Episcopalians were turning some of their attention from spiritual to social questions." [90] The Proper Philadelphian's attitude toward social inequality, for instance, is probably stated as well as anywhere else in the following remarks of Phillips Brooks, taken from a sermon he preached in Boston many years after he had left the Quaker City:

> There can be no doubt, I think, whatever puzzling questions it may bring with it, that it is the fact of privilege and inequalities among men for which they do not seem to be responsible, which makes a large part of the interest and richness of human experience. . . . I believe that the more we think, the more we become convinced that the instinct which asks for equality is a low one, and that equality, if it were completely brought about, would furnish play only for the low instincts and impulses of man.[91]

Despite Christian doctrine to the effect that poverty is a virtue and great wealth conducive to sin, complete material equality— the basis of pernicious ideologies in every age—has not always been stressed by the Church. It is hard to understand, however, how good Christian men and women with advantages of "wealth, influence, Catholic traditions, and ceremonial," as one rector once described his parishioners at St. Mark's, could have remained unconcerned with the underlying causes of corruption and cruel inequalities such as the sweat-shop and child labor, which festered beneath the calm surface of the Victorian drawing rooms on Rittenhouse Square. At any rate, aristocrats such as the Harvard-educated "Socialist Priest," Father J. O. S. Huntington, founder of the Order of the Holy Cross, were never bred on Rittenhouse Square. Perhaps George Wharton Pepper's honest and frank confession of his own inability "to appreciate the anxieties of the so-called 'underprivileged' " may be indicative of the state of mind of his class. In 1944, over half a century after the days of his youth on the Square, he wrote in his autobiography:

> In the past I have repeatedly tried to imagine what it is like to be hungry and cold and harassed by debts but I have always ended by admitting the inadequacy of mere imagination. Rolling along in a comfortable car, spending my days in congenial work, going back at

nightfall to a happy home without fear of landlord or sheriff, I simply could not imagine what it is like to be an elevator boy or a taxi driver or a share cropper or a coal miner or a veteran too old to be employed or a man with a sick wife or child and unable to afford medical care or nursing comforts or a white-collar worker conscious of inherent capacity but up against a dead end with no chance of promotion.[92]

The mores of Proper Philadelphia society allow and even foster individuality and eccentricity but never nonconformity. At the turn of the century, Lincoln Steffens found Philadelphia "corrupt and contented." He might also have added "unimaginative."

The glory of Rittenhouse Square, and the fashionable Episcopal churches in the neighborhood, reached its height in the 1890's. On Saturday afternoon, January 20, 1894, the pomp and power of Philadelphia's and America's business upper class were symbolized at a service held in memory of the city's greatest Victorian banker, Anthony J. Drexel, who had recently passed away at the height of the panic of 1893.[93] Although A. J. Drexel was baptized a Roman Catholic in infancy, he and his brother, Joseph W. Drexel, who married a Wharton, eventually went over to the Episcopal Church. The memorial service, attended by fashionable, official, and business gentlemen from Philadelphia, New York, and other cities along the eastern seaboard was held at Drexel Institute of Technology in West Philadelphia. Bishops of the Protestant Episcopal Church led the ceremonies. The opening prayer was given by William B. Bodine, Rector of the Church of the Savior, the memorial address by the Right Reverend Henry Codman Potter, Bishop of New York, and the final benediction by the Right Reverend Ozi William Whitaker, Bishop of the Diocese of Pennsylvania.

The older brother, Francis A. Drexel, remained a Catholic and one of the Church's leading benefactors. For years, on specified occasions, Holy Mass was celebrated at "St. Michel," the estate of this branch of the family in Torresdale, on the Delaware, and at 1503 Walnut Street, their winter residence. Francis A. Drexel's daughter, Katherine, eventually became a nun and founded the Sisters of the Blessed Sacrament, which used the Drexel country place, "St. Michel," as a novitiate.[94]

The Twentieth Century: Decline of the Urban Family Church

After World War I, the fashionable churches around the Square gradually ceased to be family parishes and increasingly ministered to a mobile population of apartment-dwellers and a few members of the older generation whose children had moved to the suburbs. This trend, of course, started much earlier. The historian of St. Mark's, for example, writes that in 1909, "the Sunday School numbered about 50 pupils as compared with 100 pupils in 1894." [95]

Although St. Mark's and Holy Trinity survived the suburban exodus, St. James' eventually became a casualty when it was sold to the Atlantic Refining Company (a convenient spot to refuel before taking the Parkway to the suburbs) during World War II.[96] St. James' struggle for survival in its last years provides an interesting case history of the atomization of urban life in the twentieth century. The exodus of old families to the suburbs accelerated in the twenties. Finally, in 1925, it was decided to do away with the "family pew" at St. James'. At that time, the Philadelphia *Evening Bulletin* reported the decision as follows: "St. James' is finally open to the masses. Pew rents have finally been dropped. It is reported that some of the pews here rent for as high as $2,000 a year. Often the same family rents the same pew for several generations." [97]

The final step in attempting to reach the urban masses at St. James' was taken when the vestry called the Reverend Joseph Fort Newton to be co-rector along with Dr. John C. H. Mockridge, rector of the parish since 1915. John C. H. Mockridge had been one of the most respected high churchmen in the city for many years. He was a strict Anglo-Catholic, born in Canada, and educated at Trinity College, Toronto. He was often mentioned as the High Church candidate for Bishop of the Diocese of Pennsylvania and was well known in church circles and throughout the city as a vigorous opponent of divorce. For many years he was president of the board of the Episcopal Academy and an overseer of the Philadelphia Divinity School. For the sake of his beloved St. James', he finally consented to the appointment of Dr. Newton in 1930.[98]

During World War I, Joseph Fort Newton had gained a world-wide reputation as the rector of the City Temple, often referred to as "The Cathedral of Nonconformity," in the heart of London.[99] A few years before coming to St. James', Dr. Newton had been confirmed before a small group of Episcopal clergymen and later ordained at an "imposing ceremony in Old Christ Church." Together with other plans for popularizing the work of St. James'—concerts, recitals, lectures, and sermons—the appointment of a "man of vigorous and vital utterance, eloquent, and with a voice which charms" should have revived the staid, old, first-family church.[100] If not exactly a typical Anglo-Catholic rector, Joseph Fort Newton was certainly in the tradition of the best American pastors.

He was born in a small town in Texas, graduated from the Southern Baptist Seminary, and ordained in the Baptist ministry in 1893.[101] During his vigorous career, he had written some thirty books and numerous pamphlets on patriotic, religious, and Masonic subjects. Dr. Newton's career was a personification of the secular twentieth century's attempt to compromise with Christianity. His pastorships included the First Baptist Church, Paris, Texas, the Non-Sectarian Church, St. Louis, Missouri, the People's Church, Dixon, Illinois, the Liberal Christian Church, Cedar Rapids, Iowa, the City Temple, London, and the Church of the Divine Paternity, New York City.

Both Joseph Fort Newton and John C. H. Mockridge were listed in *Who's Who* in 1940, but only the latter was listed also in the *Social Register*. Dr. Newton left St. James' in 1938, and Dr. Mockridge retired in 1940. The church did not survive the pressures of urban democracy.

The Twentieth Century: Rise of the
Suburban Church

During the second half of the nineteenth century, urban centers went through a period of rapid growth. The wealthier classes in Philadelphia moved away from the older parts of the city, west to Rittenhouse Square and West Philadelphia, and north on Broad Street. At the same time, the development of the railroad made it possible for more and more families to escape from urban congestion altogether by moving out to the suburbs. All the suburban churches listed in Table 13–2 had been built by 1900.

The two oldest Episcopal churches in the Philadelphia suburbs are Old St. David's in Wayne, on the Main Line, and St. Thomas' Church in the Whitemarsh Valley. In the eighteenth century these rural churches were served by circuit missionaries sent from London by the "Society for Propagating the Gospel in Foreign Parts." [102] The first congregation at St. David's, interestingly enough, was composed of Welsh Quakers who had gone over to the Church of England as a result of the Keithian schism mentioned above.[103] These two churches served the local people primarily and did not become fashionable suburban churches until the last two decades of the nineteenth century. In 1880, for example, one finds that Mr. W. H. Drayton and Mr. J. W. Sharp, two fashionable Philadelphians, were the senior wardens of St. Thomas' and St. David's, respectively.[104] Since the total annual offerings of these two parishes in that year were $92.42 and $60.76, however, they were hardly thriving suburban churches. Their eventual growth into full-fledged suburban (rather than rural) churches between 1920 and 1940 is indicated by the fact that each church recorded total annual offerings of over $10,000 (St. David's) and over $40,000 (St. Thomas') in 1940.

In the 1850's, new Episcopal churches came to Chestnut Hill and the Main Line. In 1852, the Church of the Redeemer was built on a hill overlooking the old Bryn Mawr Hotel in Lower Merion Township.[105] St. Paul's became the first Episcopal church in Chestnut Hill when it was completed in 1856.[106] Both churches

were founded by fashionable Philadelphians, many of whom were
still parishioners in St. James', St. Mark's, or Holy Trinity during
the winter months. Continuity, always dear to the hearts of
Proper Philadelphians, was maintained in the person of the first
rector of St. Paul's, William Hobart Hare, who was the son of
one of the great headmasters of Episcopal Academy and a grandson of Bishop Hobart of New York.[107]

The construction of these two Episcopal churches marked the
beginning of the suburban trend. Both Chestnut Hill and Lower
Merion Township, of course, were old communities in 1850. In
Chestnut Hill, for instance, the Baptist, Methodist, Presbyterian,
and Roman Catholic churches, all still standing on their original
sites in 1940, were all built before St. Paul's.[108] There was no
Quaker meetinghouse in the early days of Chestnut Hill because,
although the original settlers were German Friends, they were
members of the Germantown meeting.[109] Lower Merion Township was settled by Welsh Quakers in 1681 and the old Meeting
House was built in 1695. The Lutheran and Baptist churches were
built well before the advent of the Church of the Redeemer, in
1765 and 1808, respectively.[110]

Both the Redeemer and St. Paul's were relatively small parishes
before 1900 and went through their period of most rapid growth
during the first four decades of the present century. Due to the
pressures of an expanding congregation, a large and impressive
Gothic church, built on the same site as the original St. Paul's, was
completed in 1929, under the leadership of Reverend Malcolm
Peabody, son of Endicott Peabody of Groton.[111] St. Paul's Church
in Chestnut Hill has always maintained a close relationship with
St. Paul's School, in Concord, New Hampshire (see below). The
rector of St. Paul's Church in 1940, listed in both *Who's Who* and
the *Social Register*, had been a master at the school for a short
period, while the rector of St. Paul's School at its one hundredth
anniversary in 1956 had once been a young curate in Chestnut Hill
under Dr. Peabody.[112]

The other St. Paul's Church, along the Old York Road in Elkins
Park, was built in 1861, largely due to the generosity of the master of "Ogontz," Jay Cooke.[113] For many years Jay Cooke was a
vestryman at St. Paul's where he took an active part in the Sunday
School and other church activities. In 1940, Charles D. Barney,

Jay Cooke's son-in-law, kept up the family traditions at St. Paul's where he was the senior warden.[114]

The four remaining fashionable churches listed in Table 13–2— St. Martin's-in-the-Fields in Chestnut Hill, and the Church of the Good Shepherd, St. Asaph's, and St. Martin's on the Main Line— were all built in the 1880's. The first was named as a private chapel for the "Druim Moir" estate of Henry Howard Houston. The Church of the Good Shepherd, with its fine Gothic architecture and Anglican form of service, is the St. Mark's of the Main Line. St. Martin's-in-the-Fields, St. Martin's in Radnor, and St. Asaph's in Cynwyd, have been intimately allied with the Houston, Chew, and Roberts families, respectively, from their very beginning. In 1940, moreover, the same families were all active in these three churches: Samuel F. Houston, for example, was a warden at St. Martin's in Chestnut Hill, Benjamin Chew was a warden at St. Martin's in Radnor, and I. W. Roberts and T. W. Roberts, sons of George Roberts, late president of the Pennsylvania Railroad, were wardens at St. Asaph's.[115]

The Episcopal Church probably played a lesser role in the social life of the Proper Philadelphians in 1940 than it did in the Victorian period. No clergyman had the same influence on either the upper class or the rest of the city's population as did Phillips Brooks in Boston and Philadelphia, or Henry Codman Potter in New York. The Church was, nevertheless, still intimately connected with Philadelphia's contemporary, suburban upper class. Five of the eight Episcopalian clergymen listed in *Who's Who* in 1940, including the Bishop of the Diocese of Pennsylvania, were also listed in the *Social Register*. Of the five members of the Standing Committee of the Diocese of Pennsylvania and the four Delegates to the General Assembly—the nine most important lay positions in the Church hierarchy—seven were listed in the 1940 *Social Register*.[116] At the same time, the presidents of the Pennsylvania Railroad, the Philadelphia Savings Fund Society, the Fidelity Philadelphia Trust Company, the Real Estate Land Title and Trust Company, and the president of the University of Pennsylvania, all were active church leaders, as wardens of their respective suburban parishes or lay officials in the Diocese. Finally, in 1940, *all* the wardens of the churches listed in Table 13–2 (with the exception of the two West Philadelphia churches which were no longer fashionable) were listed in the *Social Register*. It is no wonder that in the diocesan headquarters and in the parish offices the little orange and black book is always available for convenient reference.

By 1920 the urban churches in Philadelphia reached their peak in number of communicants. By 1940, however, the fashionable suburban churches became the center of upper-class Episcopalianism. As a fitting symbol of this change, in 1940, the First City Troop, always, and still, closely connected with St. Peter's, marched to the Church of the Redeemer where a service was held to mark its departure for active service.[117]

Notes

1. Liston Pope, "Religion and the Class Structure," *The Annals of the American Academy of Political and Social Science*, CCLVI (March 1948), 89. See also the classic work on this subject, H. Richard Niebuhr, *The Social Sources of Denominationalism* (New York: Henry Holt and Co., Inc., 1929).
2. Matthew Josephson, *The Robber Barons: The Great American Capitalists, 1861–1901* (New York: Harcourt, Brace and Company, 1934), pp. 320–321.
3. George Eaton Simpson and J. Milton Yinger, *Racial and Cultural Minorities: An Analysis of Prejudice and Discrimination* (New York: Harper and Brothers, 1953), p. 515.
4. Liston Pope, *Millhands and Preachers* (New Haven: Yale University Press, 1942), p. 124.
5. Max Weber, *The Protestant Ethic and the Spirit of Capitalism*, translated by Talcott Parsons (London: Allen and Unwin, 1930), p. 1.
6. *Congregationalist*, June 21, 1876, p. 196. Quoted in Henry F. May, *Protestant Churches and Industrial America* (New York: Harper and Brothers, 1949), p. 51.
7. Clarence Day, "God and My Father," *The Best of Clarence Day* (New York: Alfred A. Knopf, 1948), p. 5.
8. George Wharton Pepper, *Philadelphia Lawyer* (Philadelphia: J. B. Lippincott Company, 1944), p. 98.
9. Dixon Wecter, *The Saga of American Society* (New York: Charles Scribner's Sons, 1937), p. 478.
10. Carl Bridenbaugh, *Cities in Revolt* (New York: Alfred A. Knopf, 1955), p. 152.
11. See W. J. Cash, *The Mind of the South* (New York: Doubleday Anchor Books, 1954).
12. See James Thayer Addison, *The Episcopal Church in the United States, 1789–1931* (New York: Charles Scribner's Sons, 1951), pp. 65–73. An excellent description of the founding of the Episcopal Church.

13. Frank Cousins and Phil M. Riley, *The Colonial Architecture of Philadelphia* (Boston: Little, Brown and Company, 1920), p. 221.
14. Ellis Paxson Oberholtzer, *Jay Cooke, Financier of the Civil War* (Philadelphia: George W. Jacobs and Company, 1907), II, 483–485.
15. Matthew Josephson, *op. cit.*, p. 319.
16. James Thayer Addison, *op. cit.*, p. 205.
17. Frank D. Ashburn, *Peabody of Groton* (New York: Coward McCann, Inc., 1944), p. 30.
18. Cleveland Amory, *The Proper Bostonians* (New York: E. P. Dutton and Company, Inc., 1947), p. 107.
19. Boston *Daily Herald*, May 15, 1836. Taken from a student's dissertation-in-progress.
20. Andrew Landale Drummond, *Story of American Protestantism* (Boston: The Beacon Press, 1951), p. 187.
21. Van Wyck Brooks, *New England: Indian Summer, 1865–1915* (New York: E. P. Dutton and Company, Inc., 1940), pp. 184–203.
22. Cleveland Amory, *op. cit.*, p. 105.
23. Charles J. Cohen, *Rittenhouse Square* (Philadelphia: Privately Printed, 1922).
24. Alexander V. G. Allen, *Life and Letters of Phillips Brooks* (New York: E. P. Dutton and Company, 1901).
25. Dixon Wecter, *op. cit.*, p. 478.
26. Robert K. Bosch, *Ecclesiastical Background of the American Episcopate* (Unpublished manuscript in the author's possession).
27. See Vida Dutton Scudder, *Father Huntington, Founder of the Order of the Holy Cross* (New York: E. P. Dutton and Company, Inc., 1940).
28. *Ibid.*, p. 35.
29. See George Hodges, *Henry Codman Potter, Seventh Bishop of New York* (New York: The Macmillan Company, 1915).
30. Dixon Wecter, *op. cit.*, p. 479.
31. Gustavus Myers, *History of the Great American Fortunes* (New York: The Modern Library, 1937), p. 378.
32. Dixon Wecter, *op. cit.*, p. 480.
33. See Frederick Lewis Allen, *The Great Pierpont Morgan* (New York: Harper and Brothers, 1949).
34. *Ibid.*, p. 240.
35. *Ibid.*, p. 153.
36. *Ibid.*, p. 133.
37. Spencer Miller, Jr., and Joseph F. Fletcher, *The Church and Industry* (New York: Longmans, Green and Company, 1930), p. 219.
38. *Ibid.*, pp. 52–111.
39. Henry F. May, *Protestant Churches and Industrial America* (New York: Harper and Brothers, 1949), p. 186.
40. George Hodges, *op. cit.*, pp. 343–344.
41. Spencer Miller, Jr., and Joseph F. Fletcher, *op. cit.*, p. 71.
42. *New York Times*, June 25, 1955.
43. *Time*, April 19, 1945, p. 62.
44. Carl and Jessica Bridenbaugh, *Rebels and Gentlemen, Philadelphia in the Age of Franklin* (New York: Reynal & Hitchcock, 1942), p. 16.
45. Nicholas B. Wainwright, *A Philadelphia Story, The Philadelphia Contributionship for the Insurance of Houses from Loss by Fire* (Philadel-

phia: Privately Printed, 1952), p. 30. Amos Strettell was married at Christ Church in 1752, and was one of the petitioners for land on which to build St. Peter's in 1754.
46. Frederick B. Tolles, *Meeting House and Counting House, The Quaker Merchants of Colonial Philadelphia, 1682–1763* (Chapel Hill, The University of North Carolina Press, 1948), p. 221.
47. *Ibid.*, p. 229n.
48. *Ibid.*, p. 45.
49. *Ibid.*, pp. 115–116.
50. *Ibid.*, p. 19.
51. William W. Montgomery, *Pew Renters of Christ Church, St. Peter's and St. James's, From 1776 to 1815* (unpublished manuscript, Philadelphia, 1948).
52. Carl and Jessica Bridenbaugh, *op. cit.*, p. 17.
53. *Ibid.*, p. 208.
54. *Ibid.*, p. 211.
55. C. P. B. Jefferys, *The Provincial and Revolutionary History of St. Peter's Church, Philadelphia, 1753–1783* (Philadelphia: Privately Printed, 1923), p. 14.
56. "Society Hill" was so called long before St. Peter's and the mansions of wealthy Philadelphians were built there. According to Christopher Tunnard, Society Hill may have been the first suburban development in America. See Christopher Tunnard, *The City of Man* (New York: Charles Scribner's Sons, 1953), p. 113.
57. Frederick B. Tolles, *op. cit.*, p. 27.
58. Quoted in J. Thomas Scharf and Thomas Westcott, *History of Philadelphia, 1609–1884* (Philadelphia: G. Everts & Co., 1884), I, 296n.
59. C. P. B. Jefferys, *op. cit.*, pp. 66–76.
60. J. Thomas Scharf and Thomas Westcott, *op. cit.*, I, 393.
61. C. P. B. Jefferys, *op. cit.*, p. 63.
62. John W. Jordan, editor, *Colonial Families of Philadelphia* (New York: The Lewis Publishing Company, 1911), II, 1746.
63. Nicholas B. Wainwright, *op. cit.*, p. 132.
64. William W. Montgomery, *op. cit.* Even the great sociologist of religion, Ernest Troeltsch, called Franklin a Quaker. *Le bon Quaker*, of course, was part of the *philosophes'* heavenly city in the eighteenth century.
65. C. P. B. Jefferys, *op. cit.*, p. 88.
66. John W. Jordan, *op. cit.*, Vol. I, p. 293.
67. Rufus M. Jones, *The Quakers in the American Colonies* (London: Macmillan and Co., Limited, 1911), pp. 457–458.
68. A. E. Browne, *A Sketch of St. James's Parish* (Philadelphia, 1899), p. 7.
69. J. Thomas Scharf and Thomas Westcott, *op. cit.*, II, 1352.
70. *The Church of the Savior*, 100th Anniversary, November, 1950 (pamphlet).
71. A. E. Browne, *op. cit.*, pp. 23–27.
72. C. P. B. Jefferys, *op. cit.*, p. 89.
73. See summary of these reports in A. E. Browne, *op. cit.*
74. Claude Gilkyson, *St. Mark's, One Hundred Years on Locust Street* (Philadelphia, 1948).
75. *Ibid.*, p. 9.
76. *Ibid.*, p. 9.

77. *Ibid.*, p. 45.
78. *Ibid.*, p. 60.
79. *Ibid.*, pp. 26–33.
80. *Ibid.*, p. 33.
81. *Ibid.*, pp. 16–25.
82. Alexander V. G. Allen, *op. cit.*, Vol. I, p. 293.
83. *Ibid.*, II, 113–114.
84. *Ibid.*, II, 113.
85. Cordelia Drexel Biddle (as told to Kyle Crichton), *My Philadelphia Father* (Garden City, N. Y.: Doubleday & Company, Inc., 1955), p. 71.
86. George Wharton Pepper, *op. cit.*, p. 313.
87. Cordelia Drexel Biddle, *op. cit.*, p. 71.
88. *Ibid.*, p. 135.
89. *Ibid.*, p. 91.
90. Henry F. May, *op. cit.*, p. 64.
91. *Ibid.*, p. 65.
92. George Wharton Pepper, *op. cit.*, p. 278.
93. *Service in Memory of Anthony J. Drexel, Founder of the Drexel Institute of Art, Science and Industry* (Philadelphia: privately printed, 1896).
94. Sister M. Dolores, *The Francis A. Drexel Family* (Cornwells Heights, Pa.: The Sisters of the Blessed Sacrament).
95. Claude Gilkyson, *op. cit.*, p. 63. Even in the 1880's parishioners were moving out to the country. In 1883, for example, while twenty-six children entered the parish school, twenty-seven left because their parents had moved from the neighborhood. *Ibid.*, p. 39.
96. St. James was sold to the Atlantic Refining Company "due to financial difficulties caused by changing neighborhood conditions." Philadelphia *Evening Bulletin*, September 8, 1945.
97. Philadelphia *Evening Bulletin*, December 21, 1925.
98. *Ibid.*, November 7, 1930.
99. *Ibid.*
100. *Ibid.*
101. *Ibid.*
102. John T. Faris, *Old Churches and Meeting Houses in and around Philadelphia* (Philadelphia: J. B. Lippincott Company, 1926), p. 203.
103. *Ibid.*, p. 206.
104. Journal of the *Annual Convention of the Protestant Episcopal Church in the Diocese of Pennsylvania* (Philadelphia, 1881).
105. Ernest C. Earp, *The Church of the Redeemer, Bryn Mawr, Lower Merion, Montgomery County, Pennsylvania.*
106. *Centennial History of St. Paul's Church, Chestnut Hill, 1856–1956.*
107. James Thayer Addison, *op. cit.*, pp. 254–262. William Hobart Hare became one of the pioneering missionary bishops of the Episcopal Church. He devoted the prime of his life to the Indians of the Dakotas.
108. *Centennial History of St. Paul's Church.*
109. Horace Mather Lippincott, *A Narrative of Chestnut Hill, Philadelphia, with some account of Springfield, Whitemarsh, and Cheltenham Townships in Montgomery County, Pennsylvania* (Jenkintown, Pennsylvania: Old York Road Publishing Company, 1948), p. 29.
110. Ernest C. Earp, *op. cit.* (no pages are numbered).

111. *Centennial History of St. Paul's Church.*
112. *Ibid.*
113. Ellis Paxson Oberholtzer, *op. cit.*, II, 483–485.
114. Journal of the *Annual Convention*, 1941.
115. *Ibid.*
116. *Ibid.*
117. Ernest C. Earp, *op. cit.*

❧ 14 ❧

Eric L. McKitrick

THE STUDY OF CORRUPTION

The investigation of corruption, in the analytical sense, does not seem to present a subject of very intense interest to social scientists these days. Past research in this area has for the most part taken its stimulus from a basic commitment to reform, rather than from the intrinsic charm of the subject, and most of it has tended to be done during times when a general concern with reform was fairly high. We are not living in such a period today. Actually such periods have been very productive, yielding rich materials in the form of journalism, histories, memoirs of reformers, and treatises on "good government" which, in their very devotion to the overthrow of the "machine" system, could hardly help producing, in the course of things, a number of insights into the nature of that system. Such bursts of energy have, in their turn, even begotten certain idiosyncratic by-products, such as an occasional "apology" for the system, or occasional sympathetic sketches of the more legendary "bosses," showing the genial side of their activities—all of which has not only multiplied the raw data, but has also given them depth.[1]

It may be regrettable—in the interest of sustained energy—that the moral tensions which formerly served to foster such investigation are at present so noticeably relaxed. But, on the other hand, there may also be reason to think that this very relaxed emotional

Eric L. McKitrick is Professor of History at Columbia University. He is the author of *Andrew Johnson and Reconstruction*.

Reprinted from *Political Science Quarterly*, LXXII (December 1957), 502–514, by permission of the author and the publisher.

climate itself offers a peculiarly promising setting in which future work might take a new and fruitful turn. In this setting, we are now able to recognize that further "reform" activity, for its own sake, will probably yield us very little that we do not already have in the way of insights; it is difficult, for instance, to mistake the indiscriminate Kefauver diggings for much that resembles "knowledge." Moreover, we have come to perceive that, amid the conflicting claims of a disorderly democratic political society, the corrupt machine system has historically performed certain stabilizing functions: it was David Riesman who referred to the local politician as "soaked in gravy which we can well afford." And finally, it is in this same setting of detachment that we are free to appreciate the attributes of that remarkable technician—and gentleman—DeSapio of Tammany Hall. These, at any rate, are a few of the straws in the wind.[2]

What we ought to see in the future, assuming a picking up of interest, will be various studies in which political machines and their auxiliary activities are examined in a structural and functional way: that is, in terms of such questions as, what have they done for society—how do they work—what gaps have they filled in our political life—what has been needed to maintain them— what are the limits within which they have had to operate—what sort of future may be expected for them?

The closest approach to a theoretical model for dealing with such questions has been that offered by Robert K. Merton in his *Social Theory and Social Structure*,[3] and no new investigation could very well afford not to take this model as its starting point. So far as I know, very little, if anything, has been done with it. I am not even sure that it has been subjected to critical examination.

An important thing to note with regard to the Merton scheme is that it seems to have been postulated for what might be called a "classical" period in the history of American machine politics. The most perceptive field work ever done in this area is still probably that of Lincoln Steffens—and since it is from Steffens that Mr. Merton has taken his major cues, it is inevitable that the balance and arrangement of his categories should be most appropriate to a state of things which existed during a period roughly centering on the year 1905.

This is not meant to intimate that the model does not apply

today. It is valid and accurate in all its major details. It is so set up that any alterations in it would have to be more in the nature of refinements than of basic changes. But the subject matter itself has changed in a great many ways since Steffens' time, and I emphasize this in order to make my key point. In the absence of outside stimuli—such as a general public interest in "reform" (or, for that matter, a primary need for reform)—pressure for new work and new insights will have to come from somewhere within the social sciences, and, specifically, I would say that it will have to come from the field of American history. Its raw data will be found in the form of substantial materials which must now be called "historical": material covering the period in which our cities underwent their most phenomenal phases of growth—material which dates back at least to the end of the Civil War. Any theoretical model for the explanation of social phenomena has a tendency, in spite of all precautions, to be static. But if there is anything about our social scene that is insistently dynamic, it is the tempo of our political life—and to get the sense of dynamism in political structures (that is, change, and the things that produce it), one needs the sense of time. We know a great deal about the functions of such structures at given points in time. But of equal, if not greater, importance to political sociology today is the course of transformation which these structures—these "machines"—have undergone over the past two generations. This is now what makes "history" such a vital dimension. An understanding of such change, and of the reasons for it, is bound to feed back into one's understanding and judgment of the very functions themselves.

What are—or have been—these "functions"? To repeat, they have been no better itemized than by Mr. Merton, and probably the best way to set up points of reference for the present discussion would be to recapitulate very briefly the principal elements of his model.

A "structural context" is first established: a general setting or environment in which, for one reason or another, the "need" for such an establishment as the political machine has arisen. The principal element in this environment is the diffusion and fragmentation of power—and therefore of responsibility—which tends to be inherent in a transitory, non-authoritarian, elected, democratic officialdom. It is easy to see how this could emerge as a critical limitation in the mushrooming cities of the United States during the seventies, eighties and nineties, amid an urban life proliferating in complexity and tangled with a bewildering maze of conflicting needs and claims. Here an alternative, informal focus of responsibility was located in the "boss," a leader of unofficial executive status who had a freedom and flexibility made possible by his ability to work, as it were, in the back room. Another element in this context—if I myself may add one—would be the fact that any organization of a political nature which did have the power and numbers to furnish these needs and umpire these claims was bound to have no more than a semiprofessional status. Such an organization, constantly requiring money to keep itself going, would have to derive a certain amount of it from sources no more than quasi-official in nature. All this would follow in the absence of centralized, professionalized, bureaucratic traditions of administration.[4]

In this setting, Mr. Merton enumerates four of the major "latent functions" which have been performed by the machine system, in relation to the various subgroups making up its constituency. The first of these functions involves various kinds of welfare services for the poor and powerless; such services would include the widest range of things—food, jobs, intercession with the law in times of difficulty, and so forth. Their price, quite logically, would be votes. Another set of functions appears in response to some of the manifold and perennial problems of businessmen—such problems as the need of smaller businessmen for protection against each other, the occasional need of larger businessmen to have cumbersome and expensive projects expedited, and the constant need of all classes of businessmen for unofficial protection against a snarl of contradictory and overlapping laws, codes, and regulations. The prices here, graded as they would be according to the services, add up to "routine graft"—the "oil" that keeps the machine in running order. A third type of function is one which requires a certain conceptual subtlety to recognize. For certain critical ethnic groups, and for groups situated in lower social brackets generally, the large urban political machine has traditionally afforded very important channels of social mobility—avenues to personal advancement—which would doubtless otherwise be closed.[5] For example, the availability of careers in politics served as a significant safety valve for the surplus social energies of the New York Irish from the 1870's on. The price which these groups were asked to pay was, from their viewpoint, hardly excessive: unstinting party loyalty—unquestioning devotion to the organization. A final category of functions is one in which services analogous to those performed for "legitimate" business were also made available to the underworld—to "illegitimate" business. Here the machine could actually operate as a kind of stabilizing mechanism: by maintaining communication—and actual connections—with the underworld, it could act as an umpire for activities carried on outside the law; it maintained, in effect, a measure of control; it could set standards and define limits. The price, of course, was the familiar "protection money"— the kickback.

Such, then, is the pattern. To what extent does it hold today? It is a pattern whose formal outlines are still in some way to be recognized in all our major cities. However, the specific activities and operations represented by these formal categories have been so immeasurably altered and transformed as to change the very symmetry of the pattern, and to raise certain very crucial questions. Has the old system for practical purposes (as some writers have begun to assert) really "broken down"? Or does it continue to operate within a more limited area? What has been the effect of the reform tradition? Has the boss "gone straight"? What kinds of loyalties can the machine command today? What kinds of things can it still do—and are there things that it can no longer do?

Certain kinds of historical problems immediately suggest themselves—problems having to do with the persistence of the "corrupt machine." For instance: under what conditions has it been possible for a reform movement to be successful? We find that it has never quite been a matter of civic affairs reaching a given point of "rottenness," with the honest citizens at that point making common cause to strike down the machine. What seems to have been required, as a matter of historical experience, is the combining of other factors, fairly complex and not always easy to identify. Such factors include points at which the machine has ceased to serve its clients responsibly—points at which services could no longer be considered worth the prices asked. The arrival of hard times could quickly precipitate such a situation. An even more sensitive point could be the one at which (for whatever reason) the machine's internal solidarity had become weakened—because of power struggles, some temporary loss of internal responsibility, perhaps a weakening of loyalties resulting from inequitable distribution of spoils. Variations on these themes will be found, if one is looking for them, recurring again and again in the literature. They are admirably spelled out in the downfall of the Tweed machine. Here we see the Boss having lost all bearings, all sense of proportion, launching a series of insane depredations, and alienating his followers by refusing to distribute the loot honorably. The Ring had become virtually a personal operation, with Tweed's raids upon the city treasury far exceeding what could reasonably be afforded. Here, moreover, we see the critical increment of reform energy coming from within: Samuel Tilden's success was in large measure owing to strategic assistance from the Tammany organization, and to the invaluable inside knowledge which was the product of having himself worked, for years, with Tammany Hall.

A situation of this sort may undoubtedly be matched by numerous others—and, in fact, by still others turned, as it were, inside out. For, conversely, it may be assumed that a reform government which offers nothing as a substitute for the functions performed by the machine will find itself very shortly in a state of paralysis. The mayoralty of Seth Low in New York in the early 1900's furnishes such a case; another is found in the efforts of Joseph Folk to "reform" St. Louis in 1902; and numerous others may be located all through the reform annals of the Progressive Era.

Such might be called the "functional" approach on the simplest and most straightforward plane. But it leads into parallel problems of even greater interest and greater subtlety. Take this question: What is the function of the reform movement—not for destroying the machine but for reinvigorating it, for renewing its vitality, for helping it to persist? At this point the "machine" metaphor itself becomes misleading. It has in no case, apparently, been a thing that could be smashed in the way that an engine can be rendered useless by the destruction of a few key parts. Rather, its very complexity, the very functional autonomy of so many of its parts, makes it more like an organism. For instance, solidarity at the ward level seems to persist almost by habit: Plunkitt of Tammany Hall—then a ward leader—survived the destruction of Tweed and flourished, and his experience must have been re-enacted by many another in comparable circumstances. How might this be explained?

Taking this situation as the focal point for a whole range of problems, one might attempt to picture the scene at local headquarters the day after an election in which smashing victories had been won by the reform ticket. One may picture the post-mortem (a proceeding built into American politics): it would most surely include a highly critical reappraisal of the power situation in the ward—and those present would be the first to understand why the organization had lost. A further result would compare very closely with Durkheim's analysis of what happens at funerals: a ritual reaffirmation of group solidarity. Still another consequence would be that the demands normally made on the machine would (in view of lean times to come) tend to drop off. Therefore—assuming that the lean period did not last too long—it might be predicted that the aftermath of defeat would coincide with precisely that phase of the machine's greatest moral solidarity.[6] Some highly interesting conclusions might be expected to flow from this. Granting any other functions remaining for the machine to perform—and by definition they always exist—might not these be precisely the conditions in which they would be discovered? A crude example is afforded by the breakup of the Whisky Ring in Grant's time; the "army of termites" (as Matthew Josephson put it) promptly marched into the Post Office Department. Or, let the setting be a little less extreme and more refined: such conditions as those just described might simply serve as a test for activities whose style must be altered from time to time in order to remain acceptable. Boss Kelly of Chicago, according to legend, was always pleased to have Paul Douglas somewhere on the scene; his use of Douglas was as a standing threat to "any of the boys who got too hungry." A final point to be made along these lines is that the very informal nature of the machine will set limits at any time upon its stability—which would mean that its internal leadership must remain aggressive and dynamic to keep from being unhorsed by disaffected henchmen. The most natural alliance that an insurgent group could reach for would be an alliance with reformers. Other factions standing by could then, like Lord Stanley on Bosworth field, take their choice. The machine, in other words, has been anything but a torpid institution: a perennial state of internal yeastiness has made it a dynamic one.

Another set of problems, in which historical analysis and the use of historical materials are indispensable, would have to do with long-term changes in the entire system of machine rule. Here the reform tradition must be given its due in another way, for the very process of evolution in civic politics has been accompanied by reform groups taking up the slack and calling the turn as change occurs. The city manager and city commission plans never quite produced—in themselves—the effects hoped for by their early exponents, but they may still be considered as symptoms of a long-term process whose tendency has been toward ever-continued extension, rationalization, and stabilization of official administrative agencies. Probably the most specific and most important single expression of this has been the extension of civil service into municipal government. Today, for example, a considerable sector of Tammany's former patronage preserves in New York City is blanketed by a very efficient system of civil service.

The notion of evolutionary change could be carried directly into the specific functions enumerated in Mr. Merton's conceptual scheme. Upon the welfare functions, for instance, time has unquestionably left its mark. Here, a considerable number of the services once performed for unassimilated immigrant groups and for the economically underprivileged are today no longer needed. The need has been eroded away by the assimilation process itself, by the development of scientific welfare on municipal and state-federal levels, and, most especially, by a relatively long period of full-employment capitalism. The result has been mobility, a constant turnover of population in urban areas—all of which has been deeply subversive of neighborhood solidarity.[7] Or, take those functions performed for legitimate business. If it is kept in mind that the protection, the controls, and the umpiring have been "*un*official," as opposed to "official," there can be little doubt as to which direction the curve has gone over time, since one of the most dramatic features of our political history since 1933 has been the extension of official public controls into every aspect of business and over all kinds of businesses. Such change is, of course, anything but absolute; the old pattern, in some form, is still there. I am only indicating what the time dimension has been doing to it.

The most fascinating changes of all, and by far the most complex and difficult to trace down, are those connected with Mr. Merton's other two functions—the functions involving social mobility and relationships with the underworld. One of the most remarkable of recent discoveries in the social sciences has been the manner in which these two areas are related—the manner in which (whether the political machine is directly involved or not) they grade into each other. It has become apparent that not only do the values of mobility, status, and respectability operate in the underworld in a way precisely analogous to their workings in the "upperworld," but also that the extent to which the two worlds overlap in shared values is considerable. All of this furnishes us a final set of problems directly related to those already touched upon.

In drawing a pattern of corruption (loosely used here as a generic term for covering a wide variety of things) might it not be possible to trace not only the obvious shifts and transformations but also a pattern of energy? What happens when obstacles are placed in a particular area of corruption? Is the result an alternative pattern? Perhaps—but what about the stabilization of existing patterns? The same question could be put in another way—in terms of the social-mobility function (either in politics or in the underworld) for socially deprived ethnic groups. Is there a possible correlation between the rise to social acceptability and the stabilization of particular forms of corruption in which members of these groups have specialized? Might not the very high value which American society at large sets upon mobility serve over a time as a built-in check—as a stimulus for (say) "cleaning up" the rackets? [8] This surely goes back at least to the days of Plunkitt— he was the man who made the virtuous distinction between "honest" and "dishonest" graft.[9]

The Italian community of a generation ago may provide the clue to the way the mechanism works. Assume at the outset a series of status gradations all the way up through narcotics, prostitution, and ultimately gambling—and in which the gamblers would be, as it were, the "gentlemen." Costello would handle the gambling, Luciano the girls and dope. Now what has, in fact, happened between then and today? As the entire Italian community has moved up, the higher-status brackets of the underworld have apparently come under tremendous crowding and pressure (gambling at large having become almost respectable), whereas the lower grades have been vacated to unorganized riffraff. No one of comparable prestige has arisen to fill the shoes of Lucky Luciano, and probably no one will. Moving up, then, into politics, we see the New York civic scene today liberally dotted with substantial citizens of Italian origin.[10] Indeed, it appears that the same mechanism just described (simple mobility—with or without an ethnic dimension) has been at work within Tammany Hall itself. The "Boss" is not finding it easy to give away what patronage he has, since the very people to be rewarded are turning out to be better placed elsewhere, in business and in the professions.[11]

Let me now return to my original point. I would like to repeat my belief that those studies which can most appropriately embrace the kinds of questions I have raised will come more and more to have a historical framework. An excellent type of investigation, simple in format but with the flexibility needed for moving into any number of related areas, would be the life-study of a machine. Here, with the historical dimension, one could get the very crucial sense of a cycle. For cycles are long, and they embrace much change. One might further predict that the historian to whom this kind of project will be of interest will tend more and more to come into it equipped with analytical tools which he has appropriated from elsewhere but modified for his own special requirements. They may not ease his task, but they will make him sensitive to a whole range of vital connections which, admittedly, past historical studies (and many "scientific" ones as well) have left untouched.[12]

I cannot resist a final question. Is the machine headed for extinction? Is it getting "cleaner and cleaner"? Conceivably not—not necessarily. New predictions could very well center on a new mobility-cycle for ethnic groups still not yet "arrived"; and this might involve a period of renewed machine activity in which the tone of politics could once more drop quite noticeably. For instance, what might happen when municipal patronage and civil service jobs are no longer attractive to (say) bright young Jewish and Italian lawyers—no longer within their dignity? One clear sign of rising mobility among Negro and Puerto Rican groups would be the appearance of substantial numbers of them in minor political leadership roles. Along with it would come, of course, a great deal of tension as such groups increased in power and numbers, and the first phase would probably not be attractive in its quality and style. We might expect, moreover, that the very same liberal, socially conscious groups now urging a fair shake for our minorities may themselves soon be embarking on new reform crusades without quite realizing what was happening. It has all happened in the past.

But what *would* be happening? It would be the same process of assimilation and socialization, the same "mobility-cycle" (though they did not call it that) which was undergone by the Irish after the Civil War, and after them the Jews and Italians. It is a process full of corruption and full of vitality. What we know about those groups may well give us the clues we need for plotting what is still to come.

Notes

NOTE: This chapter is adapted from a paper read before the 33rd Annual Institute of the Society for Social Research, University of Chicago, June 1, 1956.

1. The work which combines all the best in the tradition is, of course, that of Lincoln Steffens: *The Shame of the Cities* (New York: 1904), and especially the *Autobiography* (New York: 1931). Early inquiries (more or less theoretical) from a reform viewpoint are Robert C. Brooks, *Corruption in American Politics and Life* (New York: 1910); John J. Hamilton, *Government by Commission: The Dethronement of the City Boss* (New York and London: 1911); Frank J. Goodnow, *City Government in the United States* (New York: 1904); and Frederic C. Howe, *The City: The Hope of Democracy* (New York: 1906). A more recent summation of early reform efforts is Clifford W. Patton, *The Battle for Municipal Reform* (Washington: 1940). That "muckraking" itself is not quite dead is evident in Estes Kefauver's *Crime in America* (Garden City: 1951). The machine, on the other hand, had its literary apologists as early as the 1890's: Daniel Greenleaf Thompson, *Politics in a Democracy* (New York: 1893); Alfred Henry Lewis, *Richard Croker* (New York: 1901) and *The Boss* (New York: 1903). Material on Tammany Hall is very rich. It includes Denis Tilden Lynch, *"Boss" Tweed* (New York and London: 1927) and *The Wild Seventies* (New York and

London: 1941); M. R. Werner, *Tammany Hall* (New York: 1928); Roy V. Peel, *The Political Clubs of New York City* (New York and London: 1935); William L. Riordon, *Plunkitt of Tammany Hall* (New York: 1948); and especially Lothrop Stoddard's fascinating *Master of Manhattan: The Life of Richard Croker* (New York and Toronto: 1931). A number of active reformers have left us their memoirs. Outstanding among them are Brand Whitlock, *Forty Years of It* (New York: 1914); Fremont Older, *My Own Story* (San Francisco: 1919); Tom L. Johnson, *My Story* (New York: 1911); and Carter Harrison, *Stormy Years* (Indianapolis and New York: 1935). An attempt to deal "scientifically" with city politics is Harold F. Gosnell, *Machine Politics: Chicago Model* (Chicago: 1937); also in this vein is Sonya Forthal, *Cogwheels of Democracy: A Study of the Precinct Captain* (New York: 1946). More humane, and consequently more illuminating, is John T. Salter, *Boss Rule: Portraits in City Politics* (New York and London: 1935).

2. Another such "straw," surely, is the immense popularity of Edwin O'Connor's novel, *The Last Hurrah* (Boston: 1956).

3. Glencoe, Ill.: 1949. See pp. 71–81.

4. Max Weber, acutely sensitized to bureaucracy and its implications, was very impressed by the responsibility of the American "boss," recognizing that in him and in his organization lay the natural functional substitute for bureaucracy in a growing democratic political culture. See "Politics as a Vocation," in *From Max Weber: Essays in Sociology*, translated and edited by H. H. Gerth and C. Wright Mills (New York: 1946), pp. 108–111.

5. The significance of this function may be confused unless an important analytical distinction is made. It should be thought of in terms, not of the "number" of careers it provides for these groups at large, but rather of a critical ratio of outlets for the potential *leadership* among such groups.

6. I have been told that some of the Wallace groups reached the high point of their solidarity about a month *after* the 1948 election. After this high point—with nothing to look forward to—the groups tended to disintegrate.

7. Some present-day consequences of this mobility are discussed in G. Edward Janosik, "Suburban Balance of Power," *American Quarterly*, VII (Summer 1955), 123–141; and Harvey Wheeler, "Yesterday's Robin Hood," *American Quarterly*, VII (Winter 1955), 332–344.

8. A real landmark of analysis in this area, one whose importance cannot be too much emphasized, is Daniel Bell's brilliant essay, "Crime as an American Way of Life," *Antioch Review*, XIII (Summer 1953), 131–154.

9. There have, of course, been exceptions, but it appears that city bosses (who have by definition "risen to the top") have in general tended to be men who were fairly honest personally, and who remained aloof from police corruption (the "shaking down" of disorderly houses and other illegal enterprises), even while tolerating it among their vassals. Such activity was considered dirty and disreputable, and beneath their personal dignity. "Honest graft," on the other hand (business dealings to which the city was a party, and in which the politician, as businessman, had advantages of prior knowledge), was on a considerably higher moral

plane. See Riordon, *Plunkitt*, pp. 3–8. For a comparative survey in standards of honesty—standards surprisingly high—see Harold Zink, *City Bosses in the United States* (Durham, N. C.: 1930).

10. Throughout William Foote Whyte's *Street Corner Society* (enlarged ed., Chicago: 1955) are examples of how the universally coercive values of respectability and the drive for status and success operated among the Italian community both in the rackets and in politics, as well as elsewhere. Especially illuminating is Mr. Whyte's story of how a leading racketeer of "Cornerville" forbade his son to play with the riffraff of the neighborhood, and how gratified he himself was to associate with a Harvard professor—until he discovered the "professor" hanging out with the street-corner and poolroom crowd. Very perceptive observations on the social, political and geographical mobility of the Italian community are also to be found in chapter 4 ("The Frontier Reappears") of Samuel Lubell's *The Future of American Politics* (New York: 1952), pp. 62–80.

11. See Robert L. Heilbroner, "Carmine G. DeSapio: The Smile on the Face of the Tiger," *Harper's Magazine* (July 1954), pp. 23–33.

12. Since the above was written, an excellent and illuminating monograph, conceived along these very lines, has come to my attention. It is A. Theodore Brown's "The Politics of Reform: Kansas City's Municipal Government 1925–1950" (Ph.D. thesis, University of Chicago: 1956).

Thomas C. Cochran

THE "PRESIDENTIAL SYNTHESIS" IN
AMERICAN HISTORY

Rapid growth in the social sciences has had surprisingly little effect on the general content and synthesis of American history. The main props of the synthetic structure, erected, more or less unconsciously, by such pioneers as Channing, Hart, McMaster, and Turner, are still securely in place. Although much new trim in the form of discussions of artistic and social movements has been added, the old skeleton of wars, presidential administrations, and the westward movement still holds the edifice together.

Examining the contents of the few interpretations of American history for the general reader or of recent college textbooks, including two first published in 1947, one is struck by the uniformity of the traditional synthesis. From the Constitution to the Civil War scholars have not strayed far from the paths trod by the turn-of-the-century pioneers. Jeffersonian and Jacksonian Democracy, the War of 1812, the Westward Movement, Territorial Expansion, and Sectional Conflict form a standard pattern. In the period between 1865 and 1896, then too recent for the pioneers to set in a definitive mold, the present synthesis offers somewhat more diversity. But the suspicion that the more varied

Thomas C. Cochran is Professor of the History of the People of the United States at the University of Pennsylvania. His publications include *The Age of Enterprise* (with William Miller), *The American Business System,* and *Railroad Leaders, 1845–1890.*

Reprinted from *American Historical Review,* LIII (July, 1948), 748–759, by permission of the author and the American Historical Association.

treatment may also be due to the obvious inadequacy of national politics to serve as the thought-saving standby is supported by the resumption of the old pattern as soon as the presidency again becomes interesting. From Theodore Roosevelt on, presidential administrations and national political issues, including wars, again become the center of the narrative. For this reason I am going to refer to the standard pattern as the "presidential synthesis," realizing fully that the presidential chronology is not continuously adhered to, that many other themes are included, and that, in any case, such emphasis is only a superficial manifestation of more fundamental inadequacies.

Judged either by the complex of values and standards that may loosely be referred to as humanistic or by those of the social sciences, the presidential synthesis is a failure. It satisfies a follower of Toynbee, for example, but little better than it does the devotees of the dismal science. But, at present, I shall discuss only its inadequacy in dealing with the type of problems in modern society that most interest social scientists, or what may be termed from their point of view history's lack of social realism. To members of the disciplines that have to study the problems of industrial society, the basic data or trends with which the historian has traditionally dealt do not seem of the highest importance, and the studies themselves seem to the social scientist correspondingly futile. A consensus of the problems dealt with by social scientists would include such topics as the causes and conditions of economic growth or stagnation; the effect on enterprise of community approbation, competition, monopoly, and regulation; the social difficulties stemming from great urban centers, new types of employment, and changing levels of opportunity; the psychological frustrations developing from urban insecurity, badly selected social goals and altered family relationships; and the origins and continuing support of social manners, attitudes, and beliefs. The rapid rise of such group problems has characterized the history of the nineteenth and twentieth centuries, but, needless to say, they are not the central feature of the presidential synthesis. Moreover, cursory study of general European history writing indicates that this weakness is not confined to the history of the United States.

How has this situation arisen? Why should an important intellectual discipline, occupying the time of many thousands of scholars, fail to keep pace with the spiritual and material problems of its civilization?

An obvious part of the answer lies in the fact that the writing of history is a time-honored and traditional occupation long antedating the modern emphasis on empirical method in the social sciences or present-day problems of source materials. The historical record prior to 1800 here or abroad is relatively scanty. The historian has to use the materials he can find rather than those that might best answer his questions. To begin with, these materials are largely governmental, and the fact that the modern syntheses were developed in a period of growing nationalism led to a still greater preoccupation with political sources. Historians, used to confining themselves to these old and easily available records for the earlier periods, failed to make use of new types of material as these became available in the later nineteenth century. The habits of the older historian, educated to a scarcity of records, perpetuated themselves amid a later-day abundance. Statistical data, specialized periodicals, new types of correspondence, and the records of many organizations, profit-making or otherwise, were all relatively neglected, while the traditional sources were reinterpreted again and again.

This tendency has been noted or implied in various ways from the time of Buckle and Green in England and of the graduate seminars of the eighties in America. Yet, in spite of an increasing recognition of the importance and complexity of the elements in modern society that are but faintly reflected in national politics, no well-formulated rival synthesis is even contesting the sway of the presidential. No new texts and few other general histories have attempted to shatter the mold. No recognized "social science" synthesis of American history is challenging the traditional formula.[1]

The explanation of such a striking intellectual anachronism is bound to be subtle and complex, for if the antequated structure rested on one or two easily recognized errors it could not have withstood the pressures of new generations of historians. A long list of causes must therefore be investigated, the absolute importance of any one of which is hard to evaluate, but all of which together seem largely responsible for the general failure of the historian of recent times.

The written record itself, particularly when buttressed with systematic documentation, exercises a tyranny that has been commented on frequently by students of the nature of language but often overlooked by scholars in other fields. The mere fact that a previous writer has organized his material and phraseology in a certain way creates a predisposition in its favor. The later writer can no longer respond entirely freshly to the original data; he may agree with or object to what has been said, but in either case his orbit of thought has been made to include the existing interpretation. A. M. Schlesinger, Jr., and Joseph Dorfman, for example, may argue about the interpretation of "Jacksonian Democracy," but they both accept the traditional concept as central to the synthesis of the period. Charles A. Beard introduced new economic factors, but he employed them within the presidential synthesis. With its great quantities of traditional literature, and its lack of accepted conceptual tools for fresh theoretical analysis, history probably suffers more than any other discipline from the tyranny of written models.

In still another way, the inner compulsions of writing have ruled the historian. The traditional basis of history has been narrative. The "great" histories of the past such as Gibbon's *Decline and Fall*, Macaulay's *England*, or Motley's *Dutch Republic*, have been exciting "stories." Furthermore, since historians like to have their books published, and are not averse to sales, the popular dramatic frame of reference has been used whenever possible. This general approach is often valid when applied to the actions of a single individual, but neither narrative nor popular drama is usually suited to the analysis of mass phenomena. While drama will still be found in the conflict and resolution of forces or in group challenge and response, this is likely to be drama on a nonpopular abstract level. The historian has, of course, been aware of this dilemma, but, faced with the choice of retaining a false emphasis on colorful individuals and exciting events or of giving up the narrative style, he has clung as long as possible to storytelling and treasured most those source materials that permitted narration.[2]

By taking the written record that was easiest to use and most stirring from a sentimental or romantic standpoint, that is, the record of the federal government, the American historian prepared the way for one of the major misconceptions in American synthesis: the primary role of the central government in our historical development. While political scientists carefully pointed out that up to World War I, at least, most of the formal governmental contacts of the citizen were with his state, and historians dwelt on the importance of sectionalism and states' rights and joined with business leaders in emphasizing the laissez-faire doctrines that were a part of the nineteenth century kept government impotent and unimportant, the same men, influenced perhaps by nineteenth century European training, persisted in writing a national history revolving around presidential administrations and constitutional law. In the early stages of the economic development of each region, government and politics were in truth of great importance, but government was that of the state and the politics revolved around such material questions as loans or subsidies to banking and transportation, practices of incorporation, and the degree of government ownership thought desirable. In a later stage of economic growth the states led the way in regulating business and economic activity in the public interest. In neither stage, prior to 1900, was the federal government of major importance except for the initial disposal of public land, adjustment of the tariff, and widely separated changes in banking policy. The sporadic transference of ultimate power from state to federal government by decisions of the Supreme Court and acts of Congress from the 1880's on, at first freed certain citizens from state controls without imposing effective federal ones. Not until the second decade of the twentieth century was the theoretical shift in power implemented by much effective federal action.

The realistic history of nineteenth and even early twentieth century politics, therefore, whether viewed from the standpoint of political parties or of the community, should be built around the states. This, of course, imposes an enormous burden on the historian. The situations in from thirteen to forty-eight states must be synthesized. Furthermore, the older state histories are inadequate as a basis for such synthesis. Scholars must first write new monographs on business and government in the states, and new cultural interpretations of state politics.[3] Indeed, at present, a general American history has to be more a series of suggestions of what needs to be known than a comprehensive analysis.

A somewhat similar obstacle in the path of the historian who approaches the problem of synthesis is the extent to which our existing knowledge of the past is based on the writings of a small group of cultural leaders. He will tend to see events not only through the eyes of men of more than average vigor, property, education, and intelligence but also in the light of the metaphors of those who wrote the most enduring and readable prose. The circle of possible deception is completed when the statements of such abnormal citizens are read back as typical of their class, section, or society as a whole, and the resulting analysis is used to explain still other situations. The brilliant John Taylor of Caroline was not the typical Southern planter, Susan B. Anthony's problems were not those of the average woman, nor was Herbert Croly a good representative of many phases of the progressive movement.

A major reason for this reliance on leaders is that historical data on average people and everyday situations is hard to find. What was the typical rural community of 1840 from the statistical standpoint? What were normal ideas among its average citizens? Until there are answers to such questions, generalizations regarding the role of ideas in social change must rest on tenuous deductions.[4] Both quantitative and typical studies are sadly lacking. Some of these data can be assembled from better use of published and manuscript census reports, others will have to be examined by sampling methods, governed by proper statistical controls. The normal ideas of the average citizen in any time and place will have to be assembled from many indirect sources, such as the speeches of astute local politicians who, knowing what their constituents wanted to hear, mirrored public prejudices; the blurbs of discerning advertisers who sought in local papers to cater to public taste; and the letters of businessmen discussing public reactions that vitally concerned the future of their trade. Such materials are relatively hard to find and to use, but there are many indications of their widespread existence.[5]

Research in such sources immediately brings the scholar to a level of social relations deeper than that of conventional historic events, and exposes another major reason for the persistence of the presidential synthesis. As long as history consists of a series of important unique acts, thought to symbolize or cause change in society, a narrative account based on national happenings has a certain logic. But once the historian penetrates to the level of the social conditioning factors that produce people capable of such acts and tries to find the probability of the occurrence of any type of event, the acts themselves become a surface manifestation of more fundamental forces. While events are an indispensable part of the data of history, and even chance events, granting there are such, may have strong repercussions on their environment, the social science approach focuses attention on the aspects of the event that reveal the major drives of the culture rather than those that appear to be most colorful or unique. The latter elements, by definition not being representative of the general culture pattern, will presumably have only a limited effect or significance. Southern secession, for example, had its roots in cultural factors underlying such events as the tariffs, the acts of abolitionists, or territorial laws that seemed to produce the friction. These events are chiefly useful as clues to the nature of the basic differences between the sections. Similarly the American people in the early 1930's, facing a new cultural situation, displayed qualities of resignation not easily explicable on the basis of either the traditional or immediate events of their past.

Historical change on this level of basic social conditioning is, to be sure, a difficult, and, in the present stage of social science knowledge, a highly speculative study. Furthermore, the large quantities of material to be examined and the various types of special knowledge required often make group, rather than individual, research essential. The generally individualistic work habits of the historian, therefore, suggest another reason for the failure of historical scholarship in this area. But the topography of this field has been charted sufficiently to allow even individual historians to make rewarding sorties into its intricate terrain.[6]

In the space of an article one can suggest only a few of the many types of research that will help build a social science synthesis. As a beginning, it should be possible with patience and ingenuity to assemble the large number of career lines of different types of social leaders, essential for a picture of who succeeded in the society and how. Beside the pattern of how men succeeded in fact, should be further study, from qualitative sources such as private correspondence of the alternative goals that influenced men's expectations.[7] How did their "level of expectation" from material or intellectual standpoints vary? What was the true "American dream"? Such considerations would lead not only to a higher level of generalization in our social history writing but to possible scientific comparisons between American and other cultures.

A more difficult excursion into the field of basic historical factors is the tracing of the changing character of family relations including both the relationships within the family circle and the aims and aspirations of the members of the family in their real and imaginary contacts with the outside world. Whether one uses a striking term like Kardiner and Linton's "basic personality" [8] or some time-honored word like "background" to cover the effects of familial conditioning, few scholars will deny the fundamental importance of this factor in shaping the course of civilization.[9] But the investigation of the precise reaction to change is difficult, calling for psychological and sociological knowledge seldom possessed by the historian, and hence the family does not appear as a factor on the level of historical events.[10] An additional deterrent to historical analysis is that there are many "American families" at any given period. The variation in conditioning between the family of a back-country mountaineer and a rural professional man, or a city slum dweller and a Fifth Avenue millionaire, may easily be greater than the variation between the Maori family and the Maricopa.[11] As in current studies in cultural anthropology, such as *Plainville, U.S.A.*, or the "Yankee City Series," half a dozen different types of families based on income and occupational levels must be studied.[12] The upper-class groups offer an abundance of data in the form of memoirs, letters, and contemporary comments;[13] the poorer groups, particularly before 1890, offer only a challenge to the investigator. But the scholar striving to check theories and hypotheses regarding the family against historical data, and the one not so motivated should essay the task, will doubtless find many values that have been concealed from the "uneducated" eyes of the conventional historian. Perhaps some day it will be possible to guess wisely at the degree to which group aggressions, political radicalism, or instability in mass reactions were due to the stresses and strains of a family conditioning that became unsuited in varying degrees to the changes in surrounding society.

Looking at the situation more broadly, the new psychological problems of Western civilization by 1900 can be seen as the result of contrary types of conditioning: family and school conditioning in youth, based either here or abroad, on mores and folkways largely inherited from a preindustrial society; in maturity, conditioning in urban offices and factories, based on new mores and folkways that were evolving from the needs of business; and almost from birth to death, conditioning by pulpit, press, or other media of communication, based on a heterogeneous mixture of traditional and pragmatic doctrines.[14]

Shifting attention on this fundamental level from psychology to the pace of urban industrialism, the chief external pressure that upset existing family patterns, one enters a field where historians have done considerably more work but have in general subordinated their findings to the events of the presidential synthesis, and have failed, because of their disinterest in theory, to deal with many of the problems basic to urban sociology. Even A. M. Schlesinger, Sr., who did much to start urban study among historians and whose general synthesis in the latter half of *Land of the Free* is one of the best, keeps the city in a relatively subordinate position.[15] Special sociological areas of first-rate importance, such as urban demography and its social consequences, are not properly considered in our general histories. The whole argument on this score might be summed up by saying that we have many "social" accounts of American historical data but few sociological interpretations.

In all this confusing historic picture of shifting ideas, folkways, and mores, of new family relationships and of growing urban problems, the massive physical force producing change has been industrialism. Yet, judging from the presidential synthesis, the obvious fact that it was industrialism that moved us from the world of George Washington to that of the present day apparently needs still more emphasis. The spearhead of the multiple pressures of industrialization has been business, and businessmen have been of necessity the human agents who transmitted to society the physical changes born of science and industrial technology. The institutions of business, therefore, became the central mechanisms in shaping a new society and imposing industrial customs upon it.

Before mid-century, the sensitive New England intellectuals were well aware of the change. "In America, out of doors, all seems a market," Emerson complained in 1844.

> . . . I speak of those organs which can be presumed to speak in a popular sense. They recommend conventional virtues, whatever will earn and preserve property; always the capitalist; the college, the church, the hospital, the theatre, the hotel, the road, the ship of the capitalist—whatever goes to secure, adorn, enlarge these, is good, whatever jeopardizes any of these is damnable.[16]

From 1840 to 1860 the new impact of business and its urbanism upon American culture was perhaps greater relatively than in any other equal period, yet such forces appear only in the form of a few isolated phenomena in the presidential synthesis of the pre-Civil War era.

In the post-Civil War years the continuing cultural pressures of business, on which the Civil War had relatively little effect, are better recognized by our general historians. But a new difficulty now appears. Just as in the study of public opinion, the family, or urbanism, only the spectacular or exotic has been able to force its way into the traditional synthesis.[17] Our textbooks, for example, tell much of the resistance of certain farm groups to elevator and railroad practices but little of the growing force of business folkways and mores in the rural community.[18]

In this case the approach to a realistically balanced synthesis will be much easier than in those previously discussed. Business records of all types are becoming available in increasing quantities.[19] Monographic literature is readily accumulating.[20] The general historian surveying this field, however, will find that while existing studies, in economics as well as in history, give much of the internal picture of the workings of business, the connections between business and society are not elaborated.[21] The business leader or entrepreneur, for example, was the arbiter not only of change within his company but also, to a large extent, of change in his community.[22] Since his money, and hence his approbation, was generally necessary for community welfare and improvement, he sat on the boards of the educational, charitable, political, and business institutions that dominated social habits and set social goals.[23] And necessarily, he carried into these other fields the habits formed by the needs of survival in business. He strove to make education, charity, politics, and social life "businesslike." Generations of historians have analyzed the thought of Clay, Webster, and Calhoun to extract every last vestige of social meaning, while Nathan Appleton, John Murray Forbes, and a host of other important business figures of the same period, awaiting their first social interpreters, do not appear in the presidential synthesis.

The modern corporation, a new social instrumentality developed primarily by business leaders, must also be given a much larger place in a social science synthesis. Here the problem is a very difficult one, challenging the scholar not so much from the standpoint of data or materials of research as from that of theory. The role of the corporation in modern society has never been adequately thought through by legal, social, or economic theorists. Noncorporeal, but quite real, the corporation, of both the profit and nonprofit variety, has established substates and subcommunities within our political and geographical divisions.[24] It has created both highly responsible and highly irresponsible entities with which all citizens are forced to deal, and under the jurisdiction of which most citizens spend a large part of their lives. The resultant problems of historical interpretation are too complex to discuss here and have been in fact too complex for the wisdom of modern society, but complexity and difficulty are not valid excuses for historial neglect.

In summary, at the center of any social science synthesis, determining its topical and chronological divisions, should be the changes, whether material or psychological, that have most affected, or threatened most to affect, such human conditioning factors as family life, physical living conditions, choice of occupations, sources of prestige, and social beliefs. While the historical analysis itself must, in our present stage of psychological knowledge, be concerned with concrete physical, political, or social changes or events, these should be assigned place and importance on the basis of their estimated relation to underlying social forces. The precise social effect of the rapid rise of the corporation from 1850 to 1873, for example, cannot be measured, but the social scientist is reasonably sure that it is of more importance than the presidential aspirations of Horatio Seymour.

For the period since the middle of the nineteenth century, the source material exists to make and ultimately to amplify a synthesis based on changes in major social forces.[25] While my personal bias leads me to believe what business and economic changes should be recognized as the most dynamic elements, further investigation may reveal alterations in family life or in social beliefs not stemming directly from business sources as more powerfully operative. But as long as the historian will equip himself with the knowledge necessary to probe these deeper levels, and approach the problems with the tools of theory and hypothesis, all social scientists must applaud the results as steps in the direction of historical realism.

Such a backbone of synthesis would not only sweep away the presidential structure but demolish most of the other familiar landmarks as well. War studied as a social institution would preserve its importance, but war as an arbitrary milestone for historical periodization would probably disappear. The Civil War, for example, that great divide of American historiography, viewed in the light of these long-run social criteria, shrinks in magnitude. Even in the Deep South, the dramatic change in race and property relations brought on by the war will lose some of its importance when measured against a deeper background of the gradual social changes coming from the increase in middle-class farmers and industrial workers.[26] In any case, for nations as a whole, basic social change seems to come less cataclysmically than is indicated by wars or revolutions. Periodization should be recognized as wholly arbitrary and dependent upon the central focus of the synthesis employed. From the business and economic standpoints, for example, 1850 and 1885 are available points for periodization, the one symbolically marking the beginning of the rapid opening of a national industrial market, the latter roughly coinciding with the rise of a number of large semimonopolistic business units and the beginning of federal regulation; but if the family or urbanism is made the central phenomenon other dates might be selected.

For those historians who will mourn the passing of the historiographic day of Jeffersonian and Jacksonian Democracy, the Era of Good Feeling, the Irrepressible Conflict, the Tragic Era, the Square Deal, the New Freedom, and the New Deal, there is the poor consolation that time must, in any case, doom the ancient subdivisions. When the United States is even two hundred years old, it will no longer be possible to take up each presidential administration. Broader and less detailed syntheses will be demanded by the exigencies of space and time, and it will be up to the historian to choose whether he will avail himself of the help offered by the social sciences or attempt an intuitive resynthesis of the past presented by Spengler or Toynbee.

Notes

1. Guy Stanton Ford pointed out the need for such a synthesis over a decade ago in "Some Suggestions to American Historians," *American Historical Review*, XLIII (January, 1938), 267–268. High school textbooks, while reflecting the social scientific approach more than college, have not attempted any radical resynthesis. Henry B. Parkes, *The American Experience* (New York: 1947), while presenting an interpretation based on conflicting social ideologies, rather than the presidential synthesis, does not, in general, employ social science concepts or methods. Thomas C. Cochran and William Miller's *Age of Enterprise* (New York: 1942) offers a general synthesis, based on the social sciences, but puts specific emphasis on the role of business. See also Caroline F. Ware, ed., *The Cultural Approach to History* (New York: 1940).

2. The time and energy that have been lavished on collecting and publishing even relatively unimportant letters of famous statesmen compared with that expended in trying to learn something of the communities in which they lived strikingly indicates the historians' leanings.

3. The Committee on Research in Economic History, of the Social Science Research Council, has sponsored studies of government in relation to economic life in the pre-Civil War period for four sample states. Oscar and Mary F. Handlin, *Commonwealth: Massachusetts, 1774–1861* (New York: 1947); and Louis Hartz, *Economic Policy and Democratic Thought: Pennsylvania, 1776–1860* (Cambridge, Mass.: 1948), are the only ones that have been published.

4. See Theodore C. Blegen, *Grass Roots History* (Minneapolis: 1947).

5. See Merle E. Curti, *The Roots of American Loyalty* (New York: 1946), Lewis E. Atherton, *The Pioneer Merchant in Mid-America* (Columbia, Mo.: 1939), Thomas D. Clark, *Pills, Petticoats and Plows: The Southern Country Store* (Indianapolis: 1944), and Everett Dick, *The Dixie Frontier: A Social History of the Southern Frontier from the First Transmontane Beginnings to Civil War* (New York: 1948), for use of such material.

6. For a number of suggestive articles, see *Conflicts of Power in Modern Culture*, a symposium edited by Lyman Bryson, Louis Finkelstein and R. M. MacIver (New York: 1947). Abram Kardiner with the collaboration of Ralph Linton, Cora Du Bois, and James West (pseud.), *The Psychological Frontiers of Society* (New York: 1945), and Talcott Par-

sons, *The Structure of Social Action* (New York: 1937), are examples of the type of social-psychological and sociological literature that merits the attention of all historians.

7. See Frank W. Taussig and C. J. Joslyn, *American Business Leaders: A Study in Social Origins and Social Stratification* (New York: 1932). William Miller has assembled data on 350 business and political leaders of the decade 1900 to 1910. I have similar material for some 75 railroad executives of the period 1850 to 1890.

8. Kardiner *et al.,* p. viii.

9. See, for example, Talcott Parsons, "Certain Primary Sources and Patterns of Aggression in the Social Structure of the Western World," *Conflicts of Power in Modern Culture,* pp. 29–48.

10. Arthur W. Calhoun in his *Social History of the American Family, from Colonial Times to the Present* (3 vols., Cleveland: 1917–1919), assembled a large mass of random material that has been rather uncritically drawn upon by historians. Sociologists studying the dynamics of the family have been more interested in the inner psychological tensions than in tracing historically the changing external pressures that altered the inner patterns. See, for example, Willard Waller, *The Family: A Dynamic Interpretation* (New York: 1938).

11. The Maricopa are Southern Arizona Indians, the Maori are Polynesians.

12. James West (pseud.), *Plainville, U.S.A.* (New York: 1945); W. L. Warner, ed., "Yankee City Series," I–IV (New Haven: 1941–1947).

13. By the biographer or historian these materials have been used chiefly to enrich and support narrative, but to the cultural anthropologist or psychologist they present clues to social and psychological patterns. Social scientists have made as little use of these historical materials as historians have of the techniques necessary to analyze them.

14. See Thurman Arnold, *The Folklore of Capitalism* (New Haven: 1937).

15. Homer C. Hockett and Arthur M. Schlesinger, *Land of the Free* (New York: 1944).

16. Ralph W. Emerson, *English Traits, Representative Men, and Other Essays* (New York: 1908), pp. 370, 371.

17. See Thomas C. Cochran, "A Plan for the Study of Business Thinking," *Political Science Quarterly,* LXII (March 1947), 82–90.

18. See again, *Plainville, U.S.A.*; and also the extensive bibliography of older sociological studies of the rural community in Walter A. Terpenning, *Village and Open-Country Neighborhoods* (New York: 1931). Recent analyses such as Paul H. Landis, *Rural Life in Process* (New York: 1940), are still weak in tracing the gradual infiltration of business mores and folkways in the rural community.

19. A National Business Records Management Center has been organized by a committee of the Social Science Research Council.

20. See "Harvard Studies in Business History," N. S. B. Gras, ed. (Cambridge: 1931); and New York University Business History Series," Thomas C. Cochran, ed. (New York: 1948).

21. See such studies of the current situation as Robert A. Gordon, *Business Leadership in the Large Corporation* (Washington: 1945); and Peter F. Drucker, *Concept of the Corporation* (New York: 1946). N. S. B. Gras, *Business and Capitalism* (New York: 1939) is a historical study of business organizations. Some studies, such as Carl F. Tausch, *Professional*

and Business Ethics (New York: 1926), and Max Radin, The Manners and Morals of Business (Indianapolis: 1939), deal with limited aspects of the relations of business to society.

22. See Arthur H. Cole, "An Approach to the Study of Entrepreneurship," Journal of Economic History, VI, Supp. (1946), 1–15; Joseph A. Schumpeter, "The Creative Response in Economic History," Journal of Economic History, VII (November 1947), 149–159, for general discussion of the socioeconomic role of the business leader; and Thomas C. Cochran, "The Social History of the Corporation in the United States," in Ware, The Cultural Approach to History, pp. 168–181, for discussion and bibliography on social aspects of business.

23. See, for example, H. P. Beck, Men Who Control Our Universities (New York: 1947); and Merle E. Curti, The Social Ideas of American Educators (New York: 1935) pp. 210–232.

24. For discussion of the subcommunity or subgovernmental aspects of corporations, see A. M. Schlesinger, "Biography of a Nation of Joiners," American Historical Review, L (October 1944), 1–25; Guy Stanton Ford, On and Off the Campus (Minneapolis: 1938), pp. 149–151; and Stuart A. Daggett, Chapters on the History of the Southern Pacific (New York: 1922). For some suggestions of needed studies, see Charles A. Beard, "Corporations and Natural Rights," Virginia Quarterly, XII (July 1936), 345 ff.

25. See, for example, the forthcoming handbook of historical statistics prepared by the United States Census Bureau in cooperation with a committee of the Social Science Research Council.

26. See Herbert Weaver, Mississippi Farmers, 1850–1860 (Nashville, Tenn.: 1945); and other studies directed by Frank Owsley at Vanderbilt University.

Paul F. Lazarsfeld

THE HISTORIAN AND THE POLLSTER

During the past few decades public opinion agencies have built up rather reliable techniques for describing attitudes of people on public affairs. One would think that historians would welcome this way of obtaining information which in previous periods was available only indirectly, if at all. However, there is little collaboration between historians and "pollsters." [1] The difficulty seems to be the problem of significance; pollsters ask questions meant to furnish headlines in the newspapers instead of using their techniques for the collection of data which have lasting value. As a result, the historian does not pay attention to their work; he does not give them the benefit of a broader view which would lead to the selection of more significant topics. Consequently, a vicious circle sets in which keeps separate two professions which could cooperate to mutual benefit. Here I will try to remedy the situation by inquiring into the various ways in which the historian and the pollster could aid the future historian to interpret our times.

It might be instructive to begin with an example in which a famous historian was confronted with this exact problem of explaining the past to his contemporaries.

Paul F. Lazarsfeld is Quetelet Professor of Social Science at Columbia University. He is the author of *Mathematical Thinking in the Social Sciences* and co-author of *The People's Choice: How the Voter Makes Up His Mind in a Presidential Campaign*.

Reprinted from Mirra Komarovsky, ed., *Common Frontiers of the Social Sciences* (Glencoe, Ill.: The Free Press, 1957), pp. 242–262, by permission of the author and the publisher. © 1957 by The Free Press, a Corporation.

In the fifteenth century Machiavelli wrote what is probably one of the first examples of modern and careful analysis of political behavior. And yet, for several centuries afterward, "Machiavellian" stood for everything evil in public affairs. At the beginning of the nineteenth century a reaction set in, and in 1837, the English historian and statesman, Macaulay, wrote an essay to set the matter straight. He wanted to explain why Machiavelli was so misunderstood. His answer was that *The Prince* was written at a time and in a social setting where people had a very different way of looking at things. His argument runs about as follows: At the end of the Middle Ages the Italian cities had developed a middle class culture of artisans and merchants, while the countries north of the Alps, like England, France, and Germany, were still in a barbarous state. In the north, courage was the main means of survival; courage to withstand the hardships of life and courage to repel hostile hordes which were incessantly threatening each other with war. In the Italian cities, ingenuity was the most cherished ability; ingenuity in improving the protective value of the community, and ingenuity in meeting the competition of their fellow citizens in an essentially democratic society. "Hence while courage was a point of honor in other countries ingenuity became the point of honor in Italy." The pertinence of this passage to Macaulay's main topic is obvious. He feels that a great thinker living in what we today would call "an ingenuity culture" was judged by people who lived and are still living in the aftermath of a "courage culture."

From our point of view it is important to see what evidence Macaulay tried to adduce for his thesis. The great English historian struggles hard to make his point clear and convincing to his reader. First of all he compares an English and an Italian hero. Henry V was admired by the English because he won a great battle, in spite of his personal crudeness and cruelty. Francis Sforza was admired by the Italians because he was a successful statesman, in spite of his personal treachery and faithlessness.

And still Macaulay is not yet quite sure that the reader has seen the matter clearly. He finally hits upon what seems to him a useful literary device, and what today we can consider probably the first projective test recorded in the literature. He writes:

We have illustrated our meaning by an instance taken from history. We will select another from fiction. Othello murders his wife; he gives orders for the murder of his lieutenant; he ends by murdering himself. *Yet he never loses the esteem and affection of Northern readers.* His intrepid and ardent spirit redeems everything. The unsuspecting confidence with which he listens to his adviser, the agony with which he shrinks from the thought of shame, the tempest of passion with which he commits his crimes, and the haughty fearlessness with which he avows them, give an extraordinary interest to his character. Iago, on the contrary, is the object of universal loathing. . . . *Now we suspect that an Italian audience in the fifteenth century would have felt very differently.* Othello would have inspired nothing but detestation and contempt. The folly with which he trusts the friendly professions of a man whose promotion he had obstructed, the credulity with which he takes unsupported assertions, and trivial circumstances, for unanswerable proofs, the violence with which he silences the exculpation till the exculpation can only aggravate his misery, would have excited the abhorrence and disgust of the spectators. The conduct of Iago they would assuredly have condemned; but they would have condemned it as we condemn that of his victim. Something of interest and respect would have mingled with their disapprobation. The readiness of the traitor's wit, the clearness of his judgment, the skill with which he penetrates the dispositions of others and conceals his own, would have ensured to him a certain portion of their esteem.

It is clear what Macaulay is striving for. He wishes someone had conducted attitude studies in Florence and in London of the fifteenth century. Let us suppose that a polling agency existed at the time, and was hired by Macaulay to test his hypothesis. In a somewhat facetious way, we can imagine how they might have proceeded. The Othello story could have been written up in one or two paragraphs, without giving either Othello or Iago any advantage. Pretests could have been conducted to make sure that the wording was quite unbiased. (Perhaps they might have concealed the fact that Othello was a Negro because that might bias some respondents.) The crucial question would have been: How many Florentines and Londoners, respectively, approve of Iago, how many of Othello, and how many say "don't know"? Nothing less, but hardly much more, would have been needed to provide empirical evidence for Macaulay's brilliant conjecture.

Few historians will make such elaborate efforts to document their statements about public attitudes. It is much more likely that we shall find statements which read like a Gallup release, except, of course, that the tables are missing. See, for instance, the following account from Merle Curti's, *The Thrust of the Civil War into Intellectual Life.*

A growing number of men and women in both sections, distrustful of their leaders, sympathetic with the enemy, or merely war-weary, preferred compromise or even defeat to the continuation of the struggle. The fact of war affected the thinking not only of these dissidents but of the great majority of people who accepted it as inevitable and hoped that good would come from it.

Here are all the ingredients of a statement on the distribution of attitudes. We find quantitative statements like "a growing number" or "the great majority of people." There are suggestions for comparisons between men and women and between different sections of the country. The passage which we have quoted even implies certain cross-tabulations between attitudes toward the war and attitudes toward other issues of the day.

No wonder, then, that the historians of a later period for which polls were already available would eagerly incorporate them into their writings. Dixon Wecter writes about *The Age of the Great Depression.* At one point he discusses the growing acceptance of birth control. To document this trend, he first uses the traditional, indirect methods of the historian, trying to derive attitudes from their manifestations. He points to the change in terms from "race suicide" to "birth control" and finally to "planned parenthood." Then he goes at his topic more directly.

A poll among Farm and Fireside readers early in the Depression showed two to one for giving medical advice on planned parenthood, and during the thirties the Sears, Roebuck catalogue began to list contraceptive wares. A straw vote of subscribers by the Protestant Churchman in January, 1935, revealed almost unanimous approval for birth control, while in the next year, among all sorts of conditions, a Gallup poll agreed with a Fortune survey in finding two out of three favorable. This majority, moreover, rose steadily in later years, with women outranking men in the warmth of their indorsement.

We could cite other similar examples to show further the place of attitude and opinion research in historical studies; but it might suffice instead to point out that some of the most enduring works of historiography, such as Taylor's *The Medieval Mind* and Weber's *The Protestant Ethic*, are those which dealt with the attitudes, value systems, and prevailing beliefs of the period. By the historian's own testimony, there is a place for attitude and opinion research in their field, but this still leaves open the question of what kind of polling data the future historian will need. How can we fit at least some of our findings into the stream of intellectual work as it extends into the future?

We can expect guidance from three directions. For one, we can study historical writings; second, we can turn to certain works on the contemporary scene; finally, we can scrutinize existing speculations on the probable course of the future. It should be helpful to illustrate briefly each of these points.

The Pollster Reads a Book

It would be worthwhile for a scholar to review typical historical texts from our point of view. Where do competent writers show, either explicitly or implicitly, the need for attitude material of the kind a sampling survey can furnish? Short of a careful scrutiny we cannot know the prevailing modes of analysis. Furthermore, the specific need for opinion data will vary according to the topic under investigation. But a few expectations are rather obvious.

In at least three areas the historian will be confronted with the need for opinion data. The most obvious, of course, is when "prevailing values" are themselves the object of his study. There are a number of classical investigations of major changes in the climate of opinion such as the transition from medieval traditionalism to the individualistic thinking connected with the Protestant Reformation. During the first half of the nineteenth century a counter-trend started, stressing public responsibility for individual welfare. This trend could be observed in the United States as well as in other countries. Curti, for instance, points out that, before the Civil War, there was considerable resistance against accepting tax supported public schools.

Men of power and substance frequently argued that education had been, and properly so, a family matter. . . . What could be more potent than the certainty that if free schools were granted, the concession would not end short of socialism itself? To provide free schooling for the less well-to-do would result in the loss of their self-respect and initiative.

Today, hardly anyone feels this way. But how did this shift of public opinion come about? Among which groups did it start and how did it spread? How long did it take for the initial resistance to disappear? What external events precipitated or retarded the development?

Such knowledge would be of considerable practical importance today. If we substituted the words "housing" for "schooling" in the preceding quotation, we would describe the way in which many people feel about public housing projects. It is probable that this sentiment is now in the process of historical change. So far as public health insurance is concerned, the resistance is still very great. More detailed knowledge of such developments in the past would help us to predict better what turn our contemporary problems are likely to take. If we know better the patterns of past change, we can perhaps extract from them some recurrent paths of development. Therefore, incidentally, we can expect that those historians who look at history as one sector of a general social science will be most likely to welcome attitude data.

This leads to a second area in which the historian would undoubtedly need public opinion data. Wherever a new type of institution or a major legislative development was investigated, he would be greatly helped by data on the interaction between the diffusion of attitudes and the sequence of social actions. One of the most thoroughly investigated phenomena of this kind is the turn from laissez-faire to social legislation, which took place in England during the second half of the nineteenth century. Karl Polanyi has pointed out that the free market system never really worked well in any event. He summarizes Dicey's famous investigation of *Law and Public Opinion in England* in the following way:

Dicey made it his task to inquire into the origins of the "anti-laissez-faire" or, as he called it, the "collectivist" trend in English public opinion, the existence of which was manifest since the late 1860's. He was surprised to find that no evidence of the existence of such a trend could be traced save the acts of legislation themselves. More exactly, no evidence of a "collectivist trend" in public opinion prior to the laws which appeared to represent such a trend could be found.

Here is a challenging suggestion that major legislative events may not be preceded, but rather followed, by changes in public opinion. Before one could accept such a conclusion one would certainly want to know how safe it is to make inferences of this kind merely by examining newspapers, pamphlets and recorded speeches. Could it not be the case that there was an undercurrent of public opinion in the direction of social legislation which did not find expression in the kind of material available to the historian, but which would have been caught by systematic public opinion research at the time?

A third area of overlap between the historian and the pollster ought to be those writings in which specific events are to be explained. There is virtually no American historian, for example, who has not tried at one time or another to explain the outcome of some presidential election. Robert Bower has collected a whole folklore of stories which have arisen in connection with elections of major importance, such as those of 1840, 1882, and 1896. He analyzes these explanations of election outcomes and shows that all of them imply the type of knowledge about issues and personalities of the day which might have been obtained through polls. Even with poll data it is not easy to arrive at safe conclusions. This is known by everyone who followed the efforts to understand Truman's election in 1948. Bower's *Opinion Research and Historical Interpretation of Elections* shows how much more tenuous the conjectures are for previous periods.

Historians themselves are, of course, aware of this task. A group of medievalists started, in their professional journal, *Speculum*, to appraise the status of their work. The first article, by J. L. LaMonte, was called "Some Problems in Crusading Historiography." It was of interest to read there that "the decline of the crusading ideal in spite of papal propaganda is a little known subject." One is reminded of the studies of returning veterans reported in *The American Soldier* when the author deplores how little is known about "the social effects of the change in material status of such crusaders as returned after considerably bettering their position in the East."

In such a reappraisal of historical writings, we should be sensitive to the effect which opinion surveys have had in changing the notion of a "fact." There was a time when only political documents found in archives were considered appropriate evidence for the historian. That made him focus on political events; everything else was interpretation. Then the "new history" centered attention on data such as economic and social statistics. This enlarged considerably the area of what were considered facts. Still, sentiments and attitudes remained a matter of interpretation. Now, however, they too have become facts. The result of a public opinion poll is as much a fact as the content of a political document or the crop and price statistics of a certain region.

In turn, the term "attitude and opinion research" should not be taken too narrowly. Let us remember that we have always known and discussed among ourselves that much more than simple "yes-no" questions belongs in our equipment. In connection with the historian's problem, two techniques in particular will certainly need considerable refinement on our part. One derives from the problem of saliency. The fact that a respondent answers a question which we put to him still does not tell us whether he would have asked himself this question or whether the matter is of particular concern to him. The historian will certainly want to know what issues were in the foreground of attention at various times and in various sectors of the population. Published polling material does not contain enough of such information; as a matter of fact, considerable methodological progress on this point is still needed. The diffusion of opinion in time and social space is a second problem which we do not yet handle with enough emphasis or enough technical skill. In many more of our surveys we should find out where people get their ideas and how they pass them on. All of this has thus far been a matter of conjecture for the historian; we are supposed to turn it into an enlarged array of "facts." Thus the study of historical writings will not only be a source of significant topics; it could also be a spur for methodological improvements.

Signs of the Times

A second source of ideas, interesting hypotheses and leads for significant field surveys may be found in many efforts to understand the meaning of what is going on around us right now. It has been said that each generation must rewrite history, because hitherto unconsidered aspects of the past become interesting in the light of the changing present. But there is certainly a limitation to this rule. If there is no data at all on certain aspects of the past, not much can be done, even under the impetus of a strong new curiosity. The pollster as a contemporary historian thus takes on considerable importance. What he considers worthy of a survey will, in later years, influence the range of possible historical inquiries.

Therefore, the question of where the pollster can get leads for significant investigations is an important one. Again, we cannot exhaust the possible choices, but a few clear avenues suggest themselves at the moment. There is, first, the critic of the contemporary scene. There are always social commentators who are especially sensitive to the shortcomings of our times; it is not unlikely that they hit on topics about which the future historian will want to know more. Let us quote passages which are characteristic of the type of statement we have in mind.

Much too early do young people get excited and tense, much too early are they drawn away by the accelerated pace of the times. People admire wealth and velocity. Everybody strives for them. . . . Here they compete, here they surpass each other, with the result that they persevere in mediocrity. And this is the result of the general trend of the contemporary world toward an average civilization, common to all.

We can visualize translating this social comment into a research program. It would not be too difficult to develop an index of competitiveness, and to study at what age individuals exhibit a marked increase in their average scores. But that would not be enough. We are also called upon to follow the consequences of such developments for broader areas of society; for "not the ex-

ternal and physical alone is now managed by machinery, but the
internal and spiritual also. . . ."

Has any man, or any society of men, a truth to speak, a piece of spiritual work to do, they can nowise proceed at once and with the mere
natural organs, but must first call a public meeting, appoint committees,
issue prospectuses, eat a public dinner; in a word, construct or borrow
machinery, wherewith to speak it and do it. Without machinery they
were hopeless, helpless. . . .

Here a more sociological type of data is required; number and
types of meetings, attendance figures, etc. Most of all we will
want to study the statistical interrelationship between attitudes
and kinds of social participation in intellectual enterprises.

Most interesting about these quotations, however, are their
dates and their sources. The first is from a letter which Goethe
wrote in 1825. The second is a characteristic portion of an essay
written by Carlyle in 1830. Here are two leading minds in two
different countries voicing the same apprehension in terms which
might well be used today. Undoubtedly experts could provide us
with similar statements for any other century, for we are always
likely to find evidence of a feeling that matters were very
different sometime ago. There are certain standbys which recur
in many discussions: the tensions of daily living have become so
much worse; people are now more apathetic politically than they
were previously; the cultural taste of the country has been de-
praved. We shall not be able to decide the truth of such issues in
retrospect, but we can at least lay the ground for more responsible
discussion of the problem in the future.

The social critic will focus our attention primarily on certain
contents and subject matters which are important for our times.
There is another group of analysts who are more concerned with
the kinds of dimensions which are useful in describing the social
scene. They are likely to be interested mainly in comparisons between various countries, for instance, or between social groups. It
should never be forgotten how difficult it is to make the social
scene "visible." When we deal with nature, many objects, like
trees or stones or animals, force themselves on us visually. Social
entities are much more the product of creative intelligence. The

notion of a clique, for instance, or of a reference group, the inner gallery for which so many of us play the drama of our lives, or the distinction between an introverted and an extroverted personality are real conceptual inventions. In social observations we are often in the position of a bird which flies across the sky with a flock of other birds. For the external observer, the flock has a clearly visible geometric shape; but does the bird within the flock even know about the shape of his "group"? By what social interrelations among the birds is the form of the group maintained?

When we translate these sketchy considerations into problems of survey research, we meet them in a familiar form. Every self-respecting pollster will report his findings nowadays "subclassified by age, sex, and socioeconomic status." We know from our findings that these are useful classifications. But are they the most significant ones? Wouldn't we be helped in the work of today, and wouldn't we help readers of the future if we were alert to additional variables according to which we might classify our samples and analyze our findings?

It is on such an issue that we can get guidance from writers who have tried to obtain the best possible view of the contemporary scene. Let us turn for a moment to the patron saint of modern public opinion research, James Bryce. He makes an effort at one point to compare the political scene in England and that prevailing in this country. To this end he distinguishes "three sets of persons, those who make opinion, those who receive and hold opinion, those who have no opinions at all." After elaborating on this distinction, he comes to the conclusion that the first group is somewhat larger in England than in the United States of 1870, while the proportion in the second group is very much larger on the American continent than in Britain. From this he draws a number of interesting conclusions. The "power of public opinion in the United States," for instance, seems to him related to the inordinately large ratio of opinion holders to opinion makers.

To find significant variables for political classifications continues to be a challenge for writers of this kind. It is quite possible that an index of political participation and interest might prove a useful instrument for a great variety of surveys, on a national as well as an international scale. As a matter of fact, some research organizations are reported to be working on the development of just such devices.

In the writings of contemporary social scientists, the pollster will find other classificatory suggestions which are worth pursuing. David Riesman, for instance, in 1950 published a book centered on the distinction between three types of social character. One is the tradition-directed type; the person who behaves as he thinks his social group expects him to, does not believe he should change anything in his environment, and feels shame if he violates any of the rules under which he lives. The second is the inner-directed type; the person who is guided by strong moral standards, has a kind of psychological gyroscope which controls his conduct, and who feels guilt if he does something which is not right. Finally, there is the other-directed type; the backslapper who wants to get along with everyone, who has few convictions of his own, and who feels general anxiety if he is not successful in receiving all the signals which he tries to catch on his psychological radar system. In chapter after chapter of *The Lonely Crowd* Riesman tries to spell out the political correlates of these three types. He is especially interested in the other-directed type, which he considers characteristic of modern American life. Riesman discovers in him a dangerous kind of political apathy. He wants to get all the inside dope on politics just as on baseball, but he has lost all belief that he, individually, has any influence and therefore refrains from giving public affairs any serious thought or any active devotion. A careful reading of Riesman's chapters on politics will show how much empirical research could and should be geared in with such speculations.

Finally, the literature of the so-called cultural anthropologists belongs here. They are not only concerned with singling out significant topics or finding variables which would be useful to make more clearly visible the main character of the contemporary scene. They also want to uncover the mechanisms by which the scene develops. Distinguished equally by brilliance and by irresponsibility of factual evidence, they challenge the pollster to try to bring about effective cooperation. But the challenge is worth accepting, for from an interaction between the two groups could develop really new insights into human affairs. No newspaper

reader can be unaware of the writings on "national character."
The main thesis is that each society and each national subgroup
develops its own way of looking at the world, and its own way of
giving satisfaction to basic needs. It is the function of the family
to raise children in such a way that they "want to act in the way
they have to act as members of the society or as a special class
within it." Like a group of expert ball players giving a public
exhibition, the anthropologists toss their variations on the basic
theme from one to the other. Margaret Mead describes in great
detail the small American family with its lack of tradition and its
uncertain goals in a quickly changing world:

. . . while the child is learning that his whole place in the world, his
name, his right to the respect of other children—everything—depends
upon his parents . . . he also learns that his own acceptance by these
parents, who are his only support, is conditional upon his achievements,
upon the way in which he shows up against other children and against
their idea of other children.

Gorer picks it up from Mead. He agrees with her that there is a
strong element of uncertainty in the emotional life of the American family. The parents do not quite know what is right and
therefore can love their children only if they are successful in
their own peer group, the school class or the gang. But Gorer
does not think that ambition or success drive develops in children
as a result; he has a different notion:

The presence, the attention, the admiration of other people thus becomes for Americans a necessary component to their self-esteem, demanded with a feeling of far greater psychological urgency than is
usual in other countries. . . . The most satisfying form of this assurance is not given by direct flattery or commendation (this by itself is
suspect as a device to exploit the other) but by love.

The two writers, if confronted with their statements, would
probably say that there is a strong relation between ambition and
the desire to be loved. Yet how do they know that these desires
are more frequent or more intense among Americans than among
other people? They give many examples from Rotary meetings
and from double dates in colleges which make their idea plausible.
We pollsters are accustomed to asking for a better definition of

terms and for more precise evidence; so we are inclined to criticize these anthropologists. But are we fully justified? Have they not seen here topics which are considerably more worthy of investigation than the rating of movie stars or even the attitudes of voters toward a local candidate?

Here are writers who have challenging ideas on the structure of our social relationships and their effect on attitudes and opinions. Does this not suggest that we have neglected the first link in this chain? To cite one specific example: in the writings of the social anthropologists, the authoritarian structure of the family plays a large role. Who among us, either in this country or abroad, has collected answers to questions like these: To what extent do young people make their own occupational choices and to what extent do their parents influence their decisions? In what countries and in what groups does a young suitor still ask the girl's parents for consent to marriage? How are conflicts between father and son resolved when they both want the car or both want to use the living room? Where do children still spend their holidays with their families, and where do they go off on their own? How much visiting of relatives is there, how frequent are family reunions, and so on? What would adolescents consider the main complaints as to the way they are treated by their parents? What activities are parents most eager to forbid in their young children and what principles are they most anxious to inculcate in their older ones?

Useful contributions along such lines could be made, especially by those among us who conduct international polls. But in this discussion we are not interested in the present for its own sake; we want to look at it from the point of view of tomorrow. What should we watch as the present slowly turns into the future?

Glancing into the Future

Scrutinizing writings on the past will give us an idea of the kinds of data which historians have missed prior to the appearance of the pollster on the scene. Studying the literature on present-day society will give us a chance to confront theoretical thinking with empirical data. A final, and probably the most important, possibility develops when we make efforts to guess what the future will want to know about today. Quite a number of political scientists feel that the best way to study the present is to see it as a transitional stage to future events. Harold Lasswell has emphasized the need of "developmental constructs."

In the practice of social science, . . . we are bound to be affected in some degree by our conceptions of future development. . . . What is the function of this picture for scientists? It is to stimulate the individual specialist to clarify for himself his expectations about the future, as a guide to the timing of scientific work.

We should form expectations of what major changes might come about within the next decades. It is in connection with these changing conditions that the historian will expect that we, today, have initiated a series of trend studies. This is undoubtedly the most difficult task. It not only requires of us pollsters that we translate more or less vague ideas into specific instruments of inquiry; there is so little thinking along this line that we shall even have to assume some responsibility for guessing what will be of importance a few decades hence. The best we can do in the present context is to give a few examples of the kind of effort which will be required.

There can be little doubt that the history of the next decades will be centered around the effects of the rapidly increasing industrialization characteristic of our times. Perhaps the reaction to contemporary mechanization will be found in strong religious movements. If this is the case, what will the future analyst, in retrospect, wish that we had ascertained today? An interesting lead for this is found in *The American Soldier*. The importance of this work lies in the fact that, for the first time, we really know something about the experiences and feelings of an important sector of the population. As far as religion goes, the following observation is reported. About three-fourths of the soldiers said that prayer was a source of strength in battle, but the minority who did not find this so had certain interesting characteristics: they experienced less fear, laid more stress on their relations with other soldiers, and seemed, in general, to be what modern psychologists would call better adjusted personalities.

Here, in one result, may lie the seeds of an important bifurcation. Increasing industrialization may lead to a compensatory dependence on religious beliefs. Or, it may create a new type of personality, differently adjusted to new social demands. We cannot tell in which direction the future will tend; as a matter of fact, we do not even know whether any really new developments will take place in the religious sphere; but general considerations and bits of research evidence seem to indicate that systematic work is called for.

At the same time that we try to answer these more general questions about the intensity of religious beliefs, we should analyze the specific character of religious movements as they develop. In this connection Julian Huxley has provided an impressive set of predictions. In his essay on "Religion as an Objective Problem," he distinguishes between the "old" religion and the "new." According to him, the old one developed as a result of fear and ignorance of the external physical environment. Modern science has given us enough insight into and control over the forces of nature so that religious beliefs as we have known them so far are likely to fade away slowly. Now we are faced with a new set of problems emerging from what he calls the "internal environment"; the disorganization of our economic and social life, war, poverty, and unemployment. New religious movements are likely to develop, centered less around the worship of a supernatural being than around the worship of a single solution for social evils.

The process, of course, has already begun. Many observers have commented on the religious elements in Russian communism—the fanaticism, the insistence on orthodoxy, the violent "theological" disputes, the "worship" of Lenin, the spirit of self-dedication, the persecutions, the common enthusiasm, the puritan element, the mass-emotions, the censorship.

The new religion is now in its most primitive forms, with Communism and Fascism as typical examples. But just as the old religion moved from simple paganism to a refined monotheism, so will the new religion outgrow its present crudeness.

Accordingly, we can prophesy that in the long run the nationalistic element in socialized religion will be subordinated or adjusted to the internationalist: that the persecution of minorities will give place to toleration; that the subtler intellectual and moral virtues will find a place and will gradually oust the cruder from their present pre-eminence in the religiously conceived social organism. We can also assert with fair assurance that this process of improvement will be a slow one, and accompanied by much violence and suffering.

Here, indeed, is a research program. First we must find appropriate indices for the various shades of belief which Huxley distinguishes. Then we shall want to get our information separately from a large number of social subgroups. Trend data will have to be assembled over a long period of time; and wherever possible, these trends should be linked with external events. If a special movement starts somewhere, if a related book becomes a best-seller, if some special legislation is passed or a voluntary association established, we shall want to study the pertinent attitudes "before and after."

This is not the place to propose a concrete study design, but we should warn against oversimplifying the whole problem. The attitudes in which the historian will be interested are certainly complex in nature; and, in order to cover one single concept, it may be necessary to employ a whole set of interlocking questions. As a matter of fact, it might very well be that future trends will be different for different dimensions of the same notion. To exemplify what this means in terms of our work, we shall choose for our second example the problem of class tensions.

There is an abundance of prophecies in the literature which can be loosely labeled as Marxist. Conflicts of interest between the working class and the influential business groups will become more acute. The workers will become more class conscious, and more aggressive toward the privileged groups. The latter, in turn, will defend more strongly their class interests and more and more neglect the democratic forms of politics. These ideas are too well known to need further elaboration. Instead, let us pick out of this whole complex the notion of class consciousness, and see whether we can develop a kind of barometer by which to measure trends in the next few decades.

In recent times, a large number of business companies have conducted surveys to determine their standing with the public, but this by no means meets the task. There could very easily be an intensification of class consciousness among workers which does not express itself immediately in invectives directed toward General Motors or Standard Oil. Not even the recently increased interest of social psychologists in this problem covers it fully. Richard Centers, in his *The Psychology of Social Classes,* has developed a set of questions pertinent to two elements: readiness to accept the government as an agent in economic affairs; and a feeling that avenues of economic advancement are closing up, that social rewards are not fairly distributed.

The total picture has many additional aspects, however. We should study whether workers have a feeling of identification with their class. If a worker's son becomes a lawyer, should he work for a union rather than for a big corporation? Is there an increased interest in reading stories about workers rather than about movie stars? Is there an increased interest in leisure-time associations especially designed for workers? Another aspect of the problem would be whether workers are concerned with the power structure in the community. Do they think that the courts handle poor and rich alike? Do and can the councilmen in the city represent both poor and rich? Do they feel that the rich have special influence with the police? Even if there is growing uneasiness on this score, the questions still to be raised is whether it is channeled into political reactions. Does "going into politics" become a more respected and desirable pursuit? Is voting the "right" way something which becomes an important criterion for judging people? Do political issues become a factor in one's own personal plans?

This example, incidentally, raises a serious problem of strategy for the pollster. Topics relevant to the work of the future historian are likely to come from the area of social change. Polls dealing with such areas can easily become suspect as "subversive" or "inflammatory." It will therefore be important to make clear, both to the general public and to specific clients, that the public opinion researcher is not taking sides when he focuses part of his attention on more unconventional issues. As a matter of fact, it might very well be that some of the work suggested here might best be done under the joint sponsorship of several agencies or perhaps under the aegis of a professional organization like the American Association for Public Opinion Research.

What Should Be Done?

We pollsters cannot be expected to tackle the whole problem by ourselves. We should seek the assistance of a "commission for the utilization of polls in the service of future historiography," whose specific task it would be to furnish us with appropriate ideas. This commission should consist, on the one hand, of historians and other social scientists who have given thought to questions such as those we have raised, and, on the other hand, of research technicians who can translate research suggestions into actual study designs.

There certainly will be no scarcity of topics. There is much evidence to show that people in this country were inclined to shy away from concern with international relations. Suddenly we are thrust into the position of being the leading power in the world. How will people in this country adjust to this change, and what will be the mutual interaction between the distribution of attitudes and the actions of our policymakers? At what rate will Americans really become aware of the existence of the Far Eastern people? When will they notice that the famous destruction of the "human race" by the atomic bomb might really mean the replacing of the Western sector of humanity by their Asiatic fellow men? Another element of our tradition is the belief that one man is as good as another. But in a society which becomes ever more complex, the expert plays an increasingly important role. How will this proverbial anti-authoritarian tradition adjust to the increasing, and probably unavoidable, "bureaucratization" of the modern world? Or one might turn from the political to a more personal sphere. Increasing amounts of available leisure time will force more people to review their "designs for living." How will they use the time over which they themselves have control: will they use it to have a richer personal life, to equip themselves better for competitive advancement, or will they just fritter it away? There is certainly an obvious interrelation between these questions and new technical developments such as television.

Whatever topic we select, the procedure for research will always be the same. We must first formulate clearly a number of alternative assumptions about future developments. Then we must decide on the kind of indices which are pertinent for the problem at hand; this is where the research technician can make his main contribution. To set up the machinery for collecting the data is a matter of decision and funds. As to the selection of respondents, a certain flexibility will be necessary. For some problems a national cross-section will be most appropriate. For other problems very specific population groups will have to be sampled. When it comes to studying the diffusion of attitudes, attention will have to be focused on elite groups. In other cases specific occupations or special age groups will command our interest. And at all times we shall want to collect "background information": documentation on major events, on the activities of organizations, community leaders, etc.

At this point, we should warn against a possible misunderstanding. Previously we stressed that attitude surveys provide a new type of "facts" for the historian. But this does not imply that they are more important than the more traditional kind of data. It is just the interplay between the "objective" facts and attitudes which promises a great advance in historiography. If for a given period we not only know the standard of living, but also the distribution of ratings on happiness and personal adjustment, the dynamics of social change will be much better understood. Let us add that sampling surveys will enlarge our ideas on social bookkeeping in still another way. Nothing is more characteristic of this trend than what has happened in the decennial census of the United States. As long as we thought only in terms of complete enumerations, we could afford to include only a few questions. Now that we use 5 per cent and 1 per cent samples on specific items, we are able to cover a much wider range of topics. This is undoubtedly only a beginning. Since small sample designs have been perfected, there is no reason why sociography should not develop on a much broader scale. Cultural activities and other living habits may soon be added to the more conventional trends in the birth rate or export trade. It is certainly no coincidence that the Kinsey reports did not appear before 1948.

As early as 1908, in his *Human Nature in Politics*, Graham Wallas pointed to such changes in what he called the methods of

political reasoning. He compared the reports of two Royal commissions, both of which were concerned with the reform of the
English poor laws. One was established in 1834 and the other in
1905. The earlier one dealt with "a priori deduction, illustrated,
but not proved by particular instances." Now (in 1905) things
are different.

Instead of assuming half consciously that human energy is dependent
solely on the working of the human will in the presence of the ideas of
pleasure and pain, the Commissioners are forced to tabulate and consider innumerable quantitative observations relating to the very many
factors affecting the will of paupers and possible paupers. They cannot,
for instance, avoid the task of estimating the relative industrial effectiveness of health, which depends upon decent surroundings; of hope,
which may be made possible by State provision for old age; and of the
imaginative range which is the result of education; and of comparing all
these with the "purely economic" motive created by ideas of future
pleasure and pain.

As can be seen, Wallas did not want to replace, but to comple-
ment, principles with social surveys. And so we too do not suggest that attitude data are better than "hard" facts, but that they
add, so to speak, a new dimension.

There is one more suggestion for the work of the new commission on polling and historiography. We are all aware that prediction is one of the touchstones by which a science can justify itself.
So far our predictions have been confined mainly to the outcomes
of political elections; many have felt that this is a rather insignificant pursuit. There is no reason, however, that we should not
predict future sentiments and then, later on, study whether we
were right. One of the most impressive chapters in *The American
Soldier* is that on "The Aftermath of Hostilities." In the summer
of 1944, the Research Branch prepared a document predicting
what attitudes they expected among soldiers at the end of the war.
In 1945, many of those predictions were tested: At some points
the predictions were correct, and at others, wrong. But no person reading this chapter can escape the feeling that here might be
the substitute for laboratory experiments, so often impossible to
carry out in the social sciences. Interestingly enough, without
knowing about the experience of the Research Branch, an histo-

rian, Helen Lynd, saw this very link between her field and ours. In writing about *The Nature of Historical Objectivity*, she stated:

> . . . we know surely . . . that the future which lies ahead will become present, and that hypotheses which we may now make can be tested by the course of events. If we are in earnest about historical objectivity, why do we not more often frame precise hypotheses about what may be the course of events in a given area in a given time? . . . With all that can be said against the recent opinion polls in this country there is this to be said in their favor: they at least made their errors public so that they could be subject to the verification of events.

It may be faint praise to say that pollsters at least make their errors public. It would also be helpful if the historians became more aware of their lack of data on matters about which they often write with considerable confidence. The present chapter does not mean to claim that another "new history" is here just because public opinion data are now available. As a matter of fact, the main purpose was to point out that the historian has always wanted public opinion research and has used whatever best substitute he could find for it. By more collaboration the sophistication and the significance of polls could be improved. The historian of the future would be better served.

Note

NOTE: This chapter is an extended version of the author's presidential address to the American Association for Public Opinion Research; it was first published in *The Public Opinion Quarterly*, Winter 1950–1951.

1. I adopt in this chapter a derogatory term to describe a profession which I intend to defend, and, in a way, represent in its academic form. This should not be a surprising procedure for historians, who should remember many similar examples; for instance, the party of Dutch Protestants who called themselves "Beggars" after the lady lieutenant of the Spanish king had tried to deprecate them by this word.

Index

abolitionist movement, 28
academic history, development of, 6–7
achievement orientation, 33
Adams, George Burton, 6
Adams, Henry, 4, 318, 340
Adams, James Truslow, 139
Adams, John, 141
Adams, John Quincy, 31, 238–240
Adams, Sam, 333
Ad Hoc Committee to Collect the Basic Quantitative Data of American Political History, 213
administrative process, decision-making and, 218–219
Administrative State, The (Waldo), 221
Age of Enterprise, The (Cochran and Miller), 371 *n.*
Age of Reform, The (Hofstadter), 66
Age of the Great Depression, The (Wecter), 389
Allen, Frederic Lewis, 322
Alley, J. B., 260
American Aristocracy, An (Baltzell), 311 *n.*
American Association for Public Opinion Research, 403
American Business System, The (Cochran), 371 *n.*
American character, study of, 181
American dream, 378
American Federation of Labor, 322, 324

American Friends Service Committee, 317
American Historical Association, 10, 181 *n.*, 213, 371 *n.*
American Historical Review, 228 *n.*, 371 *n.*
American history, "presidential synthesis" of, 371–385
American History, An (Curti), 268 *n.*
Americanism, vs. British colonialism, 145–155
American nationalism, emergence of, 138–156
American Party System and the American People, The (Greenstein), 292 *n.*
American Peace Crusade, The (Curti), 268 *n.*
American philanthropy, history of, 268–269
American Philanthropy Abroad (Curti), 268 *n.*
American Philosophical Society, 328
American Quarterly, 268 *n.*
American Revolution, 48–49, 332–333
American Scholarship in the Twentieth Century (Curti), 268 *n.*
American Social Gospel movement, 324
American Soldier, The, 392–393, 400
Americas, comparative analyses in, 35
America's Philosopher (Curti), 268 *n.*
Anderson, George W., 246
Andrew Johnson and Reconstruction (McKitrick), 358 *n.*